so~ you want to be an
innkeeper

so~ you want to be an
innkeeper

THE DEFINITIVE GUIDE TO OPERATING A
SUCCESSFUL BED-AND-BREAKFAST OR COUNTRY INN

Revised and Expanded, Fourth Edition

Susan Brown
Pat Hardy
Jo Ann M. Bell
Mary E. Davies

CHRONICLE BOOKS
SAN FRANCISCO

Library of Congress Cataloging-in-Publication Data available.
ISBN 0-8118-4110-3

Manufactured in the United States of America.

Designed by Kate Berg

Distributed in Canada by Raincoast Books
9050 Shaughnessy Street
Vancouver, British Columbia V6P 6E5

10 9 8 7 6 5 4 3 2 1

Chronicle Books LLC
85 Second Street
San Francisco, California 94105

www.chroniclebooks.com

Acknowledgments

From Susan: *Thanks to the marvelous, competent innkeepers who, when I was absent or writing, ran my inn as if they were the owners; the workshop participants who kept asking for things I didn't have on paper, forcing me to write everything down; and the aspiring innkeepers who hired me as a consultant, sharing their dream from inception to opening day and beyond, thereby enriching my life and my experience.*

From Pat and Jo Ann: *Thanks to the thousands of innkeepers (and aspiring innkeepers) who have shared their dreams, their fears, and their realities—those individuals who, every day, fulfill the fantasies of millions of guests staying at bed-and-breakfast and country inns; the past guests and staff of the Glenborough Inn, who for nine years taught us lifelong lessons about ourselves; and the subscribers to* innkeeping *newsletter and members of the Professional Association of Innkeepers International, who reminded us daily for the thirteen years that we were with PAII what it was like to run an inn.*

From Mary: *Thanks to the gang at Ten Inverness Way for holding the fort while I wrote; the other innkeepers who teach me so much when I'm a guest at their inns; my own guests, who are so quick to enjoy every little thing we do for them; and my husband, Jon Langdon, who actually believed I was the best innkeeper in the world.*

And we all thank each other for a wonderful collaboration.

Contents

The Spirit of Innkeeping

When we four stepped unsuspectingly into the exciting and new world of innkeeping in the early 1980s, we each had different reasons for becoming innkeepers. What we left, what we found, and what we made of it tell the story of what innkeeping is about. For every innkeeper, the story is different. And that, in a way, is the point.

Susan Brown spent ten years as a personnel–employee relations executive, three of those years with a Fortune 500 company for which she crisscrossed the country almost weekly. Susan snapped on the day she couldn't get the manager of the Skokie Hilton to recognize her as anything other than Room 212.

"I'd been assigned to the room in error," Susan says. "I'd ask for the room change, and he'd say, 'You're Room 212.' I'd say, 'No, I'm Susan Brown, and I'd like a different room.' When I started yelling and stamping my foot in the lobby, I realized I'd had it. I took the red-eye home to Los Angeles, sold my house, and quit my job. Hello, Bath Street Inn!

"I didn't even talk to other innkeepers about how to proceed," Susan says. "I knew what I wanted to create, because I was doing it for myself, almost in direct opposition to what I had experienced in the previous several years. For me, creating the inn was stage-managing my own fantasy."

For Pat Hardy too, her inn represented what she wants most when she travels. "I want quiet," she says, "and a chance to choose whether to be alone or with other guests. The Glenborough Inn was equally comfortable whether you preferred to curl up in a guest room and read or go to the parlor and visit."

Pat's parents owned their own business for thirty-five years, and Pat started and operated her own employment business at age seventeen. She has been a full-time mom and wife, a Girl Scout leader, a camp director and counselor trainer, and both development officer and fill-in cook for a private school. During her four years as executive director of a nonprofit agency, Pat took it from two and a half employees to twenty-five, from a $25,000 annual budget to $225,000, and from a single-community program to a countywide one. "I wanted to put the skills honed there to work in a business of my own," Pat says. "I also wanted work that would allow me to be around when my daughter Colleen, then nine years old, got home from school. The inn met both these needs. It was also great for Colleen. Because of her experience as an assistant innkeeper, handling almost every part of the business, her confidence in the workplace has brought her kudos wherever else she works."

Having created their own inn, in 1981 Pat and partner Jo Ann Bell, along with Susan and other members of the Innkeepers Guild of Santa Barbara, developed the first workshop to share their knowledge and experience with prospective innkeepers. People of all ages, sizes, incomes, and intelligence levels come to the innkeeping workshops with high hopes.

"It's exciting that this entrepreneurial opportunity exists in the United States," Jo Ann says. "You don't need half a million dollars, a franchise, and somebody else's rules and concepts to make your own business. I didn't like corporate life, to put it mildly. I didn't like wearing dark suits and high heels. Santa Barbara, our home, was wide open, with no inns at all. Developing the Glenborough Inn felt like a wonderful option. Which is not to say that I wasn't terrified I'd use all the money I'd ever had on an inn—and nobody would come." The proverbial farmer's daughter from upstate New York, Jo Ann might have been worried about the money, but she was fearless when it came to the work. Until the day they sold the Glenborough, whenever a faucet needed repair, Jo Ann just gathered up her tools and did the job.

Mary Davies enjoyed some of the most exciting and satisfying work of her life before she decided to move to the California coast. "I was deputy director of the Employment Development Department of the State of California, doing their lobbying in Sacramento and Washington and directing a staff of analysts. Matching that job, for challenge, support, and fun, would be impossible. But it ended, and in Inverness, with one grocery, a service station, a post office, and miles of beaches, the opportunities for corporate success weren't overwhelming, in any case.

"In 1979 my friend Stephen Kimball and I were working with our local realtor to find investment property. The realtor told us about a house and suggested we make it an inn. Stephen said he didn't have time to run an inn. Did I? Hey, I'd been Betty Crocker Homemaker of Tomorrow in high school—no problem! Ten Inverness Way was a dream come true before we had time to dream it!"

Eventually, reality sets in. In mid-1982, Mary was discarding in disgust an unsolicited publication with a name like *Fast-Food News*, wishing there was a publication that addressed her needs as an innkeeper, when she decided to write it herself. Her monthly newsletter, *innkeeping*, has since become the basic tool for innkeepers across the country. In 1985, Mary had to make a choice between full-time innkeeping and full-time publishing. The inn won out, and she bought out her partner. And the newsletter? She sold *innkeeping* to Pat Hardy and Jo Ann Bell!

How has innkeeping met our needs and expectations? Susan likes seeing results. "Most of us came from a business world where so much is nonproductive," she says. "As an innkeeper, everything you do counts. For the first year or two, you get direct, immediate feedback on almost everything. What must be done somehow gets done. You do it." As an executive, Susan unwound by wallpapering, slipcovering, and painting. As an innkeeper these things were "work." She also put her background in business administration and psychology to work in conferences and training sessions at the Bath Street Inn, as well as in everyday guest encounters. "I'm immensely curious about people, and whatever else our guests may have experienced at our inn, they definitely got treated as whole individuals," Susan says.

In 1988, after nine good years of innkeeping, Pat and Jo Ann launched the first inclusive association focused on the innkeeper, the Professional Association of Innkeepers International (PAII). Shortly thereafter they sold the Glenborough Inn. Until 2002, when they sold the association to a group of investor-innkeepers, they had the chance to pool their own and others' expertise, and to speak up for inns on an international level.

Jo Ann's delight was the chance to utilize her training as a licensed social worker and her experience with community organizations to help innkeepers associations develop and grow. She still speaks "computer" to anyone who will listen. Pat's phone conversations with PAII members—innkeepers and aspiring innkeepers—were the highlights of her days, as she provided some new idea or resource to callers who could find answers nowhere else.

Pat and Jo Ann developed and, for thirteen years, ran the world's largest professional association serving innkeepers of bed-and-breakfast and country inns, speaking to groups across North America and, eventually, in other parts of the world. "We had a chance to keep in touch with who innkeepers were and how they were changing the industry. What we learned about the different approaches each couple or individual took to operating their business was eye-opening. We were innkeepers who had to make the business work to feed us. Many innkeepers have this as a second job in the household. Some have a retirement or investment income and have a limit on how much they want this bed-and-breakfast job to intrude on their lives."

People often asked Pat and Jo Ann why they were not innkeepers anymore. "We could not run the inn and take on the intensity of a growing association and still do both well," they said. "While we were innkeepers we really enjoyed that, but PAII was another phase in our lives. We believed, as many others did, that we would own an inn forever. What we found was that, not unlike being a mother, that period of life was a good one—and so is this one now." The same is true for PAII. Pat and Jo Ann accomplished what they could to bring together this vital industry.

For Mary, Ten Inverness Way was a chance to share what is important to her. "I was always saying Ten Inverness Way is an inn for hikers—we were right on the edge of the Point Reyes National Seashore—and for readers, especially those who think inns were invented for curling up in front of a fire with a book after a walk in the rain. I love breakfast, so at our inn, breakfast was serious—Mom's home cooking. To me, the worst thing at an inn is an innkeeper who talks too much. We often fell into wonderful conversations, but I recognized that my guests hadn't trekked out here just to spend their wedding anniversary with me. I loved the fact that I could make the inn be just the way I wanted it." Mary sold her inn in the late 1990s, and she and her husband, John, moved to Washington State.

Naturally, we all make adjustments. As Pat says, you can set your own hours, just so long as it's twenty a day. Mary never did get to serve a breakfast of warm, homemade fruit pies in bowls with cream; too many people said it just wouldn't fly. For Susan, the adjustment was facing up to the reality that "wherever you go, there you are"—with both faults and assets. "I escaped the corporate world, with all its nonproductive cover-yourself activities," she says, "to create my own corporation and a partnership, which requires compliance with many government regulations—hence, nonproductive work. I was a workaholic in the corporate world; I still was as an innkeeper, but the work was different: more creativity, more joyful people contact, and a much more healthy work environment—beautiful rooms, wonderful gardens, not to mention the Pacific Ocean five minutes away." The creativity included taking the inn from five rooms to twelve rooms by building a new separate structure; buying an adjacent house and renovating it to start a second inn; selling this second inn after failing to raise capital for a financially necessary addition; and teaching two workshops a year. Now Susan has left all the joys and challenges of running an inn to move to San Diego to spend overdue quality time with daughters and grandchildren. She comes back to Santa Barbara twice a year to conduct the So—You Think You Want to Be an Innkeeper workshops.

We were our own bosses, much of our work we did for fun, and we were building something for the future. That's the spirit of innkeeping.

A LOOK FORWARD

All four of us have now passed our inns on to the hands of a new generation of innkeepers. Being an innkeeper has changed since the 1980s, but some of the basic ingredients remain: sharing your life and home with guests from all over the world; providing quality food and furnishings in a homey, yet sophisticated atmosphere; and acting as a concierge for strangers to your city and area. A workshop participant recently asked Susan if her approach to innkeeping was "passé." He was referring to a recent *Wall Street Journal* article that talked about an innkeeper serving breakfast in her bikini. Susan replied, "Good manners, respect, kindness, consideration, and civility will never go out of style—these qualities bring out the best in people."

But in this ever-changing world, there is an infinite variety in how innkeepers go about creating their own special atmosphere. And they have many more choices now than in the early eighties, when many inns had rooms that shared bathrooms. Shared baths—now, that really seems passé! In a very short time, the number of inns in the United States and Canada has at least quadrupled. They are everywhere.

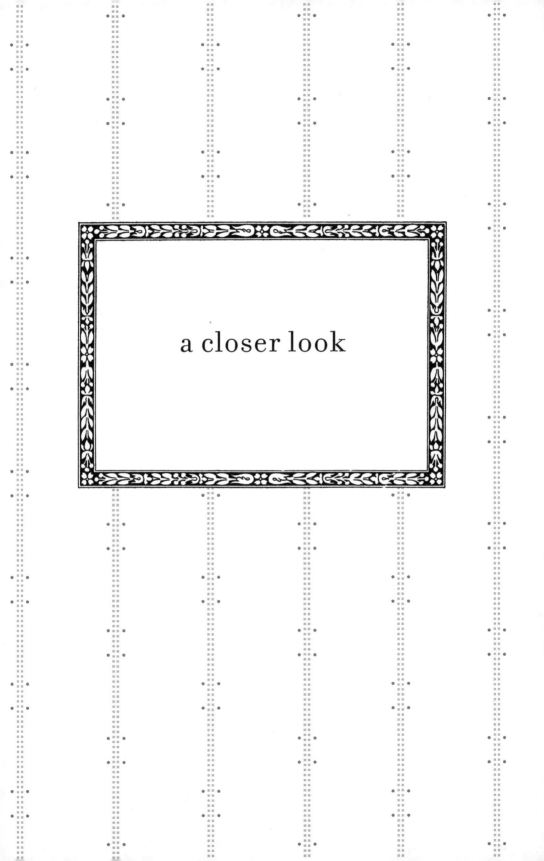

a closer look

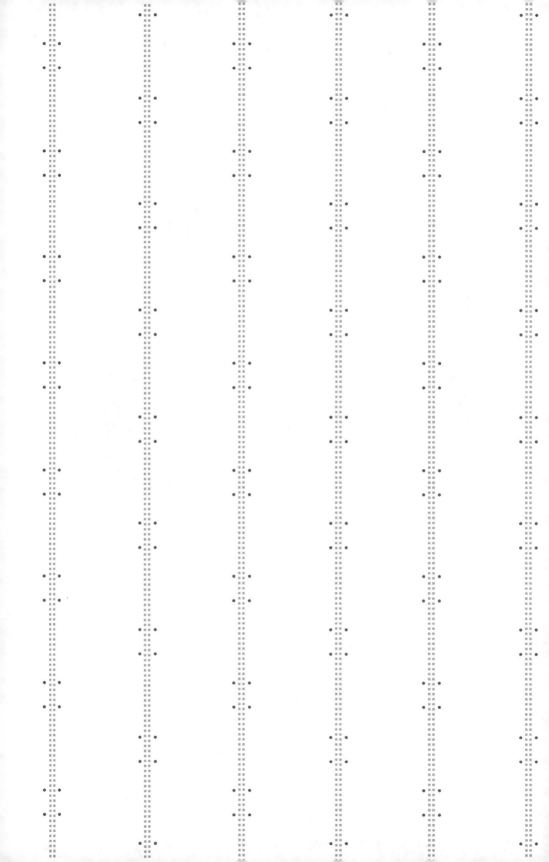

What Is an Inn?

Country inns, bed-and-breakfasts, guest houses—it's getting downright complicated to choose an escape to a simpler era. And with Nevada casinos advertising "bed, breakfast, and blackjack" on freeway billboards, somebody has to get serious about saying what's what. Travelers are often unclear on the concepts, and good innkeepers do a lot of listening to make sure prospective guests are booking reservations at a place that corresponds with the image in their heads. As a prospective innkeeper, you need a particularly clear vision of the nature of your future business.

The inn boom in the United States began in the late 1970s, but even now, staying at inns is an exciting new way to travel in many parts of the country. The origins of these hostelries are historic, based on the traditions of New England and Europe. Country inns, indigenous to New England, provided food and lodging to travelers and locals, and were often a focal point for a community. George Washington slept there. Bed-and-breakfasts in Great Britain and tourist homes and guest houses in the United States were historically the projects of widows or wives, who supplemented the family income by renting out spare rooms.

Accommodations in the United States today include both country inns and homestyle bed-and-breakfasts, as well as that unique American invention, the bed-and-breakfast inn. At the same time, hotels have responded to the traveler's love for the individuality and personal attention of inns by creating concierge floors and entire properties that, although large, seek to imitate the inn experience. What exactly are the distinctions between these properties? The Professional Association of Innkeepers International uses the following definitions.

Homestay or Host Home

This is an owner-occupied private home where the business of accommodating a few paying guests in one to three rooms is secondary to the use of the home as a private residence. The hosts are primarily interested in meeting new people and making some additional money while continuing their present employment or retirement. Breakfast is the only meal served. Since these homes are usually located in residential areas, zoning or other government restrictions may prevent the use of signs and public advertising. These homes are often members of a reservation service organization (RSO), which inspects them, but are otherwise rarely required to be licensed or inspected by local governmental agencies.

In some cases, RSOs will book unhosted apartments or cottages, where a self-serve breakfast is left in the refrigerator.

Bed-and-Breakfast (B&B)

Once a single-family dwelling, this owner-occupied establishment with four or five guest rooms is both home and lodging. The B&B is located in a legal zone, and meets all the appropriate tax, fire, building, and health requirements. The owners advertise and may legally post a sign. Like the homestay or host home, because of its size, the profits from a B&B usually cannot support a family unit, so it is often one partner's job while the other works outside. Sometimes the property is purchased specifically to be a B&B, but many are converted family homes. Reservations may be made directly with the property.

Bed-and-Breakfast

Beginning to detect the signs of burnout after seven years, innkeepers John Felton and Martie Gottron put their eight-room, year-round B&B inn on the market, figuring that the sale would take a couple of years. To their surprise, the inn sold quickly to a family who converted it into a private home, leaving John and Martie almost literally out on the street. They had not actually planned on another B&B, but the house they fell in love with in Stockbridge, Massachusetts, was already operational as a three-room seasonal inn, One Main Street B&B. The asking price was also more than what they had planned on spending. In spite of the asking price, the prospect of continuing their innkeeping career in a small B&B seemed attractive—and so back they plunged.

Three years later, both are very happy and have resumed their writing careers. Having only three rooms means more time to spend with their guests and more time for themselves as well. Because their income is no longer totally dependent on the inn, they have eliminated, or at least substantially reduced, a major source of stress. And being seasonal (May through October) allows time for recharging their batteries to pursue other interests.

Bed-and-Breakfast Inn

These are generally small, owner-operated businesses providing the primary financial support of the owner, who usually lives there. The building's primary use is for business. These inns advertise, have business licenses, produce their own brochures, comply with government ordinances, pay all appropriate taxes, and post signs. Breakfast is the only meal served, to overnight guests only. The inn may host events such as weddings and small business meetings. Room numbers range from four to twenty or even, rarely but increasingly often, as many as thirty. Reservations may be made directly with the property. Obviously, the distinction between a B&B and a bed-and-breakfast inn is elusive. In short, the B&B is as much home as business; the inn is primarily business.

Bed-and-Breakfast Inn

Chuck Ramsey and Tim Wilk, partner-owners of the Gray Goose Inn in Chester, Indiana, started out by opening two rooms to guests in the home they had owned for six years. When they were ready to expand their home-stay, they discovered that the city would grant only temporary permission: if they decided to sell, the permit would not be transferable. So they found another property in a commercial area and opened a five-room B&B. For nine years they both continued to work part-time at a steel mill, until they attended a PAII conference where they were inspired to add a meeting room, private baths, whirlpools, and fireplaces and to become full-time innkeepers. With eight well-equipped rooms today, their successful bed-and-breakfast inn serves business travelers who work with the two steel companies in the area.

Cottages—Bed-and-Breakfast Style

The guest wants it all. For those who desire a separate space and yet still want to be within reach of the personal attention from an innkeeper, the cottage concept is perfect. Innkeepers have responded by adding small outbuildings separate from the main inn where guests may take delivery of breakfast in a basket or, in many instances, choose to enjoy the company of other guests in the main dining room. Cottages can be well-appointed luxury hideaways with fireplaces and whirlpools or simple rustic cabins. However, with either style, the added attention of the innkeeper—be it a full cookie jar, twenty-four-hour hot beverages in the main house, or a manager providing direction on where to go for dinner—gives this genre that sincere and genuine B&B touch.

Country Inn

This type of inn is a business offering overnight lodging and meals where the owner is actively involved in daily operations, often living on-site. These establishments are, in fact, bed-and-breakfast inns with from six to thirty rooms. At least one meal is served in addition to breakfast, and country inns operate as restaurants as well as offering lodging. Modified American Plan (MAP) country inns serve dinner to overnight guests only, and the cost of dinner and breakfast is generally included in the room rate. A country inn with a full-service restaurant serves meals to the general public. Some lodges and dude ranches fall into this category, as do some city properties. An establishment doesn't have to be in the country to be considered a country inn.

Bed-and-Breakfast Hotel

The bed-and-breakfast hotel is a historic hotel of twenty rooms or more that offers breakfast. Only the historic structure, the included breakfast, and perhaps some decorating components provide the B&B feel.

Boutique Hotel

Because the boutique hotel is often confused with the B&B, it is important to mention it here. These properties are expensive and elaborately decorated, emphasizing hotel services with a personal touch from employees. The size ranges from fifteen to fifty or even one hundred rooms. The owner may be involved in daily operations, but generally a manager is responsible to a corporation. Meal service is usually breakfast only, but in some instances high-quality dinner, lunch service, or even room service might be available on the premises.

Trends

Where is the inn industry going? The answer depends on whom you ask, what you read, and where you look. To many who have never tried the experience it's still a new industry; however, for the general public, the novelty has worn off. As the term "bed-and-breakfast" becomes part of everyday American usage, staying in one has become an expected option when Americans look for a place to stay.

No longer do we see travel writers' fascination with this unique genre, as was so apparent in the 1980s and 1990s. Glowing coverage has moved from national media to regional publications, and even these features have become less frequent. Major travel magazines are likely to include information on inns as a part of another article on a region or a focused topic such as spas or gardens.

The transition from darling of the travel world to just another special place to stay indicates that B&Bs are here to stay. The delight of this new century's inn lies in the wide range of possibilities: from a rustic log cabin to high Victorian formality, from minimalist modern to an African theme. There is an inn for everyone.

The primary reason guests stay in small inns is pretty much the same as in the beginning—to nestle in at a welcome and special getaway with a homey feeling for a few days. And this is still the very thing that keeps this cozy little part of the travel marketplace so vital. The urban world—from whence most guests come—is impersonal, Internet-based, rushed, and lacking in human contact.

"Warmth" is still in, but "smothering" is definitely out. As much as the inn serves as an escape from a Palm Pilot–bound world, it's also given rise to cocooning, leading to the popularity of individual cottages, private entrances, and smaller breakfast tables.

Innkeepers provide many extras to guests at no extra cost. These may include use of a refrigerator; a sitting room, porch, or patio for social interaction; fresh flowers; puzzles and games; and even bicycles. Inns routinely offer complimentary wine, fruit, candy, cookies, hors d'oeuvres, social hours, or afternoon tea. In fact, large hotels have responded to these typical inn services by providing their own concierge floors with social hours, breakfast, and evening desserts; special greeters who welcome guests at the door; training programs that encourage all staff members who see guests to talk with them; all-suite hotels featuring elaborate breakfast buffets; and stocked refrigerators.

Do inns take business away from hotels? Rarely, because the total number of inn rooms is small. However, unfortunate experiences at inns can, and do, send guests running back to the anonymity of hotels. Inconsistency in friendliness and cleanliness has made the need for inspections of inns ever greater. Although thousands of inns are inspected for the *American Automobile Association TourBook* and the *Mobil Travel Guide,* many more are not eligible because they have fewer than five rooms. Most state B&B associations have taken up this challenge by designing and managing their own inspection program. In addition, a collection of inspected inns in North America known as *Select Registry* publishes a guide and implements several marketing programs for its membership.

Finding the perfect inn is not always a simple matter for inngoers. In the past, conventionally published inn guidebooks were the major resources. However, electronic guidebooks found on the Internet now occupy first place. In order to succeed today, an inn must have its own responsive and relatively sophisticated

Web site, usually promoted by a professional in B&B Internet marketing. Internet-savvy innkeepers claim that 25 to 85 percent of their new business comes from their Web presence, either through the inn's primary Web site or through listings in electronic directories. With mainstream hard-copy travel publications such as the Fodor's and Frommer's guides, as well as special focus books for the birder, gay guest, romantic, pet owner, sailing fanatic, or wine aficionado, some print guidebooks still provide a showcase for inns.

Bed-and-breakfast travel is growing steadily, but the exponential growth of the industry happened in the last century. Most areas of the country still see new inns opening, but the business has reached a level of maturity where a new innkeeper is more likely to take over an existing establishment than to start a new business from scratch.

Smaller (five rooms and under) B&Bs are likely to return to being a private home upon sale. Today's sophisticated aspiring innkeeper needs to jump into this marketplace with either good experience or hefty investments in order to buy an existing inn, where they may decide to add rooms, upgrade, or expand services. Some folks, unable to find what they need or want at a financially feasible price, choose to build from the ground up.

Given the sales tag on inns today, more aspiring innkeepers are entering the field as managers of longtime inns or as interim innkeepers. No longer "just an innsitter," many of these interim innkeepers have passed a certification program developed by the Professional Association of Innkeepers International.

Nowhere are there signs that running an inn will become less work. It is a time- and energy-consuming business, but the rewards are many and customer demand is still growing. Pundits see a bright though challenging future for the industry.

URBAN OR RURAL?

Where are inns located? We expect them on Cape Cod and in California's Napa Valley, but inns are also found in Hannibal, Missouri, Tallahassee, Florida, and fifteen minutes from Disney World.

Small-town or rural bed-and-breakfasts provide an invaluable service to communities where there is either no place at all to stay or no place other than the budget motel. And these B&Bs are making money, often functioning as a focal point for bridge groups, teas, traveling salespeople, and special occasions. Many innkeepers find that they provide the touch of class for a small town.

Urban and suburban inns have come into their own as a serious option within the bed-and-breakfast and country inn market for business travelers, providing amenities specifically aimed at them: Internet access, telephones, televisions and VCRs in guest rooms, earlier breakfast hours, breakfast-to-go bags, and facilities for small meetings. Destination cities like San Francisco attract weekend getaway travelers as well, not to mention vacationers who love inns and like the idea of staying in, for example, one of the city's characteristic Victorians.

The Business Traveler

As the world has changed, so have the ways of the business traveler. Gone are three-martini lunches and unlimited expense accounts. Corporate travel budgets have been slashed, forcing the salesperson, consultant, or executive to travel smarter, taking fewer trips but often staying away for longer periods of time. Instead of access to a great hotel lounge and an expensive restaurant, what's important now are practical room amenities, a quiet ambience, a breakfast that accommodates this type of traveler's schedule and dietary needs, and a feeling of homeyness. These guests don't live in a vacuum; they also expect the modern conveniences found elsewhere.

In true innkeeperly fashion, innkeepers are responding to their guests' requests with the addition of buildings to accommodate long-term stays. To understand your competition in this arena, stay in an all-suite hotel.

The old idea that corporate travelers can only be found in big cities is de-bunked every day by innkeepers. Some inns accommodating business travelers are located along a busy route connecting one city to another. Others may be close to a hospital, near a college, or next to the state capitol. Another may be out in the middle of a cornfield, yet near a manufacturing plant. An inn located at a tourist beach can accommodate business travelers selling products to area restaurants and hotels. People sell or service practically everything, and they all need a place to stay. They will stay at your place if they are made to feel at home.

Business travelers care about amenities, but they also care about price, at least initially. It is crucial to build into your budget lower midweek prices or special rates for regular business guests or specific companies.

The good news about adding these extra amenities and making price adjustments is that the business traveler guest is loyal and returns repeatedly. Plus, the payoff for inns focusing on the business traveler is an increased occupancy for those hard-to-fill weekdays.

From an occupancy perspective, one of the best locations for an inn is a desti-nation resort area where people expect inns. New innkeepers are often afraid to consider an area with lots of inns, but the advantages include the opportunity to buy an existing inn that is not reaching its full potential because of tired or out-of-touch owners. Areas with high property values usually mean high occupancy, but it's expensive to buy in. Seasonal locations where inns are filled every night from "twig to twig" (the first bloom to the last leaf) provide good opportunities for owners who are willing to work hard for part of the year in exchange for taking several months off to travel. If your financial projections in such a location require you to stay open and struggle during the off-season, you may be taking on more than you'll want to handle.

Locating in an area with no inns may be a great opportunity or a disaster. Maybe you're just the first to tap a rich vein, or maybe it's a ghost town. Keep in mind that there must be attractions or activities for guests at or near the inn. Few people will travel simply to stay in a nice inn if there is no other reason to go to the area.

SUCCESS

What constitutes success in the inn business today? Guests often ask innkeep-ers how they can possibly make a living. The answer, of course, depends entirely on how you define "living." A surprisingly high number of innkeepers say that if they can afford the travel, the antiques, the books, or the wines they want, they feel successful. Part of the reason financial success is so ambiguous is that inns have live-in innkeepers, most of whom are owners. As a result, the business often provides shelter, food, and sometimes even clothing, if the inn's image requires you to look more or less like George and Martha Washington. All you need—and often all you get—is an allowance.

Beyond the concrete indicators, like an ability to pay the bills, success also means that innkeeping works for you. It's a lifestyle as much as a business.

GUEST EXPECTATIONS INCREASE COMPETITION

Inn guests are sophisticated creatures, and to a great extent innkeepers foster that sophistication. The B&B tradition may have begun in the simple, private homes of Britons who needed a bit of extra income, but in the United States the bed-and-breakfast and country inn guest wants more. Inns compete for guests with furnishings, hot tubs, and Godiva chocolates.

Private baths have been de rigueur for several years. But if the inn next door puts in a swimming pool, it won't necessarily diminish your business. If you provide high-quality, caring, professional accommodations; if your inn, while retaining its uniqueness, is comparable in quality and services to other establishments in the area; and if your guests appear to depart satisfied and send their friends to you, you've no doubt met and probably exceeded their expectations.

Basically, the inn guest has come to appreciate a different mode of travel, the "inn experience." Once hooked, inn guests consider themselves part of a travel elite, discoverers of a cherished place, a secret unknown to the mainstream. Fostering this feeling is important.

The longer an inn is in business, the more likely the innkeepers will hire staff, take vacations, and even move off the premises. This is important for the innkeepers, but guests often don't like it; they tend to want to see the owner. It's a real challenge to establish an ambience that can be maintained to the satisfaction of the guests without the innkeeper doing the impossible: being everywhere, all the time.

L IS FOR LUXURY

The cute little economical B&B you remember in England has not translated well in the States. The original concept of bed-and-breakfast was that you had a couple of extra rooms in your already-paid-for home that you offered to paying guests at a low cost. As the American traveler made demands on this concept, the American B&B has strained to keep up. Starting innocently enough with the desire for private baths, the expectation of many inn travelers is now exquisite luxury.

Sure, there are still B&Bs that have shared baths, but there are also a number of high-end inns that garner the coveted AAA four- and five-diamond awards. A higher percentage of inns receive three diamonds and up than the general hotel population.

Think It Over...Very Carefully

This does not mean that every inn should strive to be luxurious, but luxury definitely has its place. Luxurious accommodations start with the services you provide. How available do you want to be to your guests? The bottom line is cheerful, really helpful, and creative twenty-four-hour assistance.

What kind of personal services do you want to offer? How are you at carrying luggage up three flights of stairs at midnight? Is there a place to eat at 10 P.M. in your tiny town? Are you prepared to make sandwiches for a late arrival? How do you feel about specially prepared breakfasts at noon for the honeymooners who struggled in at 2 A.M.? Does your guest management software record all the little things about your guests—for example, birthdays, anniversaries, whether they like sugar and cream with their coffee or are allergic to down? In other words, luxury today means going that extra step or three—or four—for your guests and getting a kick out of seeing what you can do to delight them.

Luxurious accommodations also mean physical features and amenities. Standard amenities for even the moderately priced inn today include a great breakfast and a snuggle-in comfortable bed, cookies or snacks of some kind, complimentary hot and cold beverages available 24/7, wine and hors d'oeuvres during a social hour or high tea available in the late afternoon, private use of a telephone, queen-sized beds, and twenty-four-hour refrigerator use—and, of course, everything and everyone must be spiffy and immaculately clean. According to the PAII *Industry Study*, more than 50 percent of all U.S. inns offer all these amenities.

Add to these the features in a luxurious fantasy room and you have a high-end experience. Most inns have only a few of these rooms. Not all of the following are found in a luxury room; they are presented in the general order of desirability:

- Privacy, obtained with a separate entrance or a freestanding cottage
- In-room whirlpool
- Canopy or king bed
- Fireplace that can be seen from the bed and/or whirlpool
- Spacious room
- Views, private gardens
- Large marble bathroom with separate, even multihead shower and bathtub and maybe even a sauna. If the bath is large enough and has a view, a whirlpool might be appropriate, but generally bubbles in the tub are not sufficient for a truly luxurious experience.
- Big fluffy bathrobes and maybe even slippers
- In-room telephone
- High-speed Internet connection
- Stereo system
- TV and VCR with movies available on-site
- Reservations made for dining or local adventures
- Well-appointed, high-end furnishings
- Coffeemaker
- Refrigerator stocked with soft drinks and water

Unique Quirks

- Breadmaker baking bread in your room when you arrive
- Desserts set out in the evening
- Breakfast in bed
- Dinner available by special order
- Cooking equipment and utensils for cottages (microwave, sink, dishes to match the room's theme)

Be responsive and creative in your selection of room luxury features and inn amenities.

But notice where we started: with an attitude of personal service that gets you, the innkeeper, going in the morning. These are the cornerstones of what will make bed-and-breakfast and country inns survive and thrive in a highly competitive marketplace.

SUPPORT SERVICES

A number of innkeeper support industries continue to expect a bright future, and the newest trends cluster around the specialization of services, not the plethora of broad-based industries that were so plentiful in the 1990s. For example, an Internet business that in the 1990s tried to be all things to all innkeepers now concentrates on selling Web promotion to innkeepers. Perhaps it also does some Web design and hosts innkeeper Web sites. "Internet marketing" is the key concept here, and it's one that simply did not exist ten years ago.

Most U.S. states and Canadian provinces have regional innkeeper associations. The industry has had its own trade newsletter since 1982, an international trade association for innkeepers based in the United States, and a national association in Australia. No longer are there hundreds of printed guidebooks published specifically on bed-and-breakfasts and country inns. Although several printed guidebooks remain, the "electronic guidebook," or Internet directory, is standard for both the innkeeper and for the traveler.

The inn industry is mainstream, with local and state legislation, inn realtors and consultants, a biennial international conference, and hundreds of vendors regularly serving and catering to the small-lodging-property marketplace. Seminars for aspiring innkeepers are widely available nationwide. Support services are commonplace in this ever-growing industry.

Who Makes a Good Innkeeper?

You like to cook, you're great with people, you start tingling when you're a block away from an antiques shop, and you slipcover all your own furniture. Putting all that to work is part of the reason you want to have an inn. Every one of those skills will come in handy, along with a number of others. To be successful in today's market, it's crucial that you delight in helping other people have a good time. In the rest of the travel industry, they call it a service mentality.

Innkeeping is serious business, requiring energy, responsibility, and leadership for success. It's a lifestyle change for anyone. For some, the change fits like a glove; for others, it's like a mitten: warm, toasty—and clumsy.

LIFESTYLE CHANGES

There is a timeless quality to innkeeping. The work never seems to be done, interrupted by the phone, sporadic eating patterns, late-night arrivals, a water heater that burns out when the inn is full, and a travel writer who arrives unannounced when the septic tank is being pumped.

On the other hand, there are opportunities to sit down and enjoy pieces of the day most nine-to-fivers don't have: a late breakfast in the garden on a slow weekday, an early-afternoon nap, the bargain matinee, evening wine with interesting guests.

Your whole idea of how to use time is changed. When you have a moment of peace and quiet, should you grab a needed nap or skim the newspaper for a crash course in current events? Time off tends to be in snatches: the concept of a "weekend" grows increasingly foreign; "quitting time" disappears.

Then there's the financial side. No more regular paychecks. Buying a car or a boat becomes a different kind of decision when you depend on the inclinations of the public for your income. Can-we-pay-the-mortgage panic can become a monthly event, along with juggling creditor priorities. In the meantime, you'll be describing to wealthy guests the charms of nearby expensive restaurants.

In some situations you may be able to try those restaurants, with the inn picking up the tab, because making restaurant recommendations is part of the innkeeper's job. (Consult with your accountant on this.) You also need to "shop" the competition to keep up with changes in the inn business, so your business pays for inn visits or you exchange nights with other innkeepers. If you live on the premises—and someone must—the expense of a separate home is eliminated. Guests expect a warm resident innkeeper. Your presence isn't your gift to the business. The business pays by providing housing and some meals.

All the usual employee benefits can be yours: perhaps health and life insurance; car mileage allowance or repairs and gasoline; car leasing; wages for your children who perform inn tasks. Business expenses like these are not taxable profit. So instead of a large paycheck, you will more likely receive a small allowance to supplement the essentials of life that the inn provides.

Single Innkeeper

Marie Christensen, owner of the Bath Street Inn in Santa Barbara, California, led a varied career life, all of which contributed to the skill sets necessary for the "wearing of many hats" as a single innkeeper. In 1996, Marie began working part-time for the original owner of the Bath Street Inn, Susan Brown. This apprenticeship with another single innkeeper did much to lay a useful groundwork for her eventual inn ownership.

The satisfaction of taking care of guests often fills Marie's social needs. She explains, "Having an inn is a lot of fun, a lot of work, and a truly wonderful way to be in people's lives. Guests often arrive tired and harried, and we participate in their renewal by treating them well, feeding them well (great breakfasts and lots of cookies), and providing clean, interesting, and pleasant surroundings, which are pretty but not so formal that they wonder if it's really okay to sit down. For me, it is a form of healing just as valid as that which occurs in therapy, and I appreciate being able to help guests relax and renew and return to their lives feeling better about themselves and their lives. Of course, it is also a pleasure to have guests join us when they have something to celebrate, and we support and enjoy their celebration as well.

"Retaining a staff that has a heartfelt desire to provide genuine hospitality is essential. The Bath Street Inn operates 24/7/365 and has twelve guest rooms, so as a one-woman show I definitely need help. With two full-time housekeepers, a relief housekeeper when needed, a part-time gardener, a full-time assistant manager, and three part-time innkeepers with one, two, or three shifts, I can take care of myself and live off-site." To have a definite break and some quiet time are two crucial items Marie finds essential, since she manages all aspects of the inn operation.

The satisfied guest keeps her going. "Many, many times when our guests leave they tell me what a wonderful time they had. I can see and am reminded, almost every day, that I do make a difference in a very real and practical way."

It takes almost anybody a year or two to establish a new social base and to make close friends. Meanwhile, you'll be more or less lonely during the years when you'll most need moral support. Complicating this is the intensity of the involvement and the unorthodox hours the inn will demand, making meeting and getting to know people even more difficult than normal.

WILL YOU MAKE A GOOD INNKEEPER?

To test for yourself whether the innkeeping profession is for you, fill out the following inventory as honestly as you can, checking the answer that best reflects your reaction. Have your partners fill it out too, for both themselves and for you. Use it as a tool to evaluate how well you'll succeed as innkeepers, individually and as a team.

How do you feel about people?
___I like people. I enjoy talking with a variety of people and can get along with just about anybody.
___I enjoy people in general but don't consider myself primarily a "social animal." I need private time.
___Generally, I prefer my own company to that of most others.

What was your parents' and/or your own childhood entrepreneurial experience?
___One or both of my parents or a close relative ran his or her own business, and I helped.
___I ran my own business before I was eighteen years old.
___I've been doing it now for five years or more.
___My parents and/or I have usually worked for someone else.

How persistent are you?
___I can name five projects I've worked on where I was the most tenacious in getting the job done.
___I stick to things for a while, but when I've had it, that's it. I usually finish what I start if it goes well.
___I'm not sure persistence is the answer. If I start something and then discover it doesn't appear possible, I'll give it up. Why beat your brains out?

How well do you face facts?

____I enjoy the decision-making process of learning from the event and changing my behavior accordingly.

____I believe that the way I have decided to do things is generally right and need to be shown a better way before I change.

____My experience has taught me that the way I do things is right, and I shouldn't question that.

How well do you minimize your risks?

____Although I see myself as a risk taker, I always have a backup plan if I fail. I'm open to new ideas but cautiously plan when to stop risking.

____I have an optimistic streak that leads me to play hunches. Planning usually just slows me down. I can make a budget, but usually I don't plan enough for expenses.

____I thrive on risk taking. If you listen to the naysayers, you'll never get anywhere.

What is your hands-on quotient?

____I enjoy learning by doing. I have no difficulty cleaning toilets, repairing things, and doing what needs to be done.

____I don't mind doing the everyday things, but it's really not valuable for me as owner to get involved in cleaning rooms or doing the books.

____It is not my plan to do this kind of physical work. My skills will be better utilized elsewhere.

How do you feel about business?

____I love the challenge of long-range planning, endless daily decisions, and organizing to keep a step ahead of the "other guy."

____I get bored with the repetitive problems, demands, and struggles of a business.

____Innkeeping is my escape from business.

Do you have the energy?

____I have worked in a setting demanding eighteen-hour days, seven days a week, and I thrived on it. I do, however, enjoy time off when I can arrange it.

____I have worked in a setting demanding eighteen-hour days, seven days a week. I did fine as long as I got regularly scheduled time off.

____I really need my weekend time to rejuvenate when I work forty to sixty hours a week.

____I have no interest in working more than forty hours a week.

How do you feel about providing service to others?

___I'm excited about providing my guests with a wonderful experience and look forward to going out of my way to make that possible.

___I believe that what we'll have to offer is plenty, and we'll deal as best we can with guest demands.

___I do not intend to serve anyone. A nice room and breakfast is better than our guests get elsewhere, and I think they'll be pleased with it.

What is your level of acceptance of people?

___I enjoy giving people of all kinds (including those with different moral standards, religion, lifestyle, politics, race, ethnicity, and so on) a wonderful experience. Everyone has a right to a pleasant time.

___My basic philosophy is "Live and let live," and I can accept people of all kinds.

___I have some difficulty with people different from myself and would feel uncomfortable having them in my home.

How do you handle pressure?

___I perform well under pressure. When time demands seem impossible, I enjoy the challenge.

___If I have reassurance and assistance from someone else, I do well under pressure.

___I dislike working under pressure and usually organize my life so I'm not faced with undue stress.

Your sense of humor?

___Even when things are not going well, I can always find something to laugh about.

___I tend to be somewhat serious about life but try to laugh when things are tough.

___What's to laugh about? Joking only complicates an already bad situation.

Flexibility

___I can move smoothly from one task to another without complete "closure" and not feel bothered.

___I prefer to complete one task before moving to another.

___Interruptions drive me crazy.

How do you handle conflict?

___I can usually find a way to talk to someone with whom I have a conflict without alienating that person.

____Though I dislike conflict and my stomach gets nervous, I go ahead and some-times disagree with another person even when it's very difficult; I work hard to find a solution that works for us both.

____I hit head-on and let the chips fall where they may, even if it makes the other person unhappy.

____I avoid conflict.

Like marriage and parenting, innkeeping has to be experienced; it can't be ade-quately described. But if you're willing to attend to the experience of innkeepers who are old hands and to honestly evaluate your own feelings about the behavior the job demands, you'll minimize the surprises when you hang out your own sign. Consider the comments below as you review your completed worksheet.

PEOPLE

Successful innkeepers like people. There is no quality more important. The innkeeper's appreciation and enjoyment of every guest is what keeps visitors coming back.

Innkeepers tend to begin with a feeling of "I like people night and day," then gradually become protective of their private and family time and space the longer they're in business.

ENTREPRENEURIAL BACKGROUND

Michael Phillips and Salli Rasberry, authors of *Honest Business,* point out that most people who successfully start and run small businesses had either parents or close relatives with a business, or had significant business experience themselves before the age of eighteen. "The children of taxi drivers, greasy spoon restaurateurs, and dentists have a very good chance of succeeding in business," they say. "Children of teachers, bureaucrats, and soldiers don't. A child who worked in her father's drug-store selling sodas, or in his mother's bookkeeping office doing ledgers, has a good grasp of how business works and can respond, intuitively, to business advice. All the unspoken, invisible issues of business are subtly communicated to children, and no amount of schooling can fully take the place of that process."

PERSISTENCE

This quality will be important in every area of your life as an innkeeper. As Phillips and Rasberry put it, it's "being willing to keep trying something long after your energy is used up, long after your enthusiasm has waned, and certainly long after other people have lost interest in helping you. The people who can't make it in business are the ones who give up easily or divert their attention from the long, hard parts to do the easier, more glamorous parts." It's facing life with an awareness that change comes slowly and wisdom is gained in the process.

FACING THE FACTS

Innkeepers cannot be shifting with the breeze; it takes too much energy to change your mind and your policies every day of the week. On the other hand, you must be open enough to examine the consequences of your decisions and directions, willing to learn from the evidence, and able to change in response to it. Sometimes the necessary changes will go deep; some dear principle on which you based your inn image may not work. One innkeeper found that her inherent "computerphobia" resulted in a radical decrease in her business, while her Web-savvy innkeeper neighbors were increasing their occupancy.

Another innkeeper had decided that clocks in guest rooms and televisions anywhere were an insult to her historic Victorian. When guests kept asking what time it was, showing up late for breakfast, and searching for the television, she swallowed her pride in the inn's historical accuracy. Now clock radios are at every guest bedside and a television is available upon request.

MINIMIZING THE RISKS

We all hear stories about the businessperson who takes a gamble and reaps millions; it's enough to make you believe that success requires the abandon of a gambler. But studies of successful businesspeople usually reveal not a gambler but a cautious casino owner who minimizes risks in several ways.

Developing backup plans and alternative solutions is a common strategy of successful people. Innkeepers need to be open to and seek new ideas, but they must plan carefully for their implementation, setting benchmarks for pulling back from risks too great.

HANDS-ON QUOTIENT

Innkeeping requires many and varied skills, from plumbing and cooking to bookkeeping and gardening. Using all these is for many innkeepers a highlight of the business. Actually doing a task forces you to understand the ins and outs of it. If you've cleaned rooms for a year and then hire staff, you know how long the job should take and you notice the details. You have an advantage over the innkeeper who starts out with a staff to clean rooms.

On the other hand, having and imposing your firm idea of the "right" way to do things may slow you down on delegating tasks to others and taking hold of new important areas. Your hands-on skill may conflict with your management skill.

BUSINESS ATTITUDE

Prospective innkeepers frequently explain their interest in the career change as a way to escape to a quiet country life, avoid the competitive rat race of business, and get back to the earth. In fact, owning this kind of small business brings a deluge of mundane problems and repetitive tasks, such as preparing breakfasts, doing dishes, painting, and repairing. After the first year, some aspects of innkeeping get boring. You'll be tempted to make unnecessary changes for excitement's sake.

Enjoying the challenge of providing a quality stay for every guest is crucial. You must delight in a smooth operation—accurate confirmations, prompt follow-up on mail, regular maintenance. You must thrive on a near-total commitment to the needs of your business. Persisting through the trials and tribulations is easier when you enjoy the business side of innkeeping.

ENERGY

People who consider themselves dynamos get winded operating an inn. It's not only the quantity of energy necessary; it's also a restructuring of when it must be expended. Weekends and evenings are no longer time off; weekdays and afternoons more likely are. By the same token, those spare moments when guests aren't demanding your attention are the times you'll fill with repairs, inventory, advertising, promotion, and confirming and taking reservations. The less your start-up capital, the more you'll do yourself, and the less leisure you'll experience.

SERVICE

The importance of being enthusiastic about ferreting out ways to make guests happy cannot be overemphasized. Truly happy and successful innkeepers revel in delighting their guests with little surprises. Phillips and Rasberry define service as "the conscious act of offering our talents, resources, and support to other people." This is innkeeping, and you can tell how well it's done almost the moment you enter an inn. It doesn't mean you have to become a bellhop or offer room service. It's an attitude that puts a special stay for a guest at the top of the priority list.

ACCEPTING PEOPLE

All kinds of people visit inns, and almost all of them probably offend someone: unmarried couples, mixed-race couples, gay couples, single women or men traveling alone, older men with younger women and vice versa, the unsociable and the gossips, drinkers, smokers, Jews, Arabs, born-again Christians, Buddhists, bratty kids, macho males. In some areas, such as smoking and drinking, you can set limits at your inn. In others you cannot. Beware of opening an inn if you are uncomfortable with people different from yourself.

PRESSURE

The idyllic image of unhurried, pastoral calm is for the guests, not the innkeepers. There is always some deadline to meet: breakfast at nine, rooms cleaned by two, tea at five.

The greatest pressure is often financial: how to pay too many bills, increase income, renegotiate swing loans or credit lines, make refunds, pay staff, finance necessary repairs and a new washing machine. An innkeeper makes a supermom look like a duffer.

SENSE OF HUMOR

Being an innkeeper is fun—and you'll make it that way. The longer you're in business, the less the disasters will feel like your fault, and the more humorous the problems will seem. Laughing at problems removes them from that anxious area in your stomach to a warmer place in your heart.

A healthy sense of humor helps you avoid burnout. By the same token, when situations you once could have laughed off start looking serious and like just more bad news, a red light should go on: time for a day off. Make it a habit to ask yourself, "What's funny here?"

FLEXIBILITY

If being in the center of everything happening at once sounds like fun to you, so will innkeeping. If wearing many hats is your style, innkeeping is too. If you can shift gears quickly without stripping them, innkeeping is the career vehicle you've yearned for. And if you can briefly break from a heated argument to book a room with grace, you've got what it takes.

CONFLICT

You will have to handle disagreements with staff and guests, and it will be disillusioning. Someday, some couple will take one look at the room they've reserved and ask for their money back. Some staff person will rearrange your carefully planned parlor. Unfortunately, perfection, like beauty, is in the eye of the beholder. Here's where your sense of humor and flexibility receive a good workout.

getting your act together

Preparing for Innkeeping

Here's the next step in evaluating your innkeeping potential: a checklist of skills, with comments on how they're likely to be applied in a bed-and-breakfast inn. Some of them you already have, some you've always wanted to learn, and others you wouldn't touch with a ten-foot pole. Give the skills you already have a star, the ones you want to learn a plus, and the others a zero. Your partner should do the same. Then evaluate your combined inventory.

SKILLS CHECKLIST

Financial

- **Bookkeeping and accounting:** Balancing a checkbook is just the beginning. You'll also need to balance your books—and know when they're balanced. You must understand how to track the deposits you receive and the checks you write, and how to set up your books so that they'll yield the information you want and need. Using a computer simplifies these tasks.
- **Developing and monitoring a budget:** You must know how to predict the future, so you'll know when you can expand or hire additional staff. The plan must be reviewed frequently, and changes must be made when the projections aren't panning out.
- **Understanding financial statements:** Good financial statements provide information on the equity you've built up, your return on investment, depreciation, cash flow, and problem areas. They need to be set up so that they'll tell you what you want to know, and you need to know how to read them.
- **Tax benefits and planning:** Understanding the tax structure and what it means in your particular situation is critical. How does your tax bracket affect decisions about whether your spouse should continue present employment for a while? What are the benefits of holding the inn as one spouse's separate property? Are the cash benefits of renovating a historical structure sufficient to offset the expense of it?

Computer

You'll want to be able to write checks and keep your books, establish a guest database, answer and write e-mail, manage your inn's Web site, and computerize your inn's reservations.

- **E-mail:** Are you comfortable writing and answering e-mail?
- **Web sites:** Do you know enough to hire a Web designer? Do you regularly surf the Internet? Do you understand Internet marketing?

Marketing

In an area like accounting, novices tend to recognize their need for help and gladly pay for it. In the marketing field, however, beginners more often feel they can do it themselves. Be careful; you may need more help than you realize. Getting your inn off to a slow start can be expensive in lost revenues.

- **Graphic design and layout:** You'll want brochures and stationery, and possibly advertisements, postcards, confirmation forms, gift certificates, and so on. The necessary skills range from an eye for design to the ability to create a functional reservation form that only you and your staff will see.
- **Copywriting:** Maybe you'll want to write your own brochure and regular media releases.
- **Promotion methods:** What kinds of things do people do to promote businesses? How will you promote the inn?
- **Telephone skills:** Are you comfortable talking on the phone, and is your voice pleasant and warm? Turning calls for booked Saturday nights into midweek reservations depends a lot on phone skills.
- **Media relations:** How do you get profiled in the kinds of stories you frequently see in magazines and newspapers and on television about great inns to visit?
- **Photography:** Good photographs are a must for courting the media. Sometimes writers send their own photographers, but your good shots enable you to present your inn in the best light. This is especially helpful if there's a tornado in progress when the writer's photographer arrives.
- **Organization of special events:** From your first open house to fund-raisers that benefit a favorite charity and your inn simultaneously, confidence in your ability to carry off a lulu of a party is a real asset.

Property

You may be a crack decorator, but can you fix a toilet? Read on.

- **Understanding basic building terminology and process:** You will need to work with contractors and subcontractors; you may even end up being an owner-builder.

- **Basic maintenance skills:** From changing a washer to touching up enamel, these skills will save you a lot of money.
- **Landscaping, both planting and design:** Which plants stay alive in your area? What lasts in a bouquet? What landscape design will lure passersby to your door?
- **Decorating:** Do you know how inviting a cool blue-and-white color scheme is in a snowstorm? (Not very.) Can you make a silk purse out of a sow's ear? You'll probably need to.

Food Services

- **Menu creation:** Color, temperature, and taste combinations must be more than the sum of the parts.
- **Health department standards:** Also known as Botulism 101. Protecting the public health and safety is your responsibility.
- **Serving food to a group:** There are techniques for getting it all on the table, hot or cold. Do you have them mastered?
- **Kitchen setup and organization:** If you do this wrong, you'll be annoyed by it every time you make a pot of coffee.

Staff

Some innkeepers start out convinced they will do all the work themselves. Still others believe that because they ran a corporation, they have managerial skills. Supervising a small corps of people involved in physical labor and customer relations is different from having a personnel director and a secretary, or just telling your children what to do.

- **Employing others:** Do you understand the basics of hiring, training, supervising, and terminating staff?
- **Motivating and keeping staff:** What motivates housekeepers to keep doing routine jobs perfectly? How do you keep a chef and wait staff happy through a full season, so they won't leave you high and dry two weeks before it's over?
- **Pay:** What are the going rates of pay in this market? The benefit packages?
- **Paperwork:** What forms do you need to complete? What taxes should you pay?

Getting What You Need

Now that you know the skills you want to acquire, start soon. There are numerous resources available.

Professional Resources

The Professional Association of Innkeepers International has compiled beginning resource and ongoing reference materials on staff, marketing, and financial matters. Its information and referral service, available to members, can provide assistance on property and food service skills as well.

Classes

Check the community college catalog, adult education flyers, professional organization workshops, and lecture series for classes and seminars in your areas of interest.

Computer Skills

If you don't have computer or Internet skills, take a class, hire a consultant, read a book, or ask your kids for help.

Friends

Some of your friends are undoubtedly pros in areas where you need help. Contact them for advice, possibly even instruction, and perhaps as hired consultants. This can be sticky, since you won't want to take advantage of the friendship to get for free something they make a business of selling. If you're careful and courteous about how you handle the situation, working with friends can be fun.

Consultants

If you have a good general grasp of an area but need specific answers to important questions, consider working with a consultant. A good consultant can help you design systems you'll live with for a long time. Working with someone on this short-term basis can be a good way to test whether you would work well together for the long term. For instance, if your consultant moves methodically and you think and act fast, work sessions will be frustrating and probably not very productive.

Libraries and Bookstores

People in many other businesses need much of the same information prospective innkeepers need. Books written especially for the small business can help a great deal. See Resources for specific suggestions.

Practice

Maybe you could do great layouts or write fine media releases with a little practice. Give it a shot, if it interests you. Ask friends to look over your product and give you frank feedback. To check how clearly your effort communicates, ask a friend to review it and then explain to you what it says.

Observation

Keep your eyes open for the ways others handle areas with which you'll need to deal. For example, keep a file of inn brochures and advertisements. Observe a wider field, too: How do other businesses promote? What kinds of signs attract attention and still retain a "feel" you like? What can you tell about selling by analyzing television commercials?

Volunteering

Get some on-the-job experience in budgeting, say, by working with a non-profit group. Volunteer to organize the Boy Scouts fund-raiser or to do the publicity for the women's center calendar.

Work Experience

While you're planning your inn, you may be able to work at a job that will help in your ultimate objective. If you're a retail clerk, maybe you can work in a decorator's shop. If you're a graphic designer, maybe you can take on some design work for a local inn.

Apprenticeship or Internship Innkeeping

All the research in the world can't fully prepare you for the actual experience of innkeeping. Some workshops arrange for the participants to take over an inn for a weekend, and some innkeepers take interns for varying periods. To be sure your experience serves your needs, consider the following:

- Be sure you understand the innkeeper's expectations of your time and tasks. Usually the innkeeper does not expect you to continue to carry on your other life while working at the inn, so, for example, your personal or business telephone calls may be a problem.
- Consider the inn's style, so that your experience can mesh with your future plans. If you want to serve dinner, try to find a country inn, rather than a bed-and-breakfast, for a full taste of the extra complications dinner introduces.
- Try to get a sense of how the innkeeper functions; does it fit you? Personalities are important in learning. You ought to enjoy your mentor.
- If you plan to own your inn with a partner, spouse, or friend, participate in the

internship together to get an idea of how each of you functions in this setting.

- Appreciate that even though you may be donating your time, the innkeeper is giving too. Training is hard work on both sides.
- Approach the opportunity with an open and curious mind. Evaluate your experience in relation to your own plans later, when you're back home. Of course you have your own plans and your own ways of doing things, and your unique style is important, but an apprenticeship is not the time to exercise it. You're not there to show the innkeeper how to improve, but to try out a lifestyle for yourself.

Researching Your Market and Site Selection

If you've bought the inn concept but not the inn, this section will help you make a good choice. If you've already found the perfect inn or place to create one, this information will help you review its pros and cons, which you'll want to include in your business plan.

To understand the milieu in which your inn will function, you need to research the travel field in general, as well as the bed-and-breakfast industry. Use these questions as a guide:

- What are the trends?
- What is the profile (economic position, family status, interests) of the bed-and-breakfast traveler?
- Why do people travel?
- What is the overall economic health of the travel industry in general and of the bed-and-breakfast business in particular?
- What kinds of competitive influences are there in the travel accommodations market?
- Do people travel to some areas more than to others?
- How do the policies, laws, and codes of state and national governments affect local travel?
- How do people make travel arrangements?

Be creative in finding the answers. Try these avenues:

- Watch for sales trends as you travel. Are travelers being offered unusual services or bargain prices?
- Look at what is advertised on the Internet.
- Subscribe to travel magazines and read travel ads. You can get a sense of the health of an industry and a destination by evaluating the desperation of the ads and the number and kinds of "specials."

The Perfect Search

Chuck and Robbie Slemaker, aeronautics-industry executives, set out to get educated about bed-and-breakfast inns by attending a workshop in Santa Barbara, California. They then developed a set of criteria for a site that would meet their personal needs: a four-season area with a lake and a ski resort; a town with a small village atmosphere; a location within an hour's drive of a major medical center; an affordable property; and a climate that offered at least three hundred days of sunshine a year. After hours of Internet research and a scouting trip to Colorado, they found the perfect location: Big Bear Lake in southern California, less than a hundred miles from their home.

Their marketing study revealed that within a three-and-a-half-hour drive there were over 18 million people—perfect for a focused promotion of their proposed inn. It took a trip to Switzerland for their bed-and-breakfast concept to gel. The Slemakers knew they wanted to create an inn that was modern, very luxurious, but consistent with a mountain atmosphere. In designing their remodel of an existing house to provide eight guest rooms, they worked with the American Automobile Association to make sure that their inn would meet the four-diamond criteria for rating B&Bs.

Although their remodeling and landscaping costs were high, the Slemakers succeeded in earning the four-diamond AAA rating, the only lodging facility on the mountain to do so! After three years of operation, the Alpenhorn has exceeded the area's average occupancy rate and has achieved cash breakeven. It pays to do your homework.

- Attend industry meetings, seminars, and training sessions.
- Interview industry people as you travel. Ask innkeepers, hotel managers, and travel agents the market questions listed here.
- Talk to your librarian. Find out what's new on the shelves.
- Subscribe to hospitality industry publications.

Like everyone else, people considering new careers as innkeepers have distinct likes and dislikes about where to live. Many are city-bred and intend to stay that way; for others, heaven is the desert, or the mountains, or the sea. Don't get so excited about a particular property that you ignore these personal parameters. The first criterion for selecting your site is that the environment meets your needs, your family's, and your innkeeping partners'.

Look next at recreational, social, educational, and employment needs. Does one of you intend to continue to work while another runs the inn? This naturally limits your site to areas with desirable employment opportunities. What about schools for your children? You may dream of living in the desert, but if your child is training for Olympic ice-skating events, your options will be severely limited. Whether your favorite pastime is miniature golf or amateur theater, be sure you choose a place where you can pursue it.

You can save time and money by establishing and agreeing on some basic search guidelines with the other members of the new inn family or families. The guidelines could read something like this:

- Ten to fifteen miles from the ocean, for the cool climate and because of your love of the sea.
- A city population of forty to seventy-five thousand, to satisfy your needs for community involvement, a good educational system, and cultural events.
- Not more than a day's drive to parents and grandparents.
- Employment opportunities in the computer field.

Starting from a framework like this—it can have many more selection criteria—use a map to begin choosing possible locations. You can gather a tremendous amount of information even before you leave home, by contacting the local chambers of commerce, subscribing to area newspapers, and looking at bed-and-breakfast inns advertising on the Internet.

Then the fun begins. Vacation trips become business trips. (Ask your accountant about tax write-offs for these exploratory forays.) Areas you may simply have passed through on the way to somewhere else will become important stopping places. Towns, cities, historical monuments, and scenery suddenly look different.

Not many people can start from scratch to decide where to live. Enjoy it!

Evaluating Your Selection

Now that you've found a place that meets *your* needs, you need to decide whether anyone else would like to spend time there. If not, you won't have any customers.

WHO WILL BE YOUR CUSTOMERS?

The type of customer you will attract is an important factor in the image and size of your inn, what the best location is, the room prices, and the amenities offered. Naturally, your first task will be to discover which type of visitor comes to your area: tourist or businessperson. A tourist comes to the area as a destination and normally stays at least two or three days. A traveler stops in the area on the way to somewhere else. A businessperson comes on a specific mission, perhaps to sell a product or attend a meeting.

Tourists

As our bed-and-breakfast industry has grown, a large percentage of inns are now located in rural or village areas, which are tourist destination spots. The following questions will help you evaluate your selection.

- Are you close to major highways or interstates?
- Is the climate good most of the year? Which are the down months?
- Are most of the tourists who come to the area campers, large family groups, or people who are looking for a lodging experience?
- Are you close to a large city? Americans enjoy mini vacations three or four times a year. In general, they drive no more than three hours each way for a two- or three-day vacation.
- Are there enough tourist attractions to encourage people to stay more than a day? Are there good restaurants, historical sites, museums, zoos, gardens, amusement parks, unique shopping areas, cultural events, or beautiful scenery?
- Is there a "season" and, if so, is it long enough to support the property? If snow sports are the main tourist attraction, are there also visitors in the spring, summer, and fall?
- Is there good public transportation into the area, by airplane, bus, or train?

Business Traveler

In addition to catering to the tourist business, some inns have specialized in serving the business traveler. This usually occurs in a smaller town where the lodging choices are minimal and the town has a large manufacturing facility, company headquarters, or county seat.

Next to the Courthouse

With opening day less than a month away, the inspector was signing off on the parking lot the same day the telephone lines were being installed at Bradford Place, a four-room Victorian located in a rural and isolated part of central California. With an amused grin the inspector walked over to owner Dottie Musser, a corporate refugee, and asked how many lines she was bringing to the building. "As many as I can get!" she said. "We will be catering heavily to business travelers, so each room will need its own telephone line. And I need three for the office, plus one for my personal use." He walked away shaking his head at such a seemingly foolish idea.

What no one could ever have imagined was the number of businesspeople who would decide to stay at an inn in an area known primarily for its abundant outdoor recreation, great antiquing, and sleepy little gold rush towns. Yet with only leisure guests, Bradford Place could not survive. In attracting business clientele, Dottie balances the equation this way: "The first part is location; the second part is service and value. We are centrally located in town, easy to find even at night, and in close proximity to the impressive historic courthouse. Our town is the only incorporated one in the county, and it's the hub for education, medical, and social services as well as government agencies for miles in all directions. Our reputation has been built on our superior service, our breakfast menu choices with flexible times, and our rooms, which are soothing for romantic weekend getaways but discreetly outfitted to meet the demands of the fast-paced businessperson." In 2002, after three years in business, wireless DSL became available at Bradford Place Inn and Gardens in Sonora, California—population 4,501.

This is where you apply your general field research to the specific area you are considering for your inn. This information will help you in big and little decisions about ambience, breakfast, pricing, promotion, amenities, location, specific property, and so on. Don't skip this research step. Questions to ask include:

- What is the nature of the overnight guest in the area? Consider age, economic status, children, interests and activities, purpose of visit.
- What is the occupancy percentage of nonconference hotels, motels, and inns? This step is crucial in developing income projections.
- What is the average daily room rate (ADR) of the area hotels and motels? The bed-and-breakfast inns? The resorts with golf courses, tennis courts, and swimming pools? Do these properties give AAA discounts, AARP discounts, midweek discounts, corporate discounts?
- What is special about the inns in the area?
- What is lacking in the existing inns? How would you make your inn unique?
- What is the season? Are there off-season prices?
- Is there a transient occupancy tax (bed tax) in the area, and are the tax revenues used to promote tourism?
- Where do guests come from?
- How many hotels or inns in the area are new?
- What hostelries have opened and/or gone out of business in the last two or three years?
- How many inns are there in the area? How long have they been in existence?
- What role does the government or chamber of commerce take in supporting tourism?
- What kind of recreational and cultural activities are there in the area?
- What is the restaurant scene like?
- What new commercial or recreational developments are planned?
- What special events bring travelers to the area?

HOW TO FIND OUT THE ANSWERS: A RESOURCE LIST

The sources below will have answers to the above questions. The more sources you consult, the broader and more accurate your perspective on a location will be.

- Chamber of commerce or visitors bureau. Ask for tourist materials and research materials on the area; have an in-depth discussion with the tourism director; check out the area Web sites.

- Brochures and rate sheets of lodging establishments.
- Local reference librarian.
- Local elected officials.
- Local Service Corps of Retired Executives (SCORE) consultant of the Small Business Administration (SBA).
- Web sites of hotels and inns.

Other Suggestions
- Stay in local lodgings, especially inns or the most obvious competition.
- Subscribe to a local newspaper. Take a business or travel reporter to lunch and talk about the general health of the economy and the prospects for a new inn.
- Read the ads in materials aimed at visitors to see what the best hotels stress and when they offer specials.
- Talk to experienced innkeepers in adjacent areas. They may be more willing to speak candidly about what works in your area than innkeepers located right there.
- Talk to new and longtime innkeepers in the immediate neighborhood.

Evaluating Existing Inns
How do you determine whether the bed-and-breakfast inns in an area are prosperous? Some innkeepers don't keep good records and won't be able to answer questions concretely; others are naturally hesitant about sharing such information. Here are clues to look for:
- Do they require minimum stays? This often indicates that an establishment is successful enough to be selective.
- Have existing inns expanded? When, how much, and in what way: more rooms, additional services, more baths?
- Are price ranges at the area's inns similar? If they are uniformly high, innkeepers may be prospering; if low, competition may be intense.
- How do "deals" and amenities affect prices? Do prices vary based on midweek stays, fireplaces, private baths, bed sizes, or any combination of these?
- When did prices last increase?
- Does the inn support the innkeepers financially? Is one partner working outside? Are there other apparent sources of income, such as retirement pensions?
- Is there a supportive innkeepers association in the area?
- What do innkeepers see as trends?
- What kind of media coverage have area inns received?
- What are the impressions of the inn's staff?

Most innkeepers are helpful and will be happy to talk with you, but they're also busy, and your questions aren't the only ones they get. Plan to book a room and stay at the inn on a weekday or during the off-season, when the innkeeper will not be too busy. Identify yourself as a prospective innkeeper and make an appointment to talk. Offer to pay a consulting fee.

Don't ask directly about occupancy rates. For some innkeepers, this is as touchy as inquiring about their salary level. Other innkeepers will offer the information. If they don't, ask what a new innkeeper could expect in occupancy for the first year or how long it takes for area inns to become financially successful. Or, ask what kind of occupancy other inns in the area are experiencing.

Treat the innkeeper as an expert consultant, even if you don't like the inn or the way business is done there. Innkeepers don't owe you time and information just because they've succeeded or just because you've booked a room.

Be willing to share your plans and ideas with innkeepers in the area. Don't be secretive; remember, you're getting a great deal of help from them, and you may want to join the local association.

After you've done the research, sit down and put it all together: the industry, your personal needs, and the realities of the area. If people come to the area to hike or ski, capitalize on it; don't try to open their eyes to the joys of fly-fishing. Build on the mood, energy, environment, neighborhood, and facilities that exist.

INN LOCATION

As bed-and-breakfast inns have become increasingly popular, you are more likely to find an established one for sale. The following location guidelines for buying a building to convert to an inn apply also to buying an existing inn. Even with an established property, it is important to look ahead to when you may wish to expand. Consider these factors:

Location Within the Community
· Close, but not too close, to restaurants, shops, and similar businesses.
· A "safe" area, with a low crime rate.
· Falls within the service area for police and fire departments, emergency vehicle services, and hospital facilities.
· Convenient to highways.
· Roads and utilities are developed.

The Lot
- Large enough for off-street parking for guests and owners.
- Room to expand.
- Outdoor area for the innkeepers.
- Acceptable adjoining properties, with privacy, fences, landscaping, sound insulation, animals, children, and air pollution all well explored.

The Building
- Charm, character, curb appeal, historical significance.
- Structural soundness.
- Resale value.
- Size and number of bedrooms; dining room, parlor, and kitchen areas.
- Number of bathrooms or convertible closets.
- Private innkeeper quarters and storage.
- Inn storage areas and laundry facilities.
- Utilities, water, and sewage systems.
- Ventilation, natural light, protection from sun, wind, and snow.
- Cost and future availability of energy: gas, electricity, water, solar.

Of course, no one can say you should consider only properties that meet certain very specific standards, like closets for every guest room or certifiable historic status. Your decisions will relate to many other factors, including the type of inn you wish to have, the community you've chosen, and your budget. The guidelines above are designed to help you evaluate your first-, second-, and third-choice inn locations and compare them with one another. Appendix 1 is a sample worksheet on which you can record impressions.

Zoning

By their nature, bed-and-breakfast and country inns feel like home, and they naturally tend to appear in areas with a residential character. Consequently, as the industry has grown, communities have felt the need to recognize these new lodging options and limit them appropriately.

The Professional Association of Innkeepers International periodically updates a report based on surveys of dozens of communities, including reviews of current regulations, interviews with innkeepers and planners, and traffic analyses. Of the enacted bed-and-breakfast ordinances, less than 5 percent are at the state level; most occur at local, county, and city levels.

Two planning trends indicate greater acceptance of bed-and-breakfast inns. First, planners are seriously researching the state of the industry and developing regulations where none existed before. Increasingly rare are the days when eager innkeepers-to-be appear at town meetings with plans in hand, only to be confronted by a row of blank faces of folks who have never heard of bed-and-breakfasts!

Second, existing regulations are being refined and even relaxed, reflecting the maturity of the industry and its successful incorporation into the community. For example, inns are being allowed an increasing number of rooms, resident managers, and multiple buildings.

A third trend counters the other two: local regulations are being tightened and existing inns are having to comply. These situations are often highly political and personal and, fortunately, are not too common.

However, the problem with much existing zoning is that it was established in response to one prospective bed-and-breakfast owner and a few residents, rather than as the result of a look at the industry as a whole and how it will function within a community in five or ten years. So, for example, definitions vary greatly. Not only are the terms "guest houses," "homestays," "lodging and rooming houses," "inns" and others widely used by different jurisdictions to mean the same thing, but they can also be used to mean opposite things! One jurisdiction defines an inn as having fifteen or more guest rooms, while another describes a hotel as a lodging facility with twelve or more guest rooms!

A very few jurisdictions include requirements beyond the usual zoning scope: that registration cards be retained for a period of three years; that soap, clean sheets, and towels be provided to guests; and that insurance coverage meet a prescribed standard. Interestingly, not even hotel ordinances include such requirements.

The following findings on how communities regulate inns are presented as a guide for you in reviewing and responding to your own community's approach.

WHERE DO YOU FIT?

Zoning codes generally allow homestays and small bed-and-breakfasts in single-family residential zones, and commercial B&Bs, bed-and-breakfast inns, and country inns in multiple-family, commercial, historic, or tourist zones. Communities not identifying B&Bs as a specific use in the zoning code may allow them as rooming or boardinghouses.

Inns that serve meals to the public fall under any restaurant regulations your community may have, even if you are serving dinner only to your overnight guests. This introduces additional issues, such as adequate parking for outside diners or wedding guests, and liquor-license requirements.

WHAT DO THEY WANT OF YOU?

Signs: In communities where existing sign regulations forbid signs in your neighborhood, some provision needs to be made to reduce the confusion of guests looking for their reserved lodging. Placing the sign on the building is sometimes the compromise. In any case, a large neon sign offends the very nature of the small inn. A small discreet sign placed on the front lawn with a tasteful light and a single post is the overwhelming favorite. Signs should be in keeping with the structure and the neighborhood and yet be placed where arriving guests can easily see them.

Where an inn is located on a major roadway, a sign does help to bring in business, and there will generally be a sign ordinance.

Parking: Off-street parking is frequently required, though in some neighborhoods this is not possible or necessary. In urban areas, parking is a major issue; in suburban and rural areas, less so. Recent codes require one space per guest room plus the spaces required for a single-family dwelling.

Adjacent parking or satellite parking is often permitted in communities where parking is at a premium, as is shared parking with operations that have different peak parking hours, like banks and offices. The parking requirement is often the limiting factor that discourages the inappropriate locating of a bed-and-breakfast.

Owner Residence: Zoning regulations often make specifications about who may or must live on the premises. In single-family zones, the owner-operator is required to live on the premises. In some cases this can be a part owner. For bed-and-breakfast inns or country inns located in commercial or multiple-family zones, this requirement is not common, though most states require someone to be on the premises of lodging properties in the evenings, depending on the number of rooms.

Length of Stay: To ensure that guests do not become renters, many zoning codes add regulations limiting the length of stay to seven to fourteen days, for example, or up to fourteen consecutive days in a single thirty-day period.

Food Service: Bed-and-breakfast, by definition, automatically includes the service of breakfast. However, some codes add further limitations: to continental breakfast only, for example, or breakfast served only to guests, or no other meal service allowed. Should the innkeepers wish to serve outsiders, they will face the possibility of parking problems and the requirements of any restaurant.

Problems have occurred when innkeepers expanded their business to include weddings, events, or meetings that cause parking, noise, and traffic-congestion problems. This kind of activity is not allowed or is limited in many communities' regulations.

Cooking facilities in guest rooms are generally prohibited and rarely desired, except for a few bed-and-breakfast inns or country inns with cabins, or urban inns where guests' business stays are lengthy.

Size: A restriction on the number of rooms allowed is the most common problem aspiring innkeepers face in selecting the place in a town to locate. In general, the more residential the neighborhood, the fewer rooms allowed. You may feel that with a small bed-and-breakfast, the character of your operation will be clearly residential, but in an area where townspeople prefer that businesses—no matter how small—be in commercial areas and homes in residential areas, changing these rulings or even taking on the community and the bureaucracy will waste your valuable money and time. Be sure that you understand the requirements and attitude of the community before you buy. Generally, rural areas do not seem as concerned about this issue.

Permits: Some jurisdictions require that you obtain a special permit to open a B&B. This could be a bed-and-breakfast permit or a conditional use permit. The latter is designed to permit a particular use in a specified zone but not simply as a matter of right. It recognizes that while the basic use is compatible with other permitted uses, some aspects of your proposed use could cause problems. Often, conditional use is the only course open to new bed and breakfasts in a community; however, be aware that use permits often run with the premises and the owner named on the permit. If ownership changes, the new owner needs a new permit.

MAKING THE CASE FOR INNS

Almost always, despite occasional community concerns before opening day, inns are good neighbors. Experience has shown them to play important and beneficial roles in numerous ways. Don't be shy about pointing this out.

Inns strengthen the economic base of a community by introducing a new type of nonpolluting business, deriving income from otherwise non-income-producing property, and thus bolstering the economic viability of the neighborhood without reducing its residential character. Unlike large corporations, which are likely to bring in nonlocal management and labor and use outside suppliers for construction, small inns use local contractors, subcontractors, architects, attorneys, and accountants, as well as local management, cleaning, and gardening personnel. Though one inn may not hire many employees, a community that encourages inn growth will find that ten inns with ten rooms each will actually hire more staff—and not just manual labor—than a one-hundred-room hotel. The staff-to-guest ratio in a B&B inn is closer to that of a fine resort than to that of a budget hotel.

Inns also help stabilize a community's tourism industry by increasing the choice of lodging, by providing lodging at tourism sites where commercial hotels and motels are out of place, and by relieving any lodging shortage during seasonal high occupancy periods and major events.

Inn guests are big spenders. Research on B&B guest spending done in the past by YBR Consulting and recently through PAII shows that guests spend triple the national average. An early study reported that at 40 percent occupancy, one bed-and-breakfast or country inn guest room brings $63,000 a year to the town in meals, shopping, admissions, and incidentals, not counting the income on the room and the room tax.

Inn guests are also nice folks. They're quiet, and theft is almost unknown. (With residential owner-operators in a neighborhood inn, security is better than that in neighborhoods where most residents go off to work each day.) According to industry studies, inn guests are generally married, upper-middle-class, well-educated professionals, managers, or white-collar workers seeking a quiet get-away or comfortable security on a business trip. Once a B&B has opened and the neighborhood is aware of its presence, complaints about guest noise and traffic are extremely rare. Drive-by traffic is very low, compared to other lodging. Most guests at inns make a reservation before leaving home. A recent survey of traffic flow for a Washington bed-and-breakfast inn found that traffic is actually less for the rural five-room property than for a family of four using a similar house. The typically low midweek occupancy, the elimination of the owners' commutes to work, and the need to organize one's trips away from the business tend to cause the traffic to be lighter.

Inns revitalize and conserve neighborhoods. They require the kind of large, older dwelling whose original use as a home for one family is obsolete. More than 90 percent of publicly operating B&Bs are in buildings over seventy-five years old. Innkeepers are committed to their communities, personally invested in the health of the town. Not only do B&B owners do spectacular restoration jobs on their properties, but they also often start and actively support other historic preservation efforts in their previously run-down neighborhoods, projects local agencies can rarely afford to tackle. Conversion to a B&B not only offers the opportunity to restore historic structures and provide ongoing maintenance, but it can also bring life back into neighborhoods by attracting overnight guests who will support shops, restaurants, and museums.

Finally, innkeepers are collectors and disseminators of historical information about neighborhoods and whole communities. Old pictures, stories about past generations, and furnishings of other eras are often returned to their original home—now the B&B—and used in guest rooms or as part of the lore of the inn.

YOUR ACTION PLAN

Jim Goff, once director of planning for the city of San Diego, California, and now innkeeper of the nine-room Strawberry Creek Inn Bed and Breakfast in Idyllwild, California, makes these recommendations:
- Recognize that folks who don't comply with laws and regulations cause suspicion of the industry, which can result in more stringent or even prohibitive regulations as violations become apparent.
- Be a good neighbor. Get involved with community and neighborhood councils to gain their support and show them how you can help make the neighborhood more vital.
- Don't be confrontational with neighbors and local zoning officials; it can backfire in more restrictions and prohibitions.
- Instead, work closely with local zoning officials in an education program before buying or attempting to start a B&B in a residential neighborhood.
- When dealing with legislation or regulations affecting your personal situation, take the long view for the industry as a whole. Guests are interested in all types of B&Bs and should be able to make choices, from small homestays to larger inns. The wider the range, the more likely you are to find guests who are happy at your kind of place.

For Better, for Worse: Choosing a Legal Structure

Exploring the question of legal structure for your business is a mental giant step for anyone who has been mostly an employee, especially of a large corporation or organization. These institutions are so complex that most of us don't even think about their legal structures, let alone understand them. But for the entrepreneur, choosing a legal structure is one of the most important decisions you will ever make.

There is a strong temptation to seal your business agreements with partners or investors with simple handshakes. Don't do it. It rarely makes good sense and can lead to legal, financial, and emotional chaos. It is always better to make difficult decisions while you are unencumbered by their results. The best of friends can and do part ways, leaving in their wake angry words, depleted bank accounts, and ruined businesses. Treat the planning of your business structure with the same care, respect, and professionalism you give the planning of the structure, amenities, and food service.

Your first step should be getting acquainted with the options. In addition to the information in this chapter, you might also explore the resources available from your local library, on the Internet, or from Small Business Administration publications. Then you'll want to evaluate your own personal situation in light of the options and, finally, consult an attorney who specializes in property law, a certified public accountant (CPA), and your personal financial adviser. The more you know before you see the professionals, the briefer your meeting—and the less expensive your costs—will be.

Legal language and descriptions tend to be too complicated to be clear to laypersons. The information that follows has been written for simplicity, so not every possible situation is mentioned or explained. The idea is to get you thinking of things you'll need to discuss with your attorney and your potential partners, and to give you some idea of the complexities involved.

There are five principal business structures that can be used for operating an inn: the sole proprietorship, the partnership, the corporation, the subchapter S corporation, and the limited liability company. Each has certain general advantages and disadvantages, but each must also be weighed in the light of your specific situation, plans for the future, and personal needs.

THE SOLE PROPRIETORSHIP

The sole proprietorship is basically a business owned and operated by one person or a married couple. To establish a sole proprietorship, you need only obtain necessary licenses and hang up your sign. Because it's simple, it's the most widespread form of small business organization.

Advantages of the Sole Proprietorship
· This structure requires little or no governmental approval and is usually less expensive to set up than a partnership, a limited liability company, or either type of corporation.

- Sole ownership of profits and losses flows directly to owner's tax return.
- Control of the operation and decision making is all yours, which makes for greater flexibility.
- Relative freedom from government control and special taxation.

Disadvantages of the Sole Proprietorship
- You are personally responsible for the full amount of business debts, even exceeding your total investment and extending to all your assets, including your house and car.
- The enterprise faces a potentially unstable business life, as it may be crippled or terminated as a result of your illness, death, or any other unforeseen circumstances in your life. It's more difficult to sell as a business.
- Less available capital, ordinarily, than other business structures. Your personal credit is your business credit.
- Relative difficulty in obtaining loans.
- Viewpoint and experience of management is limited—to your own!

THE PARTNERSHIP

The Uniform Partnership Act, adopted by many states, defines a partnership as "an association of two or more persons to carry on as co-owners of a business for profit." Though not specifically required by the act, written articles of partnership are usually drawn up, outlining the contributions of the partners to the business, whether material or managerial, and generally delineating their roles in management and sharing of profits and losses. Partnership agreements typically contain these articles:
- Name, purpose, domicile.
- Duration of agreement.
- Performance by partners (job descriptions of active partners).
- Kind of partners (general, limited, etc.).
- Contributions expected of partners, both up front and later on.
- Business expenses: specifically, how they are handled and what is and is not permitted.
- Authority and rights (who's responsible for what and what rights they have).
- Separate debts (a clarification of individual debts of partners as opposed to partnership debts).
- Method of general record keeping, accounting, and policy and procedures, including a specific business attorney and accountant.

- Division of profits and losses.
- Draws and/or salaries.
- Procedure for dissolution following the death of a partner.
- Release of debts.
- Sale of partnership interests in a clear and concise manner.
- Arbitration procedure in the event of an irresolvable disagreement.
- Additions, alterations, or modifications of agreement.
- Settlement of disputes.
- Required and prohibited acts.
- Absence and disability.
- Extent of liability of each partner.

Partnerships have specified characteristics that distinguish them from other forms of business organizations: limited life span; unlimited liability of at least one partner; co-ownership of assets; mutual agency, in which either partner can act for the business; share in management; and share in partnership profits or losses.

Most inns deal with an active partner—and a limited partner or partners. To the extent the law allows, limited partners risk only an agreed-upon investment, so long as they do not participate in the management and control of the business. In essence, limited partners are investors without a vote on how you do business.

Advantages of the Partnership
- Fewer legal formalities than for corporations.
- The direct sharing of profits and losses, as set forth in the partnership agreement, motivates partners. Amounts may be disproportionate to the percentage of ownership.
- More capital and a better range of skills available than in a sole proprietorship.
- Allows more flexibility in the decision-making process than in a corporation.
- Less government control and special taxation than in a corporation.

Disadvantages of the Partnership
- Less flexible than a sole proprietorship.
- Unlimited liability of at least one partner.
- Long-term financing is harder to get than for a corporation, but easier than for a proprietorship.
- The inn is bound by the acts of just one partner, who acts as the managing agent.
- Buying out a partner may be difficult, unless that possibility has been specifically arranged for in the written agreement.

- The Tax Reform Act of 1986 set limits on losses for "passive" limited partners. Consult your CPA.
- Regardless of how carefully you plan and how specific you are in your initial agreement, circumstances that occur during the course of your partnership could negatively offset your relationship with your partners.

THE C CORPORATION

The corporation is by far the most complex of the three business structures, so only its general characteristics will be discussed here.

As defined by Chief Justice John Marshall in 1819, a corporation is "an artificial being, invisible, intangible, and existing only in contemplation of the law." In other words, a corporation is a distinct legal entity, separate from the individual who owns it.

Forming a Corporation

The corporate structures from which you might select are usually formed by the authority of some state government. The procedure is, first, that subscriptions to capital stock must be taken (in other words, investors must buy shares), and then a tentative organization is created. Finally, approval must be obtained from the secretary of state, in the form of a charter for the corporation that states its powers and limitations. You should always use an attorney when establishing any type of corporation.

Advantages of the C Corporation
- Limits stockholders' liability to a fixed amount, usually the amount of investment.
- Ownership is readily transferable. How easy this transfer will be is dictated by the corporate bylaws you establish.
- Because it is a legal entity, separate from the individual, it is stable and relatively permanent. For example, in case of illness or death of a principal (officer), the corporation goes on.
- It is easier to secure capital in large amounts from lending institutions and individual investors.
- Capital may be acquired by issuing stocks and long-term bonds.
- Getting financing from lending institutions is relatively easy because you can take advantage of corporate assets and, often, the personal assets of stockholders and principals as guarantors. (Lenders often require personal guarantees.)

- Centralized control is secured when the owners delegate authority to hired managers, who are often also owners.
- The expertise and skill of more than one individual.

Disadvantages of the C Corporation
- More legal requirements and limitations than proprietorships or partnerships.
- Minority stockholders are sometimes exploited, and this can lead to legal entanglements.
- Extensive government regulations and burdensome local, state, and federal reports.
- Considerable expense in formation of corporation.
- Numerous and sometimes excessive taxes: the corporation itself is taxed, and profits are taxed again as income to shareholders.
- Can pose tax problems at sale.
- May create additional expenses at time of sale.

THE SUBCHAPTER S CORPORATION

After forming the corporation, the shareholders of a corporation may elect to make it a subchapter S corporation. This form is increasingly used by inns for the business, with innkeepers owning the property separately outside the corporation. The property is then leased to the corporation. For tax purposes, this structure is more like a partnership, but shareholders retain the "corporate shield" with respect to liability. There can be a limit on the number of shareholders allowed in a subchapter S corporation. Profits and losses pass through to shareholders in direct proportion to ownership; consult your attorney and CPA for current details.

THE LIMITED LIABILITY COMPANY

The LLC is a relatively new hybrid legal structure that combines some advantages of a corporation with those of a partnership. As with the S corporation and the C corporation, in which you file articles of incorporation with the state, the LLC typically involves filing articles of organization with the state. Think of the LLC as a partnership whose partners enjoy freedom from personal liability, like shareholders of a corporation. It is different from a limited partnership in that this liability protection allows all owners to play an active part in managing the business. Unlike the subchapter S corporation, profit and loss can be allocated differently than ownership interest, making it more attractive to investors. Since LLCs are relatively new, many legal issues have yet to be addressed by laws or courts. It is important to consult your attorney for details particular to your state.

Advantages of the Limited Liability Company
- LLC owners, like corporate shareholders, are shielded from personal liability beyond the value of their investment. Their personal assets are generally not subject to the claims of business creditors.
- Flexible management.
- Flexible distribution of profits and losses.
- One-level taxation.

Disadvantages of the Limited Liability Company
- Must have two or more owners.
- May not be suitable for converting to a corporation, as there may be tax consequences if circumstances change and the owners wish to change the legal structure.
- Highly profitable LLCs may, in some states, pay higher taxes.

APPLYING THE OPTIONS TO YOUR OWN SITUATION

Now that you have some general sense of structural opportunities, these questions should help you narrow your choice. (Although these questions are framed in terms of "I," they apply as well to couples and partners.)
- Do I want anyone else involved in owning this inn? For many, the inn is home. Owning it with someone else may not feel right.
- Do I have significant assets that will not be part of this venture that I need to protect? If you're putting all your life savings and assets into the inn, you won't have to worry about this. On the other hand, if you or your working partner have other substantial assets, you would be wise to choose a legal structure that offers protection for them.
- Do I want to share the management of the inn with someone else? Many prospective innkeepers have come from large, formal organizations. An important goal for them is being their own boss, with no one to tell them what to do. Even if you are "boss," having several partners or shareholders will infringe to varying degrees on your freedom to do things your way. On the

other hand, some prospective innkeepers feel strong in one area but weak in another, and they consider a partner with complementary skills and experience an essential part of the new venture.

- Do I have enough assets and cash to do it alone? The down payment is just the beginning. Do you have enough to pay for remodeling, furnishing, stocking, and staffing the inn until it is open? Once the inn is operational, will there be enough left over to cover your cash needs until revenue covers basic expenses? Can you qualify for loans on your own?

- Do I want full responsibility for start-up, day-to-day operations, and management of the inn? Partners and shareholders can provide a wealth of skills, but that may not matter much to you if you prefer to operate alone.

- Will I be a full-time innkeeper, or will innkeeping be secondary to my full-time employment? Naturally, if you plan to keep working outside the inn, someone else will have to cook breakfast and make beds, as well as supervise remodeling, building, decorating, and general start-up. That someone else may work harder for less money if he or she owns a piece of the action.

- Do I need a tax loss or will the potential tax benefits of the inn be wasted on me? The restoration of older buildings, plus the normal depreciation factors of buildings and furnishings used for income, will usually result in tax losses during the first years of operation. Under certain tax laws, they may be applied against current or future income, depending on which business structure you choose. The loss can be considerable and very attractive to potential investors.

- Will I be selling my personal residence or income property to get cash for the new inn? If you sell a personal residence and want to defer the gain (profit made on the sale) to avoid paying a tax, this may affect your choice of legal structure. If you sell income property, there are rigid Internal Revenue Service (IRS) rulings for tax-free exchange from one type of income property to another. Either of these transactions requires the counsel of a CPA and a tax attorney, preferably before you sell your existing property.

- Is the inn your final goal or a stepping-stone? If your inn project is a way to make money so you can move on to another career or a work-free retirement, the legal ramifications of the eventual sale of the business will vary according to its structure. Plan now for your particular situation.

In general, as you can see, the major considerations for your legal structure are personal net worth, need for capital, personal lifestyle and skills, and goals and estate plans. These all involve personal decisions for you before you see an attorney or CPA, who can help you accommodate and implement them wisely.

Prospective innkeepers range from housewives and do-it-yourself folks to corporate types who hire their attorneys to check out the options first. The real-life examples that follow illustrate the way different factors interact to affect people's decisions about their inn's business structure.

The Couple Preparing for Retirement

Mary and Harry Jones wish to sell the family home in Los Angeles and move to a quiet, seaside town in northern California to run a small bed-and-breakfast inn. Mary and Harry are in their late fifties, have raised three children, and now have four grandchildren. Harry was in the restaurant business; Mary was a teacher. Their basic assets are their home, Harry's small restaurant, Mary's pension, and $20,000 in cash, stocks, and bonds. Harry knows the ins and outs of running a small business and is a skilled handyman. Mary is looking forward to cooking, running a large household, and entertaining guests.

Using the four general considerations just outlined, let's see if we can determine which legal structure is best for the Joneses.

Personal Net Worth: Their home, purchased twenty years ago, and fully paid for, has appreciated from $40,000 to $175,000, a profit of $135,000. Under current IRS rules, this profit may be tax-free. In addition, Harry plans to sell his small restaurant (an income-producing property) for $65,000, which may qualify for a tax-free exchange if handled properly. Mary and Harry thus have roughly $220,000 in cash ($20,000 cash plus $135,000 from their home and $65,000 from the restaurant) as seed money for the new venture.

Need for Capital: Assuming they buy a property for $200,000 or less, in reasonably good shape, put 20 percent down ($40,000), and spend no more than $100,000 on remodeling, furnishing, and start-up costs, they could have $80,000 to cover the first several years' negative income flow with no further investment necessary.

Personal Lifestyle and Skills: The Joneses believe that together they have the necessary skills to run their own business. Mary and Harry recognize their need to hire competent professional help in such technical areas as bookkeeping, accounting, and legal matters. They have a large family and will wish to close the inn during holidays for family visits. They enjoy traveling, so they may not want to run the inn themselves twelve months a year. Outside investors might infringe on these plans.

Estate Planning and Goals: Owning and running the inn is their ultimate goal, so we do not need to consider the long-range effects of selling in several years.

The major consideration here appears to be estate planning. Mary and Harry will not need outside investors, will not have extensive outside assets to protect, do have the necessary management skills to go it alone, and want the freedom to run the inn as they please and when they please. Any of the legal entities would accommodate them. One form, however, may be more advantageous than another from an inheritance standpoint.

The Colleagues or Friends

Two young women, Lynn and Yvonne, have worked together for several years in a manufacturing business. They have spent many happy vacations at bed-and-breakfast inns and want to pursue innkeeping as a possible career change. Neither owns a home, but each has saved $25,000. Various wealthy family members have expressed interest in investing in an inn as a tax shelter.

Need for Capital: We know immediately that Lynn and Yvonne's personal net worth will not be adequate, and they will need capital. Their capital sources want tax shelters, so the preferred legal structure for them would probably be a limited partnership, a subchapter S corporation, or an LLC.

In a limited partnership agreement, the limited partners' liability is bounded by the amount of their investment as long as they do not participate in the management and control of the enterprise or in the conduct of the business. The rules are quite rigid, so the limited partners must be willing to let the general partner(s) run the show without interference.

In addition, there must be at least one working partner who has the financial reserves and the willingness to assume unlimited liability for business debts. If all these points can be worked out, the tax shelter advantages of this form of ownership can be very attractive, particularly because the losses can be distributed unevenly. For example, in the first year 90 percent of the losses can go to 10 percent of the investors, as agreed upon in advance.

In an S corporation, the stockholders have limited liability, usually equal to the amount of their investment, but the tax losses are directly proportional to the percentages of shares owned. For example, if Lynn owns 50 percent of the stock, she will get 50 percent of the tax loss. She may not give it to other stockholders.

In the LLC form of business, the owners' liability would be limited to the amount of their investment; both of them could participate in the management; and they could distribute the profits and loss disproportionately.

Personal Lifestyle and Skills: Lynn and Yvonne have some basic decisions to make. In addition to capital needs, they may also need a partner or stockholder who knows how to run a small business. It may be that one or both must keep their jobs for a while for financial reasons. You can see that it's complicated.

Planning and professional help are very important here for the future of the new enterprise. And innkeepers choose all kinds of variations of the options: some lease their inns instead of buying; some form limited partnerships for the first several years, then change to subchapter S corporations; some join with investors to buy and remodel property, then lease it back to a separate legal entity for management purposes.

There are many different ways to approach the structural end of your inn business, but all of them require good counsel, careful decision making, proper preparation, and conscientious execution.

Playing Politics: Who Wants What?

One of your first jobs in dealing with government is discovering which of the various levels will have a hand in your business, and then finding out what each of these wants of you. The local chamber of commerce or a citizens service office at city hall or the civic center will usually provide materials describing the federal, state, and local rules and regulations that apply.

Here are lists of the basic requirements at various levels. There may be more—the list seems to grow—or there may be fewer, depending on the area.

FEDERAL REGULATIONS

Identification Number, IRS Form SS.4

You'll be required to identify yourself on tax forms and licenses. All employers, partnerships, and corporations must have a federal employer tax identification number. If you are a sole proprietor without employees, you can simply use your own social security number. Whichever number you use, it will go on the payroll tax return forms the IRS automatically mails quarterly and at year-end, which you must complete even if you have no employees.

Self-Employment Tax

An employee's social security contribution is deducted from their paycheck and matched by the employer. When you're self-employed, you must pay the government directly. This involves a separate form and is a tax in addition to federal income tax. You may owe no income tax but still be liable for self-employment tax. When employers and employees share the cost of social security, each pays about half the total. Since no employer will supplement your contribution, it will amount to somewhat more than twice what you would have contributed as an employee. Check with your accountant and the local IRS office for details.

Sales Tax Permits

In states that require sales taxes, almost all businesses need to obtain a sales tax permit from the state. Sales taxes may be collected on the breakfast portion of room charges, gift items, books, and so on. The taxes are collected from guests and remitted to the tax collector, usually monthly or quarterly. Some local governments also require sales taxes.

State Employer Tax Identification Number

If you have employees, you will need to pay unemployment insurance taxes, which are collected by your state employment service office. You'll be issued a state employer number, which you'll need to complete the required quarterly and year-end payroll tax reporting forms. The forms will be sent to you automatically.

Alcoholic Beverage Control

Most states require you to have a license if you serve alcohol. Even if you give it away, the authorities view it as included in the room rate, and therefore a sale. Some states have special bed-and-breakfast licenses; others have reasonably priced beer and wine licenses. If you serve alcohol, you are also required to pay the U.S. Bureau of Alcohol, Tobacco, and Firearms an annual fee of $250, regardless of whether you are licensed by the state. If you do have a state license, the state will automatically inform BATF.

CITY AND COUNTY REQUIREMENTS

Fictitious Business Name

When a business operates with any name other than the operator's own, the "fictitious" name must be filed with the county clerk and published in a public newspaper for a required period of time. (Corporations, which are registered with the state, are exempt from this requirement.) There's a small fee for the fictitious business name statement, as well as a small fee to the newspaper for publishing it. This procedure also involves a check against the names of existing businesses in your area to avoid duplication. Name publication also informs the public of your business intentions. Banks require a copy of this statement before opening a business checking account for you.

Building and Zoning Department

This department, in some areas called the building and safety department, protects the community from haphazard growth and from inferior, unsafe buildings. For example, it:

- Enforces city or county regulations regarding permitted uses of property in specific areas. Would you want a bar or gas station next to your home?
- Approves structures for safety and compliance with local building codes. Some allowances may be made for historic buildings in areas where meeting codes would endanger the building's historic value.
- Approves remodeling plans to meet local setback requirements, height limitations, landscape design, and building codes. This involves an initial plan check; inspectors then sign off at different stages of construction, such as framing, rough electrical, rough plumbing, drywall, finish, and roofing. (See also the section on Zoning in "Getting Your Act Together.")

Department of Public Works

A good name for this department would be the street and sidewalks department. It enforces regulations that affect traffic patterns, safety for pedestrians, and flow of bicycles and vehicles. Some of its concerns are:

- Off-street parking: For example, this department may require one space per guest room, plus two for owners. Some jurisdictions require that parking areas be paved, striped, and have bumper guards. A rule of thumb on space requirements is that a car should be able to exit after one backup motion. In general, diagonal parking is allowed only if the driveway is one-way.
- Width of driveway, curb cut (many cities use remodeling as an opportunity to modernize curbs), and condition of sidewalk.

Fire Department

Fire departments' requirements vary from community to community, but they are becoming increasingly stringent.

- Exits: Requirements are more rigid for buildings with more than two stories. These may, for example, include two legal exits, steel doorjambs, and interior doors that can withstand fire for one hour.
- Smoke detectors: Some building codes will accept battery-operated detectors, but hardwired ones attached to a central alarm are becoming a common requirement. Ask where they should be located.

- Ability of fire hose to reach all structures on property.
- Commercial fire extinguishers on each floor and in kitchen.
- Sprinklers, though not required for many existing inns, may be required when the building changes hands or if you renovate or build a new structure. The National Fire Protection Association would like sprinklers to be required in every home. Seriously consider including sprinklers in your renovation budget.

Planning Commission

This commission approves or disapproves requests for modifications, special-use permits, variances, conditional-use permits, and rezoning. Any of these exceptions to the rule may be applied for if your project does not meet zoning or building codes.

Review Boards

- Architectural review: Many communities have standards, color schemes, or themes with which all-new projects or exterior remodels must be consistent.
- Sign reviews: Height, size, colors, and lighting may be subject to review.
- Landmark review: If you would like your inn to be classified a historic landmark, this review board must approve remodeling plans.
- Environmental review: This process requires you to prove that your project will not damage the environment. It can be expensive and involve questions of drainage, air quality, and even visual damage. Find out early if you're subject to it.

Board of Health

This is an inspecting and licensing board charged with protecting the public. Your license is renewable for an annual fee when standards, which usually relate to the following, are met.

- Kitchen and bathrooms: General condition and cleanliness of kitchen, such as washable wall and floor surfaces and absence of cracks around cupboards that would allow rodents and bugs to enter. Facilities for either high-heat or chemical sterilization of dishes, including either a commercial dishwasher or a three-bin commercial sink with drain boards. Adequate ventilation and exhaust over stove. One option may be a commercial convection oven (exhaust self-contained). Stove approval may not be necessary if only continental breakfast service is to be offered. Employee bathroom equipped with liquid soap, paper towels, and automatic door closure.
- Spas and swimming pools: There are specific requirements for tub and deck materials, grab bar, water-depth marker, and chemicals. Filter, heaters, and

other mechanical and electrical equipment must meet commercial-use standards.

- Many states require a food handler's permit for all those who work in the kitchen. This can usually be obtained by attending a special class.

Business License

Most cities require businesses to have a license, for which they pay a fee. The fee is usually annual and based on projected gross income. This agency may also collect local bed taxes, which are added to room prices.

Assessor's Office

Local property taxes are based on purchase price and reassessment of improvements. In addition, there may be an annual business tax on furniture and equipment; some local governments also have a sales tax ordinance separate from the state one.

Good intentions are not enough. The first step toward being a law-abiding business owner is discovering the laws.

LOCAL GOVERNMENT AND YOU

"Button, button, who's got the button?" Few things are as frustrating as the fourth trip to the building and zoning department to retrieve signed preliminary plans and building permits, only to discover that public works hasn't signed off yet on the parking, or the fire department took your plans last week and won't have them back until tomorrow. Meanwhile, your crew is waiting another week to get started.

Aggravating? Yes. Exaggerated? No. Few wheels turn as slowly as those of government, or of any other bureaucracy, for that matter. The people and systems that hold the future of your business in their hands have flaws, foibles, and limitations. On the other hand, you may run into individuals and even entire departments that will go out of their way to be helpful and downright expeditious.

A few communities still don't know what to do with bed-and-breakfasts. Existing zoning categories don't seem appropriate, and health regulations don't quite fit. As a result, innkeepers inadvertently create a lot of work and brand-new problems even for people with a great deal of experience. Some bureaucrats enjoy the challenge; others do not. The effect individuals have on the process is enormous: no department is the same to two different innkeepers, and no bureaucrat responds, interprets, and implements policy exactly the same as the others.

Every business faces this, but many of us innkeepers expect a warmer greeting than we get. We think we improve our neighborhoods, encourage tourist dollars, increase tax revenues, and provide unquestionably outstanding quality. Apparently, every new businessperson feels this way.

Prospective innkeepers also need to be aware of the social and political ramifications of their plans. In many towns, for example, there's a critical shortage of affordable housing. Therefore, when some well-meaning entrepreneur seeks approval to renovate a run-down Victorian presently housing six families, numerous legitimate concerns are raised. Such a situation immediately puts the prospective innkeeper in an adversarial position, at odds with the community and its governing bodies before plans are even submitted.

You can often avoid this unfortunate position. Spend some time becoming familiar with and understanding the needs of the community, especially if you are a newcomer. Newcomers start out on the defensive. People tend to be territorial and protective, and to resent outsiders "coming in and taking over." You need someone on your side who knows the ropes.

Respected architects and contractors who represent you with governing agencies can smooth the way simply because they have proven themselves with quality past performances.

In addition, any contacts you may have with longtime residents can be very beneficial. A phone call from such an ally to the mayor or city councillor can smooth the way for permit approvals. In any corporation, school district, or other bureaucracy, some people accomplish their goals with ease. You need these people on your side.

Here are some tips on the positive way to deal with codes, regulations, and inspections:

- Avoid adversarial positions.
- Sit down and talk.
- Get the experts involved to talk with each other.
- Know the regulations yourself, but listen carefully to the ones that most interest your inspector.
- Believe that modifications can happen.
- Expect everything to take time.
- Provide all the information you can, but only when it's requested.
- Don't try to get away with things.
- Go to the top gently, when problems seem insurmountable.

Finally, be there for the inspections; accompany the inspector around the site.

In many areas, bed-and-breakfast inns are operating under little or no legal authority, somewhere in the definitional crack between boardinghouses and hotels. How long this will be allowed to continue is anybody's guess. Even inns that meet all current requirements are constantly subject to political changes that may affect them: sprinkler-system requirements, earthquake-safety modifications, handicapped-access ordinances, and off-street-parking proposals, for example.

For political problems as for forest fires, prevention is the best cure. Often problems occur because somebody is angry with somebody else; on the other hand, they are often avoided because people don't want to cause their friends trouble. You can prevent problems by making friends.

At the most basic level, be a good neighbor. Be alert to problems your inn may cause the residents in the neighborhood and try to solve them. Figure out ways your inn can benefit your community: hold neighborhood meetings there, initiate a neighborhood crime-watch program, or work together on disaster-preparedness planning. Share some cuttings from your geraniums. Have a coffee klatch. Be a friend.

On the larger community level, be visibly involved in issues of concern in your town or city. Donate accommodations for the public television station fundraiser auction, hold benefit teas for a local charity, or cook the Shrove Tuesday pancake supper for the parish. Try to position yourselves as innkeepers in the best light in the eyes of your community and the media—before you have reason to need public support on a political issue. You'll not only be building goodwill, you may also get some helpful free publicity.

Know Your Officials

Make a point of getting to know the people who represent you on the city council, the county board of supervisors, the state legislature, maybe even the United States Congress. And be sure they know who you are. Invite them to an open house. Ask them to speak briefly at an innkeepers association meeting, and then follow up their remarks with a question-and-answer session. This will give you a chance to demonstrate your political interest and awareness and to present yourselves to political figures—who are always running for office—as a constituency to be reckoned with. Do some research before you become directly involved with an elected official so you will know the issues of prime interest to him or her. Take a look at where the official's support is weak and try to figure out ways you can benefit him or her by providing some good publicity or helping polish an image.

Find out your officials' positions on issues likely to affect you: development, economic growth, local control of local issues, historic preservation, and conservation, for example. Get involved in issues they care about, whether they affect you directly or not: if you're available to help your officials on their issues, you're in a good position to ask them for help on your issues.

What Are the Candidates' Needs?

Every elected official is a candidate all the time. No matter how idealistic and dedicated officials may be, they can't be effective unless they can get elected. Election is the bottom line, and in all your dealings with political people, don't forget it. You need to understand and be able to communicate how your issues can make political mileage.

For example, let's say Councillor Doe is a staunch supporter of preserving coastal access and has been taking a beating as a result, because the development community is scaring voters with stories about economic decline. If you want support in opposing an ordinance that threatens to put your inn out of business, you might approach Doe armed with data on the positive economic impact inns have had in your area, not only for inns themselves but also for local restaurants and merchants. You might suggest organizing a press conference at one of the inns to give Doe a showcase for presenting her version of economic development: using existing buildings to bring in tourism without putting the additional strain on taxpayers of paying for the new streets and educational and fire-fighting facilities that new construction usually requires.

Never approach a legislator for assistance without having a good case to make on how helping you will help him or her.

Say Thanks Loudly

When you get help from an official, be noisy about it. Write a letter of thanks and send copies to your local newspapers. If your local chamber of commerce has a newsletter, write an article about the help you got and send copies of it to the legislator's office, for constituents to see when they drop in. The help you receive may merit an award. This gives you the chance to stage a media event, presenting your legislator with something like an oversized key to the inns of your area or a handmade quilted wall hanging naming him or her the "Innsightful Legislator of the Year." Do something that will make clear to the official who helped you out, and to others who might, that helping you pays off. The publicity opportunities here are limitless, for the legislator and for you and your inn.

The political game is complicated, but you neglect it at your own risk. Plan a preventive-maintenance strategy now. If you need political solutions to problems, do your homework and get help from the friends you've made. Never, ever forget that all officials are candidates and that you get the most earnest assistance from people who stand to gain from being helpful.

Butcher, Baker, Candlestick Maker:
Selecting Your Support People

There are so many "professionals" in the marketplace today; it is difficult to know if you need them, when you need them, and how to choose them.

Naturally, you'll want to work with people who are competent in their fields. Ask friends and other professionals for recommendations, and consult local business publications. You can begin to evaluate competence on the basis of the professionalism with which initial contacts are handled. Are they on time for appointments? Do they provide reports on the outcome of meetings? Are the documents they prepare clear and attractive? Can you get in touch with them conveniently?

Once you've narrowed your choices, ask your candidates for references from local businesses; then check them out. Before you make your final decision, there's one last aspect to consider, and it's one of the most important.

Take an honest look at how you feel about your candidates. Comfort and trust must characterize your relationship with all the people you hire. Don't allow yourself to feel inferior to them because they know something you don't. Remember, they all work for you; you pay them to provide services to you and your inn. Of course you don't understand the intricacies of accounting; that's exactly why you hire an accountant. Good professionals won't encourage your feelings of inadequacy. They'll work with you, spend enough time with you to meet your needs, and give you reasonable answers to your questions, no matter how naive the questions may sound to them. Choose support people whose pace you're comfortable with. You shouldn't feel like you're racing your engine or struggling to keep up during your meetings.

What are reasonable fees? You can find out by shopping. Ask about prevailing rates in the field. The range can be very wide, and the highest-priced professionals may not necessarily be the best. Make your choice based on the balance of comfort, trust, expertise, and price that feels right to you. If you find you have chosen the wrong person, don't hesitate to end the relationship.

Tales are told of the business owner who hauls three shoe boxes of receipts to the accountant every year on April 14. Accountants worth their salt would probably smile politely and hand the boxes right back. Your inn is a business. Whether it's a corporation, an LLC, a partnership, or a sole proprietorship, well-organized financial records are imperative. The Glenborough Inn's accountant was chosen long before the doors opened, because, as Jo Ann puts it, "we were spending a lot of money, and I had no idea where or how to account for it.

"We started out with a very basic accounting system and chart of accounts. My fantasy was that I could do the bookkeeping, and it turned out to be a real fantasy. Early in our second year of business, our accountant suggested very gently that I might consider the services of a reliable bookkeeper she could recommend. I got the hint: my bookkeeping skills are nil, and the money I hoped to save by doing my own bookkeeping was being spent to correct my poor efforts."

Whether you feel cut out for the bookkeeping part of innkeeping, it's still a good idea to take a class in bookkeeping so you can effectively supervise this part of your business. Knowing your limits in this arena is crucial, but knowing what bookkeeping is about is equally helpful. Or budget time with your bookkeeper or accountant to learn some of the basics of this part of your business.

At most inns, it's unlikely that the innkeeper will be able to avoid every financial task. With the wide availability of simple computer programs for home and small businesses, many innkeepers are finding they can capably handle bookkeeping tasks like posting to general ledger and reconciling bank statements, leaving more complicated jobs like preparing quarterly returns to the professionals. The financial accounting jobs are often shared like this:

Innkeeper
- Writes all checks, including payroll.
- Assigns expenses to appropriate ledger categories, e.g., utilities, advertising, and laundry.
- Receives and records income.
- Makes all bank deposits.
- Prepares monthly bed-tax return.

Bookkeeper
- Posts to general ledger (lists expenditures in appropriate categories, e.g., utilities, advertising, and laundry).
- Reconciles bank statements.

- Prepares quarterly sales-tax return.
- Prepares quarterly payroll-tax returns.
- Readies all information for business income taxes for the accountant.
- Prepares financial reports, such as profit and loss statements, and balance sheets, after doing a financial review, checking for backup of accounts, and preparing a reconciliation report.
- Needs to work with the CPA in training the innkeeper.

Basic Things for Getting Your "Books" Set Up:

1. *Assess your skills and personalities or those of the people who will be responsible for handling the books—be aware that too many people doing the books isn't a good idea.*

2. *Take classes or do a self-study to get refreshed or learn general bookkeeping and accounting reporting as well as specific software use. Or sit down with your accountant; this is money well spent since it will be specific to your business, learning style, and time frame.*

3. *Set up a manual paper trail with organized receipt files, automobile mileage records, and petty-cash system.*

4. *Consider all the cost-benefit options of hiring a bookkeeper versus doing your bookkeeping yourself, including time, energy, and money; compare self-maintained systems (manual or computer) with an in-house hired bookkeeper and an outside bookkeeper or accountant. Don't skimp in this area.*

5. *Talk to your CPA about your reporting basis: cash, accrual, or hybrid. This affects how income and expenses are reported and what assets and liabilities you will need in your chart of accounts.*

6. *Set up a general chart of accounts ahead of time specific to you and your business needs. See www.paii.org for the industry standard.*

7. *Involving professional help to set up, organize, train, and work with yourself or your bookkeeper saves you money in the long haul.*

8. *You will need various printed forms and accounts: numbered invoices, numbered receipts, checking account, checkbook with additional deposit slips, savings accounts and deposit slips, tax receipt book-filing system, reservation package or manual system, occupancy and marketing systems, guest feedback forms and files, payroll and employee records, numbered gift certificates, mileage log, personal-use logs, and business allocations logs.*

Courtesy of Theresa August-Selover, August Selover Accounting, LLC.

Certified Public Accountant
· Prepares the business income tax return.
· Prepares any other necessary tax-related information.
· Consults with innkeeper or bookkeeper as necessary

ATTORNEYS

An attorney's skill is invaluable, and the fees reflect it! But buying a few hours' consultation at the right time can help prevent real heartache and grave financial repercussions. Negotiating contracts, deeds, and leases, and choosing the appropriate legal entity for your inn are examples of areas where you'll probably need legal advice.

In any case, do your homework before you call. With a little research, you may be able to answer some legal questions yourself. At the very least, you can clarify your problem so it's easier, faster, and therefore cheaper to resolve. Find out whether your attorney bills for every minute or will answer occasional telephone questions for free. Many attorneys are very cooperative in responding to telephone queries about whether a particular situation genuinely warrants their attention. It's something like calling your doctor to find out if an aspirin will do the job, instead of paying for an office visit to get the same advice.

INSURANCE

Surely one of the most difficult expenditures to make is one that does not apparently pay off at all, until and unless some minor or major catastrophe strikes. If that loss occurs, you will want and need the immediate, caring attention of an efficient, prompt, and fair claims service.

Choosing the right insurance agent, whatever the details of the policy, requires the same kind of analysis you use in choosing other support people. Insurance is complicated; agents should not only be willing and able to answer your questions about policies but should also spend time outlining your coverage and clarifying what it will mean in case of a loss.

As your business grows and changes, your policy should too. Even if nothing else changes, inflation can erode your coverage. Your provider should maintain a regular schedule of contact with you (probably annual) to make necessary updates.

Insurance agents make money on insurance renewals, so keeping you happy is important to them. If you're not pleased with the service you get, take your business elsewhere.

BANKERS

"Know more about your business than anyone else does," a banker will tell you. No matter how large or small your operation, bankers don't like to be told you'll have to check with your accountant when they ask a question. They want to know that you're in charge. They'll expect you to understand your cash flow and be able to discuss financial projections intelligently. (And if you've chosen your other support people with care, you'll be prepared for your banker!)

Just like anybody else, bankers lend money in situations where they feel comfortable. So choose your bank and your banker with care. Find someone interested in small businesses, and build a relationship based on professionalism. Don't hesitate to ask about special services: a business credit card, a line of credit, payroll services, and so on. But recognize at the same time that the more banking needs you handle through one bank, the more valuable a customer you are. As a result, it can pay to concentrate your banking business instead of giving it in pieces to the least expensive provider of each banking service.

go or no go

NUMBERS FOR BUYING, BUILDING, OR RENOVATING

It is not unusual for an aspiring innkeeper to fall in love with an old, tired Victorian or, at the other end of the spectrum, a luxurious beachside inn.

But though you need to love being in business, you'll want to focus those heartfelt joys on running your inn. This chapter gives you the tools to truly be your own boss and business manager. Don't skip this chapter!

Evaluating the Opportunities

Susan Brown, who does consulting with aspiring innkeepers, told us that she was asked to evaluate an inn on the California coast that was on the market for $4,000,000; it had eight guest rooms that would not qualify as luxury rooms—they were not especially large and did not have whirlpools or anything else that would set them apart from other lodging facilities in the area. This particular coastal area is not an established tourist draw, so we can guess that the area occupancy might be approximately 40–45 percent depending on how long an institution has been in business. The quick "Go, No Go" calculation looked like this:

> 8 rooms x 365 days x $200 a night = $584,000 at 100% occupancy
>
> $584,000 (100% occupancy) x 40% (estimated local occupancy) = $233,600
>
> $4,000,000 purchase price: $1,000,000; $3,000,000 commercial mortgage at 9% ARM for 25 years = annual interest and principal payment of approximately $300,000 without considering any other expenses. THIS IS A NO GO!

A word of caution: Attorneys, appraisers, and CPAs make full-time careers in matters of finance with good reason, because reporting, taxation, and financing questions are complex and continually changing. The information in this chapter and throughout the book is accurate and current but prepared by innkeepers, not financial professionals. Use it as a guide to issues and an introduction to questions you'll be handling with professional assistance.

The above example of a Go, No Go decision is very simplistic, but will give you an idea of how to determine whether a property has possibilities. The following example will give a more detailed analysis using a start-up conversion of a house to an inn.

You've found a lovely, turn-of-the-century residence that hasn't seen a coat of paint for several years, but the lines are good and you know a Queen Anne when you see one. Typical acquisition costs of houses to convert to inns will depend on property values in your selected town. They could range from $15,000 to $100,000 per usable guest room. Acquisition costs are keyed to number of guest rooms but include all the rooms of the house. Say you can buy this structure, with six bedrooms and two baths, for $350,000. After reserving one bath and bedroom for owner or innkeeper quarters, there are five guest rooms left. We'll add four baths so that all the guest rooms have private baths. The acquisition cost per room, therefore, is $70,000. (Generally speaking, wherever you go, property values are likely to be higher in cosmopolitan and tourist areas than in rural or small-town areas.) Let's look at how to evaluate whether this property will pay for itself as an inn.

STEP 1: REALISTIC OCCUPANCY RATE

Determine the realistic occupancy (number of rooms rented in relation to those available) that can be expected in the desired area. You develop this number by talking with innkeepers, hotel owners, tourist center or visitor bureaus, and the chamber of commerce. It's crucial that this number be realistic. In all of our financial calculations, we figure income low and expenses high. For further discussion of research procedures, see "Researching Your Market and Site Selection" in "Preparing for Innkeeping." If you are planning to open in an area where none of the above sources are available, try to determine when it is likely you will be full. For example, if weekends are busy but there will be very little midweek business, you can figure on 52 weekends or 104 weekend nights. To calculate occupancy, divide the number of nights filled by the nights available: 104 nights x 5 rooms divided by rooms available, which is 365 nights x 5 rooms:

$$\frac{520 \text{ rooms rented}}{1{,}825 \text{ rooms}} = 28\% \text{ annual occupancy}$$

If you can figure how many nights a year you will be full, you can calculate any occupancy. Here's an example of how this can work: area history tells us that a five-room inn we are looking at will be occupied two weekend nights all year and every night of the week in the summer; the occupancy will look like this:

number of rooms rented winter weekends: 5 rooms x 80 days = 400

number of rooms rented summer weeks: 5 rooms x 92 days = 460

total 860 rooms rented annually

number of rooms available: 5 x 365 = 1825

$$\frac{860 \text{ rooms rented}}{1{,}825 \text{ rooms available}} = 47\% \text{ annual occupancy}$$

Remember that it always takes time to develop occupancy. For new inns, we recommend that you use half of the area occupancy for the first year, and then add 10 percent a year until you reach the area occupancy. Some consultants feel that this estimate is too conservative. If you are opening in a tourist area where there are other successful bed-and-breakfast inns, you have developed a business relationship with them, and you are confident you will receive overflow referrals, perhaps you could use 60 percent or more of the area occupancy as your initial figure. Make sure you have a sophisticated Internet program up and running, have done extensive promotional marketing, and have applied for AAA and other book inclusions. Remember, always figure expenses high and income low. If, at the end of the year, it turns out you made more money than estimated, celebrate!

In our example we will use an area occupancy of 50 percent and start with half of that for our first-year occupancy projection. Our Victorian is in a small town a few miles from the coast that has the potential to become a tourist destination but at this time has only small motels. Nearby towns have successful bed-and-breakfast inns, but it can be difficult to get referrals from another town, even close by. Our town will also need to develop some good restaurants, a requirement for the upscale inn traveler. For our financial example, let's start with 25 percent the first year and add 10 percent a year until we reach the area occupancy of 50 percent.

The PAII *Industry Study* gives some general numbers for occupancy and ADR (average daily room rate) by location that may be helpful:

Rural (Country)	38%	$132.56
Urban (Cities & Suburbs)	48%	$122.37
Village (Towns & Resort Areas)	46%	$138.33

STEP 2: AVERAGE DAILY RATE

While researching the area, pay particular attention to the full range of room rates at the different lodging facilities. Those that court the more affluent traveler will set all their rates in the upper range; others will have seasonal rates; the chain motels and hotels will have a wide range of rates; and some will go primarily after commercial business. If there are no bed-and-breakfast inns in the immediate town you are researching, expand your market analysis to close-by towns. Stay at the hotels and inns that have most of the features you would like to offer in your inn. Know your competition.

Let's assume that the results of your research were as follows:

- The tourism bureau and chamber of commerce report that area occupancy for your town, and including several nearby tourist towns, is 55 percent.
- Area bed-and-breakfast inns: There are no inns in town; however, a few in a nearby tourist town have rates of $120 to $200 with 55 percent occupancy.
- Area hotels and motels: Only small motels are open; they have 50 percent occupancy with rates of $80 to $100.

Since this town is close to the ocean but not established as a tourist town, let's use the area occupancy of 50 percent and align our inn with the nearby bed-and-breakfast inns with a rate of $115. That is just $15 higher than the small motels' high end, and we include breakfast and afternoon refreshments.

STEP 3: FINANCIAL NEEDS SUMMARY

Estimate your up-front costs of getting the five-room traditional inn started and running until the inn fully reaches breakeven.

The repair and upgrade range of $15,000–$30,000, calculated using the guest rooms plus the living room or parlor, dining room, and kitchen reflects the varying conditions of older homes and whether you are planning a traditional or a luxury inn. Our Victorian has been a residence and it is in fair condition. We'll need to make sure the plumbing and electrical are up to the building code, and some seismic retrofitting of the foundation may be required. Sometimes, the building department will require an access ramp, wider doorways, and a handicapped bath to meet ADA (American with Disabilities Act) standards. We are adding four bathrooms in existing space, and this will require extensive plumbing. If there are major repairs to be done, such as roof replacement, be sure to itemize them in your estimate.

The furnishings estimate of $7,000 to $20,000 per room includes floor coverings, wall coverings, window treatments, bed linens, and furniture.

Financial Needs Summary   **Cash Needed**

Purchase price: land, building $ _350,000_
Down Payment $ _70,000_   (usually 20%–30% of price)
Closing costs, loan fees $ _7,000_   (get realtor's estimate)
Mortgage: 7%/30-year fixed-rate mortgage (residential loan);
        monthly payment $ ___$1,863___
Moving costs $ _5,000_
Other costs _____ $ _____
Working capital $ _20,000_
Organizational expenses $ _10,000_
Losses/gains first 3 years $ _7,929_

(The losses or gains figure is developed in the complete "Property Evaluation Worksheet." See Appendix 3, in Section F.)

Select One: Buying, Renovating, or Building From Scratch
  Buying an Existing Inn:
  Renovating $ _____
  Other _____ $ _____

  BUYING SUBTOTAL $ _____

Renovating (Calculate using all rooms, including guest rooms):
Renovation, repair and upgrade $ _120,000_ $15,000–$30,000 per room
Additional bathrooms $ _32,000_ $8,000–$20,000 each
Furnishings: total no. of rooms incl.common areas $ _56,000_ $7,000–$20,000 per room
Additional construction $ _____ $100–$220 per square foot
Other _____ $ _____

RENOVATING SUBTOTAL $ _208,000_

Building:
Construction Costs $ _____ $100–$220 per square foot
Add for each bathroom over 2 $ _____ $8,000–$20,000 each
Landscaping, outside patios, etc. $ _____
Furnishings—all rooms $ _____ $7,000–20,000 each
Other _____ $ _____

BUILDING SUBTOTAL $ _____

Total Cash Needed $ _327,929_

Working capital covers mortgage and living costs during the building or renovation period. In this case, let's show an estimated six months of renovation when the inn will generate no income, and during the first few months of light occupancy. In our example, financing $280,000 ($350,000 less $70,000 down payment) for thirty years at a 7 percent fixed rate will cost about $1,863 a month. For six months of renovation, the mortgage alone will cost $11,178; it is advisable to add several months for the unexpected delays and the first several months of operation. Working capital also includes utilities, office supplies, cost of first brochures, initial advertising and Web site development costs, plus licenses and permits (other than construction). We estimate working capital at $20,000. Your personal living expenses and obligations may adjust this figure upward.

Organizational expenses include legal and accounting fees for the setup of the books and the consultation and formation of your legal structure. The Internal Revenue Service does not allow these expenses to be counted in your operating expenses the first year; they must be amortized over five years.

In this example, we are planning a traditional inn. Our figure of $208,000 for renovation and furnishings will break down as shown in the next section, which compares the start-up costs of luxury and traditional inns.

STEP 4: TRADITIONAL OR LUXURY INN

Now is the time to decide whether you want a traditional inn or a luxurious inn. Don't be put off by the phrase "traditional inn" thinking it's a worn-out, bath-down-the-hall, sharing-a-closet-with-the-kids type place. Traditional is what the overwhelming majority of bed-and-breakfast inns are. And they are likely to have many of the features and amenities (including private baths) of a luxury inn, except AAA four or five diamond service, luxury baths, and the most luxurious furnishings; read more about the distinction in the section "L Is for Luxury" in the "What Is an Inn" chapter.

It is important to note here in the financial section that start-up costs and operating expenses are higher for a luxury property. Of course, the income is also higher and may compensate for increased costs. This trend toward more luxurious bed-and-breakfast inns may be the result of higher purchase prices or developmental costs pushing the need for higher room rates.

This decision should be based on your personal style and preference. What type of inn you develop or buy may also be a "niche" decision. If all the inns in the area are pretty traditional, you may wish to go with the luxury inn to attract a new segment of the market.

The $208,000 renovating and furnishings budget we have used in our example of a traditional inn will break down into costs for the remodeling of the house, including bathrooms (created out of closet space, with no additional square footage), furnishings, small equipment, linens, wall coverings, drapes, carpeting, and so on, for guest rooms and common areas. This estimate will be lower if you already have a houseful of antiques, linens, and crystal.

When you add the renovating and furnishing costs together, the range you get— $208,000 for a traditional inn to $458,000 for a luxury inn—is very wide. Let's use the extremes in both of our examples, but the costs could be anywhere in between, depending upon the condition of the house and grounds, its furnishings, and its bathroom fixtures. Your Victorian is in good condition and you plan to have traditional rooms. The following comparison shows the difference in start-up costs between the traditional room and the luxury room.

.... Renovation and Furnishings Cost Estimate ....

	Traditional Room	Luxury Room/Suite
Furnishings		
Parlor/living room	$ 7,000	$ 10,000 *
Dining room	7,000	10,000 *
Kitchen	7,000	10,000
5 guest rooms	35,000	100,000
(at $7,000–$20,000 each)		
Renovation		
Add four bathrooms	32,000	80,000
(at $8,000 to $20,000 each)		
Remodel existing bathroom	0	8,000
Paving/landscaping	20,000	50,000
Exterior painting	25,000	40,000
Electrical work	15,000	30,000
General plumbing	15,000	30,000
(e.g., new sewer, gas, and water lines)		
Carpentry, drywall, etc.	25,000	50,000
Misc., incl. decks, outdoor furnishings	20,000	40,000
Total	$208,000	$458,000

*Owners have existing living room and dining room furniture.

STEP 5: PROJECTING INCOME

The next step is to project your income for the first several years. If you are buying an existing inn, the information on actual income will be provided to you. If you are doing a start-up operation, we suggest you take 50 percent of the area occupancy multiplied by the average daily rate (ADR) of the area for guest room income for the first year, then add 10 percent a year until you reach the area occupancy. Beyond that, a 1 or 2 percent annual increase is typical; the condition of the economy can have an impact, both up and down.

Income includes all revenues from the operations of the business plus other revenue, such as interest earned on bank accounts. Typical operations income includes room rents, food sales, gift and book sales, and other services, such as rental of the inn for weddings, meetings, and so on. It is wise to keep revenue sources separate so you can evaluate the profitability of each one. For inns, income is primarily the product of room rate multiplied by the number of rooms rented. In the examples here, we are using only room rentals to keep the examples simple.

5 rooms x 365 days x $115 ADR = income at 100% occupancy = $209,875

   Year 1 projection: half of area rate of 50% = 25% x 100% occupancy income of $209,875 = $52,469

   Year 2 projection: Year 1 plus 10%: 35% x 100% occupancy income of $209,875 = $73,456

   Year 3 projection: Year 2 plus 10%: 45% x 100% occupancy income of $209,875 = $94,444

STEP 6: PROJECTING EXPENSES

The next step is projecting expenses. Again, if you are buying an existing inn, actual expense figures will hopefully be given to you. If they are not provided, use the PAII *Industry Study* as a starting point. If you are doing a start-up, we recommend using a base of $10,500 per room for operating expenses in a traditional inn and $15,000 per room for a luxury inn. Remember, operating expenses do not include interest and principal on mortgage, owners' draw or salary, depreciation, or income tax.

Property Evaluation Worksheet: Buying, Renovating, or Building

Property Type: _Five Room Traditional_

Address _Coastal, -small-non-tourist_ Owners _Dick, Jane, and dog Spot_

Research   Area occupancy rates and average daily room rates:

    Tourism bureau, visitors bureau, chamber of commerce _Regional County: 55%_

    Area bed-and-breakfast inns _No b-and-b's in-town; nearby town 60% at $120-200_

    Area hotels and motels _Small motels: 50% occupancy at $50-100_

    Derived area occupancy _50%_ Average daily room rate _$115, including full breakfast_
and afternoon refreshments

    Comparable inn sales _____

A. Financial Needs Summary

Original Building: no. of rooms _6_ no. of baths _2_

Additional no. of rooms _0_ traditional/luxury no. of baths _4_

Final: no. of guest rooms with baths _5_ traditional/luxury

Owner/innkeeper rooms with bath _1 and 1_

Cash Needed

Purchase price: land, building $ _350,000_

Mortgage _7_ %/years _30_ ARM/Fixed Res/Comm.

Monthly Payment $ _1,863_

Down Payment	$ _70,000_	(usually 20%–30% of price)
Closing costs, loan fees	$ _7,000_	(get realtor's estimate)
Moving costs	$ _5,000_	
Working capital	$ _20,000_	Exp. during const., marketing
Other costs, organizational, etc.	$ _10,000_	
Losses/gains first 3 years	$ _7,929_	

Select buying, renovating or building:

Buying an existing inn: Renovation, furnishings	$ _____	
Other	$ _____	
Buying Subtotal	$ _____	

Renovating: Repairs & upgrade, incl. common areas	$ _120,000_	$15,000–$30,000 per room _8 rooms_
Additional bathrooms (in existing space)	$ _32,000_	$8,000–$20,000 each _4_ _(LR, DR, kitch.)_
Additional construction	$ _0_	$100–$220 per square foot
Furnishings: total no. of rooms incl. common areas	$ _56,000_	$7,000–$20,000 per room _8_
Other _____	$ _____	
Renovation Subtotal	$ _208,000_	

Building: Construction Costs	$ _____	$100–$220 per square foot
Add for each bathroom beyond 2	$ _____	$8,000–$20,000 each
Landscaping; outside patios, etc.	$ _____	
Furnishings: Total no. of rooms incl. common areas	$ _____	$7,000–$20,000 per room
Other _____	$ _____	
Building Subtotal	$ _____	

Total Cash Needed $ _327,929_

B. Projected Income

___5___ rooms x 365 days x average daily room rate $ __115.00__ = Income at 100% occupancy $ __209,875__

Year 1 projection: 50% of area rate of __50__ % = __25__ % x Income at 100% occupancy *$ __52,469__

Year 2 projection: 1st year __25__ % + 10% = __10__ % x Income at 100% occupancy $ __73,456__

Year 3 projection: 2nd year __35__ % + 10% = __45__ % x Income at 100% occupancy $ __94,444__

* Buying: use Seller's occupancy rate

C. Expenses

Traditional room $10,500 per room, luxury room $15,000 per room. (Does not include mortgage, depreciation, owner's salary or draw, income taxes.)

Year 1 projection: no. of rooms __5__ x $ __10,500__ ($10,500 or $15,000) = $ __52,500__

Year 2 projection: Year 1 projection $ __52,500__ + 11% = $ __58,275__

Year 3 projection: Year 2 projection $ __58,275__ + 11% = $ __64,685__

D. Detailed Expenses

Standard Percentages of Total Revenue at 50% Occupancy	Expense Category	Column 1 Expense using Standard % at 50% Occupancy	Column 2 Seller's Actual Expenses or Adjustment For Reality (New Inn)	Column 3 Comments & $ Change in Expenses
16	Salaries/wages, including payroll taxes	$ 13,548	15,600	2 pt. time housekeepers at $10/hr.
1	Auto expense	847	847	1 car
2.5	Bank fees	2,116	1,140	factor of income
4	Taxes, fees (no bed tax)	3,387	6,000	Property tax
2	Interest: nonmortgage	1,694	100	No credit card debt
1	Dues, subscriptions	847	847	
7	Food, beverages	5,928	3,465	Lower occupancy
2.5	Insurance	2,116	3,000	
1	Legal, accounting fees	847	847	
4	Maint., repairs, fixtures	3,387	1,500	Newly remodeled
5	Marketing, advertising	4,234	5,000	Web site design
1	Office supplies, postage	847	847	
2	Outside services	1,694	0	In-house laundry
2	Housekeeping supplies	1,694	1,355	Less occupancy
1	Towels, linens	847	0	Incl. in start-up
2	Telephone	1,694	1,694	
2	Misc. expense	1,694	0	
1	Travel, entertainment	847	1,000	PA conf.
5	Utilities	4,234	5,000	More bathrooms
62%	Total operating expense	52,500 T	48,242 T	
38%	Morgage, Owner's salary	divided by 62%	22,356	
100%	Grand total	84,677 GT	70,598 GT	

1. Multiply the number of rooms x $10,500 for a traditional inn and $15,000 for a luxury inn. Put this number in Column 1T.

2. Divide this figure by .62 to calculate grand total expense GT for Column 1. The difference between the T and GT is the amount available for mortgage and owner's salary, expenses that are not included in operating expenses.

3. Take each individual percentage shown under standard percentage and multiply by the grand total GT to get the individual figures for Column 1.

4. Buying an existing inn: If you have been given itemized expenses, insert them in Column 2 for comparison.

5. If building or renovating a start-up, apply the reality test. Look at each item in Column 1 and see if it is logical and accurate for your personal circumstances and area. Put the changes in Column 2.

6. Use Column 3 for comments about changes and corrections.

E. Expenses Summary

	Year 1	Year 2 using column 2 + 11%	Year 3 using year 2 + 11%
Total operating expenses, T, from Column 2	$48,242	$53,549	$59,439
Plus mortgage expense	22,356	22,356	22,356
Plus owner's salary	0	0	0
Total Expenses	$70,598	$75,905	$81,795

F. Cash Flow and Breakeven

	Year 1	Year 2	Year 3
Gross income	$52,469	$73,456	$94,444
Less: operating expenses	48,242	53,549	59,439
Net operating income	4,227	19,907	35,005
Less: mortgage, owner's salary	22,356	22,356	22,356
Income or loss (cash flow)	<$18,129>	<$2,449>	$12,649

Total 3 year loss <$7,929>

Breakeven:	(Total Expenses)	=	$70,598	= Occupancy needed to break even
	(Income at 100% occupancy)		209,875	your first year = 34%

Comments:
Though the total three year loss is $7,929 there is a loss of $18,129 the first year, which needs to be planned for, maybe a short term family loan. The owners are residing at the inn. Perhaps a value to them of $1,000 — $1,500 a month. The breakeven the first year of 34% seems reasonably safe. Also note owners are not taking a salary in this example.

In the early years of developing your inn, it's difficult to use "percentage of income" to project your expenses because you'll probably be running in the red. "Percentage of income" is the standard used by most CPAs; it's also what PAII uses in its *Industry Study*. Michael Yovino-Young of Yovino-Young, Inc., in Berkeley, California, who specializes in appraising bed-and-breakfast inns, gives a range of operating expense to revenues of 50 percent to 65 percent for a well-established inn; he advises that inn expenses vary widely, and the smaller the inn, the higher the percentage. To keep our percentages in line with the actual operating expenses of inns surveyed by PAII, we are assuming a break-even situation—that your expenses exactly equal your income. Let's assume that this inn has a reasonable occupancy, has gone through the negative start-up period, and is breaking even at the end of the third year.

As a starting point in projecting total expense, we'll use a formula that states that 62 percent of the revenue is operating expense, the balance covering the mortgage and your personal draw or salary. We are also giving you the base operating expense of $10,500 per room for a standard room and $15,000 for a luxury room. These are, of course, estimated figures, but the basis of these numbers comes from the PAII study and the experience of knowledgeable innkeepers; they'll help you determine a starting point, which can then be adjusted for your reality. For example, to get the starting point for operating expenses, we multiply the number of rooms by $10,500 for a start-up. (See the Property Evaluation Worksheet: Buying, Building, or Renovating, Section C.) In Section D we divide the figure for total operating expense by .62 (62 percent) to get the grand total expense figure. Using this grand total, we take individual expense percentages and place them in Column 1. The individual expense percentages are averages taken from the PAII *Industry Study* based on an inn operating at 50 percent occupancy, and have been adjusted for future expectations by knowledgeable innkeepers.

Column 1 shows the break-even situation; Column 2 shows the actual reality after you have adjusted for your own circumstances. If this is the first year of operation and your occupancy is less than 50 percent, you can reduce the expenses that are sensitive to occupancy—salaries and wages, bank fees, housekeeping supplies, food and beverages, and utilities. Look at each item and adjust it according to your needs.

For example, our starting percentages show that utilities represent 5 percent of total expenses; if you are in snow country or in the opposite extreme, the desert, your utilities may far exceed the standard percentage. The Property Evaluation Worksheet gives you a procedure to adjust your expenses.

If you are buying an existing inn, you'll start the process by inserting the seller's actual operating expense figure in Column 1 at the "T," under total operating expense. Then calculate the GT (grand total) by following the procedure described at the bottom of the form.

Next, you'll take the individual percentages, which will reflect the averages of inns surveyed. Compare these with Column 2, where you have entered the actual expenses of the inn you are thinking of buying, and note variances from the norm. (Later in the chapter, where we look at buying a ten-room inn, the comparison between the two columns gives you a list of questions to ask the broker or the owner of the selling property.)

Now that you have completed the detailed expenses for your start-up, add the annual mortgage payment and any projected owners' salaries, and you'll have a grand total for Year 1 that will reflect your own operation.

Though we will hold income constant, it is necessary to increase expenses for the next years, as the savings in Year 1 derived from lower occupancy, newly remodeled inn, expenses included in start-up costs, and perhaps no salary for owner(s). Go back to Section C of the worksheet, and notice that the second- and third-year projections include an 11 percent increase in expenses. When you are preparing your financial documents in the business plan, you will calculate Years 2 and 3 as you did the first year; but to keep it simple, we will use these estimates of operating expenses for our sample:

$$\text{Year 2} = \text{Year 1 } \$48,242 + 11\% = \$53,549$$
$$\text{Year 3} = \text{Year 2 } \$53,549 + 11\% = \$59,439$$

Be as exact as possible in your expense projections. The PAII study gives some average costs per room, which are a helpful starting point. For example, the survey gives an overall average food and beverage cost per rented room of approximately \$9.93. If you take the total number of rooms you will rent in a year and multiply by \$9.93 for food and beverage, you will be able to cross-check the above percentages. This kind of information will help you check your amounts in your reality column.

Track your income and expenses by using a chart of accounts. The abbreviated chart of accounts below is a listing of all expense and income accounts typical of a bed-and-breakfast inn; using these accounts, you can project what you expect to happen financially. Develop it initially based on the figures and percentages presented here, but after six months to a year of operation, use your own real figures and project them into the next year. Comparing actual expenditures with your projections, you can discover expenses to cut, expansion possibilities, slow times that need to be promoted, and problem areas—you have become a business manager.

Standard % of Revenue at 50% Occupancy	Expense Category
16	Hourly and salaried employees, including payroll taxes
1	Auto expense
2.5	Bank fees
4	Business taxes and fees
2	Interest nonmortgage
1	Dues and subscriptions
7	Food and beverage
2.5	Insurance
1	Legal and accounting fees
4	Maintenance, repairs, and fixtures
5	Marketing, advertising, and promotion
1	Office supplies and postage
2	Outside services
2	Room and housekeeping supplies
2	Telephone
1	Towels and linens
2	Miscellaneous expenses
1	Travel and entertainment
5	Utilities
62%	Total operating and labor expenses, not including mortgage expense, owner's salary, and income taxes

The related income and expense statement uses the same categories of income and expense but also includes the noncash item of depreciation and makes adjustments to the interest figure to account for principal payments on your mortgage. The income and expense statement describes what actually happened at the end of a period, such as year-end. The chart of accounts also feeds into the balance sheet, which reflects any changes during the year in the asset, liability, and capital accounts.

In 1988 Pat Hardy and Jo Ann Bell, as editor and publisher of *innkeeping* newsletter, sponsored the first comprehensive survey and analysis of income, expenses, and return on investment for bed-and-breakfast and country inns throughout the United States. Since 1988 they have conducted industry studies every two years, as the Professional Association of Innkeepers International (PAII), and the study has been widely used by innkeepers, appraisers, brokers, and lending institutions. The following categories are consistent with PAII's study. They are recommended for all innkeepers, so that in the years to come we will always be comparing apples with apples.

Standard Chart of Accounts

In order to establish a consistent standard of comparison (as is currently available in the rest of the lodging industry), bed-and-breakfast and country inn innkeepers are encouraged to set up their accounts as delineated below. For updates, see www.paii.org.

.... **Sample Chart of Accounts** ....

Revenue Accounts

Rooms	Room rental with breakfast, excluding sales and bed taxes.
Food: restaurant	Meals served on-site, except breakfast (when included in room rate). Includes MAP allocation for meals other than breakfast.
Beverage: restaurant	Alcoholic beverages sold on-site.
Telephone	Guest use of telephone, fax charges.
Gift shop	Sale of products in gift shop, such as books and souvenirs.
Meeting/Banquet Room Rental	Room rental charges, as well as equipment charges.
Rental of Equipment	Rental fees for skis, boats, bikes, etc.
Specialty Food and Beverage	Includes services such as picnic baskets. Excludes lunch, dinner, or catering revenue.
Other Income	Income from other sources not listed above (i.e., interest income, service charges)

Expense Accounts

Payroll and Related Salary and wages	All salaries and wages for part- and full-time employees.
Employee Benefits and Taxes	FICA, FUTA, Retirement Plan, Medicare, Insurance, Workers' Compensation, etc.
Housekeeping services	Amount paid to outside contracted housekeeping services.

Country Inn (serving dinner regularly)

Cost of food: restaurant	Cost of food sold in restaurant and during banquet service.
Cost of beverage: restaurant	Cost of alcoholic beverages sold in the restaurant and during banquet service.
Other Food and Beverage: restaurant	Napkins, glassware, china, silver, pans, etc. used in restaurant and during banquet service.

Other Operating Expenses

Advertising and promotion	Brochures, magazines, newspaper ads, printing, direct mail lists, Internet, mailing, etc.
Auto expenses	Automobile gasoline, repair, maintenance, and lease.
Bank fees	Check charges, credit or debit card merchant fees, etc.
Business taxes and fees	Property taxes and business fees. Excludes income, sales, and bed taxes.
Commissions	Travel agent commissions, RSO and other booking or referral fees.
Donations	Direct cash contributions. Excludes gift certificates and in-kind donations.
Dues and subscriptions	Association dues, subscriptions to services, magazines, etc.
Equipment rental	Rental of operating equipment. Excludes land or building leases.
Food and Beverage: breakfast	Food, beverage and supplies for breakfast and special food service.
Gift shop	Cost of goods offered for sale.
Insurance	Nonpayroll insurance such as fire, theft, auto, liability, etc.
Interest expense	Nonmortgage interest on business-related loans, credit cards, etc.
Legal and accounting Fees	Fees for legal and accounting services.
Maintenance repairs and fixtures	Labor and materials including furniture, fixtures, and equipment under $300.
Miscellaneous Expenses	Fixed or variable costs that are not included in any other expense account.
Office supplies	Paper, tape, pens, letterhead, nonpromotion postage, etc.
Outside services	Services such as maintenance, gardening, etc. Excludes outside housekeeping services.
Room and housekeeping supplies	Soap, toilet paper, lightbulbs, and cleaning supplies, etc.
Telephone	Telephone and related expenses.
Towels and Linens	Nonfood and beverage towels and linens, blankets, pillows, bathrobes, etc.
Training	Fees and expenses for professional workshops and seminars.

Travel and Entertainment	Travel related expenses and business entertainment.		
Utilities	Trash, gas, electric, water, etc.		
Net operating income or loss	Income before mortgage, depreciation, income taxes, and owner's draw.		

In addition to the expense and revenue accounts listed above, there will also be asset and liability accounts, which detail the value of land, building, furniture, fixtures, autos, and the like. Under the Liability heading, there will be any loans payable, accounts payable, and owner's equity. Your CPA will help you set up your asset, liability, and equity accounts and advise you on which of the above income and expense accounts will be relative to your bed-and-breakfast or country inn.

Not every chart of accounts category is included in every budget or income and expense statement; only the categories that are useful to your particular situation should be included. And, of course, you can add more if you need to understand a certain aspect of your business in more detail.

STEP 7: PROJECTED INCOME AND EXPENSE STATEMENT

We have the projected income and the operating expenses. The difference is Net Operating Income (NOI).

	Year 1	Year 2	Year 3
Gross income	$52,469	$73,456	$94,444
Less: Operating Expenses	$48,242	$53,549	$59,439
Net operating income (NOI)	$ 4,227	$19,907	$35,005
Less: annual mortgage	$22,356	$22,356	$22,356
Net loss or gain (cash flow)	($18,129)	($2,449)	$12,649

So, in our third year we have a positive cash flow. This is fairly typical for a start-up inn. Our total deficit for the three years is $7,929, which we have planned for in our Financial Needs Summary. Now that you have the processes in mind, you can put the data up on a spreadsheet and play with different room rents, or perhaps create one or two luxury rooms to raise your ADR.

Next is a break-even calculation to determine how much occupancy is necessary to pay your total expenses. For a fair chance of success, this breakeven should be below the area occupancy or, in the case of buying an established inn, no higher than past performance.

Break-even Percentage of Occupancy: Total expenses divided by Income @ 100% occ.

$$\frac{\text{Total Expenses (Op. Exp. + Mortgage)} \quad \$70{,}598}{\text{Income at 100\% Occupancy} \quad \$209{,}875} = 34\% \text{ occ.}$$

Since the area occupancy is 50 percent, it appears there is a comfortable edge in having a breakeven of 34 percent, particularly since the area occupancy will increase as this town is developed as a tourist destination. One point to remember is that there is no owner salary included in the expense figure in this example.

You will note that we have held the room rate constant for three years for simplicity, but you will want to fully develop each of those years when you prepare your business plan, making adjustments for increased occupancy and increased ADR.

The break-even percentage at the bottom of the property evaluation worksheet is the figure important to the question of cash flow. If you do not break even, you must continue to put cash into the business. If your break-even occupancy level is too high, you will have a constant cash struggle.

And now, let's look at whether developing this property as a luxury inn will make a difference in your bottom line, assuming that the guest rooms already are relatively large.

Property Evaluation Worksheet: Buying, Renovating, or Building

Property Type: *5 Room Luxury*

Address *Coastal small non-tourist* Owners *JR, Crystal, and cat Fluffy*

Research   Area occupancy rates and average daily room rates:

Tourism bureau, visitors bureau, chamber of commerce *Regional Tourist Bureau 55%*

Area bed-and-breakfast inns *No B&B's in town—nearby town, 60% $120-200*

Area hotels and motels *Small motels — 50% occupancy — $50-100*

Derived area occupancy *50%*   Average daily room rate *$200*

Comparable inn sales *None available*

A. Financial Needs Summary

Original Building: no. of rooms *6*   no. of baths *2*

Additional no. of rooms *0*   traditional/luxury   no. of baths *4*

Final: no. of guest rooms with baths *5*   traditional/luxury

Owner/innkeeper rooms with bath *1 with 1 traditional*

Cash Needed

Purchase price: land, building $ *350,000*

Mortgage *7* %/years *30* ARM/Fixed Res/Comm.

Monthly payment $ *1,863*

Down Payment	$ *70,000*	(usually 20%–30% of price)
Closing costs, loan fees	$ *7,000*	(get realtor's estimate)
Moving costs	$ *5,000*	
Working capital	$ *20,000*	Exp. during const., marketing
Other costs, organizational, etc.	$ *10,000*	
Losses/gains first 3 years	$ *20,641*	

Select buying, renovating or building:

Buying an existing inn: Renovation, furnishings	$_____	
Other	$_____	
Buying Subtotal	$_____	

Renovating: Repairs and upgrade, incl. com. areas	$ *240,000*	$15,000–$30,000 per room
Additional bathrooms (in existing space)	$ *88,000*	$8,000–$20,000 each
Additional construction	$_____	$100–$220 per square foot
Furnishings: total no. of rooms incl. common areas	$ *130,000*	$7,000–$20,000 per room
Other _____	$_____	
Renovation Subtotal	$_____	

Building: Construction Costs	$_____	$100–$220 per square foot
Add for each bathroom beyond 2	$_____	$8,000–$20,000 each
Landscaping; outside patios, etc.	$_____	
Furnishings: Total no. of rooms incl. common areas	$_____	$7,000–$20,000 per room
Other _____	$_____	
Building Subtotal	$_____	

Total Cash Needed $ *590,641*

B. Projected Income

_5_ rooms x 365 days x average daily room rate $ _200_ = Income at 100% occupancy $ _365,000_

Year 1 projection: 50% of area rate of _50_ % = _25_ % x Income at 100% occupancy $ _91,250_

Year 2 projection: 1st year _25_ % + 10% = _35_ % x Income at 100% occupancy $ _127,750_

Year 3 projection: 2nd year _35_ % + 10% = _45_ % x Income at 100% occupancy $ _164,250_

C. Expenses

Traditional room $10,500 per room, luxury room $15,000 per room (Does not include mortgage, depreciation, owner's salary or draw, income taxes.)

Year 1 projection: no. of rooms _5_ x $ _15,000_ ($10,500 or $15,000) = $ _75,000_

Year 2 projection: Year 1 projection $ _75,000_ + 11% = $ _83,250_

Year 3 projection: Year 2 projection $ _83,250_ + 11% = $ _92,408_

D. Detailed Expenses

Standard Percentages of Total Revenue at 50% Occupancy	Expense Category	Column 1 Expense using Standard % at 50% Occupancy	Column 2 Seller's Actual Expenses or Adjustment For Reality (New Inn)	Column 3 Comments & $ Change in Expenses
16	Salaries/wages, including payroll taxes	$ 19,355	28,392	2 housekeepers at $10/hr., 20 hrs./wk.—$10,400 1 innkeeper at $10/hr., 20 hrs./wk.—$5,200
1	Auto expense	1,210	1,210	1 car
2.5	Bank fees	3,024	2,281	Based on income
4	Taxes, fees (no bed tax)	4,839	7,500	Prop tax on sale/renovation
2	Interest: nonmortgage	2,419	100	
1	Dues, subscriptions	1,210	1,210	
7	Food, beverages	8,468	8,468	Luxury foods
2.5	Insurance	3,024	4,500	Sales price & whirlpools
1	Legal, accounting fees	1,210	0	Organizational exp.
4	Maint. repairs, fixtures	4,839	2,500	Newly remodeled
5	Marketing, advertising	6,048	10,000	Web design
1	Office supplies, postage	1,210	1,210	
2	Outside services	2,419	2,419	
2	Housekeeping supplies	2,419	1,210	
1	Towels, linens	1,210	200	New linens at startup
2	Telephone	2,419	2,419	
2	Misc. expense	2,419	0	
1	Travel, entertainment	1,210	1,210	PA Conf
5	Utilities	6,048	8,000	Whirlpool & fireplace
62%	Total operating expense	75,000 T	82,829 T	
38%	Morgage, Owner's salary	divided by 62%	42,356	
100%	Grand total	$120,967 GT	125,185 GT	

1. Multiply the number of rooms x $10,500 for a traditional inn and $15,000 for a luxury inn. Put this number in Column 1T.

2. Divide this figure by .62 to calculate grand total expense GT for Column 1. The difference between the T and GT is the amount available for mortgage and owner's salary, expenses that are not included in operating expenses.

3. Take each individual percentage shown under standard percentage and multiply by the grand total GT to get the individual figures for Column 1.

4. Buying an existing inn: If you have been given itemized expenses, insert them in Column 2 for comparison.

5. If building or renovating a start-up, apply the reality test. Look at each item in Column 1 and see if it is logical and accurate for your personal circumstances and area. Put the changes in Column 2.

6. Use Column 3 for comments about changes and corrections.

E. Expenses Summary

	Year 1	Year 2 using column 2 + 11%	Year 3 using year 2 + 11%
Total operating expenses, T, from Column 2	$82,829	$91,940	$102,054
Plus mortgage expense	22,356	22,356	22,356
Plus owner's salary	20,000	20,000	20,000
Total Expenses	$125,185	$134,296	$144,410

F. Cash Flow and Breakeven

	Year 1	Year 2	Year 3
Gross income	$91,250	$127,750	$164,250
Less: operating expenses	82,829	91,940	102,054
Net operating income	8,421	35,810	62,196
Less: mortgage, owner's salary	42,356	42,356	42,356
Income or loss (cash flow)	<$33,935>	<$6,546>	19,840

3 year loss <$20,641>

Breakeven:	(Total Expenses)	=	125,185	= Occupancy needed to break even
	(Income at 100% occupancy)		365,000	your first year = 34%

Comments:

Note that the owner in this example is taking a $20,000 yearly salary in addition to living in the inn, comparable to $1,000 to $1,500 in income a month. We increased expenses 11% a year; increase in income was solely from increased occupancy with no rate increase. When doing this example for your business plan, you will want to look at each year for expenses and raise rates according to occupancy.

The following three-year investment analysis will show the net effect of the two properties at the end of the third year:

	Initial Investment	3-Year Cash Flow	Net Investment After 3 Years
5-Room Traditional Inn	$320,000	($7,929)	$327,929
5-Room Luxury Inn	$570,000	($20,641)	$590,641

Note that our investment in the luxury inn is $262,712 more than in the traditional inn. How long do you think it would take to have a return on this investment?

Let's take a look at these two inns when the area has become a sought-after tourist destination. There are now three bed-and-breakfast inns in town, along with several gourmet restaurants and a few expensive, arty shops. Our little village has come of age and is in direct competition with the nearby tourist towns. Competitive rates are $130 for the traditional inn rooms and $240 for the truly luxurious inn rooms. All are running about 60 percent occupancy. Let's do another comparison:

	Luxury Inn at 60% Occupancy ADR $240	Traditional Inn at 60% Occupancy ADR $130
Gross Income	$262,800 *	$142,350
Less: operating expenses at		
62% of Income	$162,936	$88,257
Net operating income (NOI)	$99,864	$54,093
Less: mortgage, salary	$42,356	$42,356
Cash flow	$57,508	$11,737

*Example: 5 rooms x 365 days x 240 = Inn at 100% occupancy = $438,000
Inn at 60% occupancy = $262,800

With a difference in cash flow of approximately $46,000 per year, it would take about five and a half years to see a return on your investment for a luxury inn. Further, keep in mind that we used the extremes of the renovation and furnishing budget. There is an in-between position, and many inns have a traditional inn with several very luxurious rooms to raise their ADR. Note that the owners are taking a $20,000 salary in both the luxury and the traditional inns.

Another thought is that the more expensive rooms tend to book first; because of this, it is somewhat easier to raise rates on them without losing business. Expenses for the luxury inn will usually be higher for salary and wages, room and housekeeping supplies, advertising and promotion, food and beverages, repairs and fixtures, and utilities.

If you elect to sell the luxury inn, you will see a big difference in the price you will be able to ask, as one of the crucial numbers for valuing a property relates to the net operating income. See the chapter entitled "Let's Make a Deal: Buying an Existing Inn" for these valuation formulas.

Luxury may reflect better on your bottom line, but you will work for it. Justifiably, a guest who pays more than $200 a night expects everything to be working, paint (and your staff) to be sparkly fresh, and nothing to be worn. Financial projections before you buy or build can help you make comparisons, understand all the options, and then come to an educated decision.

Analyzing An Existing Inn to Buy

The "givens" we have used to project income and expenses for the start-up inn are not necessary when looking at an inn to buy. The seller should provide the numbers listed below for the buyers to gauge the financial health of the business:

Gross income	Net operating income
Occupancy rate	Average daily rate
Number of rooms	

It would be helpful to receive this information for the past three years, but in the preliminary stages of the negotiation, most of us are grateful to receive these numbers for one year. Given these numbers, you can use the Property Evaluation Worksheet to analyze the property the same way we did for a start-up.

If the numbers are vague or you do not trust them, the PAII *Industry Study* will help you get started. Many aspiring innkeepers ask if there is any "economy of scale" in the inn business; do more rooms necessarily mean the expenses per room go down? Through the years the PAII *Industry Study* show a steady progression upward in basic expenses relative to room size, but the labor costs jump more radically. Also, the income accelerates faster than the expenses, increasing the profit for the larger inn.

Finally, let's take a look at the Property Evaluation Worksheet for buying an existing ten-room traditional inn. This will show you how the form can be used to evaluate a proposed purchase. Notice that the figures in Section D, Column 1 reflect the average percentages used previously, working off the seller's total operating expenses. You can also start with the expense and revenue figures from the PAII *Industry Study*. For comparison, insert the actual seller's expenses in Column 2. Then use Column 3 to project your own numbers; ask the seller for clarification on questionable items.

Property Evaluation Worksheet: Buying, Renovating, or Building

Property Type: _Traditional 10 Room Inn_

Address _____ _Coastal - Tourist_ _____ Owners _Tom and Sally_

Research   Area occupancy rates and average daily room rates:

Tourism bureau, visitors bureau, chamber of commerce _60%_

Area bed-and-breakfast inns _$100-150_   _55%_

Area hotels and motels _$120-150_   _65%_

Derived area occupancy _60%_   Average daily room rate _$140_

Comparable inn sales _1 at 95,000 per room_   _1 at $130,000 per room_

A. Financial Needs Summary

Original Building: no. of rooms _10_   no. of baths _10_

Additional no. of rooms _0_   (traditional)/luxury   no. of baths _0_

Final: no. of guest rooms with baths _10_   (traditional)/luxury

Owner/innkeeper rooms with bath _1 with 1_

Cash Needed

Purchase price: land, building $ _1,000,000_

Mortgage _9_ %/years _25_   (ARM)/Fixed   Res/Comm.

     Monthly payment $ _5,875_

Down Payment	$ _300,000_	(usually 20%–30% of price)
Closing costs, loan fees	$ _10,000_	(get realtor's estimate)
Moving costs	$ _10,000_	
Working capital	$ _turnkey_	Exp. during const., marketing
Other costs, (organizational) etc.	$ _10,000_	
Losses/gains first year	$_____	

Select (buying) renovating or building:

Buying an existing inn: Renovation, furnishings $ _as is_

Other $_____

Buying Subtotal $ _0_

Renovating: Repairs and upgrade, incl. com. areas $_____ $15,000–$30,000 per room

Additional bathrooms (in existing space) $_____ $8,000–$20,000 each

Additional construction $_____ $100–$220 per square foot

Furnishings: total no. of rooms incl. common areas $_____ $7,000–$20,000 per room

Other _____ $_____

Renovation Subtotal $_____

Building: Construction Costs $_____ $100–$220 per square foot

Add for each bathroom beyond 2 $_____ $8,000–$20,000 each

Landscaping; outside patios, etc. $_____

Furnishings: Total no. of rooms incl. common areas $_____ $7,000–$20,000 per room

Other _____ $_____

Building Subtotal $_____

Total Cash Needed $ _330,000_

B. Projected Income

_10_ rooms x 365 days x average daily room rate $ _140_ = Income at 100% occupancy

$ _511,000_

Year 1 projection: 50% of area rate of _60_ % = _60_ % x Income at 100% occupancy $ _306,600_

Year 2 projection: 1st year ___ % + 10% = ___ % x Income at 100% occupancy $ _____

Year 3 projection: 2nd year ___ % + 10% = ___ % x Income at 100% occupancy $ _____

C. Expenses

Traditional room $10,500 per room; luxury room $15,000 per room. (Does not include mortgage, depreciation, owner's salary or draw, income taxes.)

Year 1 projection: no. of rooms _10_ x $ _20,136*_ ($10,500 or $15,000) = $ _201,360_

Year 2 projection: Year 1 projection $ _____ + 11% = $ _____

Year 3 projection: Year 2 projection $ _____ + 11% = $ _____

Using seller's operating expenses and ADR

D. Detailed Expenses

Standard Percentages of Total Revenue at 50% Occupancy	Expense Category	Column 1 Expense using Standard % at 50% Occupancy	Column 2 Seller's Actual Expenses or Adjustment For Reality (New Inn)	Column 3 Comments & $ Change in Expenses Buyer's Numbers
16	Salaries/wages,	$ 51,963	87,356	78,000
	including payroll taxes	3,249	1,826	1,500
1	Auto expense	8,119	7,665	7,500 _1 car_
2.5	Bank fees	12,990	5,309	14,000
4	Taxes, fees (no bed tax)	6,495	550	0 _Higher Purchase Price_
2	Interest: nonmortgage	3,249	1,359	1,200 _No credit card debt_
1	Dues, subscriptions	22,734	29,409	24,000
7	Food, beverages	8,119	12,995	8,000 _Higher occupancy_
2.5	Insurance	3,249	1,359	1,200 _No health insurance for emp/owners_
1	Legal, accounting fees	12,990	14,659	7,500 _Do own books_
4	Maint., repairs, fixtures	16,239	5,000	4,000 _No deferred maint._
5	Marketing, advertising	3,248	3,500	3,000 _Established – web design good and eff._
1	Office supplies, postage	6,495	4,631	1,200
2	Outside services	6,495	3,120	6,000 _No outside laundry_
2	Housekeeping supplies	3,249	2,500	3,000 _Better amenities_
1	Towels, linens	6,495	7,000	7,000 _Upgrade_
2	Telephone	6,495	2,000	10,000 _800 line ok_
2	Misc. reserves*	3,248	1,735	1,500
1	Travel, entertainment	16,239	10,766	11,000 _PA Conference_
5	Utilities	201,360 T	201,360 T	189,600
62%	Total operating expense	divided by 62%	divided by 62%	70,500
38%	Morgage, Owner's salary	324,774 GT	324,774 GT	260,100 _Mortgage, no salary_
100%	Grand total			

1. Multiply the number of rooms x $10,500 for a traditional inn and $15,000 for a luxury inn. Put this number in Column 1T.

2. Divide this figure by .62 to calculate grand total expense GT for Column 1. The difference between the T and GT is the amount available for mortgage and owner's salary, expenses that are not included in operating expenses.

3. Take each individual percentage shown under standard percentage and multiply by the grand total GT to get the individual figures for Column 1.

4. Buying an existing inn: If you have been given itemized expenses, insert them in Column 2 for comparison.

5. If building or renovating a start-up, apply the reality test. Look at each item in Column 1 and see if it is logical and accurate for your personal circumstances and area. Put the changes in Column 2.

6. Use Column 3 for comments about changes and corrections.

* *Reserves are a common calculation by lenders and appraisers to cover unknown contigencies—roof repair, water heaters, etc.*

Questions to ask owner or broker:

- How much owner involvement?
- Who is on insurance and how important?
- What are their outside services?

E. Expenses Summary

	Seller's	Buyer's	Year 3
Total operating expenses, T, from Column 2	$201,360	189,600	
Plus mortgage expense	divided by 62%	70,500	
Plus owner's salary		0	
Total Expenses	$324,774	$260,100	

F. Cash Flow and Breakeven

	Seller's	Buyer's	Year 3
Gross income	$306,600	$306,600	
Less: operating expenses	196,450	189,600	
Net operating income	110,150	117,000	
Less: mortgage, owner's salary	unknown	70,500	
Income or loss (cash flow)		46,500	

Breakeven: $\dfrac{\text{(Total Expenses)}}{\text{(Income at 100\% occupancy)}} = \dfrac{260,100}{511,000}$ = Occupancy needed to break even your first year = *50.9%*

Comments on Buyer's Numbers:
Buyer's operating expenses represent 61.8% of revenue; the net profit of $46,500 is a return of 14% on the $330,000 cash invested up front. The $117,000 net operating income equals an overall rate of return of 11.7% on the $1,000,000 purchase price. If this was a "hot" property in a hot location, the price would likely be higher, based on a capitalization rate of 10.5%. See "Let's Make a Deal: Buying an Existing Inn" chapter, specifically the ratios. Our buyers plan a "leaner" inn. Comments on Seller's Numbers; Column 1 to Column 2: Increased staff and higher food costs are relative to higher occupancy—the standard percentages are @ 50% occupancy. It's clear that the present owners are not doing much marketing or promotion, but do have an effective Web site. Lower utilities are because of temperate climate.

When you are using the Property Evaluation Worksheets, it's best to make your comments right on the form. After you have looked at several properties and analyzed them, it helps to have everything in one place. Good luck with this adventure of buying a dream business—we think you are well informed!

Many thanks for our consultants who helped with the financial chapters:
Hugh Daniels, consultant, Ask Hugh Consulting, Utah
Michael Yovino-Young, appraiser, Yovino-Young, Inc., California
John Sheiry, CEO, Distinguished Inns Alliance, owner; Waverly Inn, Hendersonville, North Carolina
Nancy Donaldson, So . . . You Think You Want to Be an Innkeeper? Workshops and Consulting, California

your business plan
and getting a loan

At the beginning, getting the inn building in shape seems like the primary hurdle. But just as you wouldn't renovate an inn structure without a full set of plans and cost estimates, you shouldn't move ahead on your business without a comprehensive plan for its "construction" and financing.

Your Business Plan

The Small Business Administration indicates that businesses with plans have a far higher success rate. If you've been working your way through this book, you've already developed much of the information for your business plan in your head, your lists, and your files. Writing the plan will make all those pieces fall into place. It's also a check to see if you've considered everything and whether your plans can be made clear and compelling to others.

In addition, your business plan has other beneficial uses:

- **Financing**: Your plan is crucial in approaching banks, friends, and prospective partners for money. It's your "application."
- **Communication tool:** The plan is an efficient, effective summary of your business concept to share with your attorney, insurance agent, accountant, partners, and directors. They'll understand your ideas for the future better when you present them in such an organized format.
- **Organization medium**: Writing and developing the plan gives you practice in thinking and making decisions based on a business approach, not just a dream.
- **Focus:** A business plan can be the inn's "bible," to which you'll turn when nothing seems to be going right; it acts as a reminder of why you're in this business anyway. It can help keep you on track when another great idea—making widgets on the side, maybe, or adding a restaurant—threatens to sidetrack you.
- **Base from which to flex:** It's not a hard-and-fast rulebook; it's a framework. "Rolling with the punches" is different than reeling from one crisis to another, and a plan helps keep everything, including change, in perspective.

A plan that can do this much for you should be prepared carefully. It will represent your inn, so make it look professional: typed, reproduced on high-quality paper, and kept in a neat folder or binding. Copies should be numbered and dated. Keep a log of those who have the plan; it's privileged information.

Developing a plan requires time to think, and think creatively. Getting away from interruptions and routine daily pressures to work on it can be the start of a good management practice. Managers need perspective. In innkeeping, it's difficult but crucial to be far enough away to gain that perspective. Start here.

WHAT GOES INTO THE PLAN?

Naturally, plans differ in outline as well as in content, but here's a good model.

Introduction
- Title page with date, writer's name, inn name.
- Table of contents.
- Overview or summary of what plan will cover.

Description of the Business
- The type of bed-and-breakfast you will provide.
- Auxiliary services offered, if any.
- Description of physical structure.
- Location.
- Legal structure, i.e., partnership, corporation, limited liability company, sole proprietorship.
- History of business if it is an existing inn.

Marketing: Determining Sales Potential
Include the information you've gathered on site selection, researching your market, and so on, listing specifically:
- Who your customers will be (age, family, occupation).
- Who your competition is (inns, hotels, B&B services).
- The visitor statistics and accommodations occupancy rates in the area.
- What makes your inn competitive in that market.

How Will You Attract Guests?
Include here information on inn ambience, initial and ongoing marketing, plus pricing structure and policies and procedures.

Personnel

- Your own résumé(s) and business histories or list of accomplishments. The bank and others will want to know what qualifies you to be an inn owner and operator. If you have little business experience or no hotel or inn experience, you may want to include the background(s) of your outside consultants.
- Names and histories or résumé(s) of your board of directors, if you have one.
- How will work be arranged? Will you do it all or hire staff? When? How many? To do what? It may be helpful to include a simple chart of responsibilities describing who will deal with the bookkeeper, supervise the cleaning staff, and so on, to clarify roles and structure.

Consultants and Outside Resources

Successful businesses are not opened all alone, and the resources you have can help you get others. Include here all the people you can think of who have helped or will help you in your business: architect, attorney, contractor, accountant, promotion professional, consultants, insurance agent, decorator, and innkeepers and innkeeper associations.

Commitments

These are arrangements already made: building in escrow or leased, furniture already available or promised, arrangements made with antiques dealers, innkeeping class scheduled to be taken, and inn association promise of referrals.

Financial Information

Many of your readers will turn to the financial figures first. For them and for your own peace of mind, develop this section carefully and honestly. Try to follow these guidelines. First, estimate expenses high and income low. This is no time for optimism. Be as pessimistic as you can bear to be, so you build in contingency plans. You will feel much better about a low December if you've planned for it than if you unexpectedly need $2,000 you haven't set aside. If you've allocated $2,000 for the expected deficit, you'll have the satisfaction of knowing you're at least good at planning!

Second, go over your figures in detail with someone who will ask hard questions, like why you expect your gas bills to be identical in summer and winter. Talk to more than one knowledgeable person, and preferably someone familiar with hotel or inn operations.

These figures might be developed with an accountant, but there are very substantial advantages to doing them yourself. You'll be making presentations to bankers and investors, as well as making decisions based on these numbers. If you develop them, you'll know them. If your financial situation is a mystery at this stage, you'll be totally lost once you're in operation.

Try not to let sensitivity about finances get in your way. Like most people, innkeepers tend to take on the good old American value of secrecy about money. This can make it difficult both to disclose finances and to develop them honestly. Remember, the inn is not you. It's created by you, but it is not you. If it should need repairs or overhaul, it won't mean you're a loser.

WHAT TO INCLUDE IN THE FINANCIAL SECTION

For a start-up operation, the financial section should include: a summary of financial needs (including renovation or building costs), research detailing projected occupancy rate and average daily rate for your area, a pro forma (estimated or projected) profit and loss statement, and a break-even analysis. Examples of these financial forms can be found in the "Go or No Go: Numbers for Buying, Building, or Renovating" chapter (see page 67).

If you are buying an existing inn, you will need all the above information, plus the inn's financial history, including balance sheets, profit and loss statements, and tax returns for the past three years. The sellers must also provide an inventory and copies of leases, contracts, and legal documents that will carry forward. The following section includes descriptions of other financial reports that most business plans contain.

Other Financial Reports for Your Inn

YOUR PERSONAL FINANCIAL STATEMENT

Readers of your business plan who might provide loans or business support are interested in your ability to repay a loan and your collateral assets as represented by your financial situation. Potential investors will also want to evaluate your stake in the business.

The sample financial statement in Appendix 2 includes categories specifically relevant to the inn business. It's an excellent information tool for you, whether or not you plan to seek outside funding. If you do need a bank loan, a form like this will be required, along with your personal tax returns from the last three years. Financial statements include a current listing of assets and liabilities, including all real estate, stocks, bonds, insurance, loans, pension funds, personal property, and fixed expenses (child's college, alimony). You can also include here assets like the value of antique furnishings you'll use in the inn.

PERSONAL BENEFIT INCOME

Owners who live on the inn premises and are involved in daily inn operations receive related benefits of significant value. A projected breakdown of this information can help explain to bankers why you'll be able to pay back a requested loan even without a large salary.

	Past Experience	In an Inn
Housing	_____	_____
Utilities	_____	_____
Gardening service	_____	_____
Food	_____	_____
Insurance	_____	_____
Auto expenses	_____	_____
Travel and entertainment	_____	_____
Home repairs	_____	_____
Cleaning service	_____	_____

INCOME AND EXPENSE STATEMENT AND BALANCE SHEET

The two financial documents that tell the whole story of a start-up proposal or the purchase of an existing inn are the income and expense statement and the balance sheet.

Balance sheets show the relationship of current assets and liabilities; income and expense statements show the profitability—the bottom line—of your operations.

The balance sheet reflects what you own and owe at a moment in time: "at December 31, 2003" or at "June 30, 2004." It consists of a listing of all your assets and all your liabilities. The dollar difference between assets and liabilities is the owner's share of the business, which is added as "equity" and balances the totals. The income and expense statement, also called a profit and loss statement or P & L, is your formal financial statement for tax purposes. It is particularly important if you are looking for a personal tax shelter for investors. This document will cover a period of time: "twelve months ending December 31, 2003," or "three months ending May 1, 2004," or "the month of February 2005."

In addition to the actual expenses and income reported in the cash flow analysis, the P & L also includes the noncash expense of depreciation. Depreciation is the "using up" of a building, an automobile, furniture, equipment, dishes, linens, and so on. It recognizes the life expectancy of these things and their declining usefulness over the years. Your accountant or CPA will probably prepare your depreciation table.

If you buy an older house for an inn, you are buying both land and structure. Property tax bills break out the assessed values of each; you can generally find the ratio on an old tax bill. (Your CPA may not accept the ratio, but he or she will need to justify any new one.) In California coastal cities where land costs are high, the ratio may run as high as two to one, land to buildings. In rural areas or in the East, it may run two to one, buildings to land. You want the building portion to be high, because land is never depreciated—that is, it doesn't wear out, according to the IRS. Depreciation may put your business in a loss position for tax purposes even when you break even.

In addition to buildings, all other assets, such as furniture and equipment, are depreciated each year on a schedule followed by your CPA. IRS depreciation rules change often; ask your CPA about them.

Other major changes in the cash flow analysis to make it a profit and loss statement include: moving capital purchases from expenses to assets, which are then depreciated, and moving the part of your mortgage payment that is principal out of the expense portion.

The government grants tax credits that can be even more important than tax losses in restoring old buildings, since they come directly off the taxes you owe. Check with your CPA for current legislation on tax credits.

CASH FLOW PROJECTIONS MONTH BY MONTH

During the process of demonstrating to lenders or investors your ability to plan and repay, you may need to break out your projections into monthly figures. You will certainly want to do the monthly projections for your own business planning purposes. It's not enough to have income equal expenses at year-end; you must also plan for paying your property tax in April, for example, even though it's at the end of your absolutely dead season.

Financial statements are management tools. When you understand them you will be better able to recognize and respond to business problems, and you'll be able to discuss the money side of your business intelligently with anyone.

Getting a Loan

What? You say you don't *have* a couple of hundred thousand dollars to start an inn? Don't despair. Just because our examples call these enormous sums "cash needs" doesn't mean you need all of the cash in your pocket to get started.

WHERE TO LOOK FOR MONEY

If you currently own the building you wish to turn into a bed-and-breakfast inn, you have the best of all worlds. You have residential financing, which is usually at a lower interest rate, often fixed, and for a longer amortization period—up to thirty years. The longer the loan is amortized, the lower the monthly payments. These loans are obtainable because you have adequate income from other employment to convince the lender that the loan will be paid off, and because you are claiming the property as a residence.

If you are buying a building in a town distant from your home for the purpose of converting it to an inn, you will probably not be able to get residential financing, unless you have income from other continuing employment or plan to work at a new job in the new location. Some people who engage in long-range planning will buy a home suitable for inn conversion and work at a salary-paying job for years while they prepare the inn. When they open, their financing is already in place.

Friends and family are possible sources for loans. Be cautious here: since you know you will be in a negative cash flow situation for the first few years, delay repayment until a period when your projections show you'll have adequate cash flow. Extend out your projections as far into the future as necessary to reach this point. Make sure you check with your CPA, since the IRS has rules regarding interest rates and length of repayment on loans. If the terms are too lenient, they will not consider the interest deductible. Include in a formal promissory note when monthly payments of a specified amount will begin, as well as the total to be repaid in full by a specific date.

If you have substantial other property, retirement funds, stocks, or bonds that you can pledge for collateral, you may be able to obtain financing for a start-up. Most lenders like to see three years of an inn's history for loan purposes.

If you are applying to a financial institution for funds, your lender will be interested in the "five Cs" of credit:

1. **Character.** This is by far the most important quality. If you are not someone to be trusted, the lender will not want anything to do with you, no matter how good the deal is.
2. **Capacity.** What is your track record in this business or in previous businesses, and what is your financial strength?
3. **Capital.** How much of your own (and/or your investors') money is in the project? If you are not willing to put your own money in, no lender will be either.
4. **Collateral.** What is available to support the primary source of repayment on the total amount of the loan?
5. **Conditions.** What is the economy doing and how will it affect your business and the loan it is seeking?

Your loan proposal should contain the following items in a clear, clean, and concise manner. This statement should be typed, dated, and signed.

Loan request

Your complete business plan

Use or purpose(s) of the proceeds of the loan

Amount required

Source(s) of repayment

Collateral offered

Terms desired

Current personal financial statements on all owners

Some lenders will also want to see three years' worth of personal tax returns for the owners. You should also include anything else that may be pertinent, such as a partnership agreement, incorporation papers, title insurance, and photographs.

Remember the old saying "Banks only lend to people who don't need the money." This is very true when you try to borrow money for an inn. Banks are trained to always require two sources of repayment. The primary source, cash flow for short-term loans and earnings for long-term loans, should be backed up by some form of collateral, such as accounts receivable, inventory, or property. Then if something goes wrong with the original plan, the lender always has at least one fallback position.

The lender will also usually require a personal guarantee from the owner(s) of the business, because they want your psychological commitment to the success of the venture. They do not necessarily expect to gain a great deal of financial security from your personal signature, but they want your total support and dedication to making the business successful.

If you are buying an existing inn, a lender will require the business profit and loss statements, the balance sheets, and your tax returns for the past three years. Again, your ability to pledge other assets as collateral will be an important factor.

Many inns sold today carry loans guaranteed by the Small Business Administration. Check with your local banks and find several that do business with the SBA. SBA-guaranteed commercial loans are made by independent lenders, such as banks and nonbank lenders, and are guaranteed by the U.S. Small Business Administration as long as they meet certain eligibility requirements. The SBA guarantees up to 75 percent of a loan amount with some restrictions. Because of the SBA loan guarantee, lenders are often able to extend credit to small businesses that might not otherwise qualify under normal lending guidelines. SBA loans require a commercial appraisal (ordered by the bank), a loan origination fee, a business plan, a personal guarantee from the owner(s), detailed monthly projections for the first year, personal financial information of borrower(s), and evidence of all available collateral, preferably equity in owned real estate. SBA guaranteed loans cannot have a balloon payment schedule. The loans are amortized over twenty-five years for real estate; up to ten years for equipment, furniture, and fixtures; and up to seven years for working capital.

Offices of the Service Corps of Retired Executives (SCORE) throughout the country can direct you to retired professionals who donate their time to the SBA to help entrepreneurs; they can guide you through the precise, detailed, cumbersome, and lengthy application procedure.

As a rule of thumb, it's unwise to finance short-term needs like working capital with long-term financing (financing for more than a year). The reverse of the maxim is that you should finance furniture or building improvements—long-term fixed assets—with long-term loans or liabilities.

Your ability to arrange for a new mortgage will be based on your income at the time of your application, which must be high enough to support the monthly payments. If at the end of three years you are breaking even and have a three-year track record of income, refinancing should not be too difficult.

Financial institutions will ask you two questions: How much money do you need? How are you going to repay it? The more thorough your preparation for the project, documented with a business plan and financial projections, the more impressed a lender will be with your seriousness and your dependability.

Lenders invariably desire that a borrower have at least 30 percent of the total required to start a business from sources other than loan.

Despite all of the above documentation, it is difficult to convince a lender that a new business will succeed. An applicant seeking to open a branch of a recognized franchise has a better chance of securing a loan.

A business successfully established for three or more years that needs at least $50,000 for expansion has a much better chance of securing a loan. The lender will need the last three years' profit and loss statements and balance sheets.

If you are permanently handicapped, a Vietnam-era veteran, or a disabled veteran, you may be eligible for an SBA direct loan.

Quite apart from all of the above, it requires salesmanship to secure a loan. You have to sell yourself and your plan both in your interview with a loan officer and in your written plans.

let's make a deal

BUYING AN EXISTING INN

Twenty years ago, if you wanted to be an innkeeper anywhere but in New England, you almost had to start an inn. Not so today. There are plenty of inns around the country, and some of them are for sale.

Bed-and-breakfast travel is steadily growing, but the exponential growth of the industry happened in the 1980s. Most areas of the country still see new inns opening, but the inn business has finally reached a level of maturity where, as with other small, largely owner-operated businesses, inns change hands with some regularity. There is little quantitative measurement of this activity, but some patterns have emerged. It appears that the turnover runs in thirds. A third of the innkeepers leave the industry in three to five years, having been unrealistic in their understanding of the lifestyle and financial expectations. Some of the disappointed innkeepers return their inn to its original home status, while others sell to someone ready to make the next steps toward growing the business. With all the permits in place and the marketing launched, the renovation handled, and a guest base started, these young inns make good options for the future innkeeper, because the present owners don't have the longevity that would have built more value.

The next third are likely to have taken a hard look at their business and even possibly their life. By making adjustments—adding rooms, upgrading their living quarters—they last another five years, at which point they want to move on. They have been successful, but their love of innkeeping may not be as strong as that of the people in the last third. Those in this group are likely to stay on for the long haul—twenty to thirty years—because they have adjusted to the lifestyle, they are making a comfortable living, and being innkeepers is who they are. If you are looking for an average number of years, a limited study by Oates and Bredfeldt, an inn-consulting firm in Brattleboro, Vermont, tracked eighty-five inns, mostly mature properties with dinner service, over a four-year period. The average length of ownership was seven years, four months, twenty days, and twenty hours!

Start-ups may turn over sooner, often because of cash flow problems. In most cases, though, inns sell for positive reasons: the owners have achieved their original goals, their lifestyles and family relationships have changed, or a new challenge has become more attractive. More inns sell because of success than because of failure, and even problem properties can be turned around by a new owner with the necessary reserves of money and energy.

Consultants working in the field report that how long innkeepers stay in the business is directly related to having competent staff. Those innkeepers who go it alone 24/7 usually burn out after several years.

WHY BUY AN EXISTING INN?

There are several advantages to buying an existing inn. In the first place, you will be dealing with a known quantity with a measurable track record of income and expenses, occupancy rates, patterns of seasonality, and sources of business. Of course, what you'll be buying is the future, not the past. The previous performance of the inn will naturally be affected by your new style of operation. You will, however, have a starting point from which you can—and must—do your own projections.

Second, you can easily verify the existence of necessary licenses and permits. Again, do your own investigation. Permit procedures vary considerably from place to place. Since the codes change regularly, the mere existence of a permit is not sufficient. In some areas, health department licenses are issued to a location; in other jurisdictions, to individuals. A sale may or may not trigger fire marshal inspections. If you buy a place that serves alcoholic beverages, you will probably need to apply for a transfer or a new license, and that often involves investigation into your moral character and finances.

A special word of caution: You'll often hear of "grandfathered" conditions or exceptions. This term is used correctly to refer to nonconforming, preexisting uses in regard to zoning. It's often used incorrectly in relation to health, safety, parking, and fire codes. Waiver of conformance to codes may occur through forbearance, persuasion, or ignorance, but none of those have legal standing, and new ownership may be a signal for the authorities to act. Still, the existence of current licenses and permits does indicate the likelihood of their continuation. Before purchase, make that a certainty.

A third important advantage is that you will be in business the day the sale closes. An income flow, however meager, is strong psychological support, and real guests activate the learning curve in a hurry.

Fourth, you'll start out with market recognition. The *Industry Study* by the Professional Association of Innkeepers International indicates that repeat guests and their referrals of friends account for about 25 percent of the business of mature inns. An additional 15 percent comes from inn guidebooks, including

AAA's. Neither of these categories, amounting to 40 percent of a mature inn's business, is available to a start-up inn. Though having a Web site can put an inn on the map more quickly, establishing a Web presence takes additional time and energy a new innkeeper often just doesn't have.

Inns that have been around awhile are more likely to see repeat articles from travel writers who have learned to trust the seasoned inn. Inclusion of a new property in a future edition of the best guides takes time, because of publication dates and inspections that happen only once a year. Select Registry requires an inn applicant to be in business several years as well as pass an inspection.

Most people underestimate the time it takes to build a critical mass of guests sufficient to ensure a strong repeat business. Most guests try a variety of inns. Those who do return rarely come frequently. The average inn guest, according to a *Yellow Brick Road* newsletter survey, visits an inn once every eighteen months.

A fifth reason to buy an existing inn is that, contrary to popular wisdom, you can often put together a better financing package. Since you can describe the business more completely and most major renovations are already in place, financing needs are more clearly definable. A relatively mature inn will have a demonstrable cash flow to convince lending institutions of your ability to repay a loan. Finally, the selling owner will often wish to, or at least recognize the need to, participate in the financing in the form of a second mortgage or a second deed of trust.

The final advantage is the availability of transition help: ongoing, hands-on advice and assistance from the original owner, for a time you can specify in the contract (often two weeks to a month). This can help ease transition jitters, though success, of course, is in your hands alone.

As you can see, there are many good reasons to consider buying an existing inn. It's even possible, in some locations, that current zoning and other restrictions may prohibit development of new inns, limiting you to the purchase of an existing inn—and that's not bad!

Are there reasons not to buy an existing inn? It does limit you to the inns that exist and to those that are for sale. And you may face difficult price negotiations with owners who have an inflated idea of the value of their business.

Nevertheless, done right, buying an existing inn can provide a quicker and, in the long run, better economic return with less risk.

The best inn you can buy probably isn't for sale—but you can still buy it. What do we mean? Just this: it's highly improbable that you will drive up to the inn of your dreams and find a For Sale sign in the front garden. But it's still possible that the owners might be interested in hearing your proposition, even if they hadn't thought about selling.

That's one reason why the best places to find an inn for sale are innkeepers publications. Write an ad describing the inn you hope to find, place it in *innkeeping* newsletter, and it's just possible that an innkeeper will decide to sell it to you. See Resources for a listing of inn publications.

Business and real estate consultants who specialize in the inn field frequently advertise inns for sale on the Internet. You can also check the business opportunities section of the *Wall Street Journal* and of the local and major metropolitan newspapers in your target area.

If you've targeted one or two specific areas where your inn should be located, contact local innkeepers by mail or telephone for their advice on what might be for sale.

Whichever of these methods you choose, you'll be taken most seriously if you have a clear picture of what you want. Use the checklist below to "build" your model inn.

Number of rooms
Nature of innkeeper's quarters
Monthly income necessary for personal needs
Type of breakfast (sit-down, formal, in bed—affects space needs)
Ambience and decor
Geographic requirements (weather, beach, city, rural, etc.)
Amount of renovation you want and can afford
Architectural style
Special features (pool, acreage, etc.)
Services to provide (dinners, baked goods—affects kitchen requirements)
Extent of your involvement in the inn operation
Valuation

How do you know what an inn is worth? Well, it's a complicated question.

Size is a factor. Michael Yovino-Young of Berkeley, California, who has specialized in inn appraisals since 1977, says, "Small inns, under six or seven rooms, are perceived as highly personal businesses, with revenue vulnerable to the whims and abilities of a particular owner-innkeeper. Thus the ability of the inn to sustain income from year to year is judged to be at risk." A small inn is sometimes perceived to be worth its real estate value as a residence, and not much more.

Age is a factor. Bill Oates, an inn-acquisition consultant from Brattleboro, Vermont, says, "Rarely is there any business value to an inn until it is at least three years old." There are exceptions for certain very high tourist areas where the number of inns is too small for the existing market. In some very desirable areas of the country, inn prices are prohibitively high and discouraging, but there are other factors you need to consider.

First, buying an inn and becoming an innkeeper are, to some degree, emotional decisions. If being an innkeeper is what you really want to do, it may be worth it to you to, in effect, buy yourself an innkeeping job.

The second factor is property value. When we buy homes, we don't expect any yearly return on our investment, but we do look forward to reaping a gain when we finally sell. This same opportunity should exist with an inn.

And finally, in those cases where an innkeeper has substantial income in addition to that from the inn, the inn can provide considerable tax deductions, allowing the innkeeper to keep more of that other income in his or her pocket. These are the practical considerations involved in making a decision on an inn's value to you.

You need to feel good about all the money and time you'll put into your inn, so if you're going to make less on your investment than you would in U.S. Treasury bills, think again. If the figures look good only when you donate all your labor, think about how much you're paying to buy yourself a volunteer position.

But the truly critical factor for any potential buyer is whether the property makes economic sense for him or her. The most practical approach to determining this is to do the calculations used to assess value in the industry.

Here is inn appraiser Michael Yovino-Young's glossary of terms used by appraisers and banks:

Operating Expenses: Operating expenses, for a seasoned, well-run bed-and-breakfast inn, will fall into a range of 50 to 65 percent of gross revenues, excluding debt service (principal and interest of mortgage), any expenses not necessary for operation, transient occupancy and sales taxes, and owner draw or salary. Usually, the smaller the inn, the higher the operating expenses in relationship to income.

Price per Guest Room Unit: This all-inclusive index assumes that the building has a kitchen, a common area, and innkeeper's quarters and comprises real estate, personal property, including fixtures and equipment, and intangible assets of the business, such as goodwill. This index normally ranges quite widely even in one community, based on quantitative and qualitative differences among inns and the appraiser's judgment. Price per guest room is figured by dividing sales price by number of guest rooms.

Examples of prices per guest room of bed-and-breakfast and country inns actually sold:

Area	Price per Guest Room	Source
West	$121,875–$261,250	2000–2002 Yovino-Young
East: B&B Inn	$51,667–$163,636	1999–2003 Oates & Bredfeldt
East: Inn with Dinner Service	$59,757–$180,952	1999–2002 Oates & Bredfeldt

Gross Annual Rent Multiplier (GRM): This is income-based and, though time-honored in real estate transactions, must be tempered with the other valuation indexes listed here. Currently the GRM is running 4.35 to 7 in the West and 3.4 to 5.89 in the East. The lower the GRM, the better. Use this formula:

$$\frac{\text{Sales Price}}{\text{Gross Annual Income}} = \text{GRM}$$

Capitalization Rate Index: This calculation gives you the overall rate of return on your investment—it's much like figuring how much return you will make on other investments. You will want this to be between 10 and 12 percent. Use these formulas:

$$\text{Total Income - Operating Expenses} = \text{Net Operating Income}$$

$$\frac{\text{Net Operating Income}}{\text{Purchase Price of Property}} = \text{Capitalization Rate}$$

Cost Approach: In the absence of any other possible approach—for instance, when there are no sales of inns in the area and no income data to analyze—an appraiser may be forced to rely on replacement-cost or reproduction-cost methods.

The cost approach is essentially a real estate value. What are typical ratios of real estate values to other assets of a going concern? Based on a Yovino-Young sample of more than sixty inns appraised since 1983, the ratios vary as follows: real estate, 85 to 93 percent; personal property, 7 to 15 percent; and other intangible assets, 0 to 5 percent.

Placing a value on a business, particularly on an inn business, is not an exact science. There is no one way to do it. But there is one certainty: sellers will always want more than buyers wish to pay. That's not surprising. The sellers have conceived and nourished a property and business, perhaps since its inception. They're almost like parents. How do you place a fair value on something this personal? This part of your inn-search process may be the most difficult and exasperating. Owners tend to value their inns on the basis of what they've put into them, rather than on what a new owner can get out.

Hire your own value consultant or appraiser if you're uncomfortable with the price being asked. Listing agents for inns are not always well informed about the inn business, and they lack the resources to gather market data on comparable properties.

A word of caution: Don't commit yourself to an expensive appraisal—and they can cost $5,000 to $10,000—before you consult with your lender. Lenders usually have their own lists of approved appraisers and will not act upon reports from others.

Your appraiser or consultant should look at the inn for quality of location, the facilities themselves, and the consistency and reliability of the income history. Your adviser should also be able to inform you about the inn's desirability from the viewpoint of local institutional lenders. Unbiased answers to these and other practical questions are usually worth the cost of hiring an independent expert.

EVALUATING A SELLER'S NUMBERS

You have found an inn you're interested in and would like to look at some numbers. Ask the owners or the broker for the following data:

Number of rentable rooms
Average daily room rate (ADR)
Occupancy percentage
Net operating income
Gross income

Once you have these numbers, you can create a fairly accurate picture of the health of the business.

Some sellers are hesitant to give you any numbers until you make a formal offer. Even in the beginning stage of a negotiation, you should insist on receiving these basic numbers. If you are dealing directly with the owners, consult a real estate attorney for help with the formal offer; in any event, make sure that the offer is contingent upon approval of all the financial information, including transient occupancy forms and tax returns. Use these equations to check the gross income figure:

number of rooms x 365 days x ADR = income at 100% occupancy

income at 100% occupancy x actual occupancy = gross income

If your gross income total is less than the owner's stated gross, check the actual ADR against the rack-rate ADR (the brochure rate). Use these equations:

Number of rooms x 365 days = total number of rooms available for the year

total number of rooms available x actual occupancy rate = total number of rooms rented

Divide this figure into the gross income to get the actual ADR:

$$\frac{\text{Gross Income}}{\text{Total number of rooms rented}} = \text{actual ADR}$$

Once you have the actual ADR, recalculate the gross income. Multiply the number of rooms by 365 days by the new ADR to get the income at 100 percent occupancy. Then multiply the income at 100 percent occupancy by the actual occupancy to get gross income. If the seller's gross income is still higher than your calculations, ask whether sales or bed taxes are included in the gross income. These are always pass-through funds; the inn is merely the collector. They should never be included in gross income. Also ask if there are other profit centers—e.g., weddings, meals other than those included in rates, or gift shop sales.

To develop the operating expense amount, subtract the net operating income from the gross income. Typically, total operating expenses should be within the range of 50 to 65 percent of gross revenue.

ACHIEVING FINANCIAL GROWTH

How can you project the income effect of positive changes in the inn? Very carefully! Consider the ideas below, and make educated cost projections of the expense to implement them—don't ignore the cost of lost income if you need to close for remodeling—and the additional income from new rooms, more expensive rooms, higher occupancy, and additional sales and services. Be specific, and don't spend money you don't expect to get back in higher income.

Increase number of rooms
Increase room rates
Increase occupancy
Upgrade your Web site
Decrease expenses
Upgrade quality of services and
  furnishings
Add capital improvements
Hot tub
Swimming pool
Private baths
Fireplaces
Curb appeal
Increase profit centers
Retail sales
Additional food service
Wine and beer license
Special promotions
Marketing changes

Expand markets:
  Small group or conference site
  Business travelers
  Families with children
  Birders
  Seniors
  Foreign travelers
  Travel agent–generated business
  Bicycle groups

Going to the Dogs

Bobby Barker, innkeeper at the Inn at Crystal Lake in the White Mountains of New Hampshire, found a way to increase occupancy: he went to the dogs. Taking a room that has a private bath situated across the hall and thus was not a big renter, he created a "pet-friendly room," complete with queen bed, CCTV, phone, full breakfast each morning, complimentary evening cocktails, pet bed, and pet water bowl. Friendly and well-behaved pets love it, and he is not shy about asking callers if they want to bring their pets. Here is the interesting part: the occupancy for the pet-friendly room has become the same and even better than the inn's beautiful two-room suite with a canopy bed. The least desirable room (because of the bath across the hall) has become the most popular, thanks to pet lovers. This increase was very important to Barker's banker, too.

As a prospective buyer, you can't expect a seller to reveal detailed financial data until you have demonstrated that you are a qualified buyer. You are, however, entitled to summary financial information which may include gross receipts, net operating income, and occupancy percentages for the most recent year. On the basis of this data, you will be expected to make an initial offer. This often includes price, terms, management contract, covenant not to compete, disclosure requirements, and contingencies.

At this point, you will also want to specify the detailed material you will need to review during the escrow period. Naturally, it's essential to protect your interests with contingencies that make the offer invalid if the comprehensive data you receive later fails to support the summary. Now the negotiation begins.

This stage is always touchy, and you'll want to use your consultant or broker in the process. The cardinal rule of negotiation is to determine what you want and what the other person wants and then try to make it a win-win deal, so that each of you gets what you want. Of course, you must decide first what exactly you need as a bottom line. Keep that foremost in your mind as you make decisions during the negotiations.

Remember that this is a process. No major negotiation results in immediate agreement. Everyone feels hurt or insulted at one time or another during the deal making, but going back and forth is a necessary part of the successful agreement. And often, when you think all the negotiations are finished and the papers are ready to be signed, more demands are forthcoming and the process begins again.

During the negotiating period, try to maintain some distance from the owner and let your consultant or broker do the talking. This can keep the normal animosities and personal feelings separate from the working relationship you will want later. During this time, many things change or come up unexpectedly to cause both parties distress. This is normal, but keep your consultant out front and your bottom line in mind.

Once you have reached an agreement, you'll want to see: financial statements for the last three years, business tax returns and schedules for at least the last three years, transient occupancy and sales tax returns for at least the last three years, asset inventory and exclusion list, appraisals of real estate and personal property, promotional materials, inventory of goods for sale, tabulation of marketing efforts, and licenses and permits required.

You will want a contractor or person knowledgeable about old buildings to walk through the inn so you know that there are no surprises and that you are allocating adequate financial resources for renovation in your business plan. You may wish to have a formal house inspection covering wiring, heating, the roof, and so on. Have the sellers complete a disclosure statement as part of the sale and check it thoroughly with the house inspector.

It is also important to double-check that the inn is licensed, approved, and zoned for all the business being done: number of rooms, bathrooms, pool or whirlpool, kitchen, fireplaces, parking, septic system, and food or beverage service.

Most states have laws requiring the sellers and their agents to disclose all information relating to any significant historical problem the property may have suffered, such as flooding, foundation settlement, fire, or windstorm damage. You are entitled to know these facts and should protect yourself by asking direct questions. If in doubt on any point of concern, ask for a written statement from the sellers even beyond the standard "seller's disclosure statement." Be prepared to pay for your own inspections of the roof, foundation, and electrical systems—whatever seems to be marginal or flagged in the disclosure statement.

Once you have reached an agreement and have signed a contract spelling out all the contingencies, you will want to be sure to obtain the following:

Real estate transfer disclosure statement from seller and agent(s)

Use permit

Zoning ordinance and assurance that your building is in a properly zoned area

Building permits and final inspections

Health department inspection and county ordinance for kitchen

Copy of recent tests and county reports

Bed-tax ordinance and records showing the inn's payments for the last three years

Business license

Structural pest-control inspection

Contractor's inspection of building

Resale license and record of present owner's payments

Liquor license

Copy of local or state Americans with Disabilities Act requirements

Any correspondence with city regarding bed-and-breakfast use

Look at competitors' room rates and occupancy

IRS tax returns of present owner for last three years

List of all furniture, fixtures, and equipment to be transferred; include pictures, linens, dishes, pots, pans, silverware, appliances, lawn mowers, tools, etc. It is a good idea to get a list of what is not included at the same time.

List of where the sellers advertise and promote the inn and how much it costs; include guidebooks, all advertisements, Yellow Pages listings, which chamber of commerce, local and regional organizations, and referrals from other inns.

List of local suppliers and labor, including plumbers, carpenters, housekeepers, etc.

Accounting of prepaid reservations and outstanding gift certificates

MAKING THE TRANSITION BETWEEN OWNERS

If all has gone reasonably smoothly prior to closing the sale, your working relationship with the former owners will be off to a good start. Most selling innkeepers have invested a great deal of themselves in what you have just made yours, so they will want to share with you what they know about the business and the quirks of property.

Of course, you will want to make changes and to approach the inn from a fresh viewpoint. Remember to be kind. Usually the former owners know all the things that are wrong and had their own reasons for not changing them. Your ideas may not be as revolutionary as you think. If you approach the former owners asking for feedback on your plans, they will probably be able to warn you about pitfalls or suggest places to turn for more information.

To be sure you get all the information you want from the former owners, make a list, using this book as a resource. Also encourage the former owners to make a list of what they think you need to know. Be sure to go through both lists thoroughly, writing down the information for future reference.

STAFF

Staff transitions are especially touchy at inns, because the personal nature of an inn carries over into the relationships between staff and owners. Staff will usually feel loyal to the former owners, and it will take time for you to win that loyalty. On the other hand, staff people will often have ideas for you that they couldn't get the former owners to try.

A change in ownership is naturally threatening to employees, but regular communication and clear renegotiation of job descriptions and your needs will usually lay the groundwork for a strong relationship.

If you want to replace staff, however, make a clean break. (See the section on staffing in "Up and Running.")

PROMOTION

If the former innkeeper is well liked and has long been an integral part of the inn operation, you may want to ask him or her to write a letter inviting former guests to "come meet the newest member of the Long Lost Inn family." You might make a special-discount offer to former guests when you send the letter, as an extra encouragement for them to come.

New owners are news, so try to get local press coverage about the transition. Your aim will be to highlight yourselves and any new exciting direction you plan to take, such as adding dinner service or restoring the original gardens.

What if you want to disassociate yourselves and the inn from the old ownership? Even so, it will be valuable for you to understand what kinds of promotion have worked for the inn in the past, so you can develop new promotional angles along those lines.

A final caution: Do not change the inn name without a lot of thought! If you need to disassociate your inn that completely from its past, be aware that, from the viewpoint of recognition, you'll put yourself almost in the position of a start-up operation.

CHOOSING AND WORKING WITH A REALTOR OR CONSULTANT

Before you sign a contract with a realtor or consultant, interview your prospects. Ask questions and get references. Ask innkeepers or friends for recommendations of possible agents, but avoid working with close personal friends or family, unless you are very good at keeping your business life and your personal life separate. Check references carefully and beware of fast talkers, pushy people, and those who guess at answers rather than admitting they don't know.

Remember that not all realtors work with "business opportunities." The gap between evaluating "real property" and valuing a bed-and-breakfast inn is enormous.

Once you decide on a consultant or realtor, make him or her work hard; your future depends on it. But don't rely solely on your agent's judgment. You will have to do a lot of the work yourself.

being an innkeeper:
beyond owning
the building

If you don't already own the building, purchasing an inn can be a very expensive proposition. But if that yearning to serve up coffee cake and welcome guests just won't leave your heart, you do have options. These range from filling in on the weekends at a nearby inn to owning the business but not the building. You will be a "real" innkeeper even if you don't take the risk of a property investment.

The early fantasy of being a "real" innkeeper rested in owning a cute-little-inn property lock, stock, and barrel; in truth, that just isn't necessary. You can be an entrepreneur without property. Jo Ann Bell and Pat Hardy started their career in innkeeping as lessees of their nine-room inn, building a successful B&B business from day one. In the hotel business, rarely does the company that runs the hotel own the building. Yet it is still a real hotel.

Managing and Interim Innkeeping

For more than fifteen years, Nancy Smith ran a successful independent business as a sought-after innsitter. She now trains aspiring interim innkeepers (also called "interim managers," a revision of the dated term "innsitters"). You, too, can be an innkeeper without the headaches of paying a mortgage, and still enjoy much satisfaction from a thriving business and spending time with happy guests.

Being an innsitter or interim innkeeper is sometimes a retirement choice, giving a couple without the logistical requirements of supporting a family a chance to experience different parts of the country. Having a separate income helps to get you over the initial hurdle of establishing a client base or the need to work all the time. Yet many younger people are also finding satisfaction in the flexibility of selecting jobs and running their own businesses, with little overhead, and they can quit more easily when they don't have a building to support.

However, if you are still hankering to have a piece of the action, you should know that lenders are likely to pass over more financially qualified candidates to fund your B&B dream if you can demonstrate successful longevity as an innkeeper. Experience in the field gains you credibility to move out on your own.

Longtime owners are sometimes open to the possibilities of a buyout plan that you can structure together after a few years of successful employment.

The Search for Flexibility

How can you enjoy greeting guests and serving breakfast while having full responsibility for an inn, yet not work every week of the year and not have to worry about the mortgage? Innsitting was the answer for James Craig and Phyllis Slater from Brooklyn, Michigan. After retirement they were planning to buy an inn. They looked at twenty-five inns and whittled their options down to four; then an innkeeper in Montana suggested innsitting. This was a new concept that seemed to better fit their idea of retirement. They could travel, take care of family concerns, and still be "innkeepers." After James had taken an innsitting class and volunteered at an inn for several months, the newly retired Phyllis joined him. With recommendations from the inn where he had volunteered, they got their first job. Since then Phyllis and James have been interim innkeepers in Indiana, California, New Mexico, and Pennsylvania. They lease their condominium and use their motor home as their home base, learning that "you can do without all that stuff." Recently, after a six-month stint at a California inn, they were able to spend a couple of months taking care of family concerns, and then travel for a couple more months. James and Phyllis are not tied down every day of the year and can leave the worries of an inn behind when the job is done.

"The hardest part of not owning is having a huge responsibility," according to Mark Tamiso (WendMark Associates), "and being there every day and not having the final say. If you have a disagreement, you lose."

If you can live with doing it someone else's way, then one of these management options may be your "key" to someone else's inn.

Though being a "real" American seems to invoke owning property, being a "real" businessperson doesn't invoke the same prerequisite. What is important is that the numbers work and you receive both monetary and personal satisfaction from the work you have chosen. In this chapter, let's take a close look at the options available in the B&B industry: interim innkeeper, interim manager, manager, and lessee of the property.

Before going down this new road, it helps to have a map and a code in order to decipher the different directions one might take. Let's start with some history.

A Bit of History

Having a manager is not new to this industry. Innsitters were first on the scene in the early 1980s. In the 1990s, Nancy Smith established the B&B Innstitute in California to train innsitters, while a similar venture was taking place in Massachusetts by innkeeper Marie Brophy of the Isaiah Hall B&B Inn. A bit further down the road, Nancy launched the Association for Innsitters and Managers (AIM) in 1998. Since 1988, the Professional Association of Innkeepers International has embraced innsitter-supplier members and has made available a staff locator file to help owners find managers and vice versa. Workshops on innsitting and for managers have been popular at PAII conferences since 1990.

But this part of the B&B industry recently really came into its own. Shortly after the first PAII Innsitter/Manager Conference was held, in December 2002, a set of criteria for a certificate for interim innkeepers was developed, and the level of professionalism for "innsitters" made a giant leap.

UNDERSTANDING THE TERMINOLOGY

Understanding the terms for nonowners is not terribly complex; however, the terminology needs to accurately reflect what you do. This has traditionally been a very fluid field. Sometimes an *interim innkeeper* who is working for an owner during the owner's annual two-week vacation becomes an *interim manager* when the wife of the owner dies unexpectedly and the husband needs several months to collect himself and look at his future. When he decides he can't do it all alone and needs a full-time person with whom he can work, the interim manager becomes a *permanent manager.* You get the picture.

So, Who Am I?

Interim Innkeeper. *Sometimes called innsitter. Generally, this person takes over when the owner wants to go on vacation. Fully responsible for the day-to-day operation, this individual (or couple) has an independent business and works for a variety of inns. They carry their own kit bag of tools, including anything from an actual toolbox to recipes and familiar kitchen utensils. Generally the interim innkeeper interviews the owner before taking the job and collects a great deal of information on handling the inn and emergencies. Both parties sign a contract.*

Interim Manager. *This temporary employee generally comes in for several months, or even as much as a year, to assist the owner during a transition period. The owner gets the benefit of this experienced manager's viewpoint while leaving the inn completely in their hands. Unlike the interim innkeeper, the interim manager often takes on long-term projects, such as developing the marketing program and increasing occupancy. A contract is negotiated and signed by both parties.*

Manager. *Sometimes called innkeeper. This full-time employee works with the owner. The responsibilities of this position vary widely, depending on the owner and the skill of the employee. If the manager has set hours and doesn't live at the inn, standard labor laws for employees apply. Should the manager live on the premises and be expected to respond to off-hours guest needs, a contract should be negotiated and signed to protect all parties.*

Assistant Manager/Innkeeper. *Hired as an inn staff member, this individual works in conjunction with an actively participating owner. Responsibilities vary, depending upon what the owner believes should only be done by an owner. This situation is good for someone wanting to learn the business or who lives locally and enjoys working at an inn.*

Business Owner/Innkeeper. *Though this individual does not own the building, he or she is completely responsible for all aspects of the inn business. The lease that is negotiated may have a buyout clause, but it generally should be built so that the innkeeper can make money while the building owner increases value and maintains the building. Five percent of inns, many of them very well known, operate as leased properties. That number will increase as property values skyrocket in desirable areas where inns are now located.*

Throughout this section the term "owner" will refer to the business owner, whether or not that person owns the building. In some cases, the owner may actually be a general manager.

As an untrained, inexperienced owner of an inn, you can just limp along, since no one really requires that you know anything if you have enough money to buy the property. An owner will eventually pay for the mistakes they make. However, if an owner hires you, they will expect you to have experience. To get innkeepers to leave their "babies" with you, you need references from other innkeepers.

"Getting the experience without a job," the teenager's first-job lament, now rears its head for you. Innkeepers won't hire you as an interim innkeeper or manager without your having worked for someone else who can vouch for you. You are taking over their "baby," and they want to be sure you have done this work well for someone else.

If you are coming on as inn staff, owners will usually be happy to train you; but they will be more likely to take you seriously, or hire you as an interim manager or innkeeper, if you have studied this book (of course) and have taken an innkeeping workshop, attended innkeepers conferences, or taken restaurant and hospitality courses. Intern programs are available through PAII Suppliers and Inns. (Check with PAII for programs and upcoming conferences.)

Volunteer for a few weekends or a month at a nearby inn to see if the work appeals to you. After you learn the ropes and the innkeeper feels comfortable with you, offer to innsit for a weekend or a week, for pay. Be prepared to do any-thing; if all goes well, you've got a great reference! You might even be hired by one of the inns where you volunteered. It is money and time very well spent.

Interim innkeepers will also find that the above experience applies. Once you have several innkeeping situations under your belt, innkeepers are more likely to hire you as an independent contractor. Remember, these recommendations from fellow innkeepers are crucial for opening the doors of other inns. This experience will also give you valuable insights into working with inn owners, including developing your own series of questions about what you need to know in order to capably take over an inn for a short time.

Interim innkeeping is a separate business. You need all the skills of an owner, plus liability and self-employed workers' compensation insurance, a business license, certificates, a budget, and financial reports, not to mention an upbeat personality and self-promotion skills. (Contact the IRS about requirements for independent contractor.) Interim innkeepers develop their own brochures and Web sites and need to understand the basics of running a small business. All of the suggestions for inn owners regarding taking classes in bookkeeping, com-puter software, e-mail, and Internet marketing apply here as well.

As you consider these options, keep in mind, too, that few inns have large innkeeper's quarters. If you have a family, two dogs, and a llama, you're limiting your market considerably.

Since this is a new field, you may not find a great deal of written material on interim innkeeping or management, so look for a mentor who can answer your questions and give you moral support in your new venture. In today's world, this person need only be a telephone call or e-mail away and could be found through PAII's Interim Innkeeper/Manager Advisory Council.

Advice from Interim Innkeepers Given at PAII's First Innsitter/ Manager Conference in 2002

Volunteer or intern at a minimum of five inns to see if you like the field and to gain experience and references.

- *Understand the incredible responsibility and legal ramifications of what you are doing.*
- *Understand how much you are willing to give up (home, family, friends).*
- *Don't sell yourself short.*
- *Don't jump in too fast.*
- *Don't let an inn owner convince you that you are ready and have all the information you need.*
- *Come as an employee, but function as an equal.*
- *Get a mentor.*

You have to be more professional than an owner. You have two clients: the guest and the owner. Stay ahead of the trends; you are in a position to pass these along to owners who only know their inn. Take time to nourish yourself.

THE INTERVIEW

An interview between an owner and a potential inn manager, interim innkeeper, or interim manager functions as a mutual selection process.

Now that you have established yourself as capable and you have an interview with an inn owner, what are you prepared to ask?

The range of what you might do in any given position is vast, so you need to sit down and make your list of what you are able and willing to do. Be articulate about what you bring to the table. Some interim innkeepers clearly do not see cleaning rooms as part of their job, but they will take care of the pets and Grandmother. As a manager you could find yourself being a front-desk clerk and hostess or a full-charge innkeeper and dining room supervisor who also writes paychecks. Your personality and skills will determine how quickly you are ready to move into being in charge of the inn. Some of this will be trial and error; some people know that they want to work closely with the owner to learn as much as possible. Others don't want the owner looking over their shoulders and are happy to handle the necessary communication with an absentee owner to make things run smoothly for all. Before you go out into the world to be hired, know your skills and be prepared to communicate them.

Salaries for interim managers are not high, but many inns have good, unusual benefits, like great locations, simple lodgings in a terrific inn, and overnights at other inns at no charge to you—for research. Inn owners tend to overvalue these benefits and not understand the downside of a free room at the inn, so one of your goals in the interview will be to show what you can do to earn the salary or fee you desire. Since the field is still small, many managers may be the first one an inn owner has ever hired, so an educational process may be in order.

Be specific in your contract agreement. Inn management and interim management are serious positions; be careful to clearly define your hours and duties. A contract should state goals and expectations for both sides.Because innkeeping is such appealing work, it's easy to sign on for more than you can really handle. You can set yourself up for burnout. Be realistic about your abilities, and also about your salary needs, keeping in mind that this is not a get-rich business.You should, however, be able to support yourself. The interview is a chance for each of you to get a sense of whether you've found a match.

Whether you will be working for your parents or for strangers, before signing on as a manager, be sure you talk with the owner about as many specifics as you can. For example: Who will be planning, buying, preparing, cooking, serving, and cleaning up after breakfast? What hours will the telephone be answered? What authority do you have to offer discounts to last-minute reservations or to disgruntled guests? Who handles confirmations, deposits, refunds, and e-mail? Who will recruit, hire, supervise, and terminate staff? What level of involvement will the inn owner have in the daily and ongoing operation of the inn? A myriad of details should be discussed and written down, either as a job description or in a contract. (See Appendix 7 for a checklist.) You can always mutually agree to change these agreements as you get into the job—if, for example, you learn that the owners are there every day even though they said they would stop in only once a month.

Build in checkpoints. Consider setting a probationary period of thirty to sixty days after you start to review the initial agreement and to discuss how you are doing. Then expect weekly or monthly meetings with the owners so that you can check with each other on how things are going. This communication is fundamental for all of you to understand the others' philosophies and ways of doing things.

You will need to approach the inn as a business regardless of how the owners appear to deal with it. Even if the owners seem to treat the business as a hobby, when it starts to lose money they will become more serious. If you can show that you are increasing income, it will not go unappreciated. Setting goals for occupancy and income, understanding the budget and the inn's philosophy of doing business all contribute to a smoothly running business relationship.

As an interim innkeeper, you are coming in as a "substitute teacher" and must be prepared to step into the owner's shoes while they are walking out the front door. You have the incredible responsibility of taking care of the inn without the owner being there to help. Develop a list beforehand so you can get the necessary information from the owner efficiently and thoroughly prior to your taking over. (See Appendix 7 for basic information interim innkeepers need. PAII also carries a great starter list called the *Innkeepers Notebook*.) Advance communication is a basic step for success.

Innkeepers are not always aware of what it takes to run their inn, including a decent room in which to sleep. Interim innkeepers report that they have been left a mattress on a washing machine or the kitchen floor or just a bare room as a place they could retreat to when not working. You will need to determine what your limits are and ensure that they are both communicated in the initial interview and reconciled with the expectations of the owner.

Because an experienced interim innkeeper actually knows more about inns than most owners do, you are in the unique position to pass on information about what is happening in the rest of the inn world. However, this needs to be handled with delicacy. Sharing what other inns do should not break the confidential relationship that is assumed when you temporarily take over their inn. You will also find that advice may not be part of the services the owner is open to receiving. So tread lightly, and rather than make suggestions, ask questions that may open doors to further conversation. (What kind of software have you tried? Which search engines are working for you?) You will become an invaluable resource, one all too often unappreciated by the industry as a whole.

Interim Innkeepers' Ideas for Your Kit Bag

To take over someone else's baby and do it with aplomb requires some tools of one's own. Pat and Jim Yost of Inn-Ovations Interim Management/ Innsitting Services send ahead an innkeeper operations guide for the owner or manager to fill out. This later helps them find the circuit breakers and plungers, access e-mail, and even be prepared for such basics as what time breakfast is. They also keep a huge plastic storage bin with a lid ready for their assignments. It's loaded with their own favorite pots and pans, knives, spatulas, measuring spoons and cups, cookbooks, and spices, as well as their own food supply. The Yosts recommend taking "lots of clothing, because you never know what type of work might be required of you—grunge to glamorous, toilets to teatime."

Sandy Shotwell not only carries a copy of her contract but also has her list of questions for the innkeeper. That way she's sure to have on hand names and numbers of all repairpersons as well as numbers for everything you can think of: banking, emergency helpers, credit card processor. She includes her own address book and her pillow!

"One item that really upgrades our status and professionalism came from Jim's chef background," report Janis and Jim Fabok of Inn-Relief." We had chef coats embroidered with our name and logo, and we wear them while we work in the kitchen and while serving. You can't believe the difference these coats have made. Guests feel 'extra special' and always have raves about the food and service."

Wendy and Mark Tamiso, of WendMark Associates interim managers, and directors of the B&B Innstitute, share their kit bag secrets:

- *Timer*
- *Oven thermometer*
- *Sharp knives*
- *Minimuffin pans*
- *Tongs*
- *Zester*
- *Baking dishes*
- *Blender*
- *Any special or hard-to-find ingredients if you are making your own recipes*
- *A good sense of humor should not be left at home either.*

Although innkeeping isn't an industry known for its get-rich-quick reputation, you need to receive fair payment for the services you provide. As in any business deal, the buyer generally thinks the seller is asking for too much.

Many inns are on very low budgets; however, that is not your problem. Your issue is to show how you are worth every penny and more to this inn owner. Your worth may not mesh with every inn owner's vision or their capability to hire you. If a situation is close but not ideal, you may need to decide whether to keep your résumé in the marketplace or work with a good situation to make it better.

Managers work for hourly wages, for salary, on commission, or on contract, often with extra benefits thrown in, such as housing, use of a car, health insurance, dinners at local restaurants, or free theater tickets. Unless you have a great deal of experience, initially you will need to work within the payment system set up by the owner and develop your options from there. Research what is being offered at other inns for what work and evaluate the similarities between the inn at which you are applying and other inns in order to negotiate payment. Beware of signing agreements that leave you no time off and expect you to be tied to the inn day and night.

Interim innkeepers work as independent contractors and need to develop their own contracts. You are responsible for all taxes, insurance, and other business expenses. A ballpark daily fee is generally the cost of one room-night at the inn. This fee goes up when additional services are provided (cleaning rooms, caring for pets, supervising special events, etc.) and should also be negotiated at the time of the initial interview. Transportation costs and advance orientation time should be negotiated.

Interim managers function on either of the above systems. By the time you get to this level you will be very experienced and will have strong opinions on how you want things handled, so no advice is needed here.

Working at an inn can be incredibly satisfying. Taking over a business, maintaining it, and even growing it is a great feeling. With good research and ongoing communication, pampering guests, learning about a new town, helping an owner realize their dream as well as yours—all in a lovely location—can be a rewarding career.

Advice to Inn Owners

Hiring a manager or bringing in an interim innkeeper or manager calls for careful planning. Not only do you want to see references and a résumé showing business experience for these people who will be taking over your "baby," you need to plan for this transition. These relief innkeepers are not clones of you, willing and able to put in the hours you do; nor do they read your mind or know how to create your signature breakfast pancake or where to turn off the electricity.

Create a job description (contact PAII for a sample) and research local labor laws. Know your rights and the employee's before you hire.

Developing a manual that forces you to put in writing all the details that you carry in your head can start with PAII's Innkeepers Notebook. Allow a couple of weeks to transform your knowledge into useful, organized data. A good interim innkeeper or manager will come with their own sheaf of questions, but you want to be prepared before their arrival.

Figure out where they will sleep if they are to live on the premises and ensure that it's a comfortable refuge that will rejuvenate your replacements, not depress them. If you are hiring a couple, take into account their need for additional space. What hours will they be expected to be available at night for emergencies?

Communicate your philosophy of running your inn as well as the details. Give these very important inn representatives, who will shoulder the responsibility for running your inn, the authority to make decisions.

Pay these professionals as much as you possibly can afford. Remember, if you hire a couple you get double the work, so expect to pay double. Find out how they are going to add to your income with their skills. Set up goals and incentive programs that reward good work. Often inn owners find that buying worry-free time is worth much more than they originally thought they could afford.

Leasing an Inn

Leasing an inn is a viable method of becoming an innkeeper when you do not have enough cash to purchase. Two leasing modes are currently used in this industry. In one, you purchase the business portion of the inn outright and lease the real estate and, often, the furniture and fixtures as well; however, this arrangement almost always involves a purchase option on the property or, at least, a "first right of refusal" (in the event the property owners try to sell the leased real estate). In the other, you negotiate a lease with an option to purchase at a scheduled future time.

Leasing, though less expensive than buying, will still involve a substantial cash investment and, with it, a serious commitment to the business. The risk from the owners' viewpoint is great: if you destroy their business, they will have to come back and correct your mistakes after they have moved on to another life. Nevertheless, it is not uncommon to find owners who will face significant tax consequences on the sale of their longtime successful inn, and are therefore strongly motivated to lease rather than sell.

Leasing works well in several situations

- Where property values make it difficult to purchase real property at a price that makes running an inn profitable. It's not unlikely that an inn purchased five years ago may have appreciated so much that a new owner cannot afford to operate the inn and still make mortgage payments.
- When you know you need a ten-room inn but have only enough cash for a down payment on a five-room place.
- When the current debt is small in relation to the current value, normally less than 25 percent.
- When a seller's depreciated basis is small in relation to value, meaning any monies received in a sale will be subject to significant capital gains taxes. This situation is usually offset by the seller electing for a 1031 exchange, a process whereby the exchange property must be identified within forty-five days and the purchase consummated within six months. This short time frame can sometimes cause the exchanging property owner to manipulate the date for closing the sale of the inn until the exchanged property is truly identified. A lease alleviates this time crunch for the inn lessor and the would-be seller.
- When the owner's financing has roadblocks preventing a complete transfer of title (such as an outstanding debt that needs to be paid off first).

LEASE WITH AN OPTION

According to Bill Oates, many creative people have discovered that a lease with an option to purchase solves many of the problems of financing a going concern. Here is an example of how he structures a lease-option arrangement:

Assuming a going-concern inn with a current value of $895,000, there would be an up-front payment of $125,000 (or 14 percent of the price; normally, an option of this type would be 10 to 15 percent of value). This sum buys a five-year right to purchase the inn at the option price of $895,000, less the option payment. The option agreement to purchase may be exercised at any time in the five-year period. The option would cease if the concurrent lease were terminated by a default on the lease.

The option payment goes to the owner and is not refundable; nor is it taxable until the option is exercised or expires by time or default.

A concurrent five-year lease would be executed at the same time. This would be a triple-net lease (all real estate taxes, insurance, and maintenance expense would be lessee's responsibility). The base lease payment is normally comparable to a mortgage payment for the balance between option payment and purchase price. In this case the balance is $770,000. Interest on that at 8 percent equals $61,600 per year. A mortgage of that amount on a twenty-year amortization basis with a prime interest rate of 8 percent (6 percent plus 2 percent) requires an annual payment of $77,287 ($6,440.59 per month). Of that, $16,275 is principal the first year; the principal portion of the payment increases slightly each year.

Each year a portion of the payment would be construed as an additional option payment similar to a mortgage. Payments start low to ease cash flow and rise in later years to encourage exercise of the option. If the option were exercised at the end of the third year, the additional purchase price would be $740,000, as follows:

Option price	$895,000
Less option payment	125,000
Assigned option per schedule	30,000
Due	$740,000

At the end of fourth year, the amount due to exercise the option would be $725,000; at the end of the fifth year, $710,000.

For the lessee–prospective buyer, the advantages of a lease-option arrangement are:
· It achieves the objective of being an innkeeper when that might not be possible through normal means.
· It is much cheaper to get in: no bank fees, no appraisal fees, and no property transfer tax, with smaller legal and accounting fees.
· It is much faster.
· The risk is not total, though it is substantial.

When an owner does not want to sell the family homestead or you do not have enough money to buy a property, leasing the building and land and buying the inn business may be a good choice to consider. Be sure you consult a real estate attorney and your accountant in setting up a lease for your dream inn.

Leasing the real estate is the way most businesses operate, including hotels, so this is not a new idea. While 83 percent of all inns are owned lock, stock, and barrel by the innkeeper, 17 percent are leased, and that number is increasing. Unfortunately, poorly structured leases can put the lessee in a difficult financial situation, making success problematic and default probable. The best way to prevent such failures is a win-win lease where the owner doesn't get greedy and the lessee is eager to maintain a fair agreement.

In negotiating such a lease, consider the following issues:

Getting Out. Before you get into a lease, always check on how you can get out of it. The length of the lease should protect your investment long enough for you to see a return, and should allow you time to run the business at a level that would be attractively profitable to a prospective new owner. In some cases you can build in a series of points when the lease can automatically be renewed or ended. Build these into the lease in your favor.

Length of Lease. Stagger the options; three, ten, or twenty years are possible periods of duration. The three-year option protects you if you decide to get out of the business completely. The longer time periods give you an opportunity to sell at a profit, having improved the business to a level attractive to a new owner.

Percentage of Sales. If you agree to pay the lessor a percentage of sales, be sure that the base amount of the lease is very low. This type of provision makes sense in a retail operation where foot traffic is high, but it can be crippling for an inn where the number of rooms and thus the amount of business has little flexibility. If you must accept such a provision, design it so as to assure the lessor of an amount covering basic costs and a reasonable extra percentage. The innkeeper should then receive a comfortable profit, with the remainder divided between the lessor and the innkeeper.

Repairs and Renovation. Who pays for what? This part of the lease can get very detailed. One option is for the innkeeper to pay for inside work and the lessor to pay for outside repairs: roof, trees, paint, driveways, and so on.

Another possibility is for the building owner to pay for renovations that would increase the value of the property, but for the lessee to cover the costs of extra baths, carpeting, or health-code work in the kitchen, which would benefit the inn business alone. Be sure to have in writing how your additions will affect your future purchase of the building.

Leasing an Inn

The partners in the subchapter S corporation of the Inn on Mt. Ada had no other option than to negotiate a lease to use the former Wrigley Mansion, with its fantastic location: perched on a hill overlooking the tiny town of Avalon on Catalina Island, twenty-six miles across the sea to Los Angeles. All the rooms have ocean views. The original owner used to watch his Chicago Cubs during spring training from the downstairs office.

The innkeepers and their friends signed a thirty-page, thirty-year lease (renewable for another thirty years) for the building and the property with Santa Catalina Island Conservancy and the University of Southern California. The lease payment is 15 percent of the annual gross room income and 7.5 percent of the annual food and beverage gross sales, with a flat fee paid monthly. The flat fee is adjusted annually, according to the consumer price index. At year-end, the difference between the annual percentage and the monthly fee is paid to the owners. For the first five years the monthly fee was lower to allow the inn to get on its feet. A $10,000 deposit was paid to the lessors, refundable at the completion of the lease. The inn paid $1.6 million renovating the property, landscaping, and furnishing the four common rooms and six guest rooms and suites. Today, room rates range from $230 to $590 American Plan, and include use of a personal golf cart for trips up and down the hill to town, as well as evening appetizers, wine, and champagne.

Innkeepers Marlene McAdam and Suzie Griffin recommend making the lease very clear, leaving nothing to a gentleman's agreement. The people with whom they initially signed their lease are no longer with the university or the conservancy. The lease defines such things as when the lessor must be consulted about lessee spending plans, and the AAA or Mobil quality levels the inn must maintain. Good ongoing communication has helped the lessor-lessee relationship of ten years to work well. Though Suzie and Marlene receive a salary and housing from the corporation, it did not make a profit for seven years. They point out that since you don't have any real estate value at the end, you need patience to make back your money during the remaining twenty-three years on the lease.

Option to Buy. If you have any hopes of buying, get this in writing. Try to lock in a sales price, unless housing prices seem to be falling. In most cases your business operation will increase the value of the property, and you don't want to pay the seller for your efforts.

Build into the lease the opportunity for a future buyer to purchase the property at the time the inn business is sold. Structure this clearly, so as not to confuse a live prospect.

Transfer of Lease. The inn's business owner should be able to sell the business to a qualified person and transfer the building lease with no unreasonable limitations imposed by the lessor.

Sale of the Property. If the property is sold, the new owner must be obligated to honor your lease. If possible, also negotiate that you get a percentage of the profit over the value when you first leased it, especially if you are paying for renovations. You may also want a clause giving you first right to buy the property if it is offered for sale ("first right of refusal").

Special thanks to Bill Oates and Michael Yovino-Young (see Resources) for their invaluable assistance on this chapter.

getting inn shape

When you make your plans about who will do what before the inn opens, be sure to keep in mind that time is money, and this cuts two ways. On the one hand, you can save the cost of hiring people to do the tasks you're willing to take on yourself. On the other hand, every day that you spend getting ready to open means one more day that you have no paying guests.

Say you plan first to do the remodeling, then the decorating, and then the promotion. You're planning on lots of time. Hiring a contractor to do the remodel while you get started on the Web site, or vice versa, can be very cost-effective if it gets the inn open a month early.

You can calculate roughly how effective hiring help can be. For example, hiring a public relations firm to prepare a logo, brochure, stationery, signs, and a press kit might get you open four weeks early. Since most of your costs are fixed whether or not you're open—mortgage, insurance, auto—the income you receive from room rents can be applied pretty directly to your costs. You might want to reduce that income figure by the projected costs of food, supplies, and staff, if any. But the basic point is this: since your major costs are constant whether or not you're open, delaying your opening costs you money.

Ambience

Ambience is character, atmosphere, and mood. It's the consistent carrying out of a theme, such as the Victorian Mansion or Ye Olde Ski Lodge. Ambience planned and achieved with clarity during the renovation stage can be a major marketing tool over the lifetime of the inn. But before you even consider the marketability of an image, you need to be sure it fits you. You'll look as silly as an orchid at a hoedown if you wear ski boots in a Victorian mansion.

The classic advice to aspiring authors is "Write what you know." There's a corollary for aspiring innkeepers: more than anything else, your inn should be your own personal favorite, the place you would most like to stay. It must reflect your personality as well as your fantasy. Design it so it feels true to you.

How do you see yourself? Ask your partner and friends to describe you. Does their view match your own? Do you need lots of private time in the mornings, or do you love to sit down to breakfast with a crowd? Do you prefer that friends call before they drop by, or do you keep a big pot of soup bubbling to encourage impromptu gatherings? Everybody needs private time, but do you need more than the average?

Are you formal or casual? Are chats around the fireplace, feet up, your favorite way to spend the evening? Or do you prefer long gowns and tuxedos in a setting that sparkles with elegance? Do you think a little clutter makes for comfort, or do you tend to empty the ashtray before the cigarette is extinguished? Any of these styles can be a success. The question is which one is for you.

What about your community? Who comes there, and for what purpose? Is it a mountainous, rustic area or a city that hums all night long? The personality as well as the geography of your inn's community must be taken into account.

What's your inn building like? It's difficult to do art nouveau in a Federal-style building. The appearance of the structure is one of the biggest elements of the ambience your guests will experience. Inappropriate decor is an assault on the senses, but the range of acceptable choices is wide.

The look of the inn's exterior can enhance the mood, creating a quality that draws passersby to stop and stay. The way you set up your property, for example, can be expansive and open, or you can landscape to provide privacy and intimate corners. The entryway can determine what guests feel in the first thirty seconds outside and inside your door. While they wait for you, do you want them to feel formal or relaxed?

What's your family like? Do you have small children or teenagers? Who will be your helpers? Do you need a clearly separate space and physical privacy? Will you feel comfortable with guests wandering into your quarters during family arguments or while you're trying to reprimand your children? And how will your guests feel about it?

Finally, what's the field like? What are industry expectations? What's your competition doing? You'll get the best idea of the range of what's offered at inns by traveling and staying in them. Some are elegant and expensive; others have a warm family feeling; still others exude an energetic sense of the nearby beach or a romantic, intimate atmosphere and fantastic views.

The above questions should help you establish a set of "givens" against which to evaluate your image options. Keep in mind that your ambience will be a marketing tool. The more clearly you know what you are, the easier it will be to project that image.

As you visit other inns, analyze how their approaches work or don't work. Adapt ideas you like to fit your own objectives. Visit inns with an open mind and an adventurous spirit. Let yourself absorb the unique flavor of each establishment, and don't prejudge on the basis of your own great concept. Don't try to make an inn what it isn't. If you prefer a mountain cabin, don't reject a place because it's a formal, city inn. Neither one needs to be "better," but each needs to be special.

The inns you like best may differ tremendously from one another, but probably each of your favorites will communicate a definite something. Try to describe it as a starting point for taking stock of what you want. Don't even think about renovation until your unique ambience is clear to you.

Ambience

Denny Becker at A Teton Tree House in Wilson, Wyoming, is a former mountain and white-water guide who, with his then wife, Chris, decided to settle down and have children (they are now twenty and twenty-two years old). Denny gradually built their hillside inn, with each room offering a view of the trees or valley and mountains beyond. It's ninety-five steps up to the inn's two-story living room, but the climb is worth it to reach the roaring fire in the fireplace and the collection of books, games and clever puzzles. Denny (Chris lost interest in the bed-and-breakfast and subsequently left the marriage) serves a hearty and heart-healthy breakfast at a hand-carved log table, offering hot cereals with local grains, together with fresh fruits, and a creative variety of juice blends, organic homemade granola, and freshly baked breads. His knowledge of the area (a forty-year local, he doesn't remember how many times he's climbed the Grand Teton), makes for great conversation and is invaluable in finding what to do. Denny and his new wife, Sally, who fortunately loves B&Bs, help people select their day's adventures in Grand Teton and Yellowstone National Parks, offering advice on what to wear and where to hike, and providing maps and loaner backpacks. When guests return, he encourages them to replenish the fluids lost on the trail with Gatorade from the refrigerator. A bonus is his knowledge of where to raft, ride horses, eat, find plays, or listen to bluegrass, cowboy, folk, or classical music. In the inn's tiny gift shop area, guests find T-shirts, maps, and guidebooks that augment their appreciation for the Jackson Hole area.

"Green" Rooms

As public consciousness is raised and individuals grow more committed to environmental action on a personal level, lodging properties are responding for both moral and marketing reasons. Your efforts at environmental preservation will be appreciated by 80 percent of your guests, according to a survey by *Yellow Brick Road* newsletter. Creating green rooms is more than a guest-room issue; it involves actually setting up a sustainable business. In developing any green program, the bywords are *reuse, recycle,* and *reduce.* Letting the public know the concrete ways you live out your commitment to earth stewardship will bring you business—at least until green becomes the norm.

Here are some ideas:

- Use natural fabrics.
- Install low-flush toilets, low-flow showerheads, and sink-faucet water flow restrictors. Eliminate drips; keep plumbing repaired.
- Use china, cloth, and glass rather than plastic, Styrofoam, or paper.
- Recycling bottles, cans, and newspapers is routine for many people; make recycling containers available to your guests. Even flight attendants collect newspapers!
- Your guests will enjoy your special soaps, and probably won't mind a bit if you don't replace them daily for stay-over guests. Using sink dispensers as well as little bars of soap gives guests an environmentally sound choice. Wall dispensers for soap and shampoo in tubs and showers eliminate the proliferation of little plastic bottles; ask your local hotel supplier about it. Or have a central butler's basket of larger containers of luxury-type shampoo, conditioner, lotion, and so on. Give your used soap to a charity (if you can find one that will accept it).
- Give your guests an option on laundry. A Munich hotel posted this message: "Can you vaguely guess how many tons of towels are unnecessarily washed every day in the world? This means enormous quantities of washing powder polluting and burdening our water. Please decide yourself and help. Towels on the floor mean 'please change'; towels hung back on the rack mean 'I will use once more for the sake of the environment.' Thank you."

  Do be sure you have enough towel rack space in your bathrooms to dry wet towels. Innkeepers often create their own notes about towels; the Green Hotels Association also has "notes" for sale.
- Wood furniture is the norm in inns, not plastic. Because furnishings are often antique, the innkeeper is not endangering rain-forest woods. If you purchase new furniture, choose environmentally appropriate woods.

- Environmentally safe cleaning products have been tested and are being used safely throughout the lodging industry; some are even required by OSHA, to protect employees' health.
- In-room whirlpools and wood-burning fireplaces create a quandary for environmentally conscious guests and innkeepers. Consider an enclosed outdoor tub that guests can use on a private reservation basis, and consider the new gas-log fireplaces that light in an instant, do not pollute, and look good. But also remember that your guests may lead Spartan lives all year and treat themselves only rarely to the luxury of an inn; that's an acceptable ratio!
- Use metal trash baskets so you can avoid plastic bags in trash containers.
- Use metal or wicker containers and laundry baskets rather than plastic.
- Buy only containers that are recyclable.
- Start a compost heap. If you are not in the country, anaerobic containers are available that do not smell or attract flies. Or find a local pig farmer who will take your garbage.
- Patronize a local organic farm or farmers' market.
- Insulate.
- Keep your heater and air conditioner tuned and change their filters regularly. Providing room temperature controls in each room can actually reduce the cost of heating.
- Use longer-life lightbulbs, including the new warm-spectrum screw-in fluorescents—you want green rooms, not green guests! Consider installing a switch in the common rooms that turns on the lights only when someone is in there. Also consider motion-activated outdoor lighting.
- Print all of your inn materials on recycled paper with the highest percentage of postconsumer waste you can find and afford. Use soy ink. Be sure to put the recycled logo on these materials.
- Plant low-water landscaping. Use a drip system for plants and a laundry-water irrigation system for lawns.
- Using a front-loader washing machine is another way to save on water and detergent; it also saves wear and tear on linens.

> *At the Riverwalk Inn in San Antonio, Texas, a sign offered by Green Hotels Association gives guests an option: fresh towels daily, or use them another day for the environment's sake. Guests like having a choice; 90 percent of the Riverwalk guests will hang their towels up for another day, generating a substantial savings in laundry time and money, as well as in polluting detergents and bleach.*

The biggest challenge to going green is the education of the innkeepers and staff. Include everyone in the process. When people understand the *why*, the *how* is often not so difficult. Remember the underlying message of *50 Simple Things You Can Do to Save the Earth:* you don't have to be neurotically regimented about environmentalism—every little thing you do helps. Eliminate one throwaway plastic bag a day, and you'll save boxes of them over the year.

Once you're committed to creating a green room or a whole green inn, more ways of refining this vision will be suggested by guests and staff. And guest appreciation will show on the bottom line.

Renovating

This is what you've been waiting for: the difficult and expensive task of making a promising structure into the inn of your dreams.

And it can be fun! After several years of operating an inn, some innkeepers find that the most fun of all was creating it. If you've done the groundwork in visiting other inns to develop a strong sense of what you like and don't; if you have financing in hand so you can hire adequate help; and if you have allowed adequate time, then you're off to one of the most creative challenges of your life.

Renovating an inn is different from renovating a personal home. At home, we usually do a room at a time at our leisure, sometimes during vacations, often when we've decided to sell. With an inn, you'll do all the rooms at once, with a timetable and an opening date in mind, and you'll be attempting to please many different people, not just yourself and your family.

Depending on the size of the project, hiring assistance can make the difference between a challenge and a nightmare. If the job involves little more than choosing new furnishings, you may want to do it on your own. If you feel safer with the advice of a decorator, but haven't the budget or the inclination to put the whole project in a decorator's hands, you'll find many competent designers who will be happy to act as consultants for an hourly fee.

If you are adding rooms, changing the exterior, or doing anything that will require the approval of the local building department, you will probably need an architect and a general contractor. General contractors oversee jobs, bringing in carpenters, plumbers, electricians, roofers, drywallers, and so on at the appropriate times. If you decide to act as owner-builder, you will do the job of the general contractor.

Before you decide what you'll do and what you'll hire people to do, complete your financial projections and get the money. Determine and outline precisely:

- The number of guest rooms you want, from the viewpoint of staffing and serving.
- The number of rooms you need, financially speaking.
- Kitchen and dining facilities.
- Type of amenities, such as whirlpool tubs, hot tubs, fireplaces, wet bars, bathrooms, balconies, decks and outside living areas, or swimming pool.
- Innkeeper's quarters.
- Laundry facilities.
- Parking.
- Common areas: living room, TV room, library.
- Employee space and a separate bathroom for staff and nonresident guests.

Sketch out your renovation ideas. You can buy drafting paper and templates for bathroom fixtures and furniture. Play with placement in relation to entrances and windows. Consider ventilation of the rooms and bathrooms. Spend time in each room at various times of the day to check lighting and heat needs.

Use the numerous valuable resources for information on restoring old homes to avoid serious and costly mistakes. (Check Resources at the end of the book.)

Once you're clear on what you need, you have to find the people to help you do it. You find competent, reliable, honest decorators, architects, and contractors in much the same way that you find other support people.

- Architects, designers, and contractors can often recommend people for the other jobs.
- Look at older homes, inns, and restaurants that have been successfully renovated and ask their owners and managers for recommendations. If you see homes being renovated, stop and talk with the people working at the site.
- A historical society or landmark committee may also be able to give you names of people who work on older homes. Sometimes, though rarely, a building department will give you names.
- Lumber companies, wholesale hardware stores, and other building-supply providers may have recommendations.

Select two or three good prospects for each job. Call them and briefly describe your project and timetable. If some prospects are not interested, they may be able to recommend others. Set up initial consultations at the site. Usually there is no charge for this, but don't waste the time of a bidder you have no intention of hiring.

Present your list of jobs and your sketches, but also be open to the ideas of these pros. They can often solve in a moment a problem you've grappled with for weeks. Don't be afraid to discuss money. Whether you're buying an hour's consulting time or spending thousands on an architect, get rates and bids.

If your project requires an architect, he or she will probably send a draftsperson to measure your house and site as the first step in preparing working drawings. Be sure your architect is familiar with the local building and zoning departments' requirements for setbacks, zoning requirements, site plans, landscape plans, and so on. Established inns that have already gone through the process can be very helpful in this regard. Provide the architect with what you consider to be the items to include in renovation costs. Use the sample list that follows on page 157 to draw up your own list. Ask for a preliminary design and cost estimate.

When the preliminary design drawings arrive, study them closely. Go over them with someone who is familiar with all the trades and understands the symbols for plumbing and electrical work. Think through these aspects of the project in the preliminary design phase, not after working drawings have been prepared. Every change costs money.

When the changes in the preliminary design are complete, the architect you have chosen will prepare final drawings for the approval of the building department and any necessary review boards.

If you have done your homework, visited many inns, and talked with other innkeepers, you will probably be more knowledgeable about what is required for a bed-and-breakfast inn than most architects are. They tend to specialize in residential or commercial buildings, and inns don't exactly fit either category. Several years ago, a prospective innkeeper we know allowed her architect to convince her that shared baths are part of the B&B ambience! This may be true in England or Germany, but in the United States, guests want private baths.

Your architect is a good resource when selecting your contractor. Before hiring a general contractor:

- Obtain recommendations from innkeepers, building suppliers, the local building department, and owners of houses you admire.
- Verify the contractor's license; obtain copies of their general liability insurance and workers' compensation policies.
- Discuss fixed-bid versus time-and-materials contracts. Discuss the payment schedule. Discuss liens and lien releases.
- Evaluate the size of the construction company; discuss concurrent projects.

- Obtain a list of previous projects; visit them and talk to the owners.
- Discuss completion of project as promised, costs, and time; the availability of the contractor to correct problems; and the reliability and quality of subcontractors.
- Make your final selection and sign a contract. You may want to seek legal advice prior to signing it.

Read the sample contract in Appendix 5 and use it as a model for your own contract. Add a specification sheet detailing your choice of fixtures and supplies by brand names.

When the work is completed and you are settling the bills, ask each party to sign a "lien release for work done and release upon final payment" form. This form acknowledges that you have paid in full for the work performed and that the worker (plumber, electrician, painter) cannot file a mechanic's lien against your property. A mechanic's lien is where someone with whom you have done business (purchase of labor, services, equipment, and/or materials for the purpose of improvement upon real property), files a form with the state declaring that they have not been fully paid. This lien is recorded against the property and shows as a claim against the property's title. You will realize how much this affects you when you attempt to refinance or sell the property. These liens surface in a title search and all must be satisfied.

If there is a contractor supervising your renovation and you are paying them directly for work done, have the contractor sign off upon final payment that all monies owed to each subcontractor (list them all) have been paid in full.

The term for a mechanic's lien may differ from state to state, but the concept is the same. The release form can probably be picked up in your local stationery store.

Soundproofing

One of the most common complaints in hotels, bed-and-breakfast inns, and country inns is the lack of soundproofing. "Nothing is less romantic than hearing someone else's romance," quipped Sandra Soule, noted B&B author, at a PAII conference. When renovating, heavily insulate between rooms and floors. If you're already in operation but concerned about sound, well-padded carpeting and more fabric on tables, windows, and chairs can absorb sound. Special culprits are the doors between connecting rooms, which carry sound very easily.

It used to be that a good bed and a tasty breakfast were mighty fine for American guests. However, bed, breakfast, and *luxury bath* are where today's guests will spend their discretionary big bucks. E-mail responses from more than fifty innkeepers about luxury baths reinforces the idea that they look upon their spacious, well-appointed baths as right up there in importance with their guest rooms. Always including the requisite jetted whirlpool tub, these sybaritic spaces become the focal point for romantic getaways. Innkeepers gloat that these rooms bring in up to 50 percent higher occupancy, as well as $50 to $100 more in room rates during the off-season—especially, and throughout, recessionary times. Ruth Boven of Castle in the Country, a former president of the Michigan State B&B association, calls luxury baths a "weatherproof amenity."

What is luxury in bathroom terms? First, move your thoughts beyond the typical bathroom. True luxury often finds the two-person tub smack-dab in the bedroom, with a view of the ocean *and* the blazing fireplace. Or the bathroom becomes a room in itself, with a sitting area, a fireplace, and views. The number one requirement, according to Monty Turner (Run of the River B&B, in Washington State) is "space, big space." Big walk-in (or roll-in, to meet ADA requirements) showers with multiple heads might include a handheld nozzle or the ever-popular waterfall/rain feature. These accompany the proverbial spa tub, not preclude it. The Conlins (Whale Walk Inn, Massachusetts) surveyed their guests and found that men fancy steam baths and women opt for a tub, so they put in both wherever possible. The toilet has its own alcove or private room. The sink area sports two sinks, multiple huge mirrors (possibly a lighted magnifying one), and lots of space for toiletries, accompanied by plentiful amenities such as aromatic boutique soaps (Burt's Bees to Aveda), aromatherapy sachets, shampoo, conditioner, cotton balls, Q-Tips, lotion, hair dryer, makeup-remover pads, extra washcloths, a mending kit, and a shoe mitt.

Guests might also enjoy several heavy, down-soft towels, monogrammed robes, handmade slippers, aromatherapy bath gel, bath salts, bubble bath, heated towel rack, cascading green plants and live trees, upholstered chairs for relaxing, heated tile or stone floors, and marble walls. And don't forget the yellow rubber ducky!

If this isn't enough to make guests feel they are in a luxury setting, how about an entertainment center with CDs, candles encased in glass, a window shade that attaches and pulls from the bottom, and mood lighting on dimmers (sigh!). All of these signal romance and luxury and wrap up that snuggle-in feeling.

Bathrooms are an important part of selling a sleeping room, and while every feature mentioned above may not be included in every upscale bath space, luxury baths have become a competitive edge for many innkeepers.

Vinny Cusenza, innkeeper-owner of the Inn at Oyster Point in New Haven, Connecticut, observes that "ultraluxury," rather than being about bells and whistles, has just as much to do with satisfying guests' longing to be delighted and taken out of their everyday world, sprinkled with the element of surprise.

"After all," Vinny quips, "many guests know what a whirlpool tub is, have used one, and may even have one at home. But a tub under (albeit artificial) boughs of wisteria blossoms, a draped gauzy curtain, and glowing art nouveau stained glass transports them into the realm of fantasy." Guests love the sense of discovery when they peek out and find that a fantasy bathroom gives way to a private outdoor sitting porch.

Vinny also found that bathroom luxury could be convincingly conveyed without a tub at all. One of his most popular bathrooms has "just" a shower. Wall-mounted water jets complement travertine and marble touches, imparting that extra dimension beyond the ordinary bathing experience.

It's a win for everyone. Rooms with luxury baths book first, book more often, book at a premium price (an additional $30 a night), and leave both innkeepers and guests grinning.

THE BIG QUESTION: ACT AS OWNER-BUILDER OR HIRE A GENERAL CONTRACTOR?

Handy men and women often think they can run their own renovation jobs. In many cases this is true, particularly if the projects are comparatively simple, like dividing a large bathroom into two or knocking out a non-weight-bearing wall. But when you get into any structural changes or extensive plumbing or electrical work, a general contractor can be a lifesaver.

Most renovations will require building permits. (See discussion of city and county requirements on page 55.) Local officials are used to dealing with local architects and general contractors and are more inclined to give approvals to known professionals. There is also some owner security in having a third party—the building inspector—examine the work in process. You want your building to meet all the health and safety codes.

General contractors usually add a percentage of the total itemized subcontractor bids for their overhead and profit. For this fee, you are buying their knowledge, construction management skills, and the work of subcontractors they have used successfully for other jobs. Negotiating with subcontractors requires extensive experience in that field; a general contractor can usually get a better price. Timing is also critical, and a subcontractor would rather disappoint you, a one-time owner-builder client, than a general contractor who can bring him or her many more jobs.

If you decide to take on your renovation as an owner-builder, the following hints may help you. If you decide to hire a general contractor, these hints will give you an idea of what to expect from him or her.

- Plan to work every evening and early in the morning scheduling subcontractors and deliveries of supplies.
- After approval of final drawings, order enough copies to get three bids from major subcontractors: framers, plumbers, electricians, drywallers, and finish carpenters. When possible, get fixed bids, not time-and-materials contracts. (Time-and-materials contracts mean you pay an agreed hourly wage for the actual number of hours to complete the job plus the cost of materials.) Insist on products specifications in writing; a written contract should include timing, progressive payment schedules, costs for changes, guarantees, warranties, and so on.
- Do not schedule everything at one time. Plumbers do not like stumbling over electricians, and painters don't want sawdust in the air. Develop a master schedule for subcontracted work. Understand the order of the work to be done. This is the typical order for an addition: clearing the area and demolition, digging the foundation, laying the foundation, framing, rough plumbing, rough electrical, outside siding, sheet metal, roofing, insulation, doors and windows, drywall, painting, wallpapering, finish plumbing and tile, finish electrical, and finish carpentry.
- Using a large calendar and estimated schedules from your subcontractors, figure the length of the project. Anticipate delays.
- Hire manual laborers for regular cleanup. Arrange for a bin for trash. Rent a chemical toilet for workers, if necessary. Supervise the demolitions.
- Have a truck available; space for stacking lumber and supplies conveniently and safe from theft and water damage; and a ready supply of pinup working

lights and heavy-duty extension cords, brooms, hoses, miscellaneous nails, demolition tools, hammers, screwdrivers, and so on.

- Develop a master schedule for ordering materials. Some special-order items like doors, windows, and plumbing fixtures, have long lead times. Prepare space to store them when they arrive.
- On the one hand, it's awful to live in the house during renovation; on the other hand, it's a good idea to have someone on the site. If you are in the house, store as much furniture as you can away from workers, dust, and dirt. Have a telephone on the site.
- Remove windows, if necessary, and have them reputtied by a reputable glazier. Paint them prior to reinstallation. Before doors, windows, and walls are in place, consider moving into the structure large items like four-by-ten drywall sheets, one-piece shower units, armoires, and the like, which are sometimes impossible to get in later.
- Get temporary workers' compensation insurance during construction, to cover your manual laborers and anyone else you hire on an hourly basis.

It is important to determine who is an employee and who is a contractor. Independent contractors have their own businesses, provide their own tools, and establish their own work parameters. For example, it's not up to you to set a contractor's hours; they are arrived at by mutual agreement. Independent contractors pay their own social security, taxes, and unemployment and disability insurance. If your contractors have not covered their employees for workers' compensation, you're responsible if they're hurt.

At year-end, you'll need to fill out an IRS Form 1099 for each contractor to whom you have paid $600 or more. Copies must be sent to the IRS, the state income tax agency, and the contractor. The rules defining independent contractors are specific; when in doubt, check with your accountant on whether your planned arrangement applies. Always sign a contract, such as the one shown here or in Appendix 5. Ask all subcontractors to provide certificates of liability insurance and workers' compensation policies; make copies for your files.

Injuries to employees of one of your subcontractors are your responsibility if your subcontractor does not carry the necessary insurance.

Independent Contractor Agreement
Nonemployee Compensation Contract

This Agreement is entered into this _____ day of _____ 20___ by and between _____("Contractor") and _____("Client").

Contractor and Client hereby agree to the following:

1. Contractor agrees to perform the following services for Client:
    (Insert description of services to be performed or completed.)

2. Contractor will commence work on or before _____ and will perform same on a (insert "daily" or "weekly") basis. Contractor will complete the performance of these services on or before (insert date).

3. Client will pay to Contractor the following sums (or rate) on the schedule set forth below.

4. Contractor and Client intend this Agreement to be one of independent contractor and employer. Accordingly, Contractor retains the sole right to control or direct the manner in which the services described herein are to be performed, subject to the foregoing; Client retains the right to inspect, to stop work, to prescribe alterations, and generally to supervise the work to ensure its conformity with that specified in this Agreement. Contractor and Client understand that it is Contractor's sole responsibility to provide for all employment taxes, including withholding and social security, and insurance, including workers' compensation coverage and public liability insurance, arising out of or relating to this Agreement.

5. Other provisions (specify).

6. This contract contains the entire Agreement between the parties. Any amendments require the written agreement of all parties.

_____
Contractor

_____
Client

Subcontractors who have no employees should show you certificates of business liability coverage. These are a defense for you should they claim they were your employees, as well as a backup for them if a suit arises as a result of their work.

Note: Both your workers' compensation and business liability insurance require you to obtain certificates of insurance from subcontractors. Both are within their rights to charge you premiums for these contractors and their employees if you fail to have the certificates on file.

WHAT TO CONSIDER IN INITIAL RENOVATION AND SETUP COSTS

Estimating costs and obtaining adequate funding to create your inn are two of the most difficult parts of the process.

It often costs as much per square foot to renovate a building as it does to build from scratch. Furthermore, many contractors hesitate to give you firm bids on renovation since they don't know what they are going to run into. So add 50 percent to whatever figure you are quoted for the work. This may seem high, but take it from innkeepers who have been down the path: the job will cost at least twice as much and take twice as long to complete as the contractor estimates.

As you plan your renovation and landscaping, keep in mind that you are creating something today that you must be able to maintain tomorrow—and forever. It's worth a little extra expense for long-lasting paint and a high-quality preparation job. It's worth working with a designer on a low-maintenance landscaping plan. And it's worth selecting appliances and plants that minimize energy and water use. Before you begin making changes, survey the list below and set some priorities.

Outdoors
    Parking area: cleared, paved, striped
    Lights along paths, porches, parking areas
    Enlarged sewer, water, gas lines
    Sign and light for sign
    Timers to turn lights on and off
    Landscaping: design, labor, materials
    Fencing
    Sprinkler system and timer
    Outdoor electrical outlets for gardening equipment and party appliances

House painted, scraped, blasted, etc.

Roof: reroof, cover old and new material (tiles, shakes, shingles), add skylights

Rain gutters: plastic, metal, or aluminum

Stairs and walkways: improve for safety, access for wheelchairs, crutches, canes

Door locks: rekey exterior door locks, add dead bolts and peephole

Alarm system

Outdoor barbecue, spa

Indoors

Electrical and Appliances

Shaver, blow dryers (short cord, ground fault interrupters)

Reading lamps

Electric blankets

Lamp switch close to door

Washer and dryer

Stove, oven ventilation

Dishwasher

Vacuum cleaner

Separate circuits for coffeemakers, other small appliances

Heating and cooling systems

Televisions, cable

Stereo systems

Intercom

Smoke detectors

Doorbells

Telephones

Jacks in rooms

Separate telephone line for each room or central answering system

Portable phone

Cell phone

In-room Internet access: modem or high-speed connection

Electronic credit card processing and computer, modem, and fax lines

Office

Computer

Fax machine

Copy machine

Printer

Credit card machine

Common Rooms and Bedrooms

Windows and doors: double-glazed, easily and safely operable, keyed, private, screened

Decorating: wallpaper, paint, molding

Floors: carpet cleaning, floor refinishing

Soundproofing and insulation: between bedrooms and baths, between bedrooms, between floors, above common rooms, insulation for energy conservation (everywhere you can!)

Sinks in room: plumb while walls are open, even if installation is in the future

Fireplaces: add units, stack units, repair, clean and outfit, plumb for gas, install permanent screen, heat-output improvements (such as Heatilator), wood stove

Closets: linens close to rooms, cleaning supplies close to rooms

Smoke detectors (battery operated or AC)

Bathrooms

Consider layout and floor plan: stacking or back-to-back arrangement saves plumbing costs

Shower stalls: tile or modular, combination or tub with separate shower stall

Shower fixtures, handheld showerhead

Tub refinishing or painting

Lighting near mirrors

Grab bars for entering and exiting tub, access for the handicapped

Soap holders or dispensers

Bathroom features: whirlpool tub, whirlpool tub with showerhead, shower only, tub only, combined shower and tub, toilet and sink

Towel racks, heated or not

Ventilation: fan, window (frosted glass?)

Heater or heat lamp

Hot-water heater, adequate size; wrap pipes, install circulating pump

Toilet: water-saver, commode with pull chain, types of seats

Pipes: galvanized (quieter) or PVC

Fixtures and stoppers: sink, tub, and shower

Water-saver fixtures

Counter space: vanity, antique piece, additional dressing table

Handicapped requirements

Laundry

Electrical outlets	Laundry chute
Gas	Dumbwaiter
Plumbing	Table for folding
Machine space for extra dryer	

B&Bs Mix Business with Pleasure

In response to this growing marketplace, innkeeper Carole Ballard of the Thurston House in Maitland, Florida, started a Web site called www.Inn-BusinessTravel.com, dedicated to the accommodation needs of the business traveler. For an inn to be listed, it must have committed to providing all the amenities a business traveler needs and wants. The inn also must meet the third level of inspection by AAA, Mobil, or a similar group. An inspection by a member of www.inspectedinns.com is also accepted.

In-room desk with comfortable chair and good lighting

Telephone with data port, or high-speed Internet access (DSL, cable)

In-room TV

Private bath with shower

Availability of ironing board and iron

Availability of hair dryer

Availability of fax machine

Corporate rate

Flexible check-in and checkout times

Flexible breakfast times

Flexible cancellation policy

Accept major credit cards

*Good lighting and easy access to electricity (don't expect guests to crawl
    around on the floor and move furniture)*

Other amenities not required but often appreciated are: twenty-four-hour snacks and beverages, light supper options, newspaper(s), hangers with skirt and pants holder, breakfast-to-go, access to a copier, exercise facilities, VCR with movies, and airport transportation.

High-Speed Internet Access in an Inn

After twenty-three years in business, Ann and Gene Swett of the Old Monterey Inn in California decided to bite the bullet and put a TV and VCR in each guest room. My only requirement," said Ann, "was that it had to be hidden. Thank heavens we started before September 11, because for months afterward our guests, as the world, were glued to the TV."

Before they started, she notes, "A longtime guest suggested that if we were 'pulling' cable for each room, we might as well add a DSL line at the same time. *As it happens, he had brought his laptop and was using our only guest-accessible modem outlet at the time, which was in the living room."*

Ann and Gene offer the following suggestions:

When should you do it?

Installation needs to be done when it fits into the pattern of things but always during a slow time of the year.

Where should it be placed?

That takes some thought and careful planning. They chose to place the DSL and phone jack outlets together with a mutual cover plate, and have labeled each of them so there is no confusion. These also should be near an electrical outlet. A place to sit and surface area need to be available for the laptop; either provide a table in the room or offer to bring in one as needed. Good lighting is also essential. Of course the guest's computer must have Ethernet capability for a DSL connection. And be sure to keep a few spare Ethernet cables if guests haven't brought their own.

Cable or DSL?

The Old Monterey Inn chose DSL (digital subscriber line) because it was available in their geographic area and they were already using it at the inn.

Cost:

They estimate that the cost to install DSL in their seventy-five-year-old building with thick lath-and-plaster walls was around $1600 (for ten rooms).

Does it bring business?

They are not sure yet, but "it sounds great and that's what counts," says Ann. "Some of our guests bring their computer and then decide they are having too lovely a time and opt not to connect!" Gene adds, "To the computer, that is!"

Extra charge to guest:

It costs the inn $60 a month and they do not charge the guest, instead viewing DSL access as an extra service provided.

Who did the installation:

The inn's electrician was very knowledgeable and willing to do the installation, which meant they did not have to involve the cable or phone people. This was a big relief for Ann and Gene as it takes "a special person who is willing to deal with this old house with care."

Reception area, common or public rooms, dining room

Furniture

- Desk or reception counter
- Sofas and armchairs
- Occasional tables and chairs
- Bookcases
- Sideboard, cabinets, or shelves
- Serving carts
- Game table(s)
- Guest refrigerator
- Equipment for guest self-service beverages (carafes, instant hot-water faucet, cups, glasses, etc.)

Accessories

- Reading lamps, general lighting
- Draperies and curtains
- Carpeting or area rugs
- Pictures and decorative items
- Plants, plant stands, and vases
- Fireplace screen, tools, wood box
- Doilies, throw pillows
- Fans, air conditioners
- Magazines, books, games, cards
- Wastebaskets

Dining and kitchen equipment

- Dining table(s) and chairs
- Tablecloths, place mats, napkins
- Knives, forks, spoons, serving pieces
- Plates, bowls, fruit cups, saucers
- Glasses, pitchers, wine goblets
- Champagne and ice buckets
- Sugars, creamers, salt and pepper shakers
- Butter dishes, jelly dishes, bread baskets
- Coffeemakers (with timers)
- Teapot(s) and thermos containers for regular coffee, decaf, and hot water
- Usual kitchen equipment and small appliances

- Commercial dishwasher or—truly the poorest choice—three-bin stainless-steel sink
- Icemaker
- Refrigerators (most inns have at least two; many have a guest refrigerator)

Optional
- Key cabinet or holder
- Hat and coat racks
- Stereo system, CDs, cassettes
- TV, VCR, DVD, and videos
- Writing desks for guest use
- Ashtrays
- Books and maps on the community
- Emergency lighting system
- Formal coffee or tea service
- Napkin holders
- Candlesticks, candles

Required
- Fire extinguishers
- Smoke detectors

Bedrooms
- Doors with locks and key, master-keyed. If you wish to be listed in the AAA Tour-Book, dead bolts are required. For details, contact your regional inspection office.

Furniture
- Beds (queens, kings if you have room, twins only if your client base expects it; the best option here is a queen with a twin daybed, which doubles as comfortable seating)
- Box springs and mattresses (comfortable, firm, pillow-top mattresses)
- Armchairs or straight chairs (ideally a minimum of two comfortable chairs per room)
- Tables (especially if you plan to serve breakfast or any meals in the room)
- Writing desks (sturdy enough to handle a computer, placed near an outlet and telephone)
- Nightstands (one on each side of the bed and easily reached when lying down)
- Dressers
- Armoires

Linens

- Mattress pads
- Sheets, fitted bottom and flat top, two to four sets, depending on whether you do laundry in-house or have a service, and whether you have different colors for each room. If sheet sets may be used interchangeably among rooms, you will need fewer.
- Extra flats for triple sheeting (third sheet to use as a protection for blanket)
- Blankets: a light one and a heavier one on the bed, an extra one in the closet, plus extras for laundry day. Electric blankets can be used for warming up beds, but many people do not like to sleep with them so plan on having adequate blankets.
- Pillows (one soft, one firm for each person), with extras in the closet. If you use feather pillows, be prepared for allergic guests by having a nonfeather set on hand.
- Pillow covers, pillowcases, two to three sets
- Bedspread, quilt, comforter, duvet covers. Plan for emergency laundering or cleaning by having extra bedspreads that will fit in any room or one extra for each room.
- Pillow shams
- Dust ruffles
- Runners, scarves, doilies
- Tablecloths
- Canopy

Accessories

- Reading lamps (one for each side of the bed, the writing table, and each reading chair). Ideal general lighting is not an overhead fixture but a minimum of three lamps that will use one-hundred-watt bulbs.
- Carpet or rugs
- Luggage racks (one per person in the room)
- Makeup mirror (with magnifying section, especially as the population ages)
- Full-length mirror
- Draperies, curtains, and blinds or shades
- Ceiling fans, air conditioner, and an extra fan in the closet
- Glasses and ice bucket
- Water carafes
- Coat hangers (wood or plastic, but not wire; minimum of five per person)
- Plants and accessories
- Wastebaskets (at least one for each room—bath, bed, living area)
- Tissues
- Vases
- Books, magazines

- Ashtrays
- Pictures
- Smoke detectors (fire extinguisher if room has a fireplace)

Bathrooms
Furniture
- Wall cabinets or shelves (plan three square feet of surface space for overnight kits, excluding the back of the toilet.)
- Vanity
- Chair
- Storage for extra supplies

Supplies
- Soaps at sink, tub, and shower
- Bathroom tissue and toilet paper
- Soap holder
- Liquid soap dispenser at sink. Soap, shampoo, conditioner dispensers in showers and by sinks are becoming acceptable "green" alternatives to the wasteful little bottles.

Linens
- Towels: bath and face, washcloths. Plan two to four sets per person, see discussion of sheets on page 164, less for "green" rooms.
- Bathmats
- Rugs, removable. Not carpet.
- Shower curtain
- Window curtain
- Bathrobes—crucial if you have shared baths, an outdoor hot tub, or are planning an upscale inn.

Accessories
- Mirror near light
- Heat lamp or some heating essential
- Rubber tub mat inside tub for safety purposes
- Laundry basket where wet towels for the laundry can be placed
- Wastebaskets
- Drinking glasses
- Plants
- Towel racks—enough to hang each guest's towels to dry if they opt not to have them washed daily.

Optional Niceties

Often innkeepers will create "Butler's Baskets" or an "I-forgot-it cupboard" in a central place in the inn or even in each bathroom cupboard, stocked with some of these:

- Shampoo and conditioner
- Hand lotion
- Hair dryer, hair spray
- Toothbrush and toothpaste
- Deodorant
- Bath oil, bubble bath
- Sewing kit
- Condoms
- Razors, shaving cream, shaving lotion

Laundry room and cleaning area

- Linen storage area
- Cleaning equipment storage area
- Clothes washer and dryer (two, if possible)
- Ironing board and iron, for you, and small board for guests
- Vacuum cleaners (for each floor?)
- Brooms, mops, pails (for each floor?)
- Brushes, sponges, rags, cleaning supplies (for each floor?)
- Laundry baskets
- Trash baskets
- Laundry bins or chutes
- Cleaning supplies containers

Other Possible Gathering Places

(Each requires special equipment and furnishing)

- Porches and patios
- Lawn area
- Barbecue area
- Music room
- Game room
- Recreation room
- Swimming pool (plastic glasses, towels, rescue equipment, chaise lounges, tables, chairs, umbrellas)
- Hot tub
- Sauna

Utility and storage area

- Gardening tools: lawn mower, leaf blower, pruners, clippers, spraying equipment, edgers
- Firewood storage
- Bicycle storage
- Your own personal possessions

Office

- Desk
- Comfortable chair
- Good lighting
- Filing cabinet (four-drawer)
- Cabinet or shelves for books, manuals, etc.
- Answering machine with multiple-line answering capability
- Fax machine
- Copy machine ("home" version unless volume is substantial)
- Calculator with tape
- Credit card printer and electronic "swipe" (discuss with credit card processor)
- Computer with high-speed Internet access
- Printer
- Portable telephone (2.4GHz if possible)
- Cellular phone

Accommodating the Disabled

"Temporarily Disabled," by Pat Hardy

I'm a person who likes to study up on places I visit, so I can really understand them. I have "visited" being disabled while I was researching the Americans with Disabilities Act (ADA). After a hip replacement, I couldn't drive and needed a walker for about three months. The world changed. I had to find someone to take me everywhere I went. Staying home began to look more and more attractive. My independence was largely gone.

And the planning required! Are there stairs? How many? How wide? It is astounding how few elevators exist. Can I navigate safely and unobtrusively between tables at a particular restaurant or should we go somewhere else? How far do I have to walk from the parking lot to the entrance? Will I be able to maneuver into the bathroom? Will it have one of those slam-it-quick-before-anyone-can-escape door closers?

I will never forget the first time I ventured out. Terrified that everyone would be staring at me, I felt I had to dress and look especially good. In truth, no one paid particular attention unless I had to maneuver around them. To this, I usually got two responses: wondering stares—without moving one inch!—as though pondering whether I would make it, or thoughtful helpfulness.

Though I was not in a wheelchair, I still had to find curb cuts, ramps, and elevators as if I were. Since I could not bend down, my reach was also limited, as is that of a person in a wheelchair. I tried to keep my handy grabber attached to the walker, but it did not go through doors well, so I would inevitably leave it, only to search for it when I was the most tired.

My hands became extremely tender, weak, and awkward from using the walker to support myself. Childproof pill bottles were also Pat-proof.

Even when I'm able-bodied, I struggle with letting people help me. With the walker, I did nothing but receive, able to give little back. I learned that people generally don't mind helping, but I constantly feared their impatience.

I now understand how daunting an inn is to someone with even limited disabilities! Suddenly I am twenty-eight inches wide and eighteen inches deep. I think of the inns where just maneuvering into the breakfast room would be uncomfortable, to say nothing about the tiny bathrooms, or the guest rooms with little floor space.

It would be impossible to get into an upstairs room without hard work and help with my luggage. Then I would never want to leave my room to renavigate the stairs until absolutely necessary!

Before the 1900s, everyone like me was hidden in the attic or just sat in one bedroom until they got well or died. We live in a more enlightened era, but our buildings are struggling with their limiting past.

People who invite the public into their buildings must consider accommodating the guest who might be physically, visually, or aurally challenged. The Americans with Disabilities Act (ADA) requires you to do so.

When you purchase an inn, it should meet ADA requirements. If it doesn't, you should ask for some adjustment in the price to allow you to make the necessary changes. If you are starting an inn, build into your budget the cost of necessary accommodations and equipment for this growing segment of the public.

The largest hurdle in coping with the ADA is attitude. Think of it as an opportunity to attract not only guests who might currently be disabled but also a growing market as our society ages.

Start by learning all you can about the various disabilities you will need to accommodate. Talk to people with those disabilities to understand what is most important to them. In designing your plan, work with local independent-living groups or centers that serve people who are blind, deaf, or physically disabled. Invite them to do an on-site inspection. That experience alone will be enlightening. Better yet, invite them to spend the night and dine with you. This contact will not only be an education but will give you an entrée into a network that can bring you business. Document this research and these contacts, should you face noncompliance legal action in the future.

THE AMERICANS WITH DISABILITIES ACT: A PRIMER FOR INNKEEPERS

Provisions of the Law

The law does not make unreasonable demands.

- It exempts an establishment with five or fewer rooms for rent when it is occupied by the owners as their residence.
- It declares that "all physical barriers in existing public accommodations must be removed, if readily achievable," interpreted by attorneys general to mean

that removal must be easily accomplished without great expense or difficulty. If barrier removal is difficult, alternative methods of providing services must be offered, as long as those methods are, again, "readily achievable." You are not exempt just because you have an old building. A permanent ramp may injure the architectural attractiveness that "sells" your inn, but a portable ramp won't.

- Elevators are not required in newly constructed or altered buildings under three stories.
- Only one of every twenty-five rooms needs to be made wheelchair accessible and furnished for the hearing-impaired.
- If you have fourteen or fewer part-time or full-time employees, you are not required to meet the federal ADA employment standards. Check your state law for more rigid requirements. In California, for example, the standard is five or fewer employees.

Enforcement is tricky. Individuals may file complaints with the attorney general, who can levy fines up to $50,000 for a first violation and $100,000 for subsequent violations; individuals may also file private lawsuits. Victims of discrimination are expected to ferret out lawbreakers. In some areas, groups of disabled persons are active in pursuing this primary method of enforcement. Of course, if you alter or build a new structure, local building codes will be enforced by the appropriate regulatory agency.

Tax benefits are available only for barrier removal, interpreters, and readers and equipment for persons with hearing and vision impairments; benefits do not apply to new construction. Check with your accountant for full details.

Guests requiring an accessible room cannot be charged extra for accommodating the basic needs provided for all other guests.

Necessary Accommodations

Contact your local building department for required accommodations for accessibility in your town. Just so you have an idea, equipment to accommodate the guest who is hearing impaired includes a Telecommunication Display Device (TDD), for making reservations and providing the guest with telephone access, and a combination smoke detector/door-knocking transmitter/amplified telephone handset/alarm clock with strobe and bed shaker, easily movable from room to room. If you provide TVs, a closed-captioned decoder or assistive-listening device is required.

To provide accessibility for physical impairments, some facilities you'll need are signs, accessible parking space with short walking or rolling distances, a ramp for your front stairs (depending on stairway height), and lever or U-shaped door handles.

In the bathroom, things you'll need as a start are a raised toilet seat, grab bars, a portable bath seat, a full-length bathroom mirror, lever-type faucets, and padded plumbing under sinks to protect knees.

In sleeping rooms, you'll want to have tabletops twenty-seven to twenty-nine inches from the floor with nineteen-inch knee spaces; furniture arranged to allow space for sixty-inch wheelchair turnaround; a thirty-six-inch bedside clearance; and lower clothes hooks or closet bars.

To accommodate guests with visual impairments, plan adequate lighting along all exterior walkways, and large-print or Braille information materials in the bedroom and menus in the dining room. (Go to a local copy shop to enlarge print or contact your local independent living center for Braille materials.) Book tapes and a cassette player with headphones are a nice touch. Instead of purchasing tapes, check with your library and borrow a few when guests arrive.

For everyone's safety, install contrasting color strips on bottom and top steps of stairways and on unusual stairways. Be aware of fragile items or dangerous areas that need a special warning, such as low doors, uneven walkways or stairs, or vases or other decorations perched in walkways. Remove them or provide a verbal and physical warning of some kind.

Remember to check with your accountant regarding tax credits or deductions on barrier removal.

The Aging Boomer

With a huge number of inn guests moving reluctantly from the vitality of middle age to the physical limitations of being a "senior citizen" in the next ten years, innkeepers need to turn their service focus toward the maturing baby boomer. The basics of accessibility come into play for real now. Consider placing loaner over-the-counter reading glasses in every room, large-print bathroom reading materials, and larger print on shampoo bottles. Those one-hundred-watt lightbulbs are a necessity—everywhere. Do not skimp on lighting. Install lever-type handles on doors and faucets. Have extra bed boards for firmness and foam pads for softness, and let guests know they are available. Provide assistance to carry luggage. Be sure you have grab bars in all bathtubs and showers. Ask all guests for dietary restrictions and then don't cringe when they tell you. Ask some senior citizens what drives them nuts about traveling to B&Bs and you'll get a good picture of your inn's future.

Just being disabled does not make one an expert on the ADA. The following criteria for locating expert assistance can be helpful:

1. Individuals who are involved in local disability organizations representing a large population, rather than simply speaking for themselves, often have a broad perspective.
2. The federal government has developed various training programs for disabled individuals, run by the National Institute on Disability Research and Rehabilitation and through regional Disability and Business Accommodation Centers.
3. Experience in the past with architectural barrier removal or building codes can be useful, since it sensitizes the individual to the realities of compromise necessary in the construction process.
4. Disabled people who own or operate businesses or have experience working with businesses may be more knowledgeable about the needs of and economic difficulties faced by businesses.
5. Individuals with construction or building backgrounds may have a special advantage in this area, since they often understand the implications of architectural modifications, their costs, and their difficulties.

There is no perfect person for a project, so a group of consultants representing various disabilities may be best. Look for somebody with whom you can develop a rapport and who can offer insights into the needs and functional abilities of disabled people. A long-term relationship will be invaluable when the inn expands! Use these contacts to evaluate programs before implementation; you'll want to provide the greatest degree of accommodation to the widest range of people.

Fireplaces

Fireplaces and inns belong together. Guests consider a cheery fire welcoming and romantic. Fireplaces are not without cost, however, even beyond the obvious expense of creating them. The cost of wood, gas, or special fuel, as well as your time to lay fires and clean or repair fireplaces, must be taken into consideration. In addition, there are environmental effects to consider.

Fireplaces fill guest rooms, and you can charge more for rooms with fireplaces. So what constitutes a fireplace? Wood-burning fireplaces are universally considered the real thing. In an environment where chimneys are all working and safe, wood is cheap, environmental issues have not yet arisen, and the innkeeper is willing to pay close attention to what is happening, wood is it.

Gene Swett, of the Old Monterey Inn in California, solved several problems with his gas-ignition fireplaces.

- *First, there's no damper to open or close so guests don't mistakenly fill the room with smoke; glass doors control heat loss when the fireplace is not in use, thus performing the role of a damper.*
- *Second, the wood-burning fire lights with gas, which is on a timer, so that after five minutes or so, it goes off, leaving a self-sufficient, well-lit fire.*
- *Gene's third achievement was a two-by-four cubbyhole for firewood under the tiled, built-in firebox and hearth. There is no wood mess on the carpet and no clumsy wood carrier that can break or fall apart.*

Because the hearth is elevated, the flames are easily seen from the bed—guests want that.

A wood-burning, minimum-clearance fireplace can be added for under $5,000, depending on the venting required. Slatelike, fire-safe hearths come in easy-to-install slabs.

GAS

Gas logs have become increasingly popular at inns because of their cleanliness, safety, economy of fuel, easier and cheaper installation, and significant reduction of room heat loss—plus you don't have to haul wood!

Newer models look like real fireplaces and provide instant atmosphere. For fireplaces already plumbed with natural gas, installation is simple. Gas can be vented from the side through a one-foot-diameter hole. These fireplaces are safest when a pilot is part of the set. Consider putting them on a thermostat for guest comfort and energy conservation. An entire group of gas-log fireplaces are efficient heaters. They have ultrasafe permanent glass fronts and can be operated by a remote-controlled lighter, which guests can use from the bed (though innkeepers report that these remotes can be tricky to maintain).

Guests call with a variety of expectations about fireplaces; how can you be sure they're not disappointed? Most innkeepers are clear about it if their fireplaces are not traditional wood; some don't explain unless asked and find that guests are delighted with gas fireplaces.

How can you be sure that your entire investment will not burn down because of some overzealous romantic?

- Have a chimney sweep inspect and regularly clean the chimney.
- Keep a small fire extinguisher by each fireplace. The fire department will not usually require this, but will require a large one outside the rooms, nearby.
- Know your wood. If you have wet or unseasoned wood, guests will do foolish things to light it. Seasoned split wood is your best bet.
- Lay the first fire. The easier it is to light, the more likely a guest will not try to "help" an unenthusiastic flame.
- Provide clear instructions about the lighting and idiosyncrasies of your fireplace. Verbal instructions during a welcome tour are simply not enough; written directions are necessary follow-up prevention. If your fireplace draws better in the beginning with the door open, say so. Also include ideas on how to handle problems, such as what to do if it starts to smoke. Drawings help.
- Provide an adequate hearth in front of the firebox to catch sparks from a runaway log. A fireproof rug or mat helps prevent damage or cover up damage already done.
- Put all ashes in a metal container with a metal lid, even if they feel cool. Make sure the container is solid, and never use water to dampen hot wood ashes. A chemical reaction may cause them to reignite.
- Provide tools and fireplace screens that work and are easy to operate. Some fireplace tools do not make any sense. For example, giant tongs require dexterity and are generally useless except to take a burning log out of the fire and drop it on the floor.
- Place grates properly to prevent wayward logs; don't forget to train your staff in where and how to replace them after cleaning.

What About Insurance?

Insurance agents report that the presence of fireplaces in guest rooms makes no difference in premiums. Most fires occur when chimneys have not been cleaned and the fire enters the attic or walls. Ask your chimney sweep to inspect not only old chimneys but also new ones, to ensure that construction work has been done correctly.

Choosing a Computer for Your Inn

What should you buy, *how much* should you pay, *where* should you buy it, and *why* should you have it: these are the questions that plague every first-time computer purchaser—and even innkeepers who've been using computers and printers for years. The marketplace is extremely volatile. Prices drop and models change; computer consultants say you just have to reconcile yourself to the fact that the computer you buy today, even when you shop wisely, will be obsolete tomorrow. Nevertheless, many people buy haphazardly and, not surprisingly, that poor start often comes back to haunt them. Approach this purchase as a business decision.

First, let's do away with any myths about printers. A good one does not have to be expensive. Consider having two: a *laser-type* printer for doing black-and-white text, and a *color printer* for brochures, marketing pieces, and pictures. A quick search of Internet price-comparison sites (such as www.streetprices.com and www.mysimon.com) finds more than a dozen manufacturers, including Epson, Hewlett-Packard, Canon, and Lexmark, to name a few, and their products are available from hundreds of vendors. Prices range from $50 to $2,000. The more expensive the printer, the more features you get, and the more advanced standard features are—compare ppm (pages per minute), RAM ("memory"), ink-jet versus desk-jet technology, Postscript, dpi (dots per inch), and duplexing options (the ability to print on both sides).

What are the computing needs of your business? Know what you want your computer to do. Reservations, e-mail, Web design, bookkeeping, word processing (writing letters, reports), database management (labels, lists), and desktop publishing (brochures, stationery) are all tasks that innkeepers can complete using computers. This is the most important stage of preparation for computer shopping, and it's important to take the time to be extremely specific.

Will more than one person be taking reservations and entering information that is gathered manually? Will you use the computer chiefly for bookkeeping, so that you'll be the only one with your hand on the account? If everyone is going to use it, it's better to keep it simple, to reduce training time and the possibility of errors.

Once you've assessed your needs, determine your budget and set a maximum amount of money you can spend. Research market prices. Talk to other people who own and use computers as you plan to. Decide whether you want a PC (IBM or IBM-compatible, using Windows) or an Apple (Macintosh) operating system. You will never stay ahead of what is new; the world of computers moves too quickly. There will always be something newer, faster, bigger, smaller, or cheaper. So go ahead and make your purchase based on your needs.

In 2003, a PC with 256MB RAM, an Intel Pentium 4 (2GHz processor), seventeen-inch monitor, 60GB hard drive, CD drive, graphics card, integrated 10/100 Ethernet, floppy drive, and modem could be purchased for less than $1,000. A comparable Macintosh (iMac), equipped with a fifteen-inch LCD flat screen, 800MHz PowerPC G4 processor, graphics card, 256MB RAM, 60GB hard drive, CD/R, 10/100 Base-T Ethernet, two speakers, and modem, cost $1,299.

Since this is an investment, plan for the long term as well as the immediate future; don't get a system that just barely meets your needs. Get as much memory (RAM) as you can afford, and do consider an LCD flat screen. They are crisp and sharp, have great color, weigh much less, and take far less real estate on that already-crowded desk.

What about a portable? Laptops generally come with smaller screens and a compact keyboard. But are you actually going to take it anywhere? Be realistic about how you'll use it. Some innkeepers prefer laptops because they fit on the kitchen counter, where the innkeeper takes reservation phone calls while she cooks breakfast. Some manufacturers offer machines with docking systems, so that the laptop you take on the road or into the backyard "docks" into your office-based system as if it were a desktop computer.

WINDOWS OR MAC?

Choosing a personal computer used to be simpler. If you wanted a friendly machine with great graphics capabilities and could afford a premium price, you bought an Apple Macintosh. If you needed lots of cheap computing power for complicated tasks, you bought a PC. There were dozens of PC brands (and there still are). Since all used the Windows operating software, they were able to swap software and data.

These days, Windows endows the PC with Mac-like qualities. And in the other corner, Apple has reduced the prices of Macs, so they are competitive with high-quality Windows PCs.

Which kind of computer is the best to buy? About 90 percent of homes choose Windows, but the Macintosh continues to chip away at the buyer marketplace. Macs have two advantages. First, they run more efficiently than PCs and therefore require less processing power and storage capacity to accomplish the same tasks. Second, Macs incorporate features that generally cost extra on PCs.

On the other hand, the huge popularity of the PC gives Windows users important advantages. Countless software and hardware configurations are available, and because PCs vastly outnumber Macs, Windows has a built-in ticket to acceptance. And as more hardware and software companies compete to make Windows-compatible products, economic momentum is against the Mac.

But realistically, any system you buy will be out of date to some degree within a few years, so your computer selection should depend on which system you're most comfortable with, what software you need, and what you can afford—today.

Telephone Logistics

The telephone is so much the lifeline of an inn that it pays to plan an efficient, functional, handy system.

Phones should be located where you'll spend a lot of time. Since that's often hard to pinpoint in this business, most innkeepers use remote (mobile) phones. They'll go with you up to the guest rooms while you make the beds and out to the garden when you cut the flowers. If you take a scaled-down version of the reservation book along as well, you'll have all the information you need to provide immediate service. Consider a remote phone with at least a 2.4GHz range. Although it's a bit pricier than others, the extended range will be worth it.

If you choose not to install in-room phones, you will probably want at least four lines: one for business incoming calls, one for outgoing guest calls, one for your fax line, and one for your own personal use. Also consider a line for your credit card processing machine. And don't forget one for your computer modem (unless you use DSL). If you use cable, it is a separate line to the inn installed by your local cable company.

BASIC SETUP

Phones should be located in the office, the parlor, the innkeeper's quarters, and the kitchen.

The personal line should have a different ring from the business line so the innkeeper can answer calls appropriately; this will let you use a single phone without all the bells and whistles of hold buttons and flashing lights. If you use a conventional (rather than a mobile) model, this phone will also work in the event of a power outage.

The parlor phone should have no bell at all, so as not to disturb guests. This is the phone available for guests making outgoing calls. Your local phone company has a number of options for blocking long-distance calls, requiring guests to use a credit card or a calling card or to reverse the charges, thereby eliminating any potential abuse. Be careful, though, about toll calls within your area code; these are more complicated to block.

A parlor phone is cost-effective for small inns, but only one guest may make calls at a time. Phoning from the parlor is usually not very private, either, but if you provide a portable phone for guests, they can take it to their rooms. If you opt for a portable, be sure it has the necessary range capacity for good-quality communication.

Seriously consider in-room telephones. If you hope to attract business travelers, don't consider anything else; business travelers insist on immediate, private, and continuous phone availability.

A few clever innkeepers provide individual answering machines for their business travelers. This has the advantage of eliminating delays in receiving messages while the innkeeper is out, as well as reducing the number of incoming calls the innkeeper has to handle. Guests return to their rooms, retrieve their messages, and make their calls.

You'll certainly want an answering machine for yourself. A two-line model picks up calls on both your business and your personal lines. It also records separate outgoing messages for each line. Be sure to have an accurate, current message—it's not good for an April caller to hear about last February's vacancies. Return all calls promptly.

A fax is a necessity. It is necessary for business travelers and is an innkeeper's friend when you need to get complicated driving directions to guests booking a same-day reservation or have to respond instantly to an ad deadline. Don't even think of operating without one. Connect it to a separate, dedicated line so faxes can arrive and be sent without disturbing anything or anyone. It is inconvenient for an innkeeper to always be running to turn on the fax and annoying for a caller trying to get through.

Give careful thought to who will be using the inn's phones, and when, where, and for what. Letting the phone system grow like Topsy is much more expensive than figuring out at the outset how many phone jacks you'll need and having them all installed at once.

For budget reasons, you may want only a couple of separate extra phone lines to cover all of your guest rooms. Of course this will limit guest usage: eight rooms and two lines may mean six guests have to wait to make their calls. There are systems where a CPU (central processing unit) along with a computer and printer are involved; calls may be directed by the innkeeper to specific guest rooms and billing tabulated automatically (if you charge guests for local calls).

A variety of telephone systems are available for bed-and-breakfast inns and country inns, priced from around $2,000, some for lease and some for purchase. The more options you choose, the higher the cost. Evaluate what you can afford along with what telephone service you want to provide for your guests. For most inns, the high-end systems are overkill, combining computerized reservations, night audit functions, call accounting systems, and so on. A night system that allows incoming calls to be connected to a guest room using an extension number will be welcomed by parents keeping close contact with their children, and by your business travelers.

Research the marketplace; the technology and pricing change often. Don't exclude your local telephone carrier in this research phase. They may have a small-business system that works for your inn and can be purchased in installments. Be sure to check the warranty and upgrade and expansion policies. You may want only four lines now, but be sure the hardware you buy is expandable, just in case. Labor and equipment costs in the phone industry are high.

WHEN YOU'RE NOT THERE

A warm, skilled person to convey your message, your values, and your style in your absence is the first choice for handling phone calls. The second choice, and only for brief absences—ten minute or less while you check in the Joneses—is to take the phone off the hook. Then you can be sure to give the Joneses the attention they deserve. Busy signals within reason probably whet a caller's appetite.

For longer absences, such as an afternoon or an evening, a high-quality answering machine is a good idea. Make your outgoing message clear, concise, and warm, but not cute. Cute is too subjective; not everybody wants to hear an imitation of George Burns singing "Reach Out and Touch Someone."

A machine that uses cassettes allows you to program one for your basic spiel and another one for last-minute callers. You might say, "Sorry, but we're completely full for the weekend. We'd love to have you come another time. Please leave your name, address, and telephone number, and let us know if you have a specific date in mind. We'll call you right away if we have an opening for the date; if not, we'll send you our brochure and hope you'll try us again." It is important to give the caller another number to call in an emergency.

Voice-activated machines record caller messages of any length, a good safeguard against losing the last digit of the phone number of a caller who wants to book the whole inn for a week in dark, cold January. If your message tape is limited to twenty or thirty seconds, warn callers about it in *your* message.

Be honest and realistic. One inn tape says the innkeepers are out grocery shopping. It's a warm touch, until you hear it the fifth time in three days!

Cell phones are absolutely an innkeeper's best friend. They go where you go and can behave as you wish them to, such as setting the ring on "vibrate" so you can choose whether or not to answer calls during dinner.

Answering services are risky, because staffing varies. A tired operator may not only lose you a booking for a night, but may also discourage a potential guest from calling ever again. An answering machine message is canned, but at least you control the canning.

Return all calls promptly. Even at that, you will lose callers to other inns. But even if they've made other plans for the imminent trip, your courtesy, professionalism, and warmth may persuade them to try your inn next time.

Kitchen Organization

You may have been a good cook for years, but as an innkeeper, you and your kitchen are going professional. Before you can plan an efficient inn kitchen, you'll need to make some decisions.

- What meals, beverages, and snacks will you serve? Inns variously provide breakfast, lunch, dinner, wine, hors d'oeuvres, bedtime milk and cookies, picnic lunches, and high tea.
- How extensive will each meal or snack be? Full or continental? Cold cereal or gourmet? Baked, fried, or microwaved?
- How will you serve? Buffet, sit-down all at once, sit-down over a set period of time, family style, individual plates, room service?
- What service will you use? Stainless or sterling, china or stoneware, plastic or crystal, paper or linen?
- Will guests have a menu choice? Or will you serve one item to all (allowing, naturally, for dietary restrictions)?

- Will you serve large groups, such as conferences, weddings, and receptions?
- Where will you serve? In the garden, dining room, fireside, kitchen, or breakfast in bed?
- Who will cook, serve, clean up?
- How will your food service choices promote your overall inn image?
- How much will you actually prepare in your kitchen? Will you buy baked goods? A number of fine inns cook nothing on the premises, serving only fresh fruit, cheeses, and pastries, for example.

Organize the kitchen for its actual use, paying special attention to the preferences and procedures of the person who'll do most of the cooking. If you're designing a kitchen from scratch or making modifications, a few hours of consulting time from a restaurant designer could be well worth the price.

On your own or working with a pro, the second step to a kitchen plan involves listing the centers of use you'll need. For example, a baking center includes baking pans, flours, sugar, measuring tools, and so on, conveniently close at hand.

Other centers to consider are:
- Table or tray setup: silverware, dishes, glasses, linens.
- Food preparation: knives, cutting boards, food washing, garbage disposal.
- Coffee and tea: cups, spoons, sugar, lemon, and cream available outside your main work area, if guests are welcome to help themselves.
- Desk: for planning menus, answering phones (convenient but out of the way of traffic), making shopping lists.
- Family eating area.
- Guest eating area.

Some kitchens may need all of these; others will need very few. Kitchen centers often overlap, but do consider effectiveness. Draw a plan and play with it until it works well for you.

The needs of an inn kitchen will be somewhat different from those of a home kitchen, so think about these ideas when you plan the renovation:
- Health department requirements.
- Dishwasher: portable or commercial?
- Instant hot-water spout on sink.
- Water reverse-osmosis system on sink spout.
- Extra plugs for electrical appliances.
- Coffeemaker directly attached to water supply.
- Garbage disposal.
- Three-bin stainless-steel sink if you don't have a commercial dishwasher.
- Vented hood with fan over stove.
- Adequate, easy-to-clean counter space.

- Storage: Open shelves for frequently used items. Space to store items so that they are all ready to use again: coffee cups, sugar and creamer, and spoons set out for the next morning's service or individual breakfast trays set up; wineglasses on trays for evening hours. Room to store cleaning equipment and items purchased on sale and in volume.
- Adequate refrigerator and freezer space, for inn needs and family needs.
- Rest room for innkeepers and kitchen staff. (This is a health department requirement in some areas.)
- Good lighting.
- Comfortable colors.
- Adequate hot-water heater.

You've probably noticed a heavy emphasis on function in this chapter, and there's a good reason for it. Experience teaches that brass fixtures show water spots badly and fragile wineglasses can't be safely popped into the dishwasher. Don't furnish your kitchen with "cute" antiques that aren't functional or supplies that require extra work to maintain. In the inn kitchen, form should follow function.

Breakfast Ideas

The last thing most aspiring innkeepers need advice on is breakfast. Everybody seems to have good ideas for what to serve. But innkeepers find that some foods and serving strategies work better than others, and contribute more to the overall image of the inn.

An Elegant Buffet at a Queen Anne Victorian

The setting: An ornate mahogany sideboard. A delft vase of daffodils. Serving dishes of fine antique china and crystal and a silver coffee service. Guests help themselves, then take plates to tables for two and four in the dining room and sunporch. The tables are set with linen, ornate silver service, antique china and crystal, and nosegays. A discreetly available hostess refills coffee cups and prepares soft-boiled eggs on request.

The food: Three choices of home-baked breads with cream cheese, butter, and jam. Fresh fruit compote of berries, citrus fruit, and pineapple. Various domestic and imported cheeses. Crystal pitcher of fresh juice.

A Country Buffet

The setting: An antique Hoosier kitchen cabinet displays a help-yourself breakfast, served from antique crockery. The hostess serves hot beverages in country-style mugs from her kitchen counter. Guests carry their matching pottery plates to a heavy oak table set with hand-woven place mats, overlooking a stream; a dried-flower arrangement is the centerpiece.

The food: Bananas in a basket or fresh strawberries to slice over a choice of cereals in crocks—granola, raisin bran, shredded wheat. Large crockery pitchers of milk and juice. Bagels and English muffins to toast yourself, and bran muffins steaming hot. A bowl of berry yogurt.

Family-Style Breakfast

The setting: A sunny breakfast room, a large table set with a red-checked tablecloth, bouquets of daisies, simple white china, and stainless-steel flatware.

The food: As sleepy guests appear, they help themselves to a bowl of stewed fruit or homemade applesauce. Hot beverages are served by the innkeeper. When everyone has arrived for the nine o'clock meal, a huge platter of the inn's special scrambled eggs, fortified with everything but the kitchen sink, is served; a warm loaf of homemade whole-wheat bread and a cinnamon nut ring are brought out at the same time. The guests pass the foods while the innkeeper keeps mugs filled. Homemade marmalade and fluffy sweet butter are on the table.

Elegant Sit-Down Breakfast

The setting: A dining room table set with sterling silver, linen napkins, an antique lace tablecloth, crystal juice glasses, and antique china. There's a fire in the dining room fireplace. The innkeeper dresses in a period costume.

The food: First, a salad plate of fresh fruit, perhaps kiwi with brown sugar and sour cream or melon and pineapple. Hot beverages and juice are offered. The second course is spinach frittata, served with a basket of hot breads and muffins in a linen-lined silver bowl to pass. There are crystal and silver bowls of jams and butter.

Breakfast in a Basket

Delivered to the guest room at a prearranged time is a willow basket of specially designed pottery, heated to keep the decadent French toast (topped with fresh blueberries and sour cream) warm and gooey, and chilled to keep the banana-pineapple fruit bowl fresh. A quart vacuum bottle of hot coffee and a carafe of juice are tucked in under the quilted-place-mat cover, along with tableware wrapped in napkins and tiny pottery sugar cup and creamer. Cups are tied to the basket handle with grosgrain ribbon. Guests can enjoy breakfast in their rooms or carry it to the garden or the beach.

Continental Breakfast in Bed

A tray set with unique embroidered napkins holds a coffee carafe and mugs, freshly squeezed juice in stemmed glasses, and a basket of large, flaky croissants with raspberry jam and butter.

Early-Riser Breakfasts

When you don't want to arise before dawn to serve breakfast for early-departing guests, what do you do? Whether they are going bird-watching, catching an early plane, or merely come from a different time zone, not every guest wants breakfast after eight.

Innkeepers come up with all kinds of creative approaches. One innkeeper puts out a coffeepot with a timer set to start when the guests indicate they want it. With hardboiled eggs, milk, and juice in the refrigerator and some banana bread, butter, granola, and a bowl of uncut fruit on the sideboard, guests help themselves and go on their way.

Another innkeeper delivers to the guest's room, the night before departure, a paper bag with muffins, yogurt, fresh fruit, and a juice box. There's a coffeemaker already in the bedroom.

A third innkeeper leaves a breakfast bag in the guest public refrigerator identified with the name of the early-departing guest. A steaming hot-water faucet installed in the parlor buffet provides access so early guests can brew coffee, tea, or cocoa using individual packets.

Still another innkeeper always gets up to serve a hot but simple breakfast to her early-bird guests.

However you do it, all guests deserve breakfast, even if their plane departs at dawn.

PRACTICAL CONSIDERATIONS

Breakfast is a wonderful opportunity for creativity, but there are unexpected parameters. The first concerns local government health standards. For inns with only a few guest rooms, it's usually not worth investing in a complete commercial kitchen so you can scramble eggs. Be sure you find out about government restrictions in this area. The second constraint is timing. Business travelers often want to eat early, by seven or eight o'clock. Vacationers are usually happy if breakfast is available a bit later. Guests who must leave very early are sometimes offered coffee and rolls that have been set out the night before by the innkeeper.

If you decide to serve everyone at once, say at 8:30 A.M., remember that this can be a great strain on the plumbing. Also, plan ahead for gentle ways to cope with late arrivers. Perhaps you can offer them at least coffee, juice, and breads from your leftover pantry.

If you choose to serve breakfast over a range of time, say from eight to ten, whatever you provide needs to look and taste as good at ten as it did two hours earlier. Those lovely puffy German pancakes sink fast, and they take about twenty minutes to bake, longer than you may want to keep unfed guests waiting in the dining room. Make another choice. You can actually serve more guests over a longer range of time, as some people will be there at eight o'clock and some will show up at the last minute.

If you are willing to serve breakfast in bed, select foods that will still be warm or cold by the time they're delivered. Think of this kind of breakfast as a buffet. Can the foods be cut with a fork or picked up with the fingers? Don't expect guests to deal with thick slices of ham on a tray full of china that is balanced on their knees—over your antique quilts, too!

Be bountiful! Croissants and jam can look like a feast when the rolls come by the basketful and the jam is generous. It's much better to raise your rates by a dollar a person and serve more food than to charge less and scrimp.

If government regulations allow it, baking your own coffee cakes is usually much more economical than buying pastry, and it adds a homelike touch. Colette Bailey at the Grey Whale Inn in Fort Bragg, California, is always winning blue ribbons at the fair with her coffee cakes, promoting the inn as a side benefit and providing breakfast guests with a very special treat.

Innkeepers are more likely to get tired of serving the same old thing for breakfast than guests are to tire of eating it. Experimentation is not always greeted with delight. If you want to serve a Guatemalan breakfast with refried beans, you had better make granola available for the more conventional eaters. Also plan to have simple things on hand—whole-wheat toast, cereals, yogurt—for vegetarians, diabetics, or others with diet restrictions if your usual menu won't meet their needs.

Within the menu on a given day, plan variety in color, temperature, and taste. Don't serve hot-spiced cider, warm dried-fruit compote, and pancakes with syrup at the same meal.

Guests who are willing to try anything in the food line with great goodwill are nevertheless finicky about coffee; you just can't please everyone. The best guide is to serve coffee the way you like it, assuming that means it's fresh, hot, and flavorful. Offer brewed decaf as well as regular coffee, herbal tea as well as black tea, plus raw sugar and sugar substitutes.

Make your table setting creative and attractive. Garnish the plates with sliced fresh fruit or fresh herbs and flowers from the garden. Make the taste and the look of breakfast another enhancement of the overall image of your inn.

Plan the breakfast period so you can enjoy it. A frantic innkeeper makes guests uncomfortable. Don't offer what you won't be happy about delivering. If you hate to cook, don't offer a full breakfast; serve bakery croissants with a flair. Don't mention breakfast in bed in your brochure if you're going to begrudge it to the guest who wants to take you up on it.

Food should be memorable: how it tastes, where it's eaten, how it's served, and who eats with you. All these are memories guests take along and pass along to others.

The Way to a Guest's Heart

Guest hearts are a little tougher to please today, with more people taking seriously a variety of dietary restrictions. A couple of years ago, innkeepers often found that guests who stuck religiously to fat-free bran muffins all year long were ready for eggs Benedict by the time they got to the inn, and spurned the innkeeper's special low-fat preparations. While this still happens, innkeepers find more and more demand for accommodating special needs. Guests are grateful and delighted when you make them something special. It's a good idea to have a vegetarian cookbook on hand for ideas, but start simply by stocking your cupboard with special items for guests who say, "I can't eat that." Make life easy for yourself by having tricks up your sleeve and ready ingredients for diets that are fat-free, cholesterol-free (but fat is acceptable), wheat-free, dairy-free, egg-free, or sugar-free.

It's often easy to please particular palates with simple substitutions: warm corn tortillas instead of toast for people with wheat allergies; scrambled tofu for folks avoiding eggs; unbuttered toast with jam instead of coffee cake for people avoiding fat; grilled sliced polenta instead of pancakes or French toast for people who eat neither eggs nor dairy.

Just understanding what these restrictions mean is a big hurdle for those who've never had to live with them. While understanding general definitions is important, finding out what they mean to the guest is more important. Ask this question when dealing with special diets: "What do you normally have for breakfast?" Then go out and buy it. This reduces second-guessing and creates a base for creativity.

But be careful about creativity here. Mary had regular guests at Ten Inverness Way who could not eat wheat, dairy, or eggs—or even tofu. They loved her chicken-apple sausage with polenta and her Amazaki rice pudding, but actually told her they were relieved that she didn't get too creative on them: it's too risky for them not to know every ingredient they're eating!

Here are some ideas:

Sprinkle nuts, coconut flakes, or sunflower seeds over vegetables, fruits, or oatmeal.

Stir-fry tofu with vegetable salsa and serve with a warm tortilla.

Serve oatmeal with a choice of toppings: chopped dried apricots or dates, warm pecans, shredded coconut, toasted sesame seeds.

Beef up home-baked breads with nuts and seeds.

Blend even amounts of peanut butter, honey, and margarine, spread on whole-wheat toast; sprinkle with sesame seeds; and bake ten minutes at 325 degrees, then quickly broil until lightly toasted.

Broil rice cakes (which have a long shelf life) with applesauce, peanut butter, and honey, or cinnamon sugar and butter. They do not fill you up, though, so make several.

Offer peanut butter, sesame butter, or other nut butters.

You can also try:

Black beans as a side dish.

Sliced potato-and-cheese casserole.

Breakfast pizza or burrito.

Yogurt, granola, nut, and fruit parfait.

Grilled fruit-and-cheese sandwich.

Smoothies made with fruit and yogurt or soy milk.

Pancakes made with extra oatmeal and wheat germ or walnuts.

Cornmeal or whole-wheat waffles.

Egg-free French toast: dip whole-wheat bread in a mix of blended cashews, milk, and dates. Or substitute water, rice milk, or soy milk for milk for dairy-free diets.

Pancakes with sliced fresh fruit instead of syrup.

Baked whole pears in pure apple, orange, or cranberry juice and spices.

Waffles with a fruit sauce.

Breakfast nacho with corn tortilla, beans, scrambled eggs, salsa, and cheese.

Potato, green pepper, and onion casserole or stir-fry topped with cheese.

Corn pudding.

Breakfast risotto.

Crustless quiche.

Substituting cinnamon, fruit, or fruit juice for sugar in many dishes such as baked apples, crepes, or breads.

Stock your cupboard with these ingredients to be prepared for most dietary issues:

Egg whites or Egg Beaters.

Rice milk, soy cheese, soy cream cheese, and soy sour cream (found in health-food stores).

Soy milk and nondairy creamer (available at chain grocery stores).

Gluten-free bread (can be frozen until needed).

Low-sodium rice cakes.

Mashed-potato mix to use as a thickener instead of cornstarch and flour.

Oatmeal.

Nonfat and low-fat cottage cheese.

Nonfat and low-fat cheese.

Honey.

Lemons.

Flour: cornmeal, rye flour, barley flour, rice flour, spelt flour for your various bread needs.

Salt substitutes, such as Mrs. Dash or Parsley Patch.

Oil substitutes: apple juice, applesauce, mashed bananas, crushed pineapple in its own juice, or orange juice concentrates.

Bagels and cream cheese.

Whipped nonfat evaporated milk (in lieu of whipping cream).

Low-fat ricotta instead of cream cheese.

Grape-Nuts instead of nuts.

Turkey or soy sausage, bacon, or ham rather than pork.

Syrup and sauces for pancakes: have on hand fruits that can be made into sauce with a blender or food processor.

All-fruit, sugarless jams and jellies.

Check the Internet for more ideas on particular dietary restrictions.

Two final points: Ask about restrictions when taking a reservation, confirming it, or at least upon arrival; don't just hope guests will either tell you themselves or suffer in silence. And keep in mind that these folks may eat funny, but they eat big—plan on plenty. Don't be daunted by your vegan guests, who eat no meat or animal products, even milk or cheese. You can readily find soy substitutes in grocery or health-food stores.

.... **Mary's No-Fat-Added Granola** ....

Mix together:

2 1/2 pounds rolled oats

3/4 pound wheat germ

1 pound unsweetened grated coconut

2 to 3 cups sliced almonds

Mix together:

3 cups firmly packed brown sugar

2 1/2 cups water

3 tablespoons vanilla extract

Combine the two mixtures. Transfer to a shallow 11-by-17-inch baking pan. Place pan in a 350°F oven until mixture is golden, stirring every 5 to 10 minutes. The total oven time should be 40 to 50 minutes.

.... **Odd-Man-Out Shirred Eggs** ....

This is an easy dish when you have just a few guests or an odd number of them.

1 teaspoon fresh bread crumbs*

2 to 3 slices Swiss cheese

1 slice tomato

1 egg

2 slices fresh mushroom

1 tablespoon heavy cream or half-and-half

Parmesan cheese, as desired

Grease a 1-cup ramekin or custard cup with butter (or spray with a nonstick coating). Sprinkle the bread crumbs over the bottom. Arrange the cheese in the ramekin so that it reaches up the sides of the dish, forming a cup shape. Top the cheese with the tomato slice and break in the egg. Carefully place the mushroom slices on top of the egg and drizzle with cream. Finally, sprinkle with Parmesan cheese. Place the ramekin in a preheated 350°F oven and bake for 15 to 20 minutes, or until egg is firm. Makes 1 serving.

* Pat likes to use the crusts left over from making French toast to make the bread crumbs.

Put this together the night before, so you can sleep a little later in the morning.

2 tablespoons corn syrup

1 cup firmly packed brown sugar

5 tablespoons margarine or butter

16 slices inexpensive wheat sandwich bread, crusts removed

5 eggs (you can substitute Egg Beaters or 8 egg whites)

1 $1/2$ cups milk (or soy milk)

1 teaspoon vanilla extract

$1/2$ cup sour cream (soy sour cream is available)

$1/2$ cup plain yogurt

1 $1/2$ cups strawberries, hulled, or one 10-ounce package frozen unsweetened strawberries, partially thawed

Combine corn syrup, brown sugar, and margarine in a small heavy saucepan and heat, stirring, until bubbly. Pour syrup mixture into a 9-by-13-inch pan. Nestle the bread slices into the syrup, making two layers. Mix together eggs, milk, and vanilla, and pour over the bread.

Cover pan and refrigerate overnight. The next morning, remove the pan from the refrigerator and take off the cover. Place pan in a preheated 350°F oven and bake for 45 minutes.

To serve, loosen edges of bread from pan sides with the blade of a knife or a thin-bladed spatula. Invert the pan onto a serving plate so that the caramelized portion of the French toast is on top. Divide into serving portions and top each serving with a tablespoon of combined sour cream, yogurt, and some strawberries. Serve immediately. Serves 8.

1/4 pound (1/2 cup) butter

1/2 cup vegetable shortening

1 1/2 cups granulated sugar

2 eggs, beaten

1 cup sour cream

1 teaspoon vanilla extract

2 cups less 3 tablespoons all-purpose flour

1 teaspoon baking powder

1/2 teaspoon baking soda

Topping:

1/2 cup finely chopped nuts

2 tablespoons granulated sugar

1/2 teaspoon ground cinnamon

Powdered sugar

In a mixing bowl, cream together butter, shortening, and sugar. Add eggs, sour cream, and vanilla and beat well. Combine flour, baking powder, and baking soda and gradually add to butter mixture, mixing thoroughly. Combine topping ingredients and set aside.

Grease one 9-inch cake pan and pour in half of the cake batter. Sprinkle half of the topping mixture over the batter. Add the remaining batter to the pan, and sprinkle with the remaining topping.

Bake cake in a preheated 350°F oven 1 hour, or until a cake tester inserted in the center comes out clean. Remove from the oven and set on countertop. Sift powdered sugar over surface of cake. Cut in wedges to serve. Makes one 9-inch cake.

Room Planning

Hauling home the perfect armoire only to discover that it doesn't quite fit any of your guest rooms is a disaster. But you can easily avoid it with some careful planning. Since you'll have to keep all this information somewhere (and keeping it all in your head will result in a great deal of crowding), follow the plan below for making the whole purchase and decoration operation run smoothly and economically.

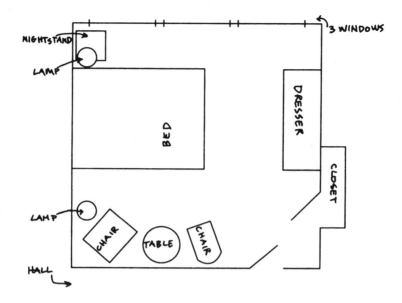

Develop a folder for each room that includes:

- A scaled floor plan for placing furniture (see drawing).
- Swatches of fabric for drapes, upholstery, quilts.
- Carpet swatches.
- Paint chips.
- Wallpaper samples.
- Photos of furniture owned or purchased; use a Polaroid camera. This is especially important when you order furniture to be delivered months in the future.
- A list of measurements of furniture acquired for the room.
- Photos from magazines that convey something of what you want for the look of the room.
- A room planning worksheet (see sample in Appendix 6).

Carry this folder, a measuring tape to measure furniture you may buy, and a small ruler to measure how pieces will fit in your scale plan.

The room planning worksheet can be used in planning your decorating for each room in the inn. A blank form is included in Appendix 6 for you to copy as necessary.

Laundry

There are three basic options for getting inn laundry done: do it yourself, send it out, or contract with a linen service, which will supply clean linens from their own stock.

In most areas, a linen service is a last resort. The sheets provided are often worn and mended; the towels tend to be small and the washcloths thin. But if your inn is in a rural area without a laundry, and if water is scarce or laundry space in the inn impossible, you have to go with a service. Shop them for quality, price, and frequency of delivery. Plan plenty of space to store the clean linens and the bags of dirty ones, in an area accessible to a delivery truck.

Doing your own laundry takes a lot of time, and it's heavy work, with all the folding and lifting involved. Before you decide to take it on yourself, calculate the cost in energy, water, and time; then compare this with the estimates you get from laundries. Remember that working with a laundry has its own time constraints and demands (such as tracking inventory every week), which must be considered before reaching a final decision.

Before contracting with a laundry, check their references carefully. When you've made your choice, try to arrange for one person at the laundry to be your contact. Reward good service with a small gift at the holidays.

If you purchase linens for the inn, the number of sets you'll need depends on how often you want to wash or how often your laundry will deliver. You'll need at least two sets of linens per room, probably more. Light colors spot with mascara and rust from water. Dark towels sometimes show lint. Sheets in prints, rather than solids, show spots less, but they fade more visibly and look worn sooner.

Contact hotel linen-supply houses in your area and compare their prices with department store sales. Look for quality, price, and consistency of supply. Will you be able to get more washcloths in this same red next January? Linen-supply houses sometimes carry products you won't be able to locate elsewhere, such as heavy, feltlike mattress pads that last for years. You may be required to order a minimum of half a dozen or more of each item.

If you decide to do laundry at the inn, design your work area carefully. Plan for storage of dirty things as well as clean ones. You'll need a heavy-duty washer, at least one dryer, shelves for supplies such as soap and fabric softener, space for folding, adequate light, and baskets. Locate the area convenient to the kitchen and office.

And make the space attractive. You'll spend a lot of time there.

Shopping: Making a List, Checking It Twice

Shopping for your inn is one of the fun parts—but there's so much to buy that it's easy to forget essential things—until a guest asks for them.

The best way to make your list is to go through an imaginary day at the inn, beginning with check-in time. Start with the entry: Where will it be? Is there a desk for holding your cash box, room keys, and reservation forms? Where is the guest registry book? Are those items on your list? (See page 162 for detailed shopping list for a B&B inn.)

Is there enough seating in the common room for all your guests at once, and do you need it? Where will they set a drink? Do you need coasters? What will you serve drinks in? How will you keep the drinks warm or cold? Will you serve only one beverage, or will any beverage you serve work appropriately in the glassware on your list?

That's the merest beginning of making your list! Now, in your mind, follow your guests to their rooms, then to the bathroom, to outdoor seating areas, and to breakfast. If you'll serve several menus, picture serving each one, and list what you'll need.

Here's a long list of things to think about when choosing specific items, as well as items you might forget!

· Smaller plates make food look more bountiful.
· Consider how the color of your china will look with the food and with your guest room (if you'll serve breakfast in bed) or dining room decor.
· Ice buckets.
· Glasses and openers for beverages guests bring themselves.
· Spares of big things: bedspreads, tablecloths, mattress pads, shower curtains. You will need these to make emergency replacements without having to wait for the laundry to finish.
· Outdoor furniture in inviting spots.
· Fancy dispensers for liquid hand soaps: they look good longer than the containers the supermarket sells.
· Bud vases for when flowers are sparse, bigger vases and bowls for midsummer.
· Adaptable tissue-box covers so you can buy tissues in the cheaper, less-attractive packages.
· Attractive baskets in all sizes for clutter: menus from local restaurants, other inns' brochures, matches, kindling, coffee filters, plants in from the garden for a week of show, cleaning supplies.
· Large canisters for baking ingredients.

- A powerful vacuum cleaner lightweight enough for quick cleanups.
- A battery-powered vacuum for smaller, even quicker cleanups, such as vacuuming up a line of ants.
- Multipurpose cleaning supplies, for efficient storage and carrying.
- China, flatware, and glassware in patterns that you'll be able to replace.
- Or wonderful old mismatches of china, flatware, and glassware.
- Thermos-type servers to keep hot beverages hot.
- Trays for serving beverages in the evening, for taking breakfast to rooms, and for guests who make a special request for a tray.
- Flashlights, candles, and other emergency equipment.
- First-aid kit.
- Kitchen things: skillets large enough, potholders you won't be ashamed to use to carry a warm plate to a guest, a lemon zester for making neat garnishes, one of those tools that will core and slice an apple in one push, and food and serving things for people who won't be able to eat your regular menu.

And this is merely the beginning!

Something Old, Something New: A Compendium of Decorating Ideas

What a guest sees in an inn reflects planning that began long before that moment, often even before the inn was selected. If your dream inn is a Victorian with large airy rooms, you may have problems finding it, since Victorian homes in reality tend toward small, dark bedrooms and larger, also dark, parlors.

Once you've chosen a structure compatible with your dreams, you must take care during renovation to ensure that electrical outlets are in the right places, that beds and other furniture will fit between doors and windows, that the floors—whether you're refinishing hardwood or underlaying uneven floors for carpet—will fit with the whole decorating scheme, and that fixtures for bathrooms and hardware for cabinetry complement the rest of the decor.

Be clear and firm about what you want, but temper it with the reality of what people will "buy." If your taste runs to black walls and ominous furniture, you should probably either rethink your taste or go all out for a "haunted" image. Listen to the suggestions of others, and there will be many, but measure them against your own instincts.

To assist you in making the myriad decisions ahead, here's a collection of ideas gleaned from the experience and research of innkeepers.

BEDS

- Where possible, use queen- or king-sized beds. King beds that can be converted to twins provide valuable flexibility in spite of occasional complaints from king bed users about the bump where the beds have been joined.
- A daybed in a spacious room can be made up to accommodate an extra person.
- Antique, hand-carved, and reproduction headboards are impressive focal points.
- Footboards can almost double the cost, but not the effectiveness, of the look. When you buy bed frames, get them without footboards, or use the footboards as heads for other beds. Very tall people can be comfortable in double beds, but not with their feet through the slats of a footboard. Leave it off for tall folks.
- Old doors with beautiful wood can be transformed into headboards.
- An interesting focal point in lieu of a headboard can be achieved by using a large antique map, a large picture or groups of pictures, or by draping the wall.
- Forming corners of drapes around the head of the bed creates a cozy feeling and an economical canopy effect.
- Antique double headboards can be attached to double or queen beds; two antique twin-bed headboards can make one king-sized headboard.
- Firm, comfortable, quiet beds are an investment in guest happiness.
- Sturdy cotton ticking on mattresses helps your sheets stay tight and smooth, unlike brocade covers.
- Pillows can be part of the room's accents: shams on bed pillows, small crocheted covers on throw pillows.
- One king-sized sheet can be made into two pillow shams and a dust ruffle.
- Dust ruffles are a country look and hide bedsprings, but they do make it more difficult to make the bed. Invest in ruffles that fit well.
- Or cover the bedsprings with a coordinated fitted sheet instead of using a ruffle.
- Guests will sleep, sit, make love, and put suitcases on your bedspreads; choose bedspreads with this in mind.
- Have a spare bedspread or two for spills and other emergencies.

BATHS

- Most Americans prefer showers to tub bathing—except at inns, where they frequently request the room with a tub. Use tubs where you can, but plan also to have showers in every room.

- Capitalize on the romance of the tub. Position a large clawfoot tub to take in the river or fireplace view. Whirlpool tubs are becoming increasingly popular and add to room prices, but here, too, placement is even more important than jets. The Rabbit Hill Inn in Lower Waterford, Vermont, placed a tub in the sleeping room, in front of the fireplace, overlooking the valley.
- Shared baths are a thing of the past. As soon as possible, make them private.
- Do include a door to the toilet and shower parts of the room.
- A sink in a guest room (separate from the bath and toilet) is a nice convenience that the owners of Canyon Villa in Sedona, Arizona, incorporated in their built-from-scratch inn. This also works well when space is tight in bathrooms converted from closets.
- Dark grout between tiles makes it easier for you to keep up with the mildew.
- Corian shower walls are easy to clean and always look fresh. And they're available in a marble pattern.
- Fiberglass tub and/or shower units are easy to install and maintain and always look spotless with reasonable cleaning methods.
- Rugs in bathrooms should be removable for washing.
- Be sure you plan enough towel bars in the bathroom for hanging the wet towels that your environmentally conscious guest has opted not to have washed every day.
- All towel bars, grab bars, and toilet paper holders need to be solidly attached either into a stud or with toggle bolts. If you don't do this in the beginning, you will do it in the end.
- Brass fixtures in the bathroom are old-fashioned and initially attractive, but they're costly and hard work to maintain.
- Install sinks in antique dressers to match your decor.
- Waterproof-fabric shower curtains launder well and quickly; apply a spot cleaner to the hem (which shows the dirt first) and put them in the washing machine with towels.
- Avoid shower curtain hooks that take both hands. The more difficult it is to unclip the shower curtain, the less often you and your staff will wash it.
- For fabric shower curtains to be used with a plastic liner, use a sheet, making buttonholes for the rings.
- Smooth glass doors for showers clean more easily than pebbly ones.
- Sliding shower doors keep the water in its place, but the tracks are hard to keep clean.
- Plan plenty of space in bathrooms for makeup and shaving gear.

If you are on a septic tank or in an area where water is at a premium, consider installing an outdoor hot tub. Since the water is reused, you will need to meet health department requirements for a public pool. It is very romantic to look up through the trees at the stars. You can enclose the tub, inviting guests to make reservations for it upon check-in, or put a tub on a private guest room patio for that room's occupants only. When the tub is available to all guests, you are likely to increase occupancy, but perhaps not guest room prices. A hot tub has become an expected necessity in ski areas. The Old Miner's Lodge in Park City, Utah, has a tub that guests scoop the snow from to climb in and soothe their ski-sore muscles.

LIGHTING

- Guests want reading lights on both sides of the bed and lights for shaving and applying makeup.
- Plan carefully: start with light sources for specific purposes like bed reading, makeup, and chair reading, and then determine if they're enough.
- A designer suggests that three or more lights are most flattering to rooms and guests because shadows are less harsh.
- Overhead lights are rarely installed today, but don't remove existing overheads. Just put in a rheostat so guests can adjust the light intensity to suit their mood. Or install a fancy fan and fixture.
- Lamps installed on the bedside wall do not take up table space. Neither do floor lamps, but they're knocked over more easily.
- Modern lamps in brass or china can complement an old-fashioned decor, and they're sturdier than true antiques and meet UL (Underwriters Lab) requirements.
- Old lampshades add a special flavor to rooms, but they're difficult to find and expensive to custom-order.
- Adequate lighting is a problem in most inns and hotels. Be sure you purchase lights that can safely accommodate one-hundred-watt bulbs. A lamp with a higher wattage bulb than approved for it can not only burn the lampshade but also cause wiring fires in the building.
- Dark lampshades reduce the lumens available to light the room. Use them where the light that escapes out the bottom or top is directed where you want it, like over a headboard rather than next to the bed.

- Candles should not be part of lighting. Fire danger and furniture damage is too great.
- Every room should have a romance light that can be turned down low enough to see but not to read. Leave this one on after you turn down the beds.

FIRST IMPRESSIONS

- The entryway sets the tone for a stay and can entice a potential guest, so the first impression is important. Use a handsome antique desk, a cabinet, or a cheerful bouquet. The entryway is a priority decorating job.
- How your inn looks to passersby involves primarily landscaping and gardens, but don't forget to step out onto the street and assess your curtains, for neatness, and your lighting, for warmth. A porch swing or a well-placed armoire visible through an upstairs window can contribute to your image.
- Wood and marble surfaces add richness to rooms. Guests appreciate them and generally are careful to protect them. The occasional water rings or iron marks are easily repaired.
- Marble surfaces are less susceptible to inadvertent guest damage, but they are also easier to overlook when cleaning; watch for barely visible rings and dust.
- Don't be so concerned with being true to the period that you provide no comfortable furniture. A few good pieces with tasteful coordinates can give an impression of consistency.
- A round table with a cloth draped to the floor adds softness and an extra surface to the room. Make the table inexpensively from a round piece of plywood and a pedestal foot from the home building-supply store, or buy an unfinished "decorator table."
- Varathane in a satin finish is good protection for fine wood surfaces.
- Dressers, shelves, closets, cupboards, and luggage racks should be selected based on the probable length of stay of your guests. Overnighters generally don't need a full dresser; guests staying longer than two days need space to store things outside their suitcases.
- If possible, guest rooms should have at least one comfortable chair.
- When stripping woodwork, remember that some of it is ugly and soft. Don't take on a stripping project without carefully evaluating whether the finished product will be worth the work.
- Window seats are a charming way to add seating, and can also be used to store blankets and pillows.
- Trunks are another decorating feature that doubles as storage.

- Quilted material for window-seat cushions softens the hard edges of cut foam, and it's durable.
- Velcro makes cushion covers easy to remove for washing.
- Cover imperfect dresser tops with crocheted doilies.
- Glass covers to protect dresser tops and tables are easy to clean, and they prevent mars.
- Mirrors can solve space problems by creating illusions of distance.
- Utilitarian mirror placement: over the sink and long enough for short and tall users; a full-length or large, tilting, over-the-dresser mirror to dress with; a lighted or small, movable tabletop mirror for makeup and hair.

WALL SURFACES

- Paint is the cheapest and easiest way to create a mood in a room.
- Painted woodwork: many old houses are dark, and can benefit from tasteful paint jobs.
- Wallpaper can hide many defects in old, repaired walls that might otherwise need resurfacing.
- Wallpaper will take incidental scuffs and scrapes without showing them.
- Wallpaper can set a tone for a room and be the starting place for the whole decorating scheme.
- Use soft things to absorb sound. Replace shutters with drapes, use tablecloths on hard dressers, and hang quilts on the wall.
- Stencil borders on walls and ceiling.
- Wallpaper accents are economical: paper a ceiling, just one wall, or halfway up the walls.
- Use a strip of wallpaper border in a painted room, around the ceiling or to frame a bed, fireplace, baseboard, or doorway. The illustrations in wallpaper sample books are a good resource for ideas.
- Paint can be creatively applied, achieving many of the benefits of wallpaper, by using sponges, rolled rags, or other items to add visual texture.
- Good vinyl-coated wallpaper is easier to maintain than paint is.
- Using the same semigloss paint on all walls that get regular scuffing in entryways or on stairs makes touch-ups easy.
- Stain and prime woodwork before installing it as trim. Then just fill in the nail holes.
- To reduce sound transmission between walls and through unused doorways,

consider installing a foam or masonite wall panel or fitted doorway panel covered with fabric.

FLOORS

- Paint and stencil a "rug" on a wood floor.
- Wood floors are beautiful, but they're noisy. Plan to use large rugs in the room, and runners in hallways and on stairs.
- Before you choose an expensive refinishing job for your wood floors, consider the folk-art look of painting them.
- Different color carpets in each guest room add interest.
- Dark carpets show lint; light carpets show spots.
- Investigate the new, easy-care surfaces for refinishing wood floors. In a satin finish, they can produce a look very much like waxed floors.

WINDOWS

- Professional installation of good-quality window shades is worth the money. A shade installed slightly askew will wear out faster.
- An alternative to blinds is an underlayer of blackout-fabric curtains on big rings to slide easily behind your regular curtains.
- Use window coverings for energy conservation, noise insulation, privacy, and light control, as well as decoration. Line them to extend their lives and accommodate late sleepers.
- Guests want the privacy provided by window coverings even if only the cows can see them.

ACCESSORIES

- Bedspreads can be tablecloths, tablecloths can be curtains, and comforters can be upholstery. Be creative.
- One good old quilt can provide fabric for several pillows, framed wall hangings, and quilted wreaths. Use the little scraps to make Christmas tree ornaments.
- Use wreaths for artwork on walls; make them of vines, herbs, fabric, and so on.
- Frame illustrations from old books. Use photos from family albums. Save handsome old calendars. Use them all for wall decoration.

- Switch plates and outlet covers can be made attractive with wallpaper or brass or wood covers.
- Make or buy linenlike easy-care cloth napkins bordered with lace.
- Solid-color napkins show stains more than print ones do. Whites can be bleached.
- If you permit smoking, provide ashtrays and matches.
- Set out books and magazines.
- Plants, dolls, old teddy bears, ducks, and shells and bottles from the beach can make a room look human and inviting. A Victorian dress or hat on a rack is another nice touch.
- However, if a room looks full before the guest arrives, it will be difficult to enjoy. Put objects in spaces guests don't need—hatboxes atop the armoire, for example. Leave valuable surface space for the guests.
- Provide two luggage racks or other accommodation for two open suitcases, since usually two people will use the room.

COLOR

- Color evokes a look, creates an ambience, and changes space perceptions. You can also target customers—upper-class, male or female, and so on—by choosing certain colors.
- Dark colors or patterns make a room smaller but hide incidental spots on bedspreads and rugs. Light colors and white expand space and look fresh, but must be cleaned more often.
- Guests seem to choose first the rooms with dark and light contrast or rooms that are bright and airy. A monochromatic color scheme is less inviting and less memorable, yet the right single-color use enhances the serenity of a room.
- Accent a simple door with paint, highlighting the panels.
- A common color running through your rooms will mean you can use the same color towels and tissues for all of them.
- Avoid ice-blue color schemes in cold climates; avoid red in hot areas. Simple changes in your basic color scheme—different throw pillows and table coverings, for example—can warm rooms for winter and cool them for summer.

MISCELLANEOUS

- Make scale drawings of rooms, measuring and marking window locations, doors, fireplaces, and built-ins. Use scale furniture pieces for model arrangements and to help you figure appropriate sizes of pieces to be purchased.

- Before you renovate a room, evaluate it very carefully. Don't incur the expense of cutting in a skylight when a lighter color paint would do the trick.
- Use closets as part of the decor. Remove the doors, wallpaper the walls in a coordinated print, and make them dressing rooms.
- Keep a notebook on decorating ideas gleaned from visits to other inns, magazines, and restoration museums.
- Don't overlook the possibility of involving a decorator or designer, especially if you have more than five rooms to do. You'll save time and possibly money, when you consider the decorator's discount purchasing power.

Before you decorate, and then on a regular schedule during your life as an innkeeper, stay a night in every room. Notice noise, cobwebs, ceiling-paint problems, lighting, mirrors, water pressure, and hot-water supply. These are all areas that affect guest comfort tremendously. And guest comfort is your chief objective.

Amenities

The amenities are the extras, and there are as many philosophies about providing these special surprises to your guests as there are innkeepers. The range of possibilities is also very broad. Here are things to consider when planning what you would like to offer.

- What do *you* especially appreciate when you travel?
- What will help your guests be comfortable in your area? Umbrellas and boots may be the perfect surprise for visitors to a rainy climate.
- What will make the visit more enjoyable? This could be anything from bikes to hot tubs.
- What is characteristic of your area? Wineglasses, salt-water taffy, or apples?
- What will increase your competitive edge? When people call and ask about prices, what amenities will make your inn look like a good value? What will encourage a guest to come back? Balance the cost of an amenity against its effectiveness.
- Do you have the energy and the money to continue to provide the amenity? For example, bowls of fresh fruit in each room are a cinch when the orchard is full but expensive in winter. Turning down beds may mean hiring extra staff when you plan to go out to dinner.
- Would guests miss it if you didn't provide it?

- What problems would providing it cause to other guests? Television in a game room is a plus to some guests, a minus to others, and the sound may carry up the stairs to the guest rooms.
- How will you feel if once every two years a guest takes the entire basket of bubble-bath envelopes from the bathroom?

Also keep in mind that the amenities you provide can and should reinforce your inn's image. Things guests take home should continue to remind them of your inn and their lovely experience there. If you can provide things guests will take to work or share with others, your amenities can extend your marketing program even further.

Here are the pluses—and in some cases the minuses—of various choices.

Flowers. The rose garden you established to create curb appeal can also be a good source of cut flowers, as well as petals to dry for potpourri. Fresh flowers make rooms smell good as well as look lovely. When cut flowers are out of season and expensive, consider flowering plants that will survive indoors, such as poinsettia, impatiens, and flowering bulbs.

Candy. Some inns put mints on pillows when they turn down the beds. At other inns, a candy jar in the parlor is a sweet stop on the way back from dinner.

Turndown Service. There's something about returning from dinner to a freshened room with lights low and bed open that makes you feel pampered. Five-star hotels must provide this, so it's a posh service. On the other hand, it can be a difficult service to staff, as you must hire someone to do it if you want to go out for the evening, and they'll have to wait around, watching for guests to leave for dinner. It can also cause problems for guests: interrupted naps, lovemaking, and so on. On the other hand, it can give the innkeeper an opportunity for a conversation with quieter guests, as well as a chance to remove wet towels from antique furniture pieces.

Menu Book. Guests really appreciate a menu book or basket of current best-restaurant menus. It also saves an innkeeper from spending hours making recommendations! Also consider a blank "restaurant-critique book," where guests can write their impressions.

Evening Beverage Service. If your parlor is comfortable for gathering, a "wine time" encourages it. Inns should also provide something nonalcoholic, such as soft drinks, mineral water and lime, lemonade, or iced tea. At some inns, guests are specifically invited to this evening gathering; at others, they're just informed that there will be drinks in the parlor at such-and-such time. Some inns serve hors d'oeuvres. This is a prime time for innkeepers and guests to spend together.

TV Area. At the Bath Street Inn, the Olympics was the catalyst for bringing a television into the inn. It's in a third-floor alcove, separate from the guest rooms.

Guests watch evening news, favorite programs, or whatever they want; it's especially appreciated by business travelers there on their own.

Videocassette Deck and Videotapes. If there's little to do in your area in the evenings, you might provide a library of classic films.

Stereo and CDs or Tapes. Choose music that you enjoy to enhance the inn's ambience.

Library. This can be a separate room or a corner of the parlor, with well-stocked bookcases and a selection of magazines. Your choice of reading material can reveal your personal tastes, and can also establish an image.

Spa, Tennis Court, Swimming Pool. Any or all of them, if provided in such a way as not to detract from the peacefulness guests desire, are pluses that will attract people.

Telephone. A small desk, message pad and pencil, directories, and good light make a comfortable spot for phone calls in a private alcove or in guest rooms.

Bathroom Items. Oversized towels or clean towels twice a day are luxurious. You might provide a basket for carrying toiletries to a shared bathroom, or stock your bathrooms with soaps, shampoos, and shaving cream.

Personal-Needs Items. Bathrobes, an iron and ironing board, and a hair dryer or blower all fit this category.

Oversized Beds. People who have king-sized beds at home will find it difficult to sleep in a standard double bed. You can order converter rails to make your antique double beds accommodate queen-sized mattresses. You can also use two twin beds together for a king.

Extra Pillows. Shams for sitting up and reading in bed are especially nice in rooms too small for easy chairs. Fancy neck rolls and heart-shaped pillows are other nice extras.

Welcome Services. Some inns offer a beverage to refresh arriving guests. Others carry luggage and provide airport pickup. A welcome tour of the inn and its services is basic to all inns.

Room Keys. Customers like the option of locking their rooms when they're out. You can ask a locksmith to make keys that will open the inn entry door and separate room doors. For example, at Ten Inverness Way, every guest room key opens the front entry door, but no one guest room key can open any other guest room.

All-Day Coffee and Tea Service. It's much appreciated, and easy and inexpensive to provide in vacuum serving bottles or by piping a hot-and-cold-water faucet in a marble sideboard with a small sink.

Dinner Reservation Service. This is simple to do and makes guests feel special. Because restaurants get frequent reservations from innkeepers, they often give your guests better service and more attention than they'd otherwise receive, and restaurateurs may return the favor, sending a late dinner guest your way.

Bicycles. This depends on your area, but if it's a nice place to bike, the bikes will be used and appreciated. Check with your insurance agent first, and provide helmets. The Bath Street Inn provides a coupon to a bike rental shop handy to the bike path, which is actually cheaper than bike maintenance, fitted helmets, and insurance would be.

Picnic Lunches. Provide them yourself, make arrangements with another supplier, or send guests to a nearby deli for do-it-yourself lunches.

Social Director. You'll be asked, and should be able to say, where to bike, ride horses, play tennis or golf, jog, hike, find antiques, see the best scenery, and get Burt Reynolds's autograph.

Postcards and Stationery. A nice giveaway that does your promoting for you! Some inns provide stamps and do the mailing.

Airport, Train, or Bus Pickup. This can be expensive in terms of insurance required, time, and gasoline, but if it's practical for you to do, it makes guests feel special.

Refrigerator. Guests like to have a place to store the oysters they brought back from the beach, to chill the wine they picked up on a tour, and to hold their doggy bags from dinner until it's time to go home. And both of you will like it when they can get ice at midnight without disturbing an innkeeper.

Miscellaneous. Games; coloring books and crayons; jigsaw puzzles; popcorn maker, stocked and ready; Polaroid camera to take pictures of guests for their albums; coffee mugs to take home; cuttings from your herb garden; and seasonal items, like heart-shaped cookies for Valentine's Day, Christmas ornaments, and Easter eggs.

Amenities are a good topic to brainstorm about with your partners. Silly things may be perfect for your inn, or you may feel that only the most elegant items reflect the image you've chosen. Whatever your direction, be innovative and have fun with this!

Sources and Suppliers

Before you buy basic inn items, check the Web site of the Professional Association of Innkeepers International (www.paii.org), then peruse the Yellow Pages for industry suppliers. Motel equipment in your Craftsman bungalow? Of course you won't use motel bedspreads and frames, but under the covers, inn beds are strikingly similar to beds in other top-quality lodgings. You can say the same for soap, towels, and tablecloths, as well as other necessities, and the discounts can be excellent.

If you find the perfect brass fixtures at a retail shop, contact the manufacturer directly and ask about industry prices, particularly when you can buy in quantity—even small quantities. Remember, however, that what you purchase in your small town may be more promptly repaired there as well.

Industry suppliers can also provide solutions to problems that you will not have encountered as a householder. For example, buying hand and body soaps by the gallon to refill attractive dispensers in guest bathrooms is not only cheaper, it is both more environmentally sensitive and convenient than stocking dozens of sixteen-ounce refill bottles.

During renovation, ask your contractors to introduce you to local suppliers of paint and plumbing and electrical supplies, and then establish your own account with them, with a trade discount.

Discount food warehouses are rarely the bargain you would expect. Price food carefully, with an eye to quality. For inns of twelve rooms or less, you're probably better off shopping at a local grocery; discuss volume discounts with them.

Don't buy retail linens until you check wholesale prices. How to find a linen supplier for your area? Look in the Yellow Pages under Linens for "Wholesale Items" and be sure you find a lodging-industry supplier, not just a wholesaler who sells to retail stores. Frequently you may find that wholesale prices will not beat your local retailer when linens are on sale, but check anyway.

An advantage to using industry linen suppliers is consistency: you can choose a type and color of towel and know you'll be able to add to your stock and buy matching replacements year after year. If you use good quality but simple white or pastel sheets, you can often buy them by the dozen at a good price.

Other ways to identify good suppliers? Attend state or national innkeepers conferences where there are exhibitors serving the inn industry. Ask your colleagues. Check innkeepers publications, particularly the classified ads in *innkeeping* newsletter and www.paii.org.

When you contact wholesale suppliers, use your inn stationery. You're a member of the lodging industry, so ask confidently for industry prices, especially for quantity purchases.

so—you want to
serve dinner

Breathes there a (prospective) innkeeper with soul so dead
That never to herself hath said,
"Why don't we serve dinners?
We already have the kitchen!"

The real question about serving dinner is not why don't we, but why *should* we? As any successful hotelier or innkeeper will tell you, "The bucks are in the beds." You need a very good reason to justify the expense, time, and effort required daily to serve meals, even if only to your overnight guests.

Not-so-great reasons are:

You throw wonderful dinner parties and have always wanted your own restaurant.

The previous owners served dinner.

You have a wonderful space to host dinners.

You feel pressured to be a "real" inn by serving food.

You love to eat.

The really good reasons to serve dinner are guest-centered:

- If you have only one good restaurant in town, you might find that guests will stay longer if you serve dinner. High-quality restaurants are important to attract inn guests.

- If you are located in a seasonal area where few restaurants stay open in the off-season, consider offering a few special package weekends that include dinner. The meals could be prepared by you in advance during the week, by a local caterer with you serving, or by special arrangement with a local restaurant or country inn that might be pleased to open and have guaranteed guests for the weekend. Gradually increase the number of weekends as you become more successful.

- If you are located some distance from restaurants, making traveling at night in bad weather a hazard, consider developing a favorite menu that is easy to prepare and have ready at the last minute. Offer your guests a hot bowl of chili with homemade bread and a salad, followed by a heaping platter of brownies. A formal, several-course dinner isn't necessary when you are doing this almost as a favor. If the problem is that restaurants in your town normally close early and your guests often show up late and hungry on Friday night, consider offering a platter of fruit and cheese from a local deli with a bowl of hot chowder; you won't want to be up much later than the restaurateurs are.

Look around at local country inns. Ask yourself a few questions: Do other inns in your area comparable to yours serve dinner? Why do they do it? Are they successful? Do the innkeepers do the cooking or do they have a chef?

Maybe you just love to cook and truly want to try your hand at this new venture. We can't give you all the answers about operating a full-service restaurant or even regular dining for guests; that's a book in itself. But we'll give you an overview of meal service as a possible additional inn feature. Read on.

Types of Meal Service

Formal sit-down dinners with many choices prepared by a chef are not the only dinner-service options, and they are too ambitious and costly for most innkeepers. But before we give you some other ideas, a couple of definitions will clarify how innkeepers approach meal service: Modified American Plan (MAP) means that breakfast and dinner are included in the price of the room. American Plan (AP) indicates that all meals are included in the price of the room. European Plan (EP) means you get the room only. Bed-and-breakfast means just that.

Here are a few of the distinctive ways inns serve dinner:

- Guests are invited to dinner in the Victorian dining room. They "dress" for dinner, then gather for a glass of wine in the parlor, a few appetizers, and conversation with the innkeeper. The doors swing open to several intimate tables set around a formal dining room with a crystal chandelier. Dinner is served as if you were a guest in someone's home, except you pay for it. It is a one-seating, fixed-price meal served only to inn guests with a set menu varied only for health or vegetarian reasons. This option provides the greatest possible control over food and labor costs.
- Guests of an eight-room inn down a country lane dress casually for dinner after a long day of cross-country skiing. They help themselves to drinks at the honor bar, then are seated at staggered times for a fixed-price meal, their choice of entrees having been selected when the room was reserved. Wine is ordered when the guests are seated.
- A local caterer dressed in tie and tails brings a romantic dinner to the guests' room; the guests have selected the menu prior to their arrival. The table is set and the meal delivered as in room service at a hotel, but all courses are left to the guests to serve in the privacy of their room. The inn owner collects the

dishes and the payment, and keeps 10 percent of the overall charge. Or the caterer brings dinner and serves it on inn china and silver in the inn dining room while the sun sets over the Rocky Mountains. The innkeepers drop in to say hello, and the caterer cleans it all up, leaving the kitchen ready for serving breakfast the next morning.

Country Inn: To Do or Not to Do a Full-Service Country Inn

Ed Butler and Les Schoof each had his own list of requirements for the perfect inn. After a couple of years of looking, they'd found several close calls, but no perfect match. One day, inn business consultant Bill Oates called to say that there was one more property they really should see.

The Notchland Inn in Hart's Location, New Hampshire, was it! It had the magical combination of character, historical significance, rooms with fireplaces, and a location near natural swimming and was surrounded by the beauty of the magnificent mountains and a national forest. It was, however, some distance to nearby restaurants. This fact went temporarily unnoticed since Les and Ed had planned to buy an inn that served dinner.

Over the past ten years, the Notchland Inn has done a superb job of presenting a five-course, multichoice dinner. For the first several years, dinner was served nightly. Ed muses, "One could say that providing dinner provides us another opportunity to interact and care for our guests—and that is very good. Having dinner service helps to create the Notchland experience. However, having to manage a small restaurant adds layers of effort, overhead, responsibility, and lots of extra work that is considerably more impressive than one might first assume."

Then they discovered there was no negative impact to their business if they took one night off. Two years later, dinners were reduced to five nights a week, and that's where they plan to stay. "Frankly, if we had it to do over again," Ed declares, "we would seriously reconsider buying a place that required dinner service. Don't get us wrong; we love where we live and the truly exciting challenge of running our inn. But, learning from our own experience and that of other innkeepers, we believe that next time we would opt to have the potential for additional personal time and choose the flexibility afforded by a bed-and-breakfast inn over a full-service country inn."

- Guests gather around a roaring fire in the great room, which opens to the kitchen, where everyone chats with the innkeepers as they prepare a family-style dinner. Guests help themselves to down-home country fare from serving dishes on each table. The fixed menu for the evening is selected and prepared by the innkeepers and served by an abbreviated staff, which also cleans up with one dishwasher and the innkeepers while the guests dine. MAP only.
- In a primarily bed-and-breakfast inn, a six-course dinner is served by a self-trained chef-innkeeper only on Saturday after a social hour. The set menu is posted on the blackboard in the combined living and dining room area as guests check in, so they can express any dietary restrictions. Tables can be for couples or combined for those who became friends during the social hour. This is the only inn in town serving dinner; they have had more media coverage than others in town because of their fine though infrequent dining. MAP only.
- When guests arrive, they are asked if they would like to dine at the inn. A reservation is made with the inn's public restaurant. Guests gather at the bar and chat with the bartender. A hostess seats them in a large room that overlooks the lake. A menu with a wide range of items is presented, and dinner proceeds with fine service and food. A bill is presented upon completion and is paid at the time or charged to the guest's room.

  Meals other than dinner and breakfast are also prepared by innkeepers to please their guests:
  - Picnic baskets for romantic in-room fireside or outside summer picnics.
  - Lunches for meetings held at the inn.
  - Theme teas for locals.

Personal Preparation

Having a restaurant or even just serving ten people will involve you, the owner, even if you plan to hire out for everything. Your inn's reputation will be resting on the success of the kitchen. So consider carefully:

- Do you want to cook? Without an accomplished chef or a great cook, your meals may be ho-hum, from the viewpoint of what is a very discriminating inngoing public. Your food need not be haute cuisine, but it does need to be tasty, fresh, attractive, and well prepared. Everyone who knows how to cook, or even eat, will tell you what is wrong with your style. You need an intact ego to prepare food for people who are paying you to cook. They are not like your family and friends, who can just laugh off the burned rice. At the same time, you must have an innkeeper with the personality to motivate, cajole, train, assist, and interact between the front and the back of the dining room; without this the food has no soul. Often, innkeeper schmoozing completes the experience for the guests. If you're cooking, who'll be the innkeeper?

- Do you have previous food service experience? How much and in what capacity? Having been a waiter or even kitchen help does not give you the experience you'll need for ordering, pricing, and supervising all aspects of a restaurant. Consider taking culinary and management classes at a local college, and working at a local restaurant. Even volunteering to do quantity cooking at a local homeless shelter will give you some practical experience.
- If you have a dinner staff and they all get sick or quit (which will happen), can you pull off dinner yourself at an acceptable quality level without affecting the other part of your business or the total guest experience? For how long?
- If you have no food experience, do you know someone you can hire to help you? Are you prepared to pay for consulting advice? Are you prepared to take that advice even if you may not like it?
- Running a restaurant is not just cooking and serving. A background in business and accounting is helpful in dealing with the increase in paperwork and reporting to governmental agencies. Handling administrative details and being organized is key. If you have a chef, you may not need to know food, but you must be tremendously organized and be a great motivator.

Is Your Building Ready?

Seating twenty people for dinner requires space not only to dine but also to store, refrigerate, serve, and cook the food, plus do the dishes afterward. Because more extensive cooking is involved in serving dinner, governmental agencies will be more interested in you. Can you handle this?

- Do you already have a commercial kitchen? If not, what would you have to do to make your kitchen "dinner ready"? Approval for a bed-and-breakfast generally does not ensure approval for dinner service.
- Are you zoned for dinner service? If not, what is the process? This is crucial, because it generally requires not only additional health department regulations but more parking and additional fire-safety requirements. Often, inns are not located in areas that allow liquor licenses, even if you can serve dinner.
- Do you have the equipment, including dishware and flatware, to present dinner? What would you have to buy? How much would that cost? Do you have that in the bank? You will most likely need to subsidize your dinner service in the

beginning. If you aren't financially ready to open the doors and operate for a while at a loss, think again.

- Does a food distributor service your area? If there is only one distributor, will you be a hostage to their standards of quality, costs, and service? If you serve dinner to a small number of people only on weekends, minimum order requirements may be unreasonable. Many innkeepers drive to discount stores forty minutes away to buy products they are unable to obtain from their one available supply house.
- Do you have a place to serve dinner that doesn't get in the way of your guests before and after dinner? It is important to evaluate the space accurately, but this is not an exact science, and it's complicated by the odd spaces available in inns. Some rules of thumb apply. Allow twenty-four to thirty-two square feet per seat for the *entire* food service space, including dining, serving, and dish-washing areas, and "ideal" kitchen space. Or, to look at it another way, production areas, including receiving, storage, preparation, cooking, and dish and pot washing require eight to twelve square feet per seat, while twelve to eighteen square feet per seat is estimated for the dining room. You'll need the larger space for luxury table service, with room on the table for flowers, a variety of crystal, silver, glasses, and side dishes accompanying the main course. Space in the aisles for fine dining needs to be large enough to accommodate iced wine buckets and the wait staff's tray stand.
- Would you serve wine? Do you need a liquor license? Can guests bring their own wine? Wine is the minimum service most guests expect, and since labor is less than on food, it's profitable.
- Are food smells from dinner going to interfere with sleeping? Are noises from the kitchen at night going to keep guests up? Dishwashers can be loud, and they are the last to shut down at night. You need a good fan system in the kitchen, which can also be noisy without proper insulation. And even with insulation, a fan just underneath a bedroom window is annoying.
- Can you handle increased quantities of garbage, trash, and recycling?

You can reduce your time and costs with a single-price, one-entree, one-seating meal without taking away from a guest's experience.

KITCHEN DESIGN

Create the menu, then design the kitchen. Or create the menu based on your existing kitchen. The wide range of possible dining services you might provide precludes a detailed list of kitchen equipment and space requirements. For example, if you plan to serve family-style, you will need ample serving dishes but not so many side plates, while if you plan to plate the salads early you'll need refrigerator storage space.

LARGE EQUIPMENT

In most cases you will already have a kitchen in place, with stove, oven, refrigerator, storage, and prep space. Plan a menu and practice preparing it there. If you do need equipment, such as commercial dishwashers or a larger range, buy used equipment. Restaurants are always going out of business (think about it!), and a great deal of good used, reasonably priced kitchen equipment can be purchased. Replace large kitchen equipment if it's old and doesn't work very well, it's an energy hog, or it's obsolete and you can't find parts. Consider first the cost to fix your existing equipment, what its useful life will be after replacement, the cost of a new one over a used one, and how much you'll need it for the present or future menu.

SMALL EQUIPMENT

The items guests actually eat with and on and that you use in preparing the food will again depend on what you serve. Here is a basic set for dinners; numbers will be higher, of course, if you do weddings or banquets:

Dishes: two per seat if you use different plates for dinner than for breakfast. Specific pieces depend on your menu.

Silver: two per seat; specific pieces depend on menu.

Linens: three per table for cloths, and three per seat for napkins.

Miscellaneous table items such as salt and pepper shakers, sugar bowl and creamer, vases, etc.: 1.5 per table

Coffee and tea service will depend on how you plan to pour.

Equipment such as a cleanup rack for dirty dishes and the container you use to clear dishes from the table need to be chosen as you walk through the dining process.

Here is where your organizational skills come into play. To serve wine, you need a corkscrew to open bottles, and a place to put them. To take food to a room, you will need a tray.

Who Will Do This Extra Work?

Serving dinner is much more labor-intensive than offering a guest room, so looking at the staff required is important. With an inn, if you get all the rooms cleaned in time for check-in, you are pretty well home free until breakfast if your staff members don't show up. When you serve dinner, you'll need three times as much staff. More questions:

- Do you like to cook? Even if you hire a chef, at some time you will inevitably end up actually cooking. Understanding the food-preparation process and enjoying it gives you a basis for supervising a chef.
- Do you have a reasonable labor market in your area for servers, kitchen helpers, dishwashers, and so on? Could you do it all yourself? A rural inn located twenty to thirty minutes from anywhere else may have difficulty getting staff to come to work. Some inns in tourist areas find that there are not enough wait staff and cleaning staff to meet the needs of all the hotels, restaurants, and inns.
- If you are the cook and your partner is the server, is there anyone else to take care of guests' needs? Who answers the phone, turns down the bed, or fixes the clogged sink when you are carving the roast?
- Do you have at least an extra three to five hours every day to plan, prepare, and present dinner? Do you have an extra two hours to supervise planning, preparing, and presenting dinner?
- Would all guests be required to dine at the inn? If not, how will you know how many will be dining? Keeping a close count for dinner is as important as it is in renting a room. You will need to know your staff and food-preparation needs in advance. Including dinner in the room price (Modified American Plan) is a way to control the dinner count. You will need to present this additional amenity properly on the phone; otherwise your price will appear too high when compared with those of bed-and-breakfast inns. If your average guest stay is three to four nights, you might want to consider not requiring MAP all nights, and encourage guests to go somewhere else one night. (Just be sure you tell them what night it is.)

What staff will you need? Here are some basic minimums:

- Sufficient housekeeping staff to allow for daily cleaning of the dining room.
- One chef or cook, perhaps you.
- One server for each twelve diners; you'll need more servers for anything greater than a single-plate presentation and wine service—for instance, if you're serving appetizer, soup, and salad courses. The server also clears dishes in a small dining room.

- One preparation assistant, dishwasher, and all-around helper in the kitchen and dining room; this person could be a second server or a kitchen assistant.
- One combined host and cashier, perhaps you.

If you are serving dinner to outside diners as well as inn guests, you will need to plan for public bathroom cleanup and cleaning the parking area.

Staffing Techniques

One of the most difficult tasks in a restaurant, whether a small dining room serving only your inn guests or a larger room open to the public, is scheduling servers. You can end up with too many waitpeople on one night, too few on another; no matter what you do, service and your bottom line seem to suffer.

As you develop your dining room you will determine an acceptable level of service and quality. The next, often overlooked, step is to develop labor standards, or the number of labor hours required to perform each task to your acceptable level. Time spent in the analysis of each position and shift will help you determine accurately how many people to schedule on each shift to achieve the desired level of service.

POSITION PERFORMANCE ANALYSIS

For one week, carefully watch the servers during the dinner shift. Daily, note how many people each server handled and the number of hours worked, thereby determining the number of guests per labor-hour. Make comments on your analysis sheet as to the quality of service, such as "Service was even," "Too rushed," or "Not enough to do."

You may be surprised to learn that your standards require more or fewer servers than you initially believed. After the week, you will be able to judge the ideal number of guests who can be accommodated by each employee. This position performance analysis can be done for each job classification: server, busser, runner, even housekeeper.

THE STAFFING GUIDE

Next, create a staffing guide. A staffing guide lists the labor standards you have set during your position performance analysis and shows the number of employees needed based on your varying business levels. Use the guide with your forecast to create a schedule. The guide not only helps you in your weekly or biweekly scheduling of servers, but can also aid you in controlling labor costs before it's too late.

After you set up the number of scheduled labor-hours, convert hours to dollars and develop a forecasted daily labor cost. By comparing scheduled hours and dollars to actual hours and dollars, you will have a positive or negative daily variance factor. Using this tool will enable you to adjust hours as needed to meet projected costs for the week.

Unless you do a single seating per evening, where all servers are on the same service sequence, the business flow is rarely constant throughout a shift. There will be busy, slow, and even times. To avoid having staff standing around waiting to rush, consider staggering work shifts. One server should arrive early to set up the room, with the second server arriving just before the guests do, giving you maximum coverage when needed. The server who arrived first leaves first, and the second server handles the last table(s) and dining room reset. This method gives you greater efficiency and fewer wasted dollars.

Sample Variable Staffing Guide
(Based on Position Performance Analysis)

Number of Guests	Breakfast (7 to 10 A.M.)			Dinner (6 to 10 P.M.)		
	Host hours	Server hours	Busser hours	Host hours	Server hours	Busser hours
1–10	0	4	0	0	6	0
11–20	0	8	0	0	12	0
21–30	0	12	0	4	12	4

CROSS-TRAINING

On evenings when your staffing guide shows you to be right on the edge of needing another server or requiring a host, cross-training can help. If a busser has been properly trained, he or she can pitch in and take a table. The assistant innkeeper or dining room supervisor can fill in as host during a busy hour in lieu of another person who would be scheduled for a full shift. Cross-training allows you to trim a few hours here or there, which can add up to a significant amount over a period of a week, and certainly throughout the year. In some inns the wait staff also turn down beds during slower seasons in lull periods of dining.

Don't be afraid to adjust the work schedule. Give your staff request forms to hand in at the beginning of one month for the next month (or longer if you need more time). Try to accommodate your staff, and they will usually work better with you. Let your staff know that in case of cancellations, more reservations, or staff illness, you will adjust the schedule. Ask for volunteers to stay home or to be "on call." (Of course, be certain to comply with any legal regulations in your area.) Work daily to keep labor hours under control. An extra labor-hour a day at $5 adds up to $35 a week, and $140 a month more than you projected. Did you really need that extra hour?

USE THE TOOLS

Labor-hours can be an invisible thief. You can lose money without being aware of it. Your dinner is served from 6 P.M. to 10 P.M. and you have always scheduled your three servers from 5 P.M. to 11 P.M., even though your busy time is 7 P.M. to 9 P.M. Schedule one server from 5 P.M. to 9 P.M., one from 6 P.M. to 10 P.M., and one from 7 P.M. to 11 P.M. You now have twelve labor-hours instead of eighteen, with essentially the same coverage.

Forecasts, staffing guides, and schedules are tools to use daily, not merely as weekly exercises. Too often, innkeepers create the forecast, guide, and schedule, and then forget about them. Learn from your business and use the tools to make adjustments that are more efficient and effective. Spending a little bit of time each day for analysis of readily available information will not only save money but can also help you improve service. And service is key.

Hiring a Chef

Even the most experienced innkeeper seems to dread the prospect of hiring and managing a chef. It is a serious task, but nothing to panic about. True, an inn chef is an extremely important member of the staff, and qualified applicants will rarely walk through the front door. But if you need a chef, there are some easy steps you can take to find potential candidates.

Before you do anything, pour a cup of coffee and close yourself in the office with no distractions. Decide:

What do you want the chef to do?
- Will he or she only cook dinner? Will the chef ever have to prepare breakfast or special parties?
- Who will do the ordering? Is this a chef responsibility, your responsibility, or is it done jointly?
- Who does the inventory? Who manages other kitchen staff or wait staff?
- Who supplies uniforms?
- Who creates the menus?
- If you do all of the menu planning, is there any room for the chef's creativity?
- How much are you willing to pay?
- Is there any bonus or incentive for increased revenues or lowered food costs?

Too often, we hire someone after describing only part of the job. In fairness to yourself and your employee, think about the scope of the job in advance so your new chef can begin with realistic expectations. Create a job description based on your consideration of the position and your answers to the above questions. Here is a model position description to use as a start; modify it for your needs.

Position Description

Position Title: Executive Chef
Reports to: Owner/Innkeeper

Position Summary
The department head responsible for any and all kitchens in a food service establishment. Ensures that all kitchens provide nutritious, safe, eye-appealing, properly flavored food. Maintains a safe and sanitary work environment for all employees. Other duties include menu planning, preparation of budgets, and maintenance of payroll, food costs, and other records. Specific duties involving food preparation are the establishment of quality standards and the training of employees in cooking methods, presentation techniques, portion control, and retention of nutrients.

Tasks

1. Interviews, hires, evaluates, rewards, and disciplines kitchen personnel as appropriate.
2. Orients and trains kitchen personnel in property and department rules, policies, and procedures.
3. Trains kitchen personnel in food-production principles and practices. Establishes quality standards for all menu items and for food production practices.
4. Plans and prices menus. Establishes portion sizes and standards of service for all menu items.
5. Schedules kitchen employees in conjunction with business forecasts and predetermined budget. Maintains payroll records for submission to payroll department.
6. Controls food costs by establishing purchasing specifications, storeroom requisition systems, product storage requirements, standardized recipes, and waste-control procedures.
7. Trains kitchen personnel in safe operating procedures of all equipment, utensils, and machinery. Establishes maintenance schedules in conjunction with manufacturer's instructions for all equipment. Provides safety training in lifting, carrying, hazardous material control, chemical control, first aid, and CPR.
8. Trains kitchen personnel in sanitation practices and establishes cleaning schedules, stock rotation schedules, refrigeration temperature control points, and other sanitary controls.
9. Trains kitchen personnel to prepare all food while retaining the maximum amount of desirable nutrients. Trains kitchen personnel to meet special dietary requests, including low-fat, low-sodium, vegetarian, and low-calorie meals.

Prerequisites

Education: Degree from a postsecondary culinary arts training program is desirable.

Experience: A minimum of five years as sous chef plus three years in another food-preparation position.

Physical: Must be able to speak clearly and listen attentively to employees, dining room staff, and guests. Must be able to stand and move about quickly for periods up to four hours in length. Must have the ability to lift pots, pans, etc., up to forty pounds in weight. Must be able to read and write.

In some areas, running an ad in the local newspaper is enough to generate applicants. If you do this, remember that the respondents will likely be from your area; in other words, you may be taking your neighbor's staff person. If you run ads in large-city newspapers to draw more people, remember that ads in New York, Boston, or Chicago will draw individuals with higher salary expectations. If you don't want to be in this position, consider some other possibilities. Contact any culinary schools in your region. Classes graduate regularly, and you may be able to interview some excellent people. New graduates will not have the refined management skills that come with years of experience, so you'll need to be more involved in training, but they should have great technique and may be more affordable.

At the same time, call your local chapter of the American Culinary Federation. Chefs in your area will generally belong to this association. Like innkeepers, chefs network and may know of someone to refer. Find the number for these associations in your telephone book.

Local hotels, restaurants, country clubs, catering halls, and other inns are also good networking sources. Applicants will often go to these places looking for work, and if you have developed positive relationships with them, they may refer people to you. If you belong to a state, regional, or national association, let them know of your recruitment plans.

The key to finding the right person for the job is to reach out to a number of different areas and then to interview thoroughly before making your decision. This can be a lengthy process; be sure to allow yourself enough time so you do not make the wrong choice in desperation. If you need to hire for your summer season, consider starting in the fall.

Once you have applications that interest you, begin the interview process. Talk with each candidate frankly. Do not exaggerate the position. Be honest about your needs and expectations. Listen, and answer questions thoroughly. After all, you are hiring an integral part of your team, and you want them to be around for a while. After you have spoken to the applicants, if possible, go to where they work now and taste their food. Would you want it to be served at your inn? Invite the candidate to come into your kitchen and prepare a meal for you. This will give both of you an idea about whether the job will work out, and it also allows you to have another conversation in a different environment. If you find a person you are excited about, check all references. If you are comfortable with everything, offer the job. Do not be afraid to set up another interview if you are not completely sure. Be absolutely certain now and avoid problems later.

Congratulations! You have hired a chef. Now is not the time, however, to breathe a sigh of relief and leave the kitchen; your most important job is just beginning. Your new staff person deserves and expects your management and time. Positive strokes as well as constructive criticism are vital.

Too often, innkeepers who have gone through all the right steps in interviewing and hiring cannot understand why the perfect person does not live up to their expectations or quits. Frequently, little or no time was spent with the employee after hiring. It is only natural that, if your new chef feels you are not paying attention or do not care, their habits will become sloppy and their motivation will disappear.

Innkeepers who have the best relationships with their chefs are not necessarily the ones with food background but the ones who are excellent communicators, not intimidated by a chef's expertise. Talk, listen, and be consistent with praise as well as criticism. Do this well, and you'll be rewarded with a happy team member for a long time. These relationships take time to grow. Give yourself time.

Budgeting

You will need to budget for the expenses of your food service. You may have twenty seats in your dining room but sometimes they'll be empty, and sometimes you'll wish they were two hundred.

There are two basic ways to treat profit at budget time. First, there's the traditional approach, which regards profit as "what is left over from sales income after subtracting expenses." It looks like this:

Profit = Sales Income - Expenses

The second method treats profit as if it were a "cost":

Sales Income - Required Profit = Allowable Operating Expenses

Since inns are likely to be on a tight budget and using the food service as a marketing opportunity, it's easy to figure that you do not need a profit. This is dangerous thinking, considering that your own time is generally not built into the budget. To be more realistic, look at the profit as owner time spent on food service, and build it into the budget at the outset.

- Analyzing sales histories will give you an idea of your heaviest season, for which type of meal, and the trends that have developed over the past couple of years. Are desserts being ordered more? Are appetizers passé?
- Reviewing current factors over which you have no control but which may affect sales gives you a broader understanding of sales. Is there new competition or is the street being repaired? What about the effect of local special events?
- Economic variables may affect the public's habits and lifestyles. As inflation rises, guests may demand greater value for their money.
- Also consider room occupancy projections.

Estimated Sales and Profits for a Ten-Room Inn with a Fifteen-Seat MAP Dining Room, Accepting Limited Outside Diners

(Assuming 50 percent year-round occupancy of inn)

A. Analysis of potential sales

Total seats (15) x estimated turnover* (1.5) = 22 dinners per day and 154 per week

Estimated average check = $25

Total potential dinner income per week, based on 50 percent occupancy

(154 x $25) x .50 = $1,925

B. Projection of costs

Cost of food (estimated at 40 percent of sales) ($770)

Cost of labor (minimum)

    1 chef $200

    2 wait staff $120

    1 dishwasher $90

Total estimated labor cost per week ($410)

All other operating costs (estimated) ($200)

Taxes, interest, amortization of mortgage† _____

Total estimated operating, food, and labor costs ($1,380)

C. Projection of potential weekly profit

(before owner's compensation for services) $545

   * Turnover is the average number of times a seat is occupied during the meal service. An average of 1.5 customers per seat is probably high, especially for an inn serving only to houseguests, where turnover will be predicated on occupancy.

   † Consider the dining room as a percentage of the entire inn space and figure in that percentage of overhead as part of the food expenses; this gives you a better handle to judge how well food is doing and how well rooms are doing.

Once sales volumes are known and profit requirements determined, expenses required to generate the projected level of sales can be estimated. To simplify this, operating costs are broken into three categories:

- *Fixed costs,* which remain constant in the short run even though sales volume may vary. Include management salaries, rent, insurance, property taxes, interest and depreciation.
- *Variable costs,* which change in relation to changes in the volume of business. Include food and beverage costs, linen laundering, labor, music, and some supplies used in food production and service areas.
- *Mixed costs,* which contain both fixed and variable cost elements, such as the telephone: it has a fixed basic charge, plus variable charges depending on call volume.

Operating costs to consider:

Food	Rent
Labor	Depreciation
Supplies	Insurance
Utilities	Property, business, or other taxes
Marketing	

The term "prime costs" is often used in the restaurant business. Prime costs are food and labor costs only; they should represent no more than 65 to 70 percent of your gross income. Figure profit, then, at 25 percent and the other costs run about 5 to 10 percent, which is why you want no waste in your kitchen.

Operational businesses often use two methods of figuring expenses, neither of which is really recommended for a new entrepreneur. The "simple markup method" adds a percentage increase in costs over the previous year. In the "percentage method," food and beverage costs are calculated as a percentage of sales income. Both systems have the potential disadvantage of perpetuating an inefficient operation if the current budget cost percentage is higher than it should be.

A third method, zero-based budgeting, avoids the errors of the other two by starting over from zero, giving you the more direct experience of developing each category based on today's costs and knowing your budget much more intimately. To a newcomer in this field, this will be time-consuming, but it will yield priceless knowledge. Do not, however, disregard previous expense histories if they are available; they are a valuable reality test.

Remember, always estimate expenses high and income low; you never know when a blizzard will blow away all your projected profit.

Fine Dinner Service: *Mise en Place*

Mise en place (pronounced "mees-on-ploss") is a French phrase that, translated literally, means "put in place." In the food service world, *mise en place* is the organization and completion of every behind-the-scenes task to prepare for the smoothest possible service for the guests. It is more than just folding and placing the napkins correctly. This physical readiness is the setting of the stage and the costuming that prepares your actor-employees to be their very best.

You need the right number of employees at the right time, so that no one ends up scurrying around doing tasks that should have been done last night or early in the afternoon. Efficient staffing will make money for you, when your people are prepared and poised enough to sell your wine list, enthuse knowledgeably about the menu, and charm your guests into dessert.

This preparatory work is vital, for once service begins—the moment the first guest walks through the door—staff must be able to devote their full attention to the needs of the guest. When guests are in the room, it is no time to fold napkins, fill salt and pepper shakers, or adjust lighting. Our guests come to us for a magical experience and pampering, and the magician needs to be physically and mentally prepared.

Wendy Denn, an innkeeper and country inn consultant, wrote this after a summer visit to New England: "This is my favorite time of the year, when I jump into my car and visit inns. I write this at the end of an excursion, and overall I'm as enthusiastic as ever about what I see, but my experiences also remind me of the importance of *mise en place* and what can happen when you don't get a chance to put the rabbit in the hat.

"I arrive at an inn midafternoon, full of anticipation. I walk into a beautifully appointed reception area, every detail surpassing my expectation. At 7 P.M. I arrive, as expected, for dinner. After several minutes, I seat myself. I watch two other couples wait awkwardly and then seat themselves as well. We all wait.

"My table is set with flatware for three courses plus dessert, and two wine-glasses. The cup and saucer have been preset, not really appropriate for fine dining, and I have no napkin nor a water glass. Clearly, there has not been time for sufficient *mise en place*. Suddenly the music comes on, the lights dim, and a waitperson rushes into the room with an armful of napkins, menus, and glasses. Gasping an apology, she thrusts a napkin onto my lap.

"Ignoring the difficult beginning, I ask several questions about the menu. I receive answers such as 'I don't know what type of salad dressing; the chef hasn't made it yet.' *Mise en place* is lacking in the kitchen also. The evening ends, however, with an absolutely lovely dinner.

"Another evening I am graciously greeted, seated at a table with a wonderful view of the sun setting behind a swan-filled pond. The sunset is overshadowed by spotty glasses, mottled flatware, and a smudgy picture-window. *Mise en place* is missing here also. I believe that all these problems are probably the result of innkeepers cutting staffing just a bit too close."

PRETEND YOU ARE THE GUEST

It is a good idea to experience your inn from your guest's perspective. Walk through your inn and sit in your dining room as if you were a guest.
- Do you know where to go and what to do?
- Do you feel comfortable?
- Do you sense a warm innkeeper's presence?
- Do you want to get up and help the server?
- Do you want to fix that dripping candle on table six?
- Are you the only one who notices the couple at table three who has no butter?
- Do you wonder why the man at table four just pushes the fish around on his plate?
- Would you come back?

The essence of *mise en place* is complete emotional and physical readiness.

Dinner Without the Daily Stress

Chef Nancy Donaldson, former owner of the nine-room Old Yacht Club Inn in Santa Barbara, California, had always liked to cook and had seriously looked at opening a restaurant before becoming an innkeeper. Her partners encouraged her cooking because it promoted the inn. Although Santa Barbara is known for its fine cuisine, Nancy established her own reputation and market niche in a competitive inn community. Serving only to guests (the city wouldn't allow her to expand to outsiders), Nancy provided a fixed-price, five-course, sit-down dinner one weekend night a few times a month. "I had a server, sometimes two. Along with my business partner, Sandy Hunt, and my faithful sous chef and dishwasher, we all pitched in to clean up after the dessert was served."

Rooms were MAP for those weekends. The rate included two nights and dinner and, of course, two breakfasts. Guests gathered for champagne before the dinner bell rang. They could also order from the wine list, for an extra charge. Up until the day she sold, Nancy loved preparing dinner. And that's quite a feat for a twenty-year innkeeper-chef.

This chapter would not have been possible without the expertise and gentle guidance of Wendy Denn. With her vast experience in food service and her knowledge of smaller properties, gained as the on-site innkeeper for Trinity Inn and Conference Center in Connecticut, Wendy brings a great depth of expertise and understanding of the MAP and full-service country inn.

marketing

YOU GOTTA HAVE A GIMMICK

If you're not careful, the opening day you've so long anticipated can be the longest, loneliest day of your life. Where are all the friends who asked you every two weeks when you'd be ready? Where are the neighbors who stopped by to check your progress? Where are the guests who are going to pay for the months of renovation you've just completed?

Marketing is how you let people know what you have to offer, and it's how you make them want it. Marketing is critical to success. You'll lose business if you don't do a good job of getting the message out there.

In today's travel world you must understand and speak the language of the Internet if you want your inn to be successful. Marketing on the World Wide Web has many facets that an innkeeper must keep up with. It begins with selecting a name and goes on to developing and marketing your own home page and Web site, deciding to post reservation availability or handle on-line booking on your Web site, purchasing space in bed-and-breakfast directories, responding to guests' e-mail requests, confirming reservations by e-mail, communicating to travel writers via e-mail, and sending out e-mail promotions to your own list of guests. Simply put, the Web has taken over the marketing of an inn.

Marketing includes many things, from the obvious ones like advertising and publicity to creating an inn image that can be presented to potential guests in an exciting, compelling way. To make sure your opening day isn't an anticlimax, put your marketing program together as you proceed with the other business of getting ready to open.

Establishing an Image

You'll have set the tone for your image before you began renovating, when you made decisions about inn ambience. The difficulty in the increasingly competitive bed-and-breakfast inn and country inn market is to define your image so clearly that you stand out from your competition in guests' minds. You want them to remember a unique experience. Yours could be the place that serves the champagne breakfast in bed, or boards guests' horses, or where you can walk to the beach or visit the barn. Notice that all of these are descriptions of the guests' experience. The more you build your image around what happens to guests when they visit, the more likely they are to think of you when they want to vacation or to tell a friend about a great place to stay.

In the amenities you offer, capitalize on what your guests do in your community. In California's Napa and Sonoma wine regions, for example, inn rooms often provide wineglasses. But don't offer something just because everyone else does. Or, if it's an important service in your area, offer it differently. The Old Yacht Club Inn in Santa Barbara is a block and a half from the beach. The innkeepers provide beach chairs and towels and picnic baskets for breakfast. They capitalize on their relationship to the ocean in every way they can, including the name of the inn.

You can dress to reinforce an image. Santa Barbara's Simpson House staff members wear similar outfits to present a more formal, upscale look at their five-diamond property. At the Garth Woodside Mansion in Hannibal, Missouri, the innkeepers give guests a chance to dress to suit the period by offering an old-fashioned nightshirt in each guest room. Of course, guests are given an opportunity to purchase the item, complete with inn monogram. Original owners Irv and Diane Feinberg were known to show up in their nightshirts at local radio stations, with breakfast for the DJ.

Don't overlook the contribution of your staff to your inn's image. If you have an Old English country house image, hire someone with an English accent. If you emphasize hiking and the outdoors, recruit staff from the local gym or Sierra Club chapter.

You'll want to maintain and extend the image of your inn throughout its lifetime, responding to the interests of your guests. If you have decided to emphasize history and a guest suggests that a library of books about the history of your area would be interesting, consider adding one. Be willing to research the history of your inn building if guests are interested in it.

Your guests will often tell you what they like. Look for moments when you can ask.

Don't let your inn image just happen. Once it's established, it's very difficult to change. Consider carefully what your inn image should be and how you will project it. Your inn guests will return in large part for your particular style.

Selecting a Name

Inn image and inn names are vitally related, of course, so the work you have done on developing an image concept is a good start on choosing the name. But there are a number of additional opportunities and limitations. Let's review them.

WEB-FRIENDLY

Do not pass Go; proceed directly to the search engines on your computer to guide you in selecting a name.

According to WebSideStory, over 64 percent of Internet users worldwide arrive at their desired site with direct navigation. Direct navigation is when you type a URL directly into the browser or click on a URL you've already bookmarked.

Major advertisers establish their brand by spending millions in advertising, which is why the statistics are so high. Folks looking for Disney World don't go to Google; they just type in disneyworld.com, and there it is. Individual B&Bs must still rely on search engines and directories like BedandBreakfast.com to drive traffic to their sites, but they can enhance branding on a smaller scale in several ways.

Make sure that the name of your inn and your URL are as similar as possible, so that travelers who learn about your inn can intuitively type it into their browser without doing a search.

If the name of your inn or your URL is a little complex or hard to spell, remember, or hear over the phone, register additional URLs that reflect common misspellings of your inn's name. For example, if you own the Captain Phillips B&B, consider registering these URLs, if available: CaptainPhilipsBB.com, Captain_PhillipsBB.com, CaptainPhillipsBnB.com, and CaptainPhillipsBandB.com. Notice the different spellings of both "Phillips" and "bed & breakfast."

Consider registering URLs that may be easier to remember than those with your inn's name. For example, if you own O'Donaghue's Inn in Smithville, try to register www.Smithvilleinn.com as well as www.odonaghuesinn.com. Registration costs are nominal, and your Webmaster (the individual who creates and makes changes to your Web site) will create a pointer to direct traffic from all these URLs to your home page.

Make sure that the name of your inn and your Web site appear on *everything* connected with your inn, from your coffee mugs to your confirmation letters, and from your press releases to your postcards.

Be sure to include your Web site URL on your voice mail, for times when you can't answer the phone personally. Be sure that your e-mail address further strengthens your brand. It should always be something like relax@myinn.com, never myinn@xazinet.com.

LOCATION

Use reference or allusion to your location to evoke a mental image for potential guests. The Inn by the Sea is a name opportunity for a coastal location, but since inns along hundreds of miles of American coastline could claim it, you might include the name of your town and make it the Kennebunkport Inn by the Sea. Maybe your inn's proximity to a landmark can lead you to a name.

HISTORY

Is there a historical event or personage that hints at a name for your inn? Many inn names are taken from the former owners of the residences. The Glenborough Inn considered this approach. According to Pat, "A Mr. Brooks was the original owner. But in Santa Barbara, there's a Brooks Institute, so Brooks Inn would have been confusing. The most famous person who lived at our inn was named Fowler. Fowler is an okay name, except 'fowl' can also be 'foul,' with obvious negative connotations. So we decided that historical names didn't work for us."

But consider the Captain Lord Mansion in Kennebunkport, Maine. All three parts of that name connote authority and even wealth: "captain," "lord," and "mansion." "Captain" also brings to mind the sea, which the inn overlooks from its top floors, where no doubt a waiting wife once paced.

SOUND

"The Captain Lord Mansion" is pleasant to say and to hear, both important tests for the inn name you select. How will it sound when you answer the phone? Will callers say "What?" The Bath Street Inn often gets mail addressed to Bass Street Inn. Susan makes a joke of it, telling callers it's "bath—as in taking one."

Does the name feel good coming out of your mouth? Does it sound crisp, clear, inviting? Does it come trippingly off the tongue? "Chambered Nautilus" is an inn name that does, and it also brings to mind the sea, "chambers," and even aquariums, all appropriate to the inn and its Seattle location.

> *The Jabberwock, an inn in Monterey, California, immediately evokes an image of playfulness, from the moment the name rolls off your tongue. If you know the Lewis Carroll poem "Jabberwocky," you're propelled instantly into the innkeepers' image of gentle fun.*
>
> *Each room name comes from the poem, and so do names for the bathroom, the telephone room, and the common refrigerator. Even the breakfast food has Lewis Carroll names. The property is landscaped in trills and trolls. The logo is ornate and intriguing; if you look closely, you'll see the Jabberwock. The playful theme is carried through with cookies and milk at bedtime, and a stuffed bear tucked between the sheets.*
>
> *Because the reference to the poem is rather erudite, while the poem itself is sheer fun, the Jabberwock appeals to both the sophisticate and the child—of any age.*

INNOVATION

Moving the words around in a name can sometimes create something fresh. For example, say a couple named King is opening an inn that they want to call King's Bed-and-Breakfast. By changing it just a little, to Bed and Breakfast with the Kings, they've made it more of an invitation. The Kings, determined to use their name, can make a rather conventional choice something different by changing the order of the words.

Designing a Logo

Your logo should be a strong visual statement of the spirit of the inn name, image, and ambience. It can be as simple as the inn's name in a pleasant typeface or as extravagant as an artist's design, commissioned and copyrighted for your inn alone. Whatever way you go, the trick for maximum effectiveness is repetition, using your logo in the same way on all your visual material, from brochures to T-shirts. This strengthens the image in your prospective guest's mind.

Whether you want the challenge of designing a logo yourself on your computer or prefer to work with a designer-artist, there's some basic conceptual work you need to do first.

First, can you tie the logo image into the name of your inn? To a drawing of it? To the street it's on? To the skyline of your city? To the tree in front of the inn? To your locale? To a special service you offer? Capitalize on the concept that will give you the strongest image. And in general, the simpler, the better. For instance, if you're the Cuckoo's Nest Inn on Pine Street, you might be able to come up with a stylized cuckoo in a pine tree.

Second, do you want or need something more than just an all-type logo? Why? Do you have the budget to have a logo created for you? Is your budget so limited that it would be wise to do a less ambitious logo very well, rather than try to do a more ambitious one poorly?

Third, make a list of specific uses for your logo, along with the minimum and maximum sizes required for those purposes. Remember that as you reduce an image, the lines become thinner, and as you enlarge it, the lines become thicker. To maintain the original quality of the design for each use, it's wise to have the artwork done in several sizes, for large and small reproduction.

Consider the appropriateness of the overall shape of the logo. For example, a long name on an essentially horizontal logo may take the entire area of a one-inch display classified ad, leaving you no room to describe the inn. An emphatically vertical logo may be a problem on a sign for your front yard.

You will want to put your logo to a variety of uses, some immediately, others several years into the business: letterhead, ads, brochure, sign, postcard, T-shirt, matchbook, soap, and display at a conference.

When the new owners bought the Rabbit Hill Inn in Lower Waterford, Vermont, the rabbit name was already in place, but they made it work—hard. Their logo is a bunny; stuffed bunnies sit next to the salt and pepper shakers on their dining room tables and perch on guest beds, on shelves, and on all sorts of unexpected places. Guests bring them rabbit gifts. Their telephone number is 800-76-BUNNY. Sound a little too cute? Not after you've stayed at the inn and discovered how serious they are about making you feel as pampered as a beloved childhood bunny.

Start by finding a designer you can work with. Artists or public relations firms may give you recommendations of who's creative, willing to share ideas, and ready to give honest feedback. Talk to a few prospects about prices and procedure, and ask to see their work. You may want to do some initial design work on your own computer, experimenting with typefaces. Many firms have flyers or booklets that show their faces in available sizes. If not, ask them to photocopy samples of your favorites for you to take home. Look them over carefully. Maybe you can combine them in an interesting way. For example, an ornate first letter can set off an otherwise straightforward, readable typeface. Be sure to look at individual letters in your inn name; some of them may be hard to read in some faces.

Once you've narrowed the choices to three or four typefaces, have your inn name set in your favorite ones, in a larger size than you'll use on a business card. If you want more than just a typeset name in your logo, review clip-art computer files or books for border shapes or illustrations, like an apple or a tree. A designer can put art and type together as you request, as well as making useful suggestions for snazzing it up or simplifying, and advising on the different sizes you'll need for the various uses you plan. Even if you decide to do much of the developmental work yourself on your own computer, do collaborate with a designer on the final product: your logo is the basic building block in your entire portfolio; don't let it look amateurish.

Think, too, about economy of reproduction. Your basic logo design should work well in black-and-white without halftones for shading. There may be times and a purpose for color or halftones, but using a logo that requires special printing techniques and inks is costly in the long run.

Show your prospective logo designs to your partners and friends for their opinions. Ask them to choose a favorite. Do some reality testing, too. Ask what each logo says to them, what ideas and feelings are evoked. Does it say homeyness, elegance, and softness? Don't prompt the answer you want to hear.

Once you've made your choice, get stats (the term is short for Photostats) in a variety of sizes at the typesetter's or from a lithographer. Stats are camera-ready art, and a file of them is handy for quick response to a well-priced ad offer or for an urgently needed flyer. If your designer can scan your logo and store it on computer disk, it can easily and quickly be resized as needed.

Some logos have a clean, still, "editorial" look. Others evoke mood, emotion, and romance. There is no right or wrong; it's a matter of taste.

Producing a Brochure and a Web Site

Producing a good brochure and a competitive Web site is astonishingly time-consuming, and it's easy to let the project slip when you're up to your armpits in sawdust. But both must be ready before you open the doors of your inn. The print brochure and an electronic Web site are the basic tools in your promotion kit. These two represent you to prospective guests who have never seen your area or your inn. The words, the pictures, the format, the style—all these choices can make or break you. Both tools should be developed to complement, but not replicate, each other. Your brochure is tangible proof reflected in paper quality, color, and design. Whether your inn is traditionally simple or extravagantly elegant, your Web site representation is most effectively reinforced by your brochure presentation.

You'll almost certainly be surprised and frustrated at how long it takes to get everything done: a month or more for design and copywriting, a couple of weeks for drawings and photography, time for you and your partners to review and react to everything, a week for the printer, another for the bindery, and even more time for the busy Web designer. The operational decisions that precede these mechanical steps can be even more time-consuming: setting inn rates and establishing deposit, children, and smoking policies and minimum stay requirements. Give the entire process plenty of time.

To start with, you need a good grasp of what you want to convey and how you want to convey it. It helps to be very analytical here about what can become otherwise too personal. You're choosing your appropriate approach within a spectrum of what other inns do, so at least six months ahead of opening day, begin collecting brochures and Web site URLs you like from other inns. Keep a collection to review for ideas on layout, color, typefaces, and the ability to project a feeling.

At the same time, begin collecting promotional materials from the big spenders in your area: the chamber of commerce, the department of tourism, and major hotels or motel chains. Analyze the way they sell the area and their business. This can give you a good idea of why people come to your community; plus, making links from your Web site to various community activities can broaden your site activity as well as credibility among potential guests (However, please don't use the materials developed by neighbors as obvious models for your own! You'll want your colleagues to be friends, you know.)

About four months before opening day, start considering how much energy and expense you want to put into developing your brochure and Web site. There are a number of approaches you can take to getting the job done. You can do it all yourself, drawing the illustrations, hand-lettering the copy, and doing the layout and pasteup, using brochure and Web-page software. If you're very good at it, this can be successful. But, the truth is, a complete do-it-yourself job fails more often than it succeeds, especially in today's competitive market.

You can take the opposite approach and hire an agency to do the whole job. You tell them what you want, and they write the copy, commission the artwork, choose and order the type, and furnish you with printed brochures and a completed Web site. You can build in stopping points along the way where they should ask for your approval. Naturally you will want to know the price of the project before you make any agreements.

Then there's a middle ground, which you design to suit your own needs and skills. Perhaps you want to write the copy, supplying it on computer disk or e-mailing it to be modified by your designer, who will do the rest. Or you may want to render the drawings. Another option is for you to handle the legwork, hiring one person to write the copy and someone else to take photographs, arranging for the Web designer, and choosing a printer. In a sense, it's like being your own building contractor.

Be careful about working with friends. Your brochure and Web site are so important that you don't want courtesy to require you to accept something less than terrific. It must be easy to say no firmly.

Brochure guru Roberta Gardner offers innkeepers this advice about working with color:

If you want to work smarter, not harder, use a color brochure and color postcards to market your inn. Color is twice as expensive as other printing, but if the work is quality, marketing in color is four times as effective, and with full-color Web sites, today's guests are thinking in color.

To avoid wasting time and money, here are some pitfalls to avoid at all costs:
- A color brochure and lavish Web site can hurt you if they outshine your inn. If you don't show truthful photos, your guests will feel duped, and they will be unhappy. And there's nothing worse than an unhappy guest. But remember, Web site visitors are looking for lots of great photos.
- Don't tell everything, and don't show everything in your brochure or even on your Web site. One of the great joys of inn travel is discovery. Show enough to attract guests, but allow them to be pleasantly surprised by the unanticipated

details. Since it is so easy to tell all on a Web site, keeping the fact that you give every guest a recipe when they leave may seem hard not to include, but save it.

- A simple message is essential. Today we have less and less time to do more and more. If recipients of your marketing materials have to scratch their heads to figure out what you're saying and what you're selling, you've lost them. Be clear, simple, and direct.
- Don't allow your designer to get carried away with a design concept at the expense of your business, indulging in design for design's sake rather than for your inn's sake. Looking at good design is like walking into an uncluttered room—a pleasant, easy experience.
- Before hiring a photographer, review his or her previous work both on the Web and on paper. Photographers specialize, just as doctors do. You wouldn't go to an eye doctor for knee surgery, so don't assume that all professional photographers can shoot interiors of buildings or even can take the kinds of shots that look good on the Web or in magazines. Once you're certain your photographer can shoot buildings, ask yourself if you like the look of the work. Some photographers use even lighting from top to bottom for a clean, still, "editorial" look. Others evoke mood, emotion, and romance. There is no right or wrong; it's a matter of taste.
- If you can't afford the highest quality design and printing, don't do color. A thoughtfully designed one- or two-color brochure (ideally with a color post-card insert) will be far more effective than ho-hum color. The cost of color is no higher on the Web, and guests can print out Web brochures from your site if they have a color printer. In case the Web traveler doesn't have a color printer, be sure to look at your color photos after copying them on a copy machine to see what they still look like in black-and-white.
- If your guests say, "Your inn is so much nicer than your brochure," you must make a change, and quickly. For every guest who gave you the benefit of the doubt, you can count on many potential guests who chose not to take a chance on your inn.

CONTENT

Put yourself in the position of a future guest. What would you want to know if you were shopping for a getaway inn? Why would you want to visit a particular inn? How would you benefit from staying there? You want your potential guests to be able to picture themselves at your inn, waking up to the smell of baking bread, opening their eyes to sun-dappled treetops. Sure, they want facts, but mostly they are seeking an experience. Don't give them a furniture inventory.

You want your inn to appear unique compared to all other choices the guest may have. When you're writing copy, eliminate every descriptive word that can be found in someone else's brochure. Eliminate nonspecific terms like "elegant," "charming," "historic," and "cozy." Always remember that the brochure is about the guests, not about the inn. For example, don't say, "There is a cozy window seat in the elegant, historic Abigail's Room." Instead, say, "Like Abigail herself in 1832, you'll burrow down into the pillows in the window seat to watch the sun set over the river. While you're there, see if you can find the secret hiding place where she kept her golden coins!"

Content has a more mundane side as well. Make a list of the questions you have as a traveler. Ask your friends, partners, and guests at inns you visit what questions they have. Three and a half months before opening, use the list as a guide and start to draw up the categories of information you want to include in your own brochure. Here are some suggestions.

- Should you include prices? The trend is to put them on an insert card, which can be altered less expensively than the entire brochure. (It is crucial to include prices on your Web site.) Some inns list a range of room prices, while others price and describe each room individually. Whether from your brochure or on the phone, guests will want to find out what their room costs and what it includes.

- How will your guests find the inn? Most will be from out of town, many from other states or countries; it will help them to know where the inn is in relation to the state or the region of the country. Plan to include a simple map and directions; not everybody is good at deciphering a road map. This will reduce the time you have to spend on the phone, repeating the same instructions. When you've drafted your instructions and drawn your map, have a friend who easily gets lost test them.

- How much space should you devote to describing your area and activities? Guests are selecting your inn partly because you know your community. Describe your area as helpfully as possible, so they'll know, for example, that you're three blocks from the Shakespeare Festival or within walking distance of ocean-view hiking trails—and, of course, let them know that you provide free maps!

- Should you describe each guest room? This is an area of some controversy, but innkeepers seem to succeed whichever course they follow. If you have sixteen rooms, it will be difficult to describe each without losing your audience; you might group descriptions by room features and prices, like "fireplace suites with Jacuzzis, $185; private bath, queen bed, $85–$110." But if your inn is small

Brochure and Web-Site Checklist

Things to consider including in your paper brochure and Web site:

- *Inn logo and name.*
- *For your Web site: lots of high-quality color photos.*
- *Innkeepers' names, both owners and employees.*
- *Mailing and physical addresses, including zip code. (Many rural areas and small towns use post office boxes, which doesn't help a prospective guest find you on a map.)*
- *Telephone with area code.*
- *TDD availability.*
- *Fax with area code.*
- *E-mail address.*
- *Web site URL (address).*
- *Map and directions. (Linking to one of the Web map sites can be helpful.)*
- *Room descriptions. (On the Web site provide photo/rates for each room.)*
- *Number of rooms.*
- *Local description: what is there to do? (On your Web site link to local sites.)*
- *Great photos, drawings.*
- *On an insert sheet or through a separate link on your home page: policies and procedures; prices; list of services included in price.*
- *One-line catchy word-picture as your image theme.*
- *Main copy: brief images actively involving guests.*
- *Easy-to-follow format with headlines and short paragraphs.*
- *A little history, woven into guest benefits.*
- *Environmental actions.*
- *Special services offered: weddings, massage, and gift certificates.*
- *Services for business travelers: Internet access, telephones, TV, early breakfast, etc.*
- *Dining on premises; menu samples.*
- *Inspections you have passed: AAA, Mobil, Select Registry, and state associations.*
- *Associations of which you are a member: PAII, state associations.*
- *Accessibility for persons with disabilities, with appropriate designations. (Use "handicapped" logos for the specific accessibility you offer—physical, hearing, sight.)*
- *Space for writing a confirmation note on your printed brochure.*
- *Recycled-paper and soy-ink logo, if you are using these.*

and there is a substantial difference in room decoration and prices, detailed descriptions will save you telephone time and help the guest fantasize about the place. It's to your advantage to promote those fantasies. In some inns, the guest rooms aren't the main draw, but the common area is. In that case, focus on the common area.

· Should you use the brochure to promote special services? Meetings and weddings, on-site therapeutic massage, bikes to rent, tours, gift certificates, and package deals are services you might offer. If some are integral parts of your inn image, mention them in the brochure. If you're not sure how certain services will be accepted, plan instead to promote them with brochure inserts. This gives you a chance to try ideas and discard them if they fail, without having to dump your whole brochure.

· What about mentioning the innkeepers' names? It adds a nice, warm touch, and guests like to know the names; it's something hotels generally don't provide. But some guests will be disappointed if they don't meet the "real" innkeepers during their stay.

· How much of your policies and procedures do you want to describe? Veteran service-oriented innkeepers know from experience that clear information saves time, confusion, and unhappiness on all sides, but they include this information on the rate-sheet insert rather than prominently on the brochure. In today's market, you don't want to sound like the inn police, but it's only fair to describe your deposit and cancellation policies, check-in and checkout times, and smoking standards.

These are the basic areas you'll want to consider for your brochure copy. You will probably think of others. This is the "function" part of brochure planning; "form" is next.

FORMAT

Even with a great Web site, you'll mail thousands of brochures during your innkeeping career. Think about the effect of various formats on cost. Some card-style designs take advantage of one-sided printing for an unusual look, but standard brochures look more professional printed on both sides. In addition, since the costs of paper, design, and postage are fixed, the marginal cost of an additional side of information is very little. If there's a brochure format you like, before you do anything else, take it to a couple of printers for informal bids on what it would cost to do something similar.

Black ink is the cheapest. Adding other ink colors or using any color instead of black is usually somewhat more expensive, but it can be effective. Ask your designer about screens, which use shading to make one or two colors look like more, and other design techniques to make an inexpensive printing job look special.

Choose your paper carefully, and make sure you understand how the color of the paper will affect the color of the inks; your printer can show you samples. Contrast is important. In general, red ink is hard to read and red paper is hard to read from. Remember, you're already competing for your reader's attention; don't put any unnecessary obstacles in the way.

Choose a paper that allows you consistency among promotional materials. Not all papers are available in the weights you may need for letterhead, business cards, and postcards. Consider whether your paper will fold nicely; heavy stock sometimes won't unless you pay a little more to have it scored before folding. Use recycled paper.

If you're on a tight budget and evaluating design, ink, and paper choices that vary widely in price, think about whether a potential guest is more likely to choose your inn if you adopt a more expensive look. If your image is elegance, the answer may be yes. If your image is more down-home, the extra cost may not be worth it.

Before you take your design to the printer, bring it to the post office to get a sense of postal limitations. A size differential of a quarter inch that makes no difference in the effectiveness of the design can nearly double your mailing costs. Putting the return address in the wrong corner of a 5 1/2-by-8-inch mailer can do the same thing. Test how well your design and paper travel through the mail by mailing samples to friends. Do postmarks cover copy or detract too much from the look of your self-mailer? If you're trying for a delicate look, is your paper too flimsy to survive the mail? A three-panel, two-fold piece will hold up better with lightweight paper than a single-fold piece.

Typefaces should be easy to read. The accepted wisdom among graphic artists is that printing in italics is not, using all capital letters is not, sans serif copy is not, and reverse type (white letters on a dark background) is not. On the whole, the more you're aware of the typeface, the less you're aware of the words. Type must be clear in small sizes as well as in large. Look at all the characters you will use, including numbers for your address (with zip code) and telephone number (with area code).

Few people feel obligated to carefully read any printed piece that comes before their eyes. Thus the best format is one that provides the basics in big letters to attract attention, followed by details in smaller letters for those who want to know more. Use short sentences and short paragraphs, with headings that tell the bare bones of your story, since most readers routinely give such material a thirty-second scan. Estimate how long your brochures will last based on how you'll distribute them. If you include room rates in your copy, you will need to reprint when prices go up, and you don't want to have to wait five years to raise rates.

Content is probably still king, as long as it's current. Take a look at the Web sites you regularly revisit. Why do you go back? Your guests are no different. They want interesting, up-to-date information. Consider no less than monthly updating; it's not that difficult. Add a new recipe, offer a new package, introduce a new room, upload your latest e-letter, or show a picture of the latest special event. People love quick and easy; give it to them.

Stephan Spencer went on a virtual field trip through various companies' Web sites. Amazed that he stayed awake through this laborious process, he offers innkeepers some quick tidbits about keeping Web sites attractive to visitors. "Forget the smoke and mirrors," says Stephan. "You want them to act."

- Convert your on-line visitors into guests by inviting them to action. Every page should have a clear call to action to get your visitors to take the next step.
- Cut to the chase. People scan Web pages, not study them, and they read at least 30 percent slower off the screen than off paper. Use active verbs rather than passive ones. It saves words and is more persuasive.
- Use "you" and "your" at least five times more than "we," "us" and "our." Your visitors are interested in what's in it for them. Potential guests don't want to read a testament to your ego.
- Don't overhype. Avoid exclamation marks and words like "premier," "leading," and "cutting-edge." In other words, keep it real.
- Search engines are your audience as much as humans, so incorporate lots of good keywords into your copy. Pick keywords that are not only relevant but also popular with search-engine users. Some B&B home pages are made up solely of images—not much for search engines to work with. Put the keywords near the top of the page, ideally in the first sentence. Don't waste this prime space with "Welcome to Our Home Page."

DOING IT YOURSELF

If you decide to write your own copy or do your own artwork, take plenty of time. Three months isn't too long. You need time to think, to work, and to get others to react, plus time to put your copy, drawings, or photographs away so you can come back and review them with fresh eyes.

HIRING WRITERS, GRAPHIC ARTISTS, AND WEB DESIGNERS

Even if you're working with a pro, do your homework first. It will save you money, because your job will take less time, and you'll probably be happier with the product, because it will reflect your inn as you see it. Start by writing out your identity concept. Give it to your artist, writer, and Web designer with a copy of your logo. Also supply any other written descriptions you may have, like the one in your business plan. Your writer and Web designer will also need a list of what information must be included in the brochure.

Before any work begins, put into writing your expectations; the artist's, writer's, or Web designer's fees; completion or delivery dates; and restrictions. Specify whether you are buying the product outright or only limited rights to its use. For example, if you're working with a photographer, will you own a specific number of prints only or the negatives, too? Be clear about what happens if you don't like the preliminary work proposed to you. With a Web designer, you should own your domain name and thus your Web site. Some unethical designers have registered innkeepers' domain names in their own name; that way the inn doesn't own it and can't easily leave the designer. Your contract should also provide for a "kill fee." This is the amount that you will pay the artist, writer, or designer to end the agreement at a specified stage if you don't like the work in progress.

Special Concerns for Web Sites

As with a brochure, you need to be in charge of all aspects of the look and read of your Web site. Even if you feel like a technodummy, never fear. You can and must become the manager of your Web presence. The Web is your primary source of new business and is crucial to the success of your whole marketing plan. Your inn's Web site is the home base for the rest of your marketing efforts. From media referrals to listings in B&B directories, your home page will be seen by tens of thousands of possible guests. Inns reap more benefits from Internet marketing than the generic hotel does, and since travel is one of the most common reasons Americans use the Web, you cannot afford to be laissez-faire about this medium.

If you enjoy Web design and you're good at it, use one of several software packages to design your own site. On the other hand, if you lack the time or the expertise, turn this very important task over to someone else. Using a designer who understands the B&B industry may give you an edge. However, not unlike a graphic designer for your paper brochure, the person who designs your Web site may not be the same one who markets it (gets your Web site listed on search engines and Web directories, links to local activities, and develops keywords); that's okay.

In selecting a designer, use the same criteria as you would when finding someone to design a print brochure with a few extras thrown in. Be sure the designer will let you make simple changes to your Web site. Being able to change rates, add special packages and links, or even revise copy such as recipes makes your Web site dynamic and more likely to be used as a resource by your guests and picked up by search engines.

Put These on Top of Your List When Choosing a Web Designer and/or Web Master

Trent Blizzard (Blizzard Internet Marketing) offers the following advice.

- *What is their experience in the B&B industry? Do they have a portfolio of client Web sites? Keep in mind that you don't have to like every Web site designed by this person, since different inns want different designs, but you should like the overall quality.*
- *Do they copyright their work? The answer should be no. All text, graphics, and HTML coding on a Web site should be owned by you.*
- *How do you make updates to your Web site? How quickly will they insert updates, and is there a charge? You will also want them to send you a follow-up report whenever something is done to your site (whether requested by you or not).*
- *Do they provide tracking software? Make sure that your Webmaster has a plan to track all the visitors to your site. This is an indication that your Web site's traffic is being taken seriously, in addition to how good it looks.*
- *What is their refund policy? Do you have to sign a contract? Make sure you are able to move your services elsewhere (and get a prorated refund) if you are not happy. Get it in writing before there is a problem.*
- *What is their fee structure? Make sure you understand exactly what you will be charged and what each fee includes. Also ask what is not included.*

Your Web Site Shouldn't Need a Manual

Users shouldn't need to learn how to use your site, notes Stephan Spencer, founder and president of Netconcepts, a Web-design agency. Put stuff where people expect it. Don't put the navigation bar on the right or the bottom or make nonclickable content indistinguishable from clickable. Don't force users to hover their mouse over a button to see what it does. And never hide the user's browser toolbar (the bit that contains the back, forward, and refresh buttons). Designers like to show off and be different, but different isn't always better on the Web, so be prepared to reel in your designer.

Here are some tips:

- *Have a search function on your site. Many people prefer searching by keyword rather than browsing.*
- *Don't have a "Flash" intro—a multimedia presentation that's played upon entering your site. Your Web site is not a television commercial. If you had to sit through an ad every time you phoned a supplier, you'd soon be taking your business elsewhere.*
- *Keep the navigation consistent across your site.*
- *Include navigation on every page of your site. Visitors who find your site through a search engine will not necessarily enter through your home page.*
- *Place a "Contact us" link on every page. Don't just link to your e-mail address; provide a fill-in form for visitors, as well as your telephone number and postal and street addresses.*
- *Don't use "frames," where parts of the Web page scroll but others stay fixed. Frames make it difficult, if not impossible, for users to bookmark your pages. Search engines don't like frames, either.*
- *Name things intuitively. Coke's Web site has a section called "Spill It"—not helpful.*
- *Minimize the number of clicks required to perform important functions on your site, such as making a reservation or an inquiry. Amazon's "1-Click Ordering" is the epitome of efficiency.*

TYPESETTING

Getting type set for a brochure or a Web site is a piece of cake today. Just type what you want, proof it well, and e-mail it off to your designers. They will copy and paste it exactly as you send it, so it better be accurate. You can even choose your typeface right on your computer.

SELECTING A PRINTER

This is a good time to establish a working relationship with a printer, since you'll be doing plenty of printing through the years. Find someone you're comfortable with. Ask to see samples. Check to see that they're crisp and clean, not smudged, not tilted, and with folds sharp and straight.

Printing prices can vary tremendously, so get bids for your first job from more than one printer. Include this information in your bid requests:
- Name of paper and its weight, texture, and color.
- Typeface and distinctive symbols, features, or a logo.
- Type of ink and colors, identified by PMS numbers found on printer's ink-color wheels.
- Size of finished piece: A rack card? A folded brochure?
- Number of halftones and screens.
- Number of folds and a sample of the finished folding format.
- Number of finished pieces.

Always ask for price breakdowns based on volume; the price per thousand of ten thousand brochures will be substantially less than the cost of a single thousand brochures. Think seriously about using recycled paper and soy ink, even if it costs more; guests will appreciate your concern for the environment when they see the recycled logo on your materials.

When you've received the bids and you've chosen your printer, provide painstakingly clear written instructions with your artwork and a mockup of the finished piece, illustrating where the folds go and which end is up. Keep photocopies of the artwork in case it is lost and to make telephone discussions with the printer easier while he or she has the job. Set a date to check a blueline to see how the material will look when it's printed, before the whole job is run. Make sure everything's coming out right at that stage, when changes, although very expensive, can still allow you to salvage a potential catastrophe. Be sure to agree in advance on the final completion date and pickup or delivery.

Then prepare for the thrill of holding your first printed brochure in your hands—put the champagne on ice!

Flashy May Be Trashy

Be sure your Web site design is clear, clean, and professional looking. Restrain yourself from overusing multiple font sizes, styles, and colors. Simplicity still reigns. Whirling animations, text that blinks, music that doesn't stop . . . be prudent with your creativity. Too much going on only encourages potential guests to get out of there, and fast. Keep the overall layout simple and uniform. Less is always better. This is your business. Guests can feel "warm and fuzzy" about your Web site without "Danny Boy" humming ad nauseam in their ears as they try to check your availability.

Curb Appeal

Drive-by guests! You will be surprised how many people who may be staying in your town have read about you in a book or on the Web and want to just drive by and see what the place looks like. In your planning you will want to consider how your inn looks to someone driving by (or walking by if you are in a section of town where guests stroll).

In designing the safety lighting you will want to consider how the building looks at night. You will want those late or last-minute winter guests to feel invited in. Find ways to make your building look as spectacular at night as it does in the day and locals, too, will remember you.

Plant the front of your building to look great year-round if you expect to be open all year. In cold climates this is more of a challenge, but it will pay off in drop-in guests during the off-season. Work with a local nursery or landscape designer with this look in mind.

The idea of a sign on a discreet little bed-and-breakfast was so offensive when this book was first written that it wasn't even included! Today's traveler expects to be able to find your place easily, and a well-lit, easy-to-read, well-placed sign is what they are looking for. A tasteful selection of materials and colors that mesh with your inn's theme (plus a vacancy sign) can set the tone for that first contact with your arriving or future guests.

Vacancy signs were really unacceptable twenty years ago, but today they are considered a kind of welcome sign to what seems like a place that is so intimate it isn't appropriate to come knocking at the door. To encourage visitors as well as define the limits to the touring, some inns announce on a removable board below the vacancy sign when tours of the inn are held.

Though most communities where you will locate will have sign restrictions, don't let this prevent you from putting out this statement of who you are and where your inn is. Just read the regulations, find a local signmaker who has worked with the sign committee, and be creative.

Your sign, above all, needs to be readable by people driving by in cars. You will want those drive-by guests to notice you.

> *The Davy Jackson Inn in Jackson, Wyoming, uses a hospitable alternative to the typical but somewhat harsh No Vacancy sign. Their sign by the front door says in two-inch letters, "Rooms Available." When they are full, a sign goes on top that says "Sorry No." It's a convenience to travelers not to have to climb the stairs or the path to find out if there's a room. A basket of brochures by the front door also gives a future guest a chance to take home a reminder of the inn, now that they have seen it from the outside.*

Ongoing Marketing

Marketing is one of your most important jobs, and the one that most often gets pushed aside in favor of things like toilet repair. It's a classic example of the urgent pushing aside the important. Don't let it happen to you, or all your urgent work will be complete, and you'll have no guests to enjoy the perfect flush.

The frustrating thing about marketing is the lack of immediate gratification. When you serve breakfast, you get not only the satisfaction of completing a task but also enthusiastic, immediate feedback. Marketing is not like that. Much of what you produce and pay for will never succeed. Then, unexpectedly, an article will appear in *Gourmet* magazine because a guest liked your coffee cake. Marketing is experimentation with uncontrollable elements, but it can be as creative as it is frustrating. And it's certainly a great educational adventure.

The best marketing you can do is a superb job of attending to details—and loving it—as an innkeeper, but that's just step one. There are lots more.

Decide who will be the marketing director of your small business. For the first three years at least, that person should set aside a regular weekly time to market, five to eight hours minimum. Use the time to send promotional material to writers, track patterns of occupancy and demographics, and plan new promotional strategies.

Develop a promotion file of names and addresses of travel writers who have done articles about other inns. Keep copies of the articles so you'll know the subjects and angles that most interest particular writers; this will help you target letters, releases, and personal contacts with them. Store these on your computer as well, so you can e-mail them to writers. Keep copies of information you send anywhere; you can often reuse it as it is, or modify it slightly to send to someone else. Keep a careful record of what you've done.

File art—drawings, logos in various sizes, and photographs—and originals of type used for ads and brochures. Much of this can be recycled, and it's all expensive to use just once. Keep additional separate files for advertising contracts, letters to guidebook publishers, and promotional ideas.

Mailing supplies should also be part of your promotion file. Getting together the envelope, cardboard backing for photographs, and appropriate postage, then leaving the inn to mail everything is not easy. Having all these items stocked away enables you to respond to media inquiries with lightning speed—which is just what the media expect. If you have it all saved on your computer, you may never need recourse to snail mail, but be prepared.

As results of your marketing begin to appear in newspaper and magazine articles and guidebooks, keep a scrapbook for your guests in the common room. It will provide them with interesting information about the inn and also reconfirm their idea that yours is the best place to stay.

Keep close track of your marketing efforts, and ask all guests and callers how they heard about the inn. Keep a close watch on your Web-site statistics. Review traffic monthly. If you don't see the return from a particular ad or approach, stop spending money on it. Computer software will help you track results easily, but don't let the counting and bookwork keep you from tallying this information, even if you have to do it by hand. The information is essential.

Also, save all names, home addresses, and e-mail addresses from any respondents to your marketing; this is your mailing list, worth its weight in gold for future promotions.

Whether you are suggesting a story idea to the travel editor of the *New York Times* or asking a guidebook writer to consider including your inn in the next edition, there are certain basic materials you will be expected to provide:

Color photographs.

Several color photo prints to entice writers, clearly labeled on the back with the name of the inn.

Photos in GIF (graphic interchange format) format, for use on Web sites.

Photos in TIFF (tagged image file format) format, for use in print (must be high-resolution).

Do not ask for photographs to be returned. Make extra copies instead, or offer to send electronic files.

A couple of great color photographs may make the difference between being included in a story or not; bad-quality artwork will go directly to the wastebasket. Most newspapers prefer color for soft-news articles.

Many writers say they prefer to see people in photographs, receiving a breakfast tray or walking up the front pathway; after all, these aren't real estate ads. However, you define and limit your audience if you show only young, white heterosexual couples. Also, make sure you have permission if you are showing people in your photos. And be sure your photographer is familiar with work for publication, so the contrast in the photographs will be good. Your objective is to have such appealing artwork available that editors who must choose which inn among several to highlight will pick yours so they can use your great photo. In some instances, a fine color photograph provided by an inn has appeared as the cover of a magazine! A winning formula is: Make it easy for the media to make you famous. Have several copies of everything in your drawer and on your Web site, so you can mail or e-mail artwork at a moment's notice. Label it with your inn name and address, so the recipient can identify the photo later. You want the media to keep it, just in case there's an emergency empty space to fill.

Try taping to the back of the photo a typed description or caption that you would like to have accompany the photo when it is published. Always include your inn name, town, and state in the copy. Also tape a business card or piece of paper with your name, address and phone number to the photo. Handwritten notes bleed or leave marks that could show through. Never use felt-tipped markers; their ink will smudge any photos they are stacked on top of.

You will need to provide the media with background material. Your brochure is an obvious source, but a detailed, easy-to-read description of the inn just for writers is a good idea. Describe the history of the inn, the locale, the innkeeper's biography, and what there is to do. Consider including a unique item that makes your inn stand out from the rest, just to attract the writer's attention: an acorn from your oak tree, rare seeds from your historic garden, or a bit of patchwork in the pattern of your handmade quilts.

Digital Photos

"If I had one wish, it would be for all innkeepers to have quality digital photos of their B&Bs. They are easy to e-mail and quick to insert into the Internet media," says Elizabeth Arneson of About.com, a wide-ranging Internet site with a B&B travel section.

Sandra Soule, at BedandBreakfast.com, advises: Forget line drawings; black-and-white photos are rarely used anymore. Slides and transparencies are passé. Digital photography has revolutionized the industry. On the Internet, digital pictures usually look crisper, brighter, and clearer than scanned prints. Digital images also offer instant gratification; shoot dozens of shots from different angles, with varied lighting, then load them into your computer. Chose the best to crop and brighten, and you'll have some great photos to add to your Web site. Quality remains essential in all photos, of course.

Checklist: What to Include in Your Promotion File and Library

· Your inn Web site and e-mail address should be on everything.
· Contracts for advertising.
· Artwork, carefully stored:
    Line drawings, originals with at least five copies ready to mail. You may use
        these in your own promotional postcards or letterhead.
    Logos in various sizes.
    Color prints for use in media kits (twenty copies).
    TIFF or GIF images stored on your computer and on a back-up disk.
· Articles written about the inn; keep five copies of each. Be sure you have permission to reprint.
· Recipes with a little background; keep original plus ten copies.
· Chamber of commerce materials about area; twenty copies.
· Written information (ten copies each, as well as stored on your computer so you can customize where appropriate and print out as needed) on:
    Inn history, architecture, rooms.

Owner's or innkeeper's background.

Special packages, events, cooperative marketing.

Your food.

- Stories about the inn to help the media write about you.
- Brochures and rate sheets.
- Menus and recipes from the dining room or breakfast.
- Mailing materials

    Twelve nice folders to hold materials.

    Twelve large (9-by-12) envelopes.

    Four overnight express envelopes (Federal Express will let you charge fees on your credit card) with telephone number and times for pickup.

    Cardboard backing to protect artwork.

    Postage stamps.
- Your special item in quantity: an oak leaf, a bit of patchwork, etc.

Also include a collection of chamber of commerce materials about your town and area; there's no need to duplicate material you probably help pay for with your membership.

Reprints of articles on your inn give media people a feeling of security, that they're not alone in being interested in you. Reprints should show dates, the writer's name, and the newspaper or book title. Select the most recent and the best coverage as the quantity grows. Be sure you have permission to reprint articles. Sometimes it is less expensive to get copies of the magazine or buy reprints from the publisher, but be sure to ask before you copy.

Many inns assemble these materials in loose-leaf binders or cardboard folders to present to writers. Some inns preprint covers with their logo; others find attractive ways to mount a business card or brochure on the cover. Your presentation should look professional, but don't be afraid to be innovative and creative; media people get kits by the hundreds.

Now you're ready to promote. In some cases, you'll want to introduce your inn to an important writer with your complete kit; in others, you'll select appropriate materials from it. Depending on the photos, artwork, and attention-getters your kit includes, it can be expensive. Use it judiciously, but don't be stingy. A major article is worth the price of a lot of kits!

INN GUIDEBOOKS

Innkeepers say inn guidebooks are no longer their largest single source of business; the Internet has now assumed that position. However, inns are regularly being included in well-known mainstream travel guides, which shouldn't be ignored. In books like Fodor's and Frommer's travel guides you'll find inns sprinkled throughout the hotel listings. Because the time lag between selecting inns for a volume and getting the guide to the bookstore can be a year or two, contacting guidebook writers can begin even before you open.

The best approach is to send a letter to the author in care of the publishing house. Indicate that you're familiar with the author's book and understand his or her particular emphasis, which might be history, cuisine, or quality. Explain why your inn is an appropriate inclusion, particularly if it helps fill an obvious gap, such as location. Always give them your Web-site URL.

Briefly describe a few additional things that make your inn different from others. Being "romantic" and "charming" is not enough. Use specific, vivid language that will help your reader get a feeling for your inn. Mention attractions and events in your area, and invite the writer to visit. Enclose a press kit or material from it: a brochure and other information that will make a visit irresistible, particularly anything that relates specifically to the author's guidebook angle. You may also want to include some reference to yourself—a hobby, something about your life before innkeeping, your close relationship to the House of Windsor—to convey that time spent with you will be interesting. Your tone should reflect your style as an innkeeper, just as it does with guests or prospective guests.

Keep the letter brief—a single page, if possible—and before you finalize it, ask someone not connected with the inn to read it and tell you what overall impression it conveys. This is a safeguard against the errors occasioned by being too close to your subject.

Naturally, this letter is going to take some time. Once you've written it, though, you'll find that with slight modifications it's a good letter to use for many other contacts, with other media, or with new businesses in your area that might need accommodations for clients. And you'll personalize it to send to writers of several other guidebooks, too.

Keep guidebook writers informed of price or other significant changes, and when they do list your inn, send a thank-you note. Guidebook writers also write for other publications and the Web and are used as consultants by travel writers, so cultivate these relationships.

Should you offer a free night's stay? Many writers make it a policy not to accept free nights, to ensure their objectivity. On the other hand, it's expensive to visit hundreds of inns a year, and some writers almost have to accept free nights. It doesn't hurt to suggest it.

According to PAII's comprehensive *Guide to the Inn Guidebooks*, less than 30 percent of guidebooks charge fees to list inns. Before you pay, ask other innkeepers who keep good guest records whether the listings are worth it. Innkeepers are inundated with offers for listings in books and on Internet sites. PAII maintains a file of offers they have researched for members, and a list of good questions to ask.

When you receive a solicitation from a guidebook writer, check the deadlines and respond clearly and on time with what they want. Most guidebook authors will not visit your inn, so the information you send is your chance to be included.

INTERNET DIRECTORIES AND WEB MARKETING

Once you are up and running, your e-mail inbox will be overwhelmed with Internet opportunities. For all intents and purposes, these directories have far surpassed the paper guide as a primary source of business for the small inn. Travel (second only to pornography) is one of the primary reasons people access the Web.

What works and what doesn't changes extremely quickly. A few years ago any small B&B could list on the Web and expect to reap many reservations. The sheer volume of lodging properties listed on the Web today has decreased the initial ease of that marketing success. These days, inns pay for every possible exposure, if not in time then definitely in money. Today the trend is "pay per click." Who knows what tomorrow will bring? There is, however, no doubt that innkeepers need to remain very attentive.

To ensure maximum exposure, list on several directories, especially those that come up highest when you search for "bed-and-breakfast" on a search engine such as www.google.com. Check out innkeeper Bill Wayne's www.InnStar.com ratings of Internet B&B directories. Before you sign up, always go to the directory and browse to find out more about it. See what properties are listed. What catches your eye as a user? How can you best be featured? Review the "Marketing and Promotion" section of Resources for more ways to evaluate a new directory offer.

How do you know which directories are working for you? Once you are listed, work with your own Webmaster to track the business you receive. Interpreting a detailed analysis of your Web-site traffic should be one of your monthly tasks; you just need to know how it works and what it means.

Also consider using different e-mail addresses for tracking. For example, use your domain name as your e-mail address, changing to whom it is addressed for each directory in which you are listed. Try listing different packages or photos on each directory, so when a guest calls about the Lovers' Package (found on www.bbonline.com) rather than the Romance Package (as seen on www.Bedand Breakfast.com) you'll know where they found you.

Get to know the directories on which you are listed. Often there are special sections for recipes or packages; these may not cost anything and can give you added exposure. Some regularly feature selected properties on their home page; usually an extra cost applies.

This section could go into great detail about the state of the marketplace, but it would be out of date tomorrow. PAII's *innkeeping* newsletter features a "Bits and Bytes" column, which has kept innkeepers up to speed since the Web first began to poke its head into our industry.

TRAVEL WRITERS

Coverage in newspaper and magazine travel articles is one of the best free promotions for inns. Sometimes getting a story is just luck, but there are also things inns can do to attract attention. To plan the most effective approach to a travel writer, consider your story from a writer's viewpoint.

Writers need to produce good articles in a reasonable amount of time. Remember that these folks are being invited to all kinds of places, all the time; a "getaway" is not the thrill to them that it would be to you. The information you provide should reassure them that they'll get a great story without a tremendous amount of work if they take the time to visit. You must provide complete information on rates, directions, special programs and deals, and so on.

Your area is as important as your inn. Innkeepers often mistakenly believe an inn makes a story, but travel writers regard inns as places to stay, not reasons to travel. A large part of your "sell" is selling the things to do in your area.

How do you identify travel writers? Start by developing a list of names and addresses of travel writers who have done articles on other inns. Save copies of the articles so you'll know the subjects and angles that most interest particular writers; this information will be helpful when you write them a pitch. Subscribe to the publications in which you'd like to be featured, and get a feel for what they look for. You might also contact the Society of American Travel Writers for their members list or search on-line for travel publications and travel editors.

Some innkeepers routinely send out press releases to writers; others insist that personal letters are the best approach. In either case, keep in mind that travel writers get stacks of mail, and many of them have perfected the art of reducing the size of the stacks at a rate of about an inch a minute. You need to attract attention and make a compelling case in your first paragraph.

On the whole, sending a mass mailing to travel writers announcing your inn opening is probably a waste of time. It would be wiser to send out specific invitations to writers in nearby large cities. Do something catchy to attract attention, like sending a box of cookies along with the invitation to an opening of Grandmother's Inn, or delivering a hot pizza along with the invitation to the opening of Albergo Lucia. Use all the pizzazz you can muster!

When you finally hear from your dream writer, what then? Here are some quick guidelines:

· Return calls and e-mails promptly. Often writers are on deadline; if you're not available, they may call the next inn on the list.
· Show enthusiasm.
· Be a good listener who is interested in the writer. You'll learn how best to meet their publication requirements and fit into their articles.
· Send promotional information as soon as possible. Use e-mail, overnight mail, or your fax to get it there fast.
· Always get the writer's name, address, phone number, and publication, even if it's just a quick phone interview. You might come up with a great new angle and want this person on your media list.
  When the writer arrives:
· Always tell the truth. If you don't know the answer, say so.
· Be ready with a colorful anecdote about your inn or yourself: how many couples were engaged at your inn, how many pancakes you've served, the biggest fish caught in the lake, and so on. Write these ideas down when you get them, so you'll be ready for writers.
· Say what is different about your place. It may be the history, the theme, or package deals—anything that makes your inn stand out from the rest.
· Give the writer something to take home: cookies, muffins, a jar of jam, flowers, a sachet—any small reminder of your hospitality. A gift of food allows writers to speak of your cooking, even if they're not there for a meal.
· Offer to introduce the writer to other tourist operators in the area, including other inns, restaurants, and attractions. Function as a tour guide.
· Don't complain about anything, including guests, being overworked, expenses, or even local government. Be positive.
· Don't ask to read and approve material before it is published, or ask for a guarantee that you'll be included. (Unless you're paying; that's advertising, a different matter.)
· Don't speak off the record; who says anything good off the record?
  What about complimentary lodging? Ask for more information before offering free lodging or a discount, whether you're responding to a letter, a call, or a visitor who has arrived unannounced. You can do this gracefully, while ascertaining whether the person is genuine or merely looking for a free room; fortunately,

there are only a few of these freeloaders. In fact, few authentic writers actually spend the night, so when they do, treat them like royalty.

It's okay to ask about the project. Who is the publisher? What is the assignment? When will it be published? Ask about previous articles so you can get an idea of the writer's interests. A professional understands your need for information and will not be insulted. Often a freelance writer can provide you with a copy of the assignment letter. If you're still doubtful, call the publication.

If, despite your best efforts, your inn is not included in an article, don't feel cheated. The writer may be able to use your information another time. Take it in stride and keep the writer on your mailing list.

And if your inn, or even just your area, is included in a story, send a warm thank-you note or letter!

SPECIAL EVENTS

Special events are gatherings done around a theme, designed to expose people to your inn, create interest, and generate publicity. The big-city paper in your area is unlikely to do more than one travel article about your inn, but if you sponsor an autumn biking tour that goes from inn to inn, Mystery Weekends, or an annual puzzle challenge, that's news.

The more angles you can come up with, the better. Some inns plan events calendars for a full year, so that every article on one event automatically leads readers to send for the full calendar. Sometimes you can get local merchants to cosponsor, saving you money and providing more hands for the work to be done. For example, the bike tour might include stops at new wineries in the area, or it might be sponsored by a worthy nonprofit group that will do much of the promotion for you. Nonprofit sponsorship of events means you can get free public-service announcements on radio and television, too.

Sometimes special events are a way to bring in paying overnight guests at slow times of the year; they can also introduce local residents to your inn, who will then think of you first for accommodating out-of-town guests. For some inns, the events themselves have provided important incomes during the early years before occupancy could support the operation.

Special events are great opportunities for creative promoters to generate consistent publicity and to develop an image of the inn as the place to be. But they're also a lot of work, so be sure you plan something that's fun for you. Even if it isn't a roaring success, at least you will have had a good time during your slow season.

Creating a newsworthy happening is just the first step; the follow-up of letters, press releases, and phone calls to the media takes a lot of time, energy, and nerve. If you've got all those, you can make events pay off.

How can a little inn put on a communitywide event that becomes a business-building tradition?

In 1980, Dane and Joan Wells established the Queen Victoria Bed and Breakfast Inn in Cape May, New Jersey, and their development of several special events over the following years helped build their business. Working with retail shops, restaurants, and other inns, the Wellses have also helped change Cape May's seasonal shore economy into a robust year-round economy.

Dane, who in a prior career supervised economic-development marketing programs, cites several basic principles that have helped make the Queen Victoria successful. "Know your 'brand' and market it," he says. "Don't just make marketing noise using popular clichés. Sing a polished tune that focuses on who you are. Better yet, work with others and sing in harmony!"

- *Know your "brand"—what Disney calls a "story." It might not be appropriate for a rustic colonial inn to do a high-style Victorian event. Market what you are. Dane and Joan saw Victorian Christmas as an event opportunity to say, "The Queen Victoria is open year-round." Their inn is very Victorian, and the Wellses thoroughly researched Victorian Christmas customs.*
- *Popular clichés: In 1981, Christmas house tours were not yet an overworked idea. Nevertheless, Dane and Joan tried to make the Queen Victoria tour different by offering interesting content, not just pretty decorations.*
- *A polished tune: It was this tour content that attracted media coverage. Christmas tours were not new, but the Wellses, with their educational content, offered a tour that was different and in style. Valuable national press coverage was the result.*
- *Who you are: Joan was a former Victorian house-museum curator and executive director of the Victorian Society; she had the knowledge, credibility, and contacts to support the content of the tours and to promote it to the media.*
- *Work with others in harmony: The first tour of the Queen Victoria at Christmas 1981 drew forty visitors. The next year the Wellses asked three other inns to join in, and the tour drew four hundred visitors. The Wellses also worked in close concert with the local arts organization, and Dane involved local merchants. The tour grew logarithmically as they added*

more inns and businesses to the event. Though the Wellses have retired from the tour, the Cape May Christmas Tours now attract tens of thousands of visitors from late November through early January.

The key concept, Dane says, is "To thine own self be true." This is critical to effective marketing of any kind. It is important to realistically analyze who you are and what your strengths are. He says he sees too many inns floundering, wasting energy and resources by trying overworked ideas that really don't fit their particular brand.

The other lesson the Wellses and the businesses in Cape May have demonstrated is the importance of working together. As a former Main Street coordinator, Dane will tell you that this isn't easy, but it pays to start small and keep trying.

For more information, see www.queenvictoria.com and select "Christmas" from the menu.

ADVERTISING

"Never buy ads or vacuum cleaners on the first contact," or so the saying goes. Ad salespeople always sound urgent, but there will always be another chance. Here are some guidelines to help you make wise advertising decisions.

- Remember that advertising is only one part of your overall promotion campaign, and that it needs to be integrated into the plan. A number of excellent, one-time articles on your inn won't help for long if readers can't find out how to contact you a few months later, when they finally plan a trip.
- The reader, or audience, is basically passive. The more difficult you make your ad to read, the less attention it will get. Some marketing studies claim you have all of three seconds to grab a reader's attention.
- Arrange the information in the ad as clearly as possible. Use the 60-40 rule: 60 percent art and 40 percent copy, or 60 percent copy and 40 percent art. If art and copy are given equal weight, the reader will be confused about what to focus on.
- The primary goal of an ad is to give your reader the basic facts: what you do, where you are, and how to reach you. The size ad you buy should determine how many more details you will be able to share.
- Are you primarily competing with inns in your area, and therefore working to differentiate your place on the basis of price, services, quality, and so on? Or is

yours the only inn in the area, and you are trying to attract a new market, pioneer-style? Determine your position—it may very well combine a bit of both objectives—to help construct more effective ads.

- How well will your ad compete on a page? If you are buying a small ad on a directory page, you have a lot of competition for attention. So how can you draw the reader's eye? Use bold borders, bold type, or black background with white type. Is your logo a real eye-catcher, or does it need to be strengthened when it's reduced? Can you use a combination of bold and lightweight typefaces or a combination of type sizes to balance the look of the ad?

- Leave room around the words or the design within the borders of the ad so the eye can focus. Graphic designers call this concept white space. Consider walking into a room with flowered wallpaper, plaid curtains, striped upholstery, and mirrors along one wall. The eye doesn't know where to look first; it has no resting place, no focus. The only obvious move is to leave the room. For the same reasons you wouldn't decorate this way, you shouldn't design ads this way.

- Repetition—alias money, money, money. A one-time placement of an ad is likely to get little or no response. When you've carefully considered all the periodicals you might buy space in, and you've made your choice(s), give the ad(s) some time. For a reader, it's a disappointment to try unsuccessfully to find an ad that was there last month in a current issue.

- When should you advertise? Do you expect a slow time you want to bolster? Advertise before you hit it. In the middle of a lull is no time to make a one-month advertising appearance. Besides, you won't have any money then. If there's a time of year when your area is flooded with tourists, you may want to advertise then, so people take your ad home to plan for the next season. You might also want to run an ad that encourages them to come back at a slower time.

- Figure out exactly what the ad's purpose is, and then buy space accordingly. The only way you can gauge the effectiveness of an ad is to be very clear from the beginning about what you want it to do.

- Never, never, never let a persuasive sales representative talk you into buying an ad during the first phone call or meeting. Ask for the rate sheets and the demographics information on the subscribing population. A professional publication will have this information for you. Then tell them you'll get back to them after you review it.Check their editorial calendar; it will list the topics to be covered in particular issues, so you can time advertising decisions or submission of copy for stories for appropriate issues. If the publication looks like a good possibility, request the same kind of information from its competitors. Compare them carefully to choose your best buy.

- In general, beware of little, "inexpensive" ads, those costing $30 to $75. The only truly inexpensive ad is one that brings in more business and income than it costs.
- Advertising lodging in the local paper is usually a waste of money. Instead, get involved in fund-raisers for community causes, and advertise the events. This demonstrates your public spirit and inclines the local media to print your media releases.
- If you're considering a particular ad buy, contact other inns that use the publication and ask about their results. Sometimes you'll get a more helpful answer from inns not in your immediate competitive area.

Advertising shouldn't be an impulse or instinct buy, and it doesn't have to be. Just make sure you know what you want your ads to do, and then run ones that accomplish your purpose and target your audience at a good price. To target your ads, you have to do your homework. Start by reviewing your guest research. Where will most of your guests come from? What professions will they represent: doctors, attorneys, teachers, carpenters, or artists? Finally, what will your guests come to the inn to do: ski, hike, or eat?

Using this information, develop a list of advertising target priorities. Be as specific as you can about your target goals. For example, maybe your very best market includes bird-watching dentists from the Twin Cities, and your next best, also from Minneapolis–St. Paul, comprises carpenters who enjoy the hot springs and mud baths. How do you reach these targets?

If your audience is chiefly made up of professionals from the Twin Cities, there may be a business journal most of them receive. If they are in small business, a chamber of commerce publication might be good. If your guest population is very broad in terms of profession and activities, you might consider advertising in the *Minneapolis Star Tribune's* travel section, a publication that targets a geographic area more than a demographic one.

The next step is designing an ad that will catch the eyes of the people you want to attract. If you're after craftspeople, how about an ad with calligraphy? Professionals may be drawn to a very sophisticated, clean look. (Caution: this may be the toughest one to achieve without the assistance of a pro.)

If you plan to work with an artist on the ad, look at several portfolios to find an artist who already does the kind of thing you like. It's much easier than trying to explain to an artist, no matter how talented, an unfamiliar style that your heart is set on.

GIFT CERTIFICATES AND GIVEAWAYS

Gift certificates for nights at the inn can generate income during slow times, like Christmas. There's also a publicity angle on gift certificates: inns are frequently asked to donate them as prizes for fund-raisers. Every time your inn is mentioned at a raffle or a silent auction, potential guests hear it. Every guest who comes at no charge, as the result of a fund-raiser, will be another satisfied customer to spread the word.

To help a good cause without loss of needed income, limit the certificate's validity period to times when the inn won't be full. Know your state's law on gift-certificate expiration dates. Track the way your donation is publicized, so you can decide whether you'll want to do it again next year. Feel free to be specific about the conditions of your offer. You can donate for the silent auction only, or perhaps reserve the right to be the only inn featured.

YELLOW PAGES ADVERTISING

The Yellow Pages are tricky because everyone has a copy, so it seems obvious that you should be in them. Their salespeople are confusing and sometimes confused, and the ads add up. Here are a few recommendations to get through the maze, from experienced ad man Rusty Pile of www.TTAadvertising.com.

Step 1: Look at the book. See who's advertising in the appropriate sections. What size are their ads? Do they use color? What information is included? Essentially, this is a reconnaissance mission. Odds are that if there are several advertisers in your directory, directory advertising works well in your area. However, if there are no advertisers in your directory, this could be your opportunity to dominate with a small, inexpensive ad.

Step 2: How expensive is it to dominate your section? Request costs from a directory representative and pay attention to any special offers they might have. Many times directories will offer upgrade deals or new-advertiser promotions that you can take advantage of. If there are no advertisers in a section, you might also be able to swing a deal as the first advertiser (directories love to stimulate competition). With some promotions it's actually possible to purchase a larger ad than your competitors yet pay less than they do. But most importantly, decide how much business you would need that ad to stimulate for an acceptable return on your investment. If you are unsure about what to do, start slowly. Test the waters with something a little larger than what you've done in the past; perhaps a bold listing or a one-inch listing. If you see a positive response, step it up the next year. Keep track of all calls (you'll do that, right?) and monitor your return on this investment. What are you paying per reservation compared with your other advertising?

Step 3: After deciding on an appropriate size and color (if any), it's time to design the ad. Unlike with other publications, you do not need to sell readers on the prospect of buying your type of product. After all, they turned to your heading because they're ready to buy and are just searching for the right property. Show off your property with a graphic or photo, if applicable. That's what they're really looking for. Make sure your property phone number is prominent. Use your logo if you can. List your amenities, address, and unique selling proposition as the headline or tag line (e.g., "Voted Finest Inn on the Island."). Finally, unless you are a true graphic-design professional who does outstanding work, pay the extra few hundred dollars and hire one. Don't cut corners here. This is your livelihood. The return on a professionally designed ad far outweighs the cost.

MARKETING TO GUESTS WITH DISABILITIES

Here is an opportunity to expand your guest population to include the over 37 million consumers with a visual, hearing, or physical disability.

Start with checking your language. Of course you wouldn't use terms like "retarded," "crippled," or "crazy," but appropriate terminology today can be confusing, even to the best-intentioned. Peter Robertson, a disabilities consultant, prefers the term "people with different physical, hearing, or visual abilities." To Robertson, the rest of the world is made up of TABs, the "temporarily able-bodied," since everyone is vulnerable to age and accidents.

Other appropriate terms include "physically challenged," "disabled," "visually impaired," and "wheelchair users." "Lame," "wheelchair-bound," and "confined to a wheelchair" are considered derogatory. "Blind" and "deaf" are acceptable, but "deaf and dumb" is not.

Language is powerful. It reflects, reinforces, and shapes perceptions. Words that inspire positive attitudes and awareness help develop great communication with happy, returning guests.

Where Can I Turn for Help?

Find out more about the needs of the otherwise abled. It is time to walk (or roll, as the case may be) in someone else's shoes (or chair). Understand your inn from their viewpoint. Invite someone from a local organization that provides services for the disabled community or ask a disabled friend to go through your inn and discuss what you need to do to increase accessibility. Talk to someone who actually experiences the disability. An architect generally knows the law, but you want more. You want happy guests.

Communication Accessibility for Hearing-Disabled Travelers

The most effective way of contacting the deaf community is through e-mail. Investing in a TDD (telecommunications device for the deaf), which attaches to your phone and has a keyboard with a screen, is no longer necessary.

Deaf callers can also dial the relay system in their state and be connected with you; a voice operator then reads their typing aloud to you, and types your response back to them during the call.

Letting the World Know

If your inn is barrier-free and has met federal guidelines, use the international blue-wheelchair symbol for accessibility. However, do not misrepresent yourself. This group of travelers has more often than not encountered serious misrepresentation regarding accessibility. Be honest and clear about any and all obstacles that exist. For example: "The bath has no turnaround and the sink has no knee clearance, but the shower and toilet have grab bars, and there is plenty of room to wheel into the bathroom. In addition, there is a one-inch threshold on the outside entry door, but it is thirty-one inches wide and has a ramp. We also have a portable ramp for entering and exiting the dining room."

Architectural and communication barriers are obvious, but attitude is an invisible barrier. You may think, "I won't get much request for this type of room, so there's no need for me to make changes." This may be true, but it also may not. If hearing-disabled individuals cannot even call you or physically disabled persons have other obviously safer choices (which advertise and market to them), why would they even bother to contact your inn? Imagine the delight of a wheelchair user when a great place like yours solicits their business!

E-MAIL COMMUNICATIONS

Personal handwritten notes are nice, but it is personal e-mail that will be your primary, and often preferred, method of communication with guests, suppliers, and other innkeepers.

Two kinds of e-mail are your friend: e-mail that comes to you and to which you respond, and e-mail you send in quantity to guests or potential guests who have signed up to receive newsletters or information on seasonal specials.

E-mail can consume you, and you can end up not doing a very good job at it if you don't keep some pretty important things in mind.

The key marketing question to answer is always, "What's in it for me?" Tempt them, entice them, and find ways to show them how they'll benefit from coming to your inn.

The key rule of writing applies here in spades: Keep it short. Of all types of communication that need brevity, this one is at the top of the list. E-mail users want information that is easy to read quickly. If you want to provide them with more information offer a link to your site or another helpful site, but don't send an e-mail that is longer than the screen. Don't expect a reader to scroll down very far to read your message.

"Don't forget the call to action," advises editor Sandra Soule of the Bedand Breakfast.com newsletter. Whether it is calling immediately for two rooms available this weekend or booking for the upcoming mystery weekend, you want to give them a reason to act—in other words, send you money.

A few e-mail quirks need to be observed as well.

Use the subject line effectively. Make it attention getting and accurate. If you are on your fourth reply to an e-mail about a reservation but now are discussing how to get to the inn, change the subject line to read "Directions to Canberra Inn." If you are sending confirmation information, you might write in the subject line: "Print this out and save: confirmation for the Have Fun Inn."

Learn to use your particular e-mail software program completely. As these change and are refined, you will find you can do layout, color, different typefaces, and all kinds of things to make the copy more interesting. Beware of being unreadable or too cutsey, and of creating messages that will take users with standard phone lines too long to receive.

Readability is basic. Never write in all capital letters; you can, however, use caps to emphasize certain sections. Text written in all capitals is hard to read and is considered the Internet equivalent of shouting.

Use signature files. Create a signature file that includes all your key contact information (name, inn name, address, phone, fax, e-mail address, Web-site URL) as well as a brief but distinctive phrase about your inn.

Make your life easier by creating e-mail that does your work for you. Develop a series of reusable enticing paragraphs about the inn you can send every time you get a specific question: room descriptions, breakfast menu, directions to the inn, special packages, check-in details. Even if these are included on the Web site, also collect them on your e-mail files for easy use. It's more polite to give the e-mailer the information than to send them back to the Web site, which is a little like telling them when they call on the phone to just look at their brochure.

Speed works for you, but it can work very much against you. Potential guests expect immediate responses, so check your e-mail early and check it often—reply within the day if not within the hour. As soon as you can get high-speed Internet access, do so; then you can stay connected all the time, rather than having to dial up many times a day. If you can't get back promptly, set an explanatory auto-responder message. Never send an e-mail when you are angry; wait until you cool off. Even then, to prevent it from being mailed unexpectedly, save it as a draft or don't address it until you have thought more about it.

E-MAIL MARKETING

With the time and increasing cost of snail mail (mailing through the post office), innkeepers are turning to e-mail to promote their special events, vacant rooms, and the new dog. Stephan Spencer of Netconcepts advises, "E-mail can be your inn's secret weapon, or it can end up biting you in the backside if it's seen as junk e-mail or spam. It all depends on the execution. You've seen companies make deadly e-mail mistakes, like listing their entire customer list in the (cc) line or flooding recipients' inboxes with thousands of copies of the same message."

The Web is a "pull" marketing medium. You are at the visitor's mercy as to whether they return or not. With e-mail, on the other hand, you can "push" a marketing message at them. E-mail marketing campaigns can generate great results. For example, you can increase repeat stays just by asking guests for their e-mail addresses and anniversary dates and then sending out e-mails reminding them of that special occasion. There are some ground rules for good e-mail marketing. Try the following helpful suggestions from Stephan.

Seven Tips for Successful E-mail Marketing

- **Get permission.** Don't buy or rent lists of e-mail addresses. Ask your guests or visitors to your Web site if they want to subscribe to your e-mail list or lists. Make your specialty lists specific: "Procrastinators" for last-minute openings, "Great Deals" for special packages for the economy-minded, "Arts Lovers" for gallery openings, plays, or special exhibitions in your area, "Food Fanatics" for recipes and new restaurant announcements. Include simple unsubscribe instructions, then abide by users' wishes if they opt out.
- **Work at your subject line.** It should have a good call to action or value proposition. Use the subject line to satisfy the recipients' needs and appeal to their interests. Consider including their first name.
- **Make it easy.** Easy to unsubscribe, to offer feedback, or to place an order by phone, e-mail or on-line. Make sure that if a recipient hits "Reply," it won't come straight back to them marked "Undeliverable."
- **Distance yourself from spammers, weasels selling weight-loss gimmicks, and other scam merchants.** Put your inn's name in the "From" line, not "Here it is" or "jm169@hotmail.com." Sign your e-mail with a real person's name. Address it to the person you want to receive it, not to "undisclosed recipients."
- **Write compelling copy.** Make the e-mail short and sweet (but appetizing), so that it can be scanned easily. Make judicious use of links, including one to your privacy-policy page (you do have one, don't you?), where you reassure subscribers you won't share their details with third parties. Make the message look good; a poorly designed e-mail begets poor results.
- **Track everything.** Calculate click-through rates, unsubscribe rates, bounce rates, "open" rates (meaning that they viewed your e-mail), and, most importantly, conversion rates, where you've successfully converted recipients into guests.
- **Test, test, test!** Test the offer, the "Subject" line, the "From" line, the message copy, the layout, the message length, the timing, and the contact frequency. Set up a control group and experimental groups, where you vary just one element per group. Pay particular attention to the contact frequency, particularly if it's a regular mailing, such as an e-mail newsletter.

As software changes, so too will e-mail, so keep up and refine your skills in this dynamic marketing and communication area. It takes writing skill and sensitivity to the written word to assure that this is positive experience every time

> *Elaine Herbert of Yelton Manor on Lake Michigan creates goodwill through her daily e-mails in which the subject line reads, "Bless You." She collects quotes, then sends one every morning to her friends' and guests' e-mail inboxes. The quotes are generally a sentence long and uplifting, a great way to start the day. (They're not biblical, despite the subject line.) Of course, she lists her name and inn details so anyone reading her message just might feel so good about Elaine and her dear thoughts that they call her up and make a reservation.*

DIRECT MAIL

Direct mail gives you the opportunity to capture a prospective guest's undivided attention—for a few seconds, at least. Compare this with magazine advertising, where readers may never see your ad at all among the competition.

Successful mail promotion makes a valuable short-term offer that is urgent, personal, and easy to understand. Even offering a percentage discount is too complex. Think about which offer would make you drop everything and run: "Stay two weeknights and get 20 percent off" or "Stay three nights and we'll give you a hundred bucks!" Be sure to describe exactly how a guest can take advantage of the offer, and tell them to do it. Many innkeepers are shy about saying, "Call now," but it works.

Traditional elements of successful direct-mail marketing are an envelope with a two-page cover letter, a brochure, and a special offer. Innkeepers are breaking ground in changing this standard, with clever, well-designed postcards, full-color photos of the inn, self-mailing brochures, and newsletters. Naturally, whatever you produce should be consistent with and extend your overall theme at the inn.

How do you know which idea will work best? Print two different offers, randomly splitting your list. Code them so you know when you get a booking whether the guest responded to the special rate, say, or the free champagne. Stick with the most successful offer on subsequent mailings.

Postcards

Promoting slower seasons takes creativity, and Betty Gladden of the Garratt Mansion in Alameda, California, has been doing theme teas for years, focusing her efforts on locals. Here is a postcard invitation from the inn. It doesn't always have to be fancy, expensive, or four-color. Betty has done four-color and one-color postcards. Both seem to work well.

The Direct Marketing Association reports that postcards are the second most likely piece of mail to be read (after newspapers and magazines) and that they are the least common piece of mail received, making them stand out. Innkeepers are sending birthday and anniversary cards generated from their computer records of guests who celebrated these events in previous years.

Newsletters

Innkeepers find that well-written newsletters sent a couple of times a year live beyond special offers on postcards when they include recipes, travel hints, and powerful, sincere personal stories. Pam Thorsen of the Rosewood Inn in Minnesota muses about direct mail, "It's about reaching out and touching our guests. We are so grateful to them, and this is a way that we have a chance to let them know." She reports that a recent mailing, sent to ten thousand former guests and prospective guests, increased business by 22 percent over the year before—just in the first two months after the mailing. Most reservations were from repeat guests.

Where do you get such a list? Your own records of former guests and inquirers is at least four times as effective as any other list you can use, according to Don Peppers and Martha Rogers in *The One to One Future*. Of course, if you are just opening, you won't have a list, but if you are taking over an existing inn, be sure you get its list of former guests—even if it is on little pieces of paper in a shoe box. Also consider purchasing lists from other inns and from inn consumer publications, the local chamber of commerce, a state association, or a list broker. Be sure you focus on zip codes that match the demographics of your inn's guest profile.

If you've got a clearly targeted audience and an irresistible idea, mail it! Once you've developed a piece that works, you can use it again and again.

The Porch Swing Awaits

Creative, clever, and succinct, this copy makes for a great e-mail marketing piece or for a print postcard. Choose your words thoughtfully and carefully, for they say much about your B&B . . . and you. For example:

"Time away doesn't just happen. You have to plan for it. Reminisce about the last time you were here. Remember the pace of this pleasant little river town, Hastings. Remember the walk downtown watching the mighty Mississippi meander by under the highway bridge, then the railroad bridge. Remember the distant sound of the train whistle.

Remember just the two of you—alone together (at last). Remember sleeping late, perhaps tucking in again after the last bite of caramel-apple bread pudding. Remember quiet, a rocker creaking, a page turning, a fire crackling, a warm effervescent whirlpool. Remember classic Rosewood."

(From the Rosewood Inn, Minnesota.)

The numbers are irrefutable. According to Eric Goldreyer of BedandBreak-fast.com, "Innkeepers report up to 50 to 90 percent of their business coming from the Internet, and the numbers increase daily." And one of the best ways to capture some of this marketplace is from the use of on-line availability or real-time booking. Understanding the differences is challenging, but inns of all sizes use these systems, both as a service to their guests and for themselves.

Definitions

Availability: You are able to show, on the Internet, which rooms are available at your inn and which ones are not.

Typically displayed in a calendar-style chart, inventory can be shown as individual rooms, categories (such as suites, fireplace rooms, etc.), or a combination of both individual and classes of rooms. Dates up to one or two years in the future can be displayed.

When potential guests are ready to make a reservation, they contact the inn directly via e-mail, fax, phone, or a secure reservation-request form. The inn confirms each booking. The cost to use one of these systems is typically an annual flat-rate fee.

Real-Time Booking (RTB): These systems both display your available inventory and sell your rooms directly to Web visitors. Confirmations are automatically generated by the booking system, the moment the Web visitor fills out the booking form. Your available room inventory can be displayed in a broad range of travel-portal Web sites and travel-booking systems. Commissions are charged, most often on a sliding scale, per room-night sold. (Definitions are courtesy of Tom Lichtman, Availability Online)

What They Have in Common

- *Display of inventory.* Both types of systems list rooms the innkeeper has chosen to make available.
- *Inventory maintained by property.* Both types of systems require regular updating by the innkeeper. This is performed either automatically, with a Web interface built into the inn's guest management software, or through a manual interface of password-protected Web pages in which boxes are clicked to indicate status.

Where They Differ

- *Exposure.* RTB systems sell your inventory through a variety of global distribution systems (GDS), such as Sabre, Travelocity, and travel-agent networks. They maintain their own central travel-portal sites. Availability systems are attached to the inn's Web site, and to Web sites of lodging associations, travel destinations, or chambers of commerce that choose to include links to availability systems.
- *Confirmations.* With availability systems, the lodging property confirms all reservation requests. The final sale rests with the innkeeper. Some type of interaction with the guest is necessary. RTB systems generate immediate confirmations automatically. No interaction with the guest is necessary to complete a sale.
- *Money.* Availability systems are not involved in financial transactions. They are limited to displaying inventory and some level of detail for rates, but do not process credit cards or collect funds. RTB systems collect funds from the prospective guest before a confirmation is issued. Payment (minus commission) will then be conveyed from the RTB to the inn.
- *Commissions.* RTB systems charge commissions on room sales confirmed through their Web sites. The rate can vary, depending on the source of the Web visitor, from lower (or zero) commissions for visitors originating on the inn's Web site to higher ones when the visitor comes through the system's portal or an affiliated travel-booking system, such as Sabre. Availability systems do not charge commissions on room sales.
- *Inventory displayed.* With availability systems, the inn typically displays all available rooms. When using a RTB system, any room displayed and sold will potentially require a commission to be paid. Innkeepers often choose not to display prime-time inventory, knowing that those nights can be sold by the property directly. Some type of "inventory blocking" is usually involved with real-time booking. This gives the system the ability to sell a room on behalf of the inn with assurance that it is available. When used effectively, blocking gives "dibs" to the RTB system and prevents double-booking.
- *Complexity.* In order to "free sell" rooms, RTB systems need to be kept up to date on precise rate schedules and minimum-stay requirements. Availability systems can show rates optionally in broad ranges, in more specific detail, or not at all.

Why Use One of the Systems

"We are all concerned about our communications with guests," say Nancy and Steve Sandstrom at the Pinehurst Inn at Pikes Creek in Bayfield, Wisconsin. "The argument is made by many innkeepers that they want a phone conversation with the potential guest in order to screen them, and to provide the potential guest the opportunity to screen us. While the need is valid, we felt it was counterproductive to go against what is an obvious trend—use of the Web to research and eventually book reservations. So the challenge has been to offer this option in a manner that still affords good communications and accurate availability information."

"Just do it," says Donna Gushue, innkeeper at the Jefferson Inn in Ellicottville, New York. "Why lose the guests who want to use on-line booking? Stop worrying that they need personal contact. It isn't them but you who wants the personal contact." Besides, one does not preclude the other. Maintaining personal contact can always be done with a phone call or a personalized confirmation letter.

Why Not Use One

"In all the years of running our B&B we have come to the conclusion that no one sells us better than us and that with on-line availability we prevent the possibility of selling another date for a potential guest. If we can speak directly to a 'live' body, we can be our own sales team," say Wendy Goldstein and Sharon Smith of the Two Sisters Inn in Manitou Springs, Colorado.

It's Not a Perfect Marriage

Until guest management software and all the availability folks can work with an "open-source" system, it is time-consuming to maintain multiple inventories. Ideally, an innkeeper would be able to work with several companies and by clicking one button would update everyone. Keeping records and updating the innumerable sites with current availability and information is a time-consuming job.

To Err Is Human, to Double-Book Is Painful

Potential guests are able to see availability on-line, but to make an actual reservation they need to either e-mail or phone. Otherwise, if you don't check with immediacy or find yourself taking a reservation on the phone at the very same time someone is making on-line arrangements for the very same room, double-booking can occur. If you have enough rooms, consider dedicating a certain number of them strictly to on-line booking. Use guest management software that interfaces with an on-line availability system and that updates your inventory automatically. Doing it manually is laborious and time-consuming at best. At the worst, it opens you to the potential that you will overbook.

Does It Make Money?

For the Sandstroms, on-line availability represented 22 percent of their 2002 business. At Indiana's Grey Goose Inn, owner Tim Wilk sees that his repeat guests call the inn directly but check on-line first for availability.

Would these folks have booked if no on-line availability or real-time bookings were offered? Innkeepers agree that they don't know the answer to that question. However, they also believe that the service meets their guests' needs and makes money while they sleep.

Do Your Research

· Investigate what other innkeepers are doing. If you are technologically challenged, find other innkeepers who are currently set up with an availability or RTB service. Ask them what they like and what they do not like.
· Purchase guest management software that integrates with several on-line availability products and updates automatically.
· Choose a service that offers convenient updating and the ability to have guests "sign off" on policies when submitting their reservation (i.e., they agree to the nonsmoking policy, understand the cancellation policy).
· Be prepared to update frequently. It's going to take time to keep it current, and it's going to add another task to your day.

"'Build it and they shall come' is a fantasy, not a business plan," cautions Eric Goldreyer. On-line availability and real-time booking products are in a great position to begin packaging services for the innkeeper. However, Gideon Stanley of GraceSoft reminds innkeepers, "On-line booking requires on-line marketing to succeed. The good news is that niche marketing, a specialty of B&Bs, is still an effective online marketing strategy."

Guests who reserve on-line are no different or more problematic than guests who call to make a reservation. People are people, whether they come by plane, train, fax, automobile, or e-mail.

TRAVEL AGENTS

For most sectors of the accommodations business, travel agents have been a significant resource for booking rooms. Though some inns work with travel agents, on average, innkeepers receive less than 3 percent of their business from them. Properties with more than nine rooms do better than smaller ones. With the increase in Web marketing, travel agents are a resource, but don't expect much business from them.

Working with travel agents is a challenge, not unlike that of working with Internet booking engines, especially for small properties with few rooms available to rent at the peak times the agent requests them. If the inn is not charging enough for the guest room to comfortably pay the travel agent, the innkeeper resents paying the 10 percent commission. However, the greatest hurdle is confusion over third-party reservations because inns are so different from one another; they don't like to miss the opportunity to set the stage for the visit with a hospitable initial contact.

Make it your goal to get organized enough to avoid the confusion. When a travel agent calls (with rare exceptions, they will identify themselves) for a "double room," be very clear about the unique features of the room, such as bed size, no TV or phone, three floors of stairs, or no facilities for children. Make a point of mentioning any policies not typical at hotels, such as restricted smoking, check-in times, or cancellation policies. Of course you want to sell the room, but be sure to find out whether their clients will be comfortable. Never book a shared-bath room unless the client has specifically requested it.

Create a warm letter of confirmation with the specific potential problem areas of your inn highlighted in the letter and again in your brochure. This works well with any third-party reservation. Enclose two letters and two brochures, one each for agent and client.

TELEPHONE MARKETING

What is the sound of opportunity knocking? In the inn business, it's the ringing of the telephone. Great beds and great breakfasts are not enough. You need a telephone presence that conveys all you have to offer.

Skill matters, too. An inviting presence on the phone is simply an empty promise if your guests arrive to find that you forgot to calendar their reservation, quoted the wrong room rate, or were too embarrassed to mention the no-smoking policy. Whoever handles the phones should understand the history, development, and relevance of your policies. There's a tendency for new staff members to apologize for policies that seem unnecessarily hard-nosed. Sometimes, too, staff people who don't have to follow the reservation process all the way through can be too casual about recording complete, accurate information. Getting names right, for example, avoids embarrassment and is a way of demonstrating to people that they're important to you. You can and must be professional and skilled, as well as friendly and inviting.

Get the details right and you'll find that your telephone can be a great promotional resource—on the customer's dime. You have paid for your callers through your advertising, your brochures, special promotions, word of mouth, and so on. Now this caller is spending time and money to find out whether your inn really is as wonderful as it's billed to be.

The first rule for tapping this resource is to make sure the phone is well tended, by you or someone you have trained. Whoever answers your phone should see it as an opportunity to transform originally interested callers, obviously shopping around by phone, into guests with confirmed reservations, so eager to stay in your inn that you know their deposits will go into the mail without hesitation.

When you or your trained staff people can't be at the inn to answer the phone, you have two options: answering machines and cellular phones. The cell phone lets you take your reservation book and make reservations wherever you go. Future guests don't know where you are and will make an immediate reservation with you rather than wait for your competitor to respond to a phone message.

Answering machines are an expected part of today's society, so using one is not a problem for guests. However, potential guests are likely to call someone else until they find an inn that will make a reservation. Be sure your message is clear, friendly, and inviting. Give the caller a reason to make the extra effort to get in touch with you. Your prompt callback is crucial. If you put an exciting message on the tape, along with your e-mail and Internet URL, the number of people leaving messages and waiting for your return call will be high. The way you handle callbacks can increase your business. Many a guest has said, "I chose your inn because you were the only one who called me back, even though you had no rooms when I wanted them."

Don't fill your message with rules and instructions. Many people are still struggling with voice mail instructions and are turned off by "If we don't have a room we won't call you back; if you want a brochure leave a name and address; if [after all this] you still want to make a reservation, leave your number, and we will call." Assume that the guest knows nothing about your place and make your message so inviting they will wait with bated breath for your return call. Again, be sure to list your Web-site address so potential guests have something to do while waiting for your return. If you have on-line availability or reservation potential on your Web site, you just might find that the answering machine has helped make a reservation in your absence.

Voice mail is also an option, although still not as good as personal contact. If you have a larger inn and want to install voice mail for nighttime guest room phones or for the manager, that may work, but remember that guests choose inns because they want to feel like a person, not a room number. Be cautious in your installation of this feature.

Be cautious too with call waiting. Many people find this inexpensive telephone service galling. Consider instead installing a second line that rolls over to an answering machine that says, "We are on another line and will return your call as soon as we hang up"—plus your usual great message. If your inn is small, this second line might be your personal line. It is also possible that a busy signal will tell callers that you are popular, so they'll try again; just be sure the primary line doesn't get tied up with long phone calls.

When speaking with a prospective guest, it's essential to articulate a sense of your place in a simple, appealing way. Have ready a few adjective-laden sentences that capture just what it is that makes your inn rare and wonderful. Develop a "script" and keep it by the phone for you or your reservation people to use.

Base it on a guest's-eye view of the experience of your inn, emphasizing the things you've picked out to highlight in your brochure: architecture, setting, sounds, scents, and activities. Use vivid adjectives to construct the most poetic description possible for your surroundings. You're not the last building on the right at the end of the road. You're at the back of a wooded canyon with no through traffic, where the main sounds are singing birds and the running river. You're not on the left side of the highway; you're on a magnificent promontory jutting out over the Atlantic Ocean. You're not five miles from town; you're high in the hills with a sweeping view of the bay.

Extract the essence into two or three sentences that can be spoken comfortably, without sounding "canned." Rather than responding to the question "What's your inn like?" with a strictly factual account of how many rooms you have and whether there are private baths, have those few lines ready to spark the caller's interest.

But don't get so involved in what you want to say that you forget to listen. Find out as much as you can about your caller's needs. For example, are they looking for a secluded place, or for one within walking distance of shops and restaurants? Point out the ways your place matches what they're seeking.

If you do have a room, your script can make your callers feel lucky to get it. If your inn sounds irresistible, callers will shop no further and will be unlikely to cancel a reservation later.

If you don't have a room this Saturday night, get in your two-liner anyway, and volunteer information about when you do have an opening. Mention that weekends book up eight weeks (or whatever) in advance, but during the week they'll have the place pretty much to themselves. Mention how wonderful it is to walk along the beach on a Tuesday morning without running into another soul or to go bicycling along a country road with no weekend traffic. Also, don't hesitate to refer the caller to an inn in your area that has openings; next time the callers will remember your helpfulness and generosity.

If they can't come midweek but sound interested in your inn, encourage them to book the next available weekend, reminding them that most of the inns in your area fill up at least that far in advance. You might also mention something that's going to be of special interest even two or three months ahead, like whale watching or spring blossoms, and suggest that they make plans now for the next outing.

If they decide to come to your area on a weekend when you are already booked, invite them to tour your inn. Seeing your place will give them a solid image to store for future vacation plans and a sample of the charm they can expect when they come back to stay.

If you can't get a booking, ask whether you can send a brochure (if they don't already have one). Add callers to your mailing list, too. Remember, you paid for this inquiry, so use it. At the very least, find out how they heard about your inn so you can keep track of the ads or sources that are working.

The telephone is a tool to help you make the most of all your other promotional techniques. Use it creatively, with a warm and light touch. Joke around a little; it's fun for you, and people respond to it.

MISCELLANEOUS MARKETING

- Cooperative marketing with other inns can increase your visibility and multiply your promotional dollar—besides, it may be fun. Initiate it yourself if something hasn't already been started.
- Open houses are a standard for new inns and new owners, but an annual one for the locals has been especially well received at the very upscale Inn on Mt. Ada, the former Wrigley Mansion on Catalina Island in California.
- Tours of inns—whether during the first week in December for the National Bed and Breakfast Open House or as a fund-raiser for a local charity—give you invaluable local exposure.
- Familiarization tours for travel writers and travel agents are best coordinated with a group of inns and/or your convention and visitors bureau.
- Hiring a public relations agency is like hiring a staff member; they should have a great deal of experience in the area where you need help. Interview and research carefully.

- Radio advertising can be costly, especially if you don't understand the lingo and the best hours, but maybe someone will trade you airtime for nights at the inn while you learn. Giving away room-nights works especially well during public-radio fund drives.
- TV advertising is expensive; try promotion via a nonprofit fund-raiser. Some television programs featuring a very few inns are being produced. Approach the producers with your press kit.
- International travelers are best reached by cooperating with the state tourism office's overseas visitors department; you'll need a color brochure.
- Outdoor advertising, such as scenic-byway signage, billboards, or freeway Adopt-a-Highway signs require research about your particular state and community. Think twice about the message a billboard conveys; be sure it fits with your image.
- Environmental marketing does more than soothe your conscience; many people will choose your inn if they see the recycled logo on your brochure and learn of your sincere efforts to preserve the earth.
- Niche markets—to bicyclists, hikers, gays, African-Americans, business travelers, and so on—are there for the plucking. Get to know their publications and needs and promote to them.
- Cookbooks are a way into another section of the newspaper, a gift your guests will use to pass your name around, and a statement on how fine your food is.

Most important of all, remember to have fun at marketing. Let your creative juices flow, but do it with a plan and a budget.

up and running

Professionalism

A variety of things will bring guests to your inn; professionalism will bring them back. Innkeepers must combine skill with flexibility, the warmth and intimacy of Grandma's with the perfection of Buckingham Palace.

Guests are usually understanding and helpful in the face of emergencies at the inn, but they expect peace and comfort. If you accompany mopping up the water from a broken commode with a litany of how tough your day has been, you are breaking the spell.

Professionalism is obvious in numerous small things. At check-in time, for example, the mood of an entire stay is established. It's an insecure time for guests, who bring high hopes along with uncertainty about what to expect; if you're scrambling around to get organized, you add to that insecurity.

Even if you spent the last four hours cleaning rooms, comforting your sick child, and installing a new sink, and even though the groceries you raced out to purchase are still spread all over the kitchen table, what really matters is how your guest feels when you open the door and say, "Hi! Welcome to the Inn on the Corner."

Among prospective and operating innkeepers, there are a few who want to escape the rat race run a laid-back establishment. Nothing, however, will more quickly destroy your efforts to relax in your new career than a double-booking, and that's just what you'll get if you refuse to run your inn in a professional way.

Do you want to be casual about innkeeping? Before you begin, take a moment to imagine what it's like to tell a young couple on their honeymoon that the room they booked and paid for has been given away because you forgot to note their reservation in the calendar book. This is nightmare stuff! Or how about failing to notice that the Smiths never sent their deposit for Saturday night, leaving you with an empty room on one of the few nights you can count on full occupancy? Emotionally and economically, you can't afford a lot of errors like these.

Whether evidenced by cold coffee, grungy sheets, or rude telephone manners, a too casual approach to innkeeping can ruin you. A professional always tries harder.

SERVICE

"Service" is the byword in the hospitality industry, but few segments of the industry are able to pull it off as effectively as the bed-and-breakfast and country inn business. If you are to succeed in today's competitive market, it will be because of your "service mentality."

Because guests expect more of inns, the possibility of disappointment is greater. When you are expected to be both the ideal mom and the world's greatest flight attendant, living up to your guests' expectations can be tough.

Service has three components: anticipating guests' needs, responding cheerfully to guests' needs and more than meeting them, and viewing problems as opportunities to serve.

Innkeepers anticipate guests' needs by paying attention. Prepare to design your inn and choose the amenities and features you will offer by visiting other inns; in good inns, what you'll experience is what the innkeepers have learned their guests want. Pay close attention to guests' requests. If they want a place to put their dinner leftovers, perhaps you might add a guest refrigerator. Do guests rearrange their rooms? If they move a lamp closer to the reading chair, another lamp may be needed. Listening to prospective guests' questions about the availability of in-room spas, fireplaces, or queen-sized beds has caused many an innkeeper to add them.

Anticipating guests' needs is more than responding to specific requests; it's also figuring out how to go beyond what the guest might expect or demand. Ask them if they are celebrating a special occasion: you may get the opportunity to present a birthday cake or anniversary champagne when they arrive. If you hear them exclaim over the lilacs as they walk up the front path, put a vase of the flowers in their room. Surprising guests with that unanticipated extra is inn-style service today.

Responding cheerfully to guests' needs is not always easy, but it's the basis of good service. The guest who doesn't like your house-special hazelnut coffee is not insulting you, just making a request. Everyone who pays you money will not necessarily like everything they have bought. Your challenge is to be thankful that they have told you their opinion and to respond cheerfully by not only meeting the request but also double-checking later that your response satisfied their needs. It's strange but true that responding well to a request may please the guest even more than if everything had been perfect for him at the outset!

Once in a while a guest will complain about something more than your coffee. The toilet is overflowing, there are fleas in the carpet, the bed collapses. These are problems. The secret to handling them is not only to fix the fixable immediately, but also to look for an opportunity to extend yourself. While you bomb the fleas, fix the bed, or repair the toilet, offer a picnic basket and a map to a secret spot for a romantic afternoon. Or simply present a bottle of champagne with a note thanking your guests for their patience.

Please Complain!

According to A Complaint Is a Gift *by Janelle Barlow and Claus Møller, the Technical Assistance Research Program's (TARP) research on unhappy customers shows that you want them to complain to you before they leave, to give you a chance to fix the problem. Twenty-six out of twenty-seven customers with complaints will never tell you, which means that in order to get an accurate count of complaints you need to multiply each complaint by twenty-seven. Those guests who complain become your most loyal customers, as TARP's research shows that 95 percent of the complainers whose problems were resolved quickly and well are likely to return. Interestingly, of guests who do not complain, only 37 percent return. TARP found that if the problem is resolved successfully, customers will tell five other people, whereas if customers receive good service initially, they will tell three others. So problems are opportunities to guarantee return guests.*

Guest-Friendly Policies and Procedures

Inns are as individual as innkeepers, and one inn's set of policies is unlikely to be perfect for any other. Nevertheless, other innkeepers may have solutions you haven't thought of in problem areas like children and pets. There's also a feeling of safety in numbers: the "industry standard" is easier to assert. Unfortunately, there are not really very many industry standards in policies and procedures among bed-and-breakfast inns and country inns.

Developing clear policies and putting them in writing will benefit your guests as well as you. Guests to whom you have sent a brochure or letter of confirmation describing your no-pets policy, for example, aren't as likely to muster up much righteous indignation when you stop them at the front door with Fido. But don't let clarity overwhelm hospitality. Some people just don't read anything you send them; it's not their way. If you care about maintaining goodwill—and studies show that a dissatisfied guest will tell more people about your inn than an ecstatic guest will—be as flexible as you can comfortably be. Some issues are clear and firm; some you'll evaluate over and over. Here are some specifics.

SMOKING

Stale cigarette odors in a guest room can take days to disperse. Not only that, fires caused by cigarettes kill more people than any other kind of fire. This is due chiefly to smoking in bed, but another common cause is cigarettes that fall into sofas and smolder until finally the upholstery ignites in the wee hours of the night. The combination of cigarettes and alcohol is especially deadly, because people become more careless when they drink.

On the other hand, some potential guests will undoubtedly decide against your inn if they're not permitted to smoke there. A middle ground is permitting smoking in some limited area outside the inn, where it will be least hazardous and least offensive. You may also want to limit *what* can be smoked: cigars get a pretty strong no at most inns; pipes can smell cozy or lousy. Most inns simply permit no smoking inside.

So what do you do when there's a problem and your clear policy is being ignored? Often a nice note by the pillow is enough to stop the smoke in a no-smoking guest room. Because it involves no face-to-face interaction, embarrassment on both sides is less.

If you encounter a smoking guest in a no-smoking area, a nice line to use is "Are you going to have trouble with our no-smoking policy?" Take it from there.

CHILDREN AND PETS

Not accepting children is age discrimination; proceed carefully. It is true that children may be a problem to guests who are taking breaks from their own progeny, and children may create noise problems. Increasingly often, innkeepers are setting up special cottages or rooms with an outside entrance to accommodate their former yuppie guests who now have children.

Families Are Welcome Here

- *Call it being part-time surrogate grandparents, but since their grandchildren are in Europe and Massachusetts, John and Betty Foy, innkeepers at Meadows Inn in New Bern, North Carolina, are happily prepared to welcome children. Their two-bedroom suite (Granny's Attic) on the third floor is private and allows the perfect setting for families traveling together. A school desk and tea set, plus books, are provided for pretend play, as well as a TV and VCR for each room. A selection of games—not requiring batteries—is available in the gathering room on the first floor. Two of their larger rooms will also accommodate a single rollaway for one child. A baby crib is available for the occasional infant. The Meadows is carpeted, and with nine rooms it is large enough that noise is minimized for the other guests.*

- *Su Casa B&B in Kansas City, Missouri, is very family friendly. From a game room with Foosball, a miniature pool table, and lots of children's books and games to a wonderful movie theater (with twenty theater seats, popcorn, soda pop, and other movie theater treats plus all types of movies, including many children's selections), this B&B knows how to welcome kids. The guest kitchen is stocked with drinks and other snacks that children love.*

  The swimming pool has both a deep end with a diving board and a shallow end. Water wings are provided for children's safety, as are other fun water games and toys. Guest rooms are equipped with children's robes and slippers, baby potty seats, baby bathtub seats, and other necessities. When families are present, breakfast is served with children in mind, with children's place settings, silverware, and cups. Oh, and let's not forget the Su Casa critters, a child's favorite. The innkeeper, Lois Hoover, will accompany the family for an interactive visit with the resident llamas, miniature donkeys, ponies, goats, and geese. A free camera comes with the rental of the suite, so that families can memorialize their children's reactions to the animals.

- *"In almost twelve years we have had only four complaints about children," recalls Camille Lawrence of the AAA four-diamond First Colony Inn on Nags Head in North Carolina. "I can't count the complaints about loud adults."*

It is increasingly desirable to accept pets at inns. You can choose to do so on a limited basis, with specific rooms designed for guests and their furry friends. Cat allergies are common among travelers, and sometimes the little critters (both dogs and cats) do bring fleas.

While many innkeepers can regale you with stories about the letters and gifts their pets receive from guests, who miss the pets more than they do the innkeepers, other guests may be allergic to cats or afraid of large dogs; they may not view your large, oh-so-friendly, bouncing-up-the-driveway German shepherd as a treat. Be sure to mention any in-residence animals in your written materials, as well as when taking a telephone reservation.

Please keep in mind the same considerations regarding the innkeeper's children and pets. Guests taking a breather from their own children may not enjoy having to converse with the innkeeper's little ones. If you believe that no children can be welcomed as guests at your inn, try this positive approach: "Because of the physical nature of our inn and our concern for your child's safety, we will be glad to refer you to another inn in the area where your family will be welcome." The whole point is to come across as guest-friendly and helpful.

Because many potential guests who want to travel with children feel that inns are inhospitable to families, "Children welcome" is not enough to entice or reassure them. Instead, try: "We truly welcome children. We'll help you plan special events for their enjoyment during your stay" or "Our cottage is perfect for families . . . come visit us and we'll all have a great time," or "You and your children will find our inn a home away from home, from a special kids' welcoming kit to a well-stocked toy box."

Whatever your policy regarding children and pets, it should reflect a sense of the character of the inn and the innkeeper and a sensitivity for your potential guests.

CASH, CHECK, OR CHARGE

"Do you accept cash?" As incredible as it sounds, guests ask it. Here's an outline of the advantages and disadvantages of various forms of payment.

Cash
Advantages
- No bank charges
- Almost always "good"

Disadvantages
- Some risk of theft
- Need to make change
- Need to receipt payments

Checks

Advantages

- No bank charges
- No change to make
- Good for mail-in deposits
- Automatic receipt of payment

Disadvantages

- Some risk of bouncing
- Risk of theft
- Can't guarantee last-minute booking

Credit Cards

Advantages

- Can confirm last-minute reservation
- Convenient for guest
- More "impulse" sales; more expensive rooms sold
- Automatic receipt of payment
- No need for change

Disadvantages

- Bank charges (2 to 4 percent)
- Authorizations take time
- Disputed charges may be difficult to collect (protection varies)
- Extra paperwork with chargebacks (when credit card companies, or guests, dispute a charge), closing out every day, etc.

Debit cards

Advantages

- Lower bank fee than credit card
- Automatic receipt of payment
- No need for change
- Used by international guests
- May be more secure than credit cards because of need for PIN number

Disadvantages

- Inn needs special equipment to process
- Small bank charge (1 percent)
- All the other disadvantages of credit cards

A deposit is the seal on a two-way commitment: the innkeeper commits that the room will be ready and waiting for the guests to arrive, and the guests commit to coming. Most inns require a deposit within a week or ten days of the date the reservation is made. For reservations made months in advance, you may wish to allow more time, but it's to your advantage in every way to get the money in hand. Deposits can be the price of one night's stay, half the price of the total stay, the price of the first and last nights' stay, or the total amount. Base your choice on how much commitment you want.

A related procedural issue involves last-minute reservations, made too late to be guaranteed with deposits (except by credit card). Take the call, make the reservation, and guarantee the stay with a credit card. Be sure to state your cancellation policy clearly so the guests understand their part of the bargain. Say, for example, "Since the reservation is for tonight, it is too late for you to mail us a check. Since we will be holding a room for you and turning others away, we'll have to charge your credit card for one night's stay even if you fail to come."

It's a tough one, warning callers that they'll be billed if they don't show for a last-minute reservation. You want to be guest-friendly and at the same time reiterate that this is a two-way commitment. You can ask them to take the Girl Scout Oath, or intimate that your people will be watching them. Whatever "friendly persuasion" you use, remember that establishing a personal connection with these callers makes it harder for them to disappoint you while you are guaranteeing not to disappoint them.

Cancellations

How much notice of cancellation should you require to return a deposit? This philosophical argument is endless. Innkeepers do not want to lose money on a guest who does not come and a room that is not filled, and guests do not want to lose money on a room they aren't going to occupy.

Cancellation policies range from twenty-four hours to seven or more days. Options on this theme include:

· Refunding all the money if the room is rebooked, except, perhaps, for a cancellation fee—generally $5 to $10. (AAA-rated properties are not permitted to charge a cancellation fee.)

· Refunding no money, part of the money, or all of the money whether or not the room is rebooked.

· Converting the deposit into a gift certificate for a later stay regardless of whether the room is rebooked.

In the past, innkeepers were quite rigid about cancellations. If the cancellation period required seven days' notice, then by golly a guest who wanted to cancel had better call seven days ahead. Times have changed; travelers are now much less tolerant of what they perceive as inflexible and inhospitable cancellation policies. Smart innkeepers have changed too. Even though it may be difficult for them to fill a room canceled at the last minute, innkeepers who respond with generosity and grace find that it pays off with satisfied, repeat guests.

The keys to handling cancellation issues successfully, from both the innkeeper's and the guest's perspective, are clarity and, even more important, flexibility. Be sure guests understand your cancellation policy when you take the reservation, and when you confirm it. Some, accustomed to the 6 P.M. cancellation policy of big hotels, will be surprised, but it's usually easy to explain the reason behind your policies: unlike big hotels, you don't overbook based on a factor for cancellations; you absolutely guarantee a room, and you need your guests to guarantee that they'll arrive. Inn guests generally book for special occasions, not last-minute impulses. An innkeeper who has turned away twenty callers for a weekend room may be unable to fill that room if it's canceled on the preceding Tuesday.

Still, things can go wrong for people, and it pays to keep that in mind when someone has to make a last-minute change. Nice innkeepers do not finish last. In the short haul, when your room sits empty and the income is gone, it may seem so. But the day will come when the phone rings and a caller says, "Michael Scott told me that I just have to come and stay at your inn. Do you remember Michael? He had to cancel a reservation and was unable to come, but you were so gracious in working with him that he says this just has to be a great place. My wife's birthday is coming up . . . " That conversation will make your day!

Besides, the longer you're an innkeeper, the more you'll realize that saving one or two hundred bucks isn't worth even an hour of your anger or unhappiness.

CHECK-IN AND CHECKOUT

How do you decide what's the best check-in time or period for your inn? In an inn with round-the-clock staff, you might base it solely on the time it takes you to get your rooms ready for the next guests. But if yours is a small operation and the only desk staff is you, limiting check-in to give yourself some time away from the inn to shop, do promotion, or play a game of tennis is also important.

On the other hand, you are in business to accommodate guests. How can you meet both sets of needs? In most cases, reasonable check-in hours can be established, say 2 to 7 P.M. If most of your guests arrive from nearby cities after a day's work, a shorter time, say 4 to 7 P.M., may be adequate. If they are chiefly vacationers, midafternoon hours may work better.

There will always be some people who arrive either without reservations or hoping to check in early. If they see a sign indicating that check-in time is hours away, those without reservations will look elsewhere; those with reservations may get irritated, no matter how clearly you have communicated your check-in hours and the reason for them. Guests are rightly concerned about beginning their inn experience, not about your needs.

How can you accommodate them? Be creative. Some inns arrange to leave keys or door-lock combinations along with special notes for guests with reservations who must arrive early or late. Some innkeepers arrange special telephone lines on the inn's front door that connect to a neighbor who comes when called to take care of early arrivals. Or perhaps that same phone rings into your quarters where you are having lunch. Or the inn doorbell rings where cleaning staff can hear it. You then have a great opportunity to say, "I'm glad you're here. You're welcome to sit in the parlor and enjoy a glass of lemonade or a cup of tea until your room is ready."

You'll be tempted to add, "And please forgive my not being terribly attentive right at this moment, but I want to finish all of the inn's preparation for our guests arriving today," but your guests won't really understand that either. Most of them won't even feel you've done anything extraordinary by greeting them so warmly when they're there early. Call on every emotional reserve to assist your guests right then in whatever way they require; don't let on that their behavior is in any way unusual.

Checkout time at most inns is eleven or noon. Few guests fail to leave on time, but it's often possible to accommodate a requested late checkout time by leaving the room until last for cleaning.

Occasionally you'll have to knock on a door in order to "encourage" a guest's departure. You might use a line like this: "I'm sorry to bother you, but did you realize that checkout time was noon? I just want to let you know that we'll be cleaning your room in about ten minutes. You're welcome to leave your bags in the office if you like, and feel free to enjoy the garden." You'll be tempted to speak with just a hint of reprimand in your tone; resist.

If it's 10:30 A.M. and nobody has shown up for breakfast, you'd better think back on whether you told them when breakfast is served, and where. You want your guests to be comfortable, and that involves partly your clear communication.

If you serve breakfast in bed, ask your guests the night before what time they'd like it. If you serve everybody promptly at 8:30 in the dining room, talk it up during check-in time when you show them the inn and their room. Some inns serve over a range of time, from 8 to 10 A.M., for example.

Many inns offer early breakfasts to business travelers. Some also provide early coffee service in guest rooms, or in the common area where guests can help themselves. This needs to be communicated to guests. If guests come down to your 8:30 A.M. breakfast and you hear someone say, "Gee, I didn't know I could get coffee at six-thirty," you've got a communication problem.

Flexibility and communication are the keys to guest-friendly policies. Every bottom line probably has its own bottom line. Mull your system over and try out variations. Policies can always be changed.

Handling Reservations

Just because you don't have fifty rooms to book doesn't mean you can afford to be casual about maintaining a proper reservations system.

THE RESERVATION FORM

A well-organized reservation form is the primary source of information that performs a variety of important functions:

- Ensures that all essential information is taken at one time, when the guest calls to make the reservation, so it's on the guest's dime.
- Ensures that all policies and procedures are described to the guest, even when you take the call at the busiest moment of the day.
- Provides a convenient and time-saving space to make calculations.
- Provides marketing data for future advertising and promotional planning.
- Provides the basis for a mailing list.
- Allows easy filing and retrieval of reservations.
- Becomes an all-in-one innsitter's resource, allowing innsitters to read or quote information accurately without hours of training.

- Helps eliminate double-bookings, cancellations, misunderstandings, and unhappy guests.
- Provides easy retrieval of information on repeat guests. Happy is the guest greeted with warm words of personal recognition based on the previous stay.

Professional inns keep useful, accurate, retrievable information. Here are the basics of how it's done.

Though specific information needs vary from inn to inn, reservation forms can follow some basic rules. Most inns devise their own forms. Some use standard 8 1/2-by-11-inch paper; others use 4-by-6-inch cards. Some innkeepers fill blank pages with information in each of several categories they keep in their heads; others use preprinted cards. Some include a lot of information; others include very little. The basic information necessary to ensure a pleasant stay for your guest and a smooth transaction for you includes:

Name. It's important to know who called to make the reservation, as well as the names and the number of persons in the party.

Address. This should be the preferred mailing address, whether home, work, or elsewhere.

Phone. Try to get home, business, and cell phones. Calling home numbers on evenings and weekends when rates are low will save you money.

Date(s) and Day(s) of Reservation. Potential mistakes usually show up here, when callers request a day and date that do not occur simultaneously. Ask for both to improve your chance of catching the error. This information can also assist you in tracking business patterns, especially midweek and weekend variations.

Room. Inngoers often book a specific room and expect to have it.

Room Price, Deposit Amount, and When Deposit Is Due. You'll probably request a deposit equivalent to a night's lodging, half of the total lodging, full prepayment, or an amount based on some other formula. Record clearly the total price quoted for the stay, the amount requested in deposit, and the date by which the deposit must arrive.

Method of Payment. Leave room for credit card number, cardholder name, and expiration date.

Policies. You will no doubt have a separate rate and policy sheet to which you refer when there are questions, but it's also a big help to have policies written out on the reservation form in a conversational style you can actually read over the phone. There should also be a space to check off when the policy is read or described to the caller.

Check-in Time. Although the only way to make sure guests arrive during a specific check-in time is to ferry them in to an island inn, the odds of their showing up on time improve if you are clear about your check-in time. You may want to work out special arrangements with guests for whom your regular check-in hours are inconvenient.

How They Found Out About Your Inn. This information, which guests are happy to share, is essential for evaluating your advertising and promotional program.

Who Took the Reservation. If more than one person takes reservations at your inn, note who took the booking in case questions arise later.

Date the Reservation Was Made. If you require prepayment within a certain period, the date of the booking is very important. It may also prove useful or interesting to see how far in advance most reservations are made.

Special Occasion and Other Notes. Important information could be that they're coming on an anniversary or honeymoon, driving up in a day from New York, or that they once lived in your area, hate carrots, or want dinner reservations.

Bookkeeping. Save space on the reservation form to record when payment arrives, the date you send confirmation, and the balance due.

The Fine Print—A Sample for a Brochure

Rates include breakfast, hot tub use, evening beverage in the parlor; rates subject to change without notice; rates do not include applicable taxes; all rooms are designed for two persons (additional persons may use the sofa beds in the suites at $10 per person extra); singles subtract $5 from listed price.

Reservations held pending receipt of one-night deposit; two-night minimum stay on weekends; MasterCard and Visa accepted.

Cancellations require seventy-two hours' notice prior to date of arrival for refund.

For the comfort of others, there is no smoking in the main house and no pets, please. Courteous smokers may smoke in the garden and may book a suite in the cottage.

Check-in time: 3 to 8 P.M. Please call to make special arrangements if you plan to arrive later than 8 P.M. If you desire an earlier check-in, please call on the morning of your arrival about the possibilities.

Checkout time: 11 A.M.

RATE INFORMATION

The lodging industry is notorious for complicated rate structures. Books may come in one basic hardback format at one regular price, but rooms vary in price from Monday to Saturday, from February to June, and for one person, two people, and three people. And you may get a different price if you're a corporate traveler or a tourist.

The reason inns get into the same complexities of rates, amenities, and package deals as the big hotels is because our objective is the same: a full house. Whatever rate variations you work with at your inn, be sure that the people who take reservations can find the appropriate rates quickly and communicate them accurately to callers. Whether the rate card is taped to the reservations book, the refrigerator, or the telephone desk, it must be handy, readable, and complete.

GIVING INFORMATION

After you've collected all the information *you* need from your callers, consciously take a moment to inquire about their needs. Perhaps they would like further information about their room, the inn, or the town. Offer to send additional tourist information on what to do and see in the area, or about special events during their stay. Ask if they'd like directions to the inn, especially if you've become aware through experience that the map or directions on your brochure are inadequate.

Describe the parking situation or any other important procedural matter. Some innkeepers have devised ingenious ways of dealing with late arrivals: staying up to greet them even at 3:00 A.M.; specially coding lockboxes for keys; leaving notes with maps and keys; installing intercoms to rouse the innkeepers; or maintaining a firm policy that no one is admitted after midnight. Whatever the late-arrival policy, it shouldn't be a surprise to an expectant guest.

THE CALENDAR

You've just gotten a four-day midweek reservation! Don't get so excited that you forget the crucial step: recording the information on your calendar. Whether you use a special form that lists rooms, dates, and so on, or simply a standard daily/weekly/monthly appointment book, post the name and the specific room on the appropriate dates immediately.

At day's end, most inns apply some form of a checks-and-balances system. Check all reservations taken that day against your calendar. If there are discrepancies, correct them as soon as possible.

FILING RESERVATION FORMS

Most inns file individual reservation forms chronologically for easy retrieval in case there's a question or problem, to record payments received, or to prepare a weekly schedule of arriving guests.

ONCE PAYMENT HAS BEEN RECEIVED

When the money is in hand, first pull the form and verify that the date, the room, and the amount received are correct. Note on the form the amount paid, the date the confirmation is being sent, and the balance due, if any.

Next, note on the master calendar that payment has been received, and send a confirmation or receipt. Finally, refile the form and go to the bank!

MODIFICATIONS AND CANCELLATIONS

While some inns use a separate form for recording this information, most inns put it on the reservation form. The essential points to note are:
· Previous arrival and departure dates.
· New arrival and departure dates.
· Name.
· Who is making the change, and their address, phone number, and position or relationship to the guest.
· What monetary differences are created by the change. Who owes what to whom.
· Today's date.
· The reason for the change.

When a change is requested by phone, ask for the previous arrival date and name, then retrieve the reservation form from the file, so you have the guest's history in front of you before you proceed. Be sure to erase the booking on your calendar immediately so that the room will show as vacant and can be rebooked. If you use a separate form for modifications and cancellations, clip it to the top of the reservation form, along with any other correspondence; the cancellation form is now the most critical information in that particular batch.

ORGANIZING FOR GUESTS' ARRIVALS

There should be a regular point when you prepare for the next day, week, or some definite period of time. Inns do this in a variety of ways. One pulls reservation cards weekly and pins them to the kitchen wall, ready for guests' arrivals. Another keeps arriving guests' cards in a desk drawer. Still another makes a weekly chart listing dates and rooms with guest names, then, in a different color ink, notes estimated arrival times, money owed, whether someone is a repeat guest, any special occasions, and so on. This sheet is taped to the back of the kitchen door, next to the room keys.

Each of these very different systems appears to work well for the inn using it. Each is a way of streamlining the usefulness of the information collected at reservation time, so it can be used at check-in time. At check-in, do ask your guests to register in some way; a big book or registration cards are two choices. Do not leave them waiting more than half a minute while you get their room key. Guests should feel welcome and expected.

ORGANIZING FOR THE FUTURE

The guest has come and gone. Retrieve the reservation forms from the kitchen wall, the desk drawer, or wherever you keep them to streamline your welcoming routine. These cards are filled with information about people you hope to see again. What do you do with them now? Here are several options for storage and retrievability.

- A simple filing system includes one expandable date file with numbers one through thirty-one on the tabs, plus twelve file folders, one for each month. The expandable file is used for the current month's reservation forms. All other months are filed chronologically in the monthly file folders, kept in a file drawer. Reservations can be filed by arrival date, then within that date section by name.
- File cards alphabetically on a Rolodex. They can be flipped through quickly and pulled out. Keep a separate Rolodex for each year.
- Computerize. Standard inexpensive software, available for most home systems, allows you to enter a number of different fields for each file record. You can enter not only names and addresses for future mailings, but also other demographics, such as reservation date, room selected, special occasion, and advertising source. This will allow you to print lists by categories, such as referral source, effectiveness of specific advertising, length of stay, where guests come

from (geographically), special-occasion business, and business travelers. Seriously consider guest management software that gives you database and reservations capability.

Guest Management Software

Most innkeepers would prefer to deal with one simple application that could handle all of their reservations—no matter when or by which method reservations are received. "Currently," says Gideon Stanley of GraceSoft, "The innkeeper may manage a desktop reservation software program, e-mail, an on-line availability system, and travel-agent bookings in order to handle all the reservations that come from their Web site, walk-ins, phone, and fax."

With today's competitive marketplace, using technology to stay on top is a must. One of the best investments an innkeeper can make is guest management software (GMS). Much more is expected from GMS today than ten years ago. Not only does it enter, record, and track reservations and provide you with a variety of reports (on housekeeping, income, etc.) but most offer an interface for automatically uploading to an on-line availability calendar on your Web site so potential guests can, at a minimum, e-mail for a specific room's availability. In addition, most offer features that track travel-agent commissions, make group reservations, generate e-mail, and synchronize with your PDA.

Select your reservation software with care. Whether your needs are simple, complex, or somewhere in between, research your options well. "When innkeepers look at purchasing GMS, they should ask very simple questions," says Bill Mitchell of RezOvation.

- Start where you live. Find out what GMS area innkeepers are using. Visit them and ask them to show you how their program works. Ask them what they like and do not like.
- Order or download demos of each GMS you want to evaluate. Take some time and look at each program carefully.
- Call each company and ask a salesperson to help you. Do not assume that all routine features function equally well. Pick two or three key features and have each company show you how they work (creating reservations, moving reservations, canceling reservations, etc.).
- Ask each company how long they have been in business, how many users they have, and what their tech-support policies are.
- How easy is it to fix things when something goes wrong?
- Take a look at how the program integrates with on-line availability companies.

- Pick the software that best fits your needs, with a look toward the future. Small B&Bs will probably not benefit from GDS (global distribution system) bookings. However, on-line availability is something from which almost any inn can benefit.
- Don't underestimate your needs. If in doubt, go with the program that offers more rather than less.
- Attend a PAII-sponsored trade show. Most of the GMS vendors will be there. Take your list and spend time at their computers with each one.

Better Living Through Technology

Dana Owens, innkeeper and owner at the Rosewood Inn B&B in Oklahoma and technology professor extraordinaire, is never without her Palm Pilot and cell phone. She and her husband, Val, who is the B&B's primary innkeeper, subscribe to the "enter information once" theory. "Originally we hired a cell phone," says Val. "That was our first employee. All calls got a real, live person." Then came the Palm Pilot, and by using the GuestTracker guest management software's PDA module, they book all reservations on their PDA. "The software is not perfect," says Dana, "but it gets us eighty percent of the way." From 1996 with a three-ring binder and telephone to 2002 with a desktop computer, PDA, synchronization (between PDA and computer), and their cell phone, these innkeepers maximize time with guests by getting technology to work for them.

Gideon Stanley believes that the future of GMS may rest with "Web ware," Internet-based software that is rented (not owned) by the innkeeper. Advantages include data security and 24/7 backup. While this concept may appear risky, in reality the information may be much more secure on a remote server than it currently is on the desktop. However, if your Internet connection goes down, your GMS information will not be accessible. Ideally, says Gideon, "An application that could automatically consolidate all sources of reservations for the innkeeper would be a dream come true." As technology and the Internet are constantly improving, so will GMS.

Staffing

"What! You want to come in here and mess up my clean inn?" When you answer the doorbell feeling like that, it's time to think about getting help.

Many innkeepers start out doing everything themselves, often thinking they'll continue this way forever. They are usually concerned about the expense, paperwork, and loss of autonomy that hiring staff means. And there's no question that the intimate, homey feeling of an inn changes when hired help takes over the jobs owners previously did. Innkeepers often fear the public reaction to this and, in addition, feel that "no one else does things the way I want them done."

When innkeepers do hire staff, it's often to make time for the things only they can do or things they can do better than anyone else, like some kinds of promotion, planning, and financial projections. Staff can also free owners to do the things they enjoy most, such as gardening, perhaps, or spending extra time with guests. In some cases, staffers provide expertise owners don't have. But most importantly, owners hire staff to give themselves time off and to avoid jobs they dislike.

A good way to decide what staff to hire is to make a list of all the tasks done in the inn. Here's a start:

Cook and serve breakfast

Clean rooms

Clean common areas and kitchen

Take phone reservations

Confirm reservations

Bookkeeping

Promotion

Flower arranging

Now put four columns next to your list, for things you like to do, things you don't like to do, things someone else can do, and things only you can do. Review your list and put check marks in the appropriate columns; ask your partners to do so as well. This process will make clear to you which tasks you might hire someone for. And it's also a beginning on writing a job description.

The job description should include each task to be done, the number of hours and days of the week required, the pay scale, and the experience and education required. Under the Americans with Disabilities Act, you must also list the physical requirements and limitations of the job. In conjunction with other hospitality-industry associations, PAII has compiled position descriptions that meet ADA requirements. When calculating hours and wages, be careful to consider seasonal variations, so you don't give applicants unrealistic expectations. Type the job description and keep it on file. It should be the first thing you give an applicant to review.

Where do you find applicants? Word of mouth works well for some owners as a method of recruitment, but this varies within each community. Asking present staff for recommendations also helps to screen potential recruits, since your staff are frequently protective of "their inn." One innkeeper uses a networking technique, calling ten people and describing his staff needs; the word spreads from there.

The success of local classified ads depends on the community's available workforce. In many small towns it becomes necessary to recruit outside the area for good employees—or any employees! Try advertising, stating clearly the nature of the position, both positive and negative, and see what happens. Different times of year may yield differing levels of success, depending on the school year or military-base transfer patterns. December is generally a difficult month to find new employees.

Local schools sometimes have internship programs that are ideal sources for specialized positions like food service, promotion, or hotel-management positions. Posting notices in high school and college employment offices can reap valuable staff.

If your town has a small workforce to draw from, be creative. Would you like someone with great handwriting to address envelopes, or an experienced breakfast cook? Contact a local senior-citizen group. Try local churches, women's groups, service clubs, or nonprofit agencies.

Different kinds of people get along well with different innkeepers. Some inns prefer to hire people who are a bit older, then give them more responsibility; other inns hire young people to do jobs like housekeeping and dishwashing. High school and college students need to schedule their work around school, which often fits in with your busy-season needs, but requires flexibility in scheduling.

If there are few suitable applicants, consider offering benefits that are especially appealing or valuable in your area. These might include the opportunity to bring children to the job, avoiding the expense and uncertainty of child care. Some inns can develop a small apartment for a staffer, or provide meals for students. Inns also offer other pluses for staff, including varied tasks and flexible scheduling, a chance to interact with guests, and often an opportunity to become an integral part of the business. Don't hesitate to mention these.

Your task is to find a good employee as directly and efficiently as possible. You do yourself and your applicants no favors by spending time with people you instantly know you will never hire. How do you work smart here?

A clear ad, posted position-available announcement, or telephone conversation with someone who has been recommended to you allows applicants to screen themselves right at the beginning, saving them and you time. Before you accept an application, confirm that the person understands the position and meets the requirements for it. Manager, public relations, or chef applicants will probably have résumés, which are unnecessary for housekeepers, wait staff, or dishwashers. Handwritten application forms (available from office-supply stores if you don't have your own) will give you, in addition to important information, an idea of the applicant's handwriting for reservation cards or mail.

Once you have gathered all the applications or résumés, review them to select the top applicants, using consistent criteria such as direct experience that relates to the job or good understanding of local tourist activities. Further screen applicants by telephone. In an inn, every position is a public-contact position; if they don't speak well or clearly to you, how will they represent your inn? Then schedule and perform in-person interviews.

For the interview, dress and act like an employer, not a harried innkeeper, to establish a tone of professionalism. If you have several people to see, schedule them consecutively, about thirty minutes apart. Be sure someone else will handle the phones while you interview, and find a quiet, private part of the inn away from guests and other staffers.

Indicate clearly to the prospective employees what the position is; don't glamorize it. Ask questions that help you assess the applicants' commitment to the area, future plans, attitude toward work, background, and present situation. Do *not* ask questions about marital status, age, race, or pregnancy; it's illegal to consider these issues in hiring. If you're concerned about age or pregnancy because it might affect a candidate's strength for certain tasks, ask about strength.

Follow a consistent format during the interviews; it will help you compare candidates more effectively. Here are sample interview questions to ask after you've introduced yourself, toured some or all of the inn, and described the job.

· Why do you think you could do this job?
· What are your strengths and weaknesses?
· How would you describe yourself?
· Why do you want this job? What circumstances bring you to apply for it?

- What was your favorite previous job, and why? What other jobs have you had and why did you leave them?
- What other jobs are you applying for?
- What things do you think would be problems with this job?
- How long a time commitment can you make to this job?
- What are your plans for the future? What do you hope or expect to be doing in five years?

You may want to send your best candidates directly to a second interview, ideally with someone else who'll supervise the new employee. After you've interviewed all candidates, check references on your best prospect(s). Some employers will limit their comments to confirming the length of the employee's service and whether or not he or she is eligible for rehire. Get a name and phone number of a previous and a present employer, if possible. If you are able to get more information, here are some suggestions:

- Describe your job opening, and ask about X's suitability for it.
- Ask what kind of work X did for the reference, for how long, and why X left.
- Ask whether the reference would hire X again.
- Ask about X as an employee. Listen hard for key words here and write them down.
- Ask what was the major problem with X. If the problem sounds like it could also be troublesome to you, ask how it was worked out in the previous position.
- Ask about X's strengths and weaknesses, and for any other information that the reference believes would be helpful.

Once you've made your choice, take a night to think about the decision, then call and offer the job. Be very specific: reconfirm the job title, salary or hourly rate, and hours. Suggest a specific time on a specific day to begin work, suggest appropriate attire, and describe what will happen on the first day and how much time it will take.

Hiring Managers

Salaries for managers of bed-and-breakfast and country inns range from $2,000 to $6,000 a month, not including room, board, and benefits. This salary is for one person, not a couple. Salaries increase with responsibility. So an assistant to an on-site manager-owner is likely to receive less than a fully-in-charge manager hired by a rarely present owner.

It's probably not wise to include the value of a room at the inn as compensation for a manager, since with the room comes a high level of stress.

In many cases owners expect managers to be exact replicas of themselves, even expecting them to work long hours without additional pay (which, of course, owners do). If the extra hours worked are not agreed to by contract or paid for in overtime, you could be liable for extra pay for hours worked over forty hours a week or eight hours a day should the employee go to the labor board in your area.

It's your job to provide time off, reasonable pay, encouragement, and moral support on the job. Without this you will eventually lose a valuable investment; and you may discover other surprises after your employee leaves, such as cash embezzlement, other unhappy staffers, tasks half done, and disappointed guests. For up-to-date details on your legal requirements regarding staff, contact your local labor board.

> *Ann and Gene Swett of the Old Monterey Inn in Monterey, California, hire a variety of people for their bed-and-breakfast inn. "Younger people are here to learn things and often do not stay more than a couple of years," Ann says. "I don't want anyone to feel obligated to stay here. We had a woman with a master's degree who really needed to move on to other things, and I encouraged her to do just that. On the other hand, our manager has been with us for ten years, and a housekeeper who we encouraged to speak English has been here for six years. We care for staff as well as we care for our guests. We are like a supportive family. For example, a student who worked for us until he graduated now works at a local bank, but when we have an emergency, he pitches in on his time off. His family is in Chicago; we're his other family. We find out what an individual's strengths are and change the job to use them. Still, there's a fine line between being nurturing and being in charge."*

TRAINING

Be prepared for your new employee on the first day. Have a training plan and a time card ready. It's obvious to most innkeepers that detail is necessary to task training, but don't overlook the importance of values training. Equipping your staff to understand what the inn is about will contribute immensely to their ability to convey the spirit of the inn and to meet your expectations. Consider spending an hour to cover the areas outlined here.

History

- Why and how you got into innkeeping. This will tell them a lot about your expectations for innkeepers and the inn. Besides, guests will ask staff for the story.
- Why you chose the area and the structure you did. Much of your own image of the inn will be revealed in this.
- What personal values were involved in your decision to open an inn. This can be especially revealing if you left another career or saw innkeeping as a way to earn a living and still spend time with your young children.

Objectives

- Complete this sentence: I will feel successful when _____. You may define success in terms of money, smooth operation, free time, or fame. Your definition makes a big difference in how you run your inn and what your staff people understand to be important.
- Set specific goals if you can, such as a regular 10 percent increase in occupancy year to year or getting paperwork and cleaning out of the way by 1:00 P.M. Make charts that convey your objectives visually and help you and your staff evaluate your achievements.

Organization

- Are you the head honcho in every area and your staff people only assistants? Or do you see your organization as a team with different people responsible for specific areas like maintenance, food preparation, and paperwork? Assistants behave differently from "division managers." Staff people like and need to know not only their own roles but the roles of their coworkers and how they fit together into a total structure.
- What about the future staff structure you envision? Is there room for advancement? Will a good housekeeper ever get a chance to be a weekend innkeeper or manage the office?

Management Practices

- If you encourage staff ideas and suggestions, make it known. And act on them when they come!
- Is there a regular period, perhaps six months or a year, after which you review performance and consider giving raises? Is there a standard increase staff people can expect?
- Describe the criteria you use for determining whether and how large a raise to give. It will probably be helpful to you and to your staff to have a formal list of standards; it gives them something to work for, as well as a very tangible

demonstration of your work values, and helps you maintain consistency and fairness in decisions about pay levels.

Then describe your method for task training. List the skills to be learned and the criteria for success. For example, the goal for a cleaning person might be to change a bed, arrange the flowers, and dust and vacuum a room in thirty minutes. You might use a checklist that shows every task involved in getting a room ready for the next guests. Be sure to plan enough time in your own schedule to explain things, demonstrate, check progress, give feedback, and correct errors. Let your new staff people know what standards must be met before they are on their own in the job.

As you go through this training process, developing a notebook will make subsequent training much easier. It also provides a reminder and refresher to staff, and reduces the need for repeating details. A loose-leaf notebook indexed for various subjects is perfect; include breakfast, room cleaning, reservations policy, and cancellation procedures.

KEEPING GOOD STAFF

The best way to keep good staff is to pay them such a good salary that no other job is tempting. Think you can't afford it? Don't forget how expensive it is in time, energy, and wages to find and train new staff over and over again.

Split tips fairly. Housekeepers, wait staff, and innkeepers are all likely to receive tips. Be sure everyone understands how they are to be handled. For example, if guests tip housekeepers at checkout, the tip should be split among all housekeepers who worked during the guests' stay.

Making your staff people feel part of the inn team is important in keeping them. Inns usually can't offer large salaries, so you need to make other job benefits clear. Be a caring, fair employer, respecting the ideas and feelings of your staff. Reward good performance, and be sure everyone knows what you consider that to be. Everybody likes to be appreciated, and encouraging and rewarding good work pays off in the spirit as well as the economics of your inn. Here are some ideas:

Contests. Start a competition among staff members who handle the telephones and reservations. Give the one who gets the most midweek bookings during a specific period a night's stay at another inn. You can probably arrange a trade, so the room won't cost you anything. A bonus for you—in addition to increased midweek bookings—may be that your staff will see the inn in a new light as they look for the words to bring in the business.

Awards. Corporations reward employees who come up with cost-saving and moneymaking ideas. Why not do this at your inn? At Ten Inverness Way, a staff member came up with an idea for saving $300 a year in the cost of dairy products by dealing directly with the local delivery company. Shopping time was reduced as well. Mary and her partner were so impressed with the idea that they instituted a standing incentive award. The rule is that any idea that produces continuing, quantifiable savings or earnings is rewarded with a check in the amount of 50 percent of the first year's cash benefits.

Gratitude. It is surprising how important it is to thank staffers. And it's equally surprising how often we forget to do it. Look for and mention things your staff members do especially well. It could be the smooth handling of a difficult phone call. It could be a creative touch with making bouquets out of next to nothing from your frostbitten garden. It could be handling a complex agenda item particularly well. You will almost certainly be amazed at how many people you will please by noticing their good work.

Promotion and Raises

Base employee rewards on the value of staff people to your business. Take care that the more responsible jobs command the higher pay, and that pay scales also reward length of employment at the inn. Don't raise pay prematurely or capriciously. Pay increases should be based on regular, individual evaluations of established criteria. If you're not entirely satisfied with a job, say, "I'd like to raise your pay to X dollars, but I need to feel confident you'll _____. When I see that this is happening regularly for a month, I'll give you the raise."

When you promote someone, they're often taking on a whole new job. Just because they've been on staff in another capacity doesn't mean they don't need thorough training in the new slot.

Don't promote and give raises just before your slow season unless you're sure you can afford it.

Benefits

Paying a competitive salary is the best way to keep good staff, but a benefits package certainly sweetens the pot. If you see yourself and your staff in this for the long haul, health insurance, bonus plans, and retirement savings plans should be in your budget and staffing plan.

A Staff Bonus Program That Works

Susan Zolla, owner of the fourteen-room Channel Road Inn in Santa Monica, California, has a staff bonus program that has reduced waste, improved morale, and reduced turnover.

"I instituted this program because I wanted the employees to take home a decent salary, especially during our good months," says Susan. Although she has a six-month employee performance review and usually gives a raise at that time, Susan was concerned that if raises were high, she would be locked into higher wages during bad months. "With a bonus, everyone shares in our extra income during busy months, when they work extra hard."

In addition, the bonus involves sharing the responsibility of expenses, including utility bills and food waste. This particular system has given Susan's eight staff members an idea of the costs of running an inn, and that they have the power to control those costs. The repeated repairs on an overloaded washer have stopped. Staff now do not hesitate to pull hair from drains, because they know the plumbing costs. Personal telephone calls are reduced. Keeping the clothes-dryer filter cleaned and taking care of the computer and copy machine have become everyone's responsibility.

How It Works

The bonus is derived from a combination of net revenue (income after expenses, also called profit) and the savings from original budgeted costs. The bonus pool is 3.5 percent of the monthly profit and 10 percent of the difference between budgeted costs and actual expenses. Ideal expenditures are 70 percent of income. Bonuses are distributed monthly among employees on the basis of hours worked during the month.

Additional details increase fairness. As much as 5 percent can be added to reward individual performance. Vacation hours are not included in monthly hours, encouraging staff to take vacations during slow seasons rather than when they could get the largest bonus. First- and last-month employees are not given bonuses. Annual expenses (taxes, insurance) are spread over the entire year rather than deducted in the month paid.

Sample Month

Income	$42,000
Income goal	$26,000
Profit	$16,000
Take 3.5 percent of Profit to create part 1 of bonus pool	$560

They try to keep expenses at 70 percent of income. A bonus pool contribution is made based on the actual amount that expenses fall below 70 percent of sales.

70 percent of sales	$28,000
If actual expenses are	$24,000
Savings	$4,000

Take 10 percent of savings to create part 2 of bonus pool $400
Total of parts 1 + 2 = total bonus pool $960

This amount is split among the staff based on hours worked. Full-time housekeepers often receive $150 to $300 extra a month.

Staff have made operational changes that saved money, which they see in their paychecks. They are happy when they are busy, but they are prepared, when it is slow, for a lower bonus amount. Some employees are upset with the variation in income. Susan tries to level the variation, controlling profit in busier months by spending for needed items then.

Once employees see the benefits that they did not receive when they worked at local hotels for the same hourly base wage, they remain with her for a long time. Susan believes that this system rewards positive behavior and attitudes in line with profitability. "Employees are the heart of this business," she says, and here is a way to reward and keep them for their hard, conscientious work.

Health insurance may be more reasonably priced through local or state associations, either chambers of commerce or lodging groups. To find the best rate for your area that meets your insurance needs, call an insurance agent in your local area who specializes in health insurance. Also check out www.quotesmith.com, a free service.

Bonus plans vary in design depending on the nature of the business. Sometimes innkeepers give a bonus to staff who complete the full season with them. Others base it on profit in relation to the individual's wages. Still others merely provide a holiday bonus. As the boss, you will want to find a way that meets your cash flow needs and motivates staff at the same time.

Retirement plans do not necessarily require a financial output by you. In the United States, you can arrange with an investment counselor to set up a plan where your employees choose to deduct from their paychecks, prior to taxes (except social security), a set monthly amount to be deposited in a retirement fund. The employees can save for retirement on their own, often with very little decrease in their take-home pay, because of the reduction of taxable income and thus of taxes, and you end up being the good guy for setting it up.

THE BOOKWORK

When you hire employees, you become responsible for maintaining records for unemployment insurance, disability insurance, workers' compensation insurance, state and federal income taxes, and social security. Your state employment services office should be able to give you current information about your legal responsibilities as an employer.

Sometimes innkeepers think they can pay housekeepers "under the table" or as independent contractors, avoiding all the paperwork and taxes. However, the penalties for this are twofold. First, if the government catches you, you'll be held responsible for all the back taxes and penalties, and your income tax records will be flagged, making an audit likely. Second, if an employee is injured, you'll be liable for all medical bills and can be sued. Furthermore, a disgruntled employee may report you to the labor board, IRS, or other government entity. In an inn, it is unlikely that you will use independent contractors except for outside or temporary help, such as gardeners or plumbers. And even then, you'll need proof that they are covered themselves for workers' compensation. The IRS can provide a very clear twenty-step pamphlet that will help you clarify whether you are stepping over a dangerous line.

For your own purposes, you'll probably want to keep a personnel file for employees, including their applications, up-to-date addresses, reference information, and work history. You'll also want to create a payroll file; records should be kept current and retained for several years. Stationery stores can provide time cards and payroll forms that will help you create records for yourself and your staff people. Here's what to look for:

- Time cards
- W-4 and W-2 tax forms
- I-9 Immigration and Naturalization Service Forms
- Payroll cards
- Quarterly tax records
- Time sheets
- Communication with employees:

Performance reviews

Letters of reprimand or commendation

Contracts

The employee's initial application materials and job description.

Also nice to have in each person's file is:

- Emergency contact person
- Family member names
- Birthdays, anniversary
- Samples of good work

Forms and Information to Gather Prior to Hiring Staff

- *Federal identification number from the Internal Revenue Service. The IRS will issue a number and will then begin forwarding forms, to be completed quarterly. An employer's guide will be sent for figuring federal income tax to be withheld and forwarded to the IRS, as well as the percentage rate for FICA (social security) for you and the employee to pay.*
- *State income tax withholding (if your state has it) from your closest state employment office. They will issue a number and will then begin forwarding forms, to be completed quarterly. Some states also require a disability tax.*
- *W-4 forms from IRS or office-supply stores.*
- *W-2 forms from IRS or office-supply stores.*
- *I-9 Immigration and Naturalization Service forms.*
- *Workers' compensation insurance from private insurance carriers or through state association plans.*
- *Health insurance from private insurance carriers.*
- *Consider a dishonesty bond from private insurance carriers, which covers all employees up to a certain amount, protecting you from potential losses due to employee embezzlement.*

FIRING EMPLOYEES

Firing employees doesn't have to be that awful if you've clearly communicated your expectations and standards all along. For example, staffers need to understand their job description and duties, as well as your expectations about hours, dress, and pace. If attitude is a problem, describe it in concrete terms. For example, courtesy to guests and staff is concretely exhibited in saying "please" and "thank you."

Put in writing any warning or ultimatum that could result in dismissal. Employer premiums are likely to increase as unemployment claims of former employees increase. When you fire someone, explain again your reasons for it. In many states, dismissal for incompetence does not preclude former employees from collecting unemployment compensation; as an employer, you're responsible for screening out the incompetents before you hire them.

Laying off employees when work is slow is a different matter completely. Be sure to discuss the situation and the possibility of rehiring when conditions change. Sometimes you can negotiate a reduced-hours arrangement with an employee you want to keep but can't currently afford.

INDEPENDENT CONTRACTORS

Independent contractors can sometimes perform necessary services, but they will not be employees. They have their own businesses, provide their own tools, and establish their own work parameters. For example, it's not up to you to set a contractor's hours; they are arrived at by mutual agreement. Independent contractors pay their own social security, taxes, and unemployment and disability insurance. If your contractors have not covered their employees for workers' compensation, you'll be responsible if they're hurt on your premises and you'll be responsible for taxes not paid!

At year-end, you need to fill out an IRS Form 1099 for each contractor to whom you have paid $600 or more. Copies must be sent to the IRS, the state income tax agency, and the contractor. The rules defining independent contractors are specific; when in doubt, check with your accountant on whether your planned arrangement applies. Always sign a contract, such as the one in Appendix 5.

In some work areas, innkeepers can choose whether to hire an employee or work with a contractor. Gardening services are a perfect example. If you're not already an employer, it would probably be wisest to work with an independent gardening service rather than to set up the necessary structure and paperwork systems to hire a gardener as an inn employee. CAUTION: Check with www.irs.gov for details.

THE AMERICANS WITH DISABILITIES ACT AND EMPLOYEES

If you have fifteen or more employees, you must reasonably accommodate the disabilities of qualified applicants and employees. This may entail modifying applications, the interviewing process, and workstations and equipment, unless undue hardship would result.

Review Job Descriptions

Job descriptions should not be worded in such a way that they would discourage applicants with disabilities. People with disabilities are deemed to be qualified for a position if they are able to perform its "essential functions." Essential functions are those the individual must perform unaided or with the assistance of reasonable accommodation. The definition does not include marginal functions of a position. For example, bookkeepers cannot perform the job without mathematical skills. However, it is not necessary, even if it would be more helpful, that they can lift boxes or even walk. In designing descriptions, break a job down into its four basic elements:

- Purpose (the reason for the job).
- Major tasks (those *essential* to accomplish the purpose).
- Job setting (the workstation and conditions).
- Worker qualifications (minimum requirements a worker must meet to perform the major tasks).

Restructure Jobs

To ensure that you can accommodate individuals with disabilities, consider restructuring the job in several ways. Restructuring schedules may mean dividing a job into two positions to accommodate someone who can work a half but not a whole day. Some disabilities occasionally necessitate brief periods of hospitalization (kidney diseases, hemophilia) or weekly therapy sessions (substance-abuse recovery, cancer, mental disorders). Appropriate time off must be granted.

Flex time may solve disability-related punctuality problems where morning personal preparations may not always last a predictable amount of time. Implementing "core hours," such as allowing an employee to work an eight-hour shift sometime between 6:00 A.M. and 6:00 P.M. may be desirable.

Reassigning incidental duties should also be considered. For example, say you have an assistant chef with a bad back. She receives and inventories provisions. Lifting fifty-pound boxes is not a necessary part of the job. With someone else to help, she can perform the essential inventory-taking part of her job.

Job Interviews

You can ask questions that determine the applicant's ability to perform the functions of the job, but you *cannot* ask an interviewee to list on an application or verbally respond during an interview to the following:

- Are there any conditions or diseases for which you have been treated?
- Have you ever been hospitalized?
- Have you ever been treated for any mental condition?
- Do you have a history of alcohol or drug abuse?
- Do you have any disabilities or impairment that may affect your performance in this position?
- Have you ever filed for workers' compensation insurance?
- What's the prognosis or expectation regarding your condition or disability?
- Will you need treatment or special leave because of the disability?

An alternative to a question like "How many days were you absent from work last year?" might be to communicate to the prospective employee that employment at your inn requires a certain number days of attendance per year. Then ask whether or not the applicant can meet this particular requirement. Avoid direct inquiries such as "What disabilities do you have that would keep you from performing this job?" This does not, however, mean that you cannot ask an applicant whether or not he or she has the ability to perform a specific job.

You may seek information regarding a person's ability to perform the essential functions of a job with questions like these:
- Based on this job description, are you able to perform these tasks with or without accommodation?
- How would you perform the tasks and with what accommodation?
- Based on what you have been told regarding our work hours and leave policies, are you able to meet these requirements?

Avoid unrelated subjects. An applicant could complain that the real reason he or she was denied a position is that the employer knew that the applicant had a child with Down's syndrome and assumed the applicant would continually be called away from work to care for the child. To preclude such charges, stay away from discussing friends and family during the application process.

Finally,
- Don't make medical judgments. Don't reject an applicant with a readily apparent disability. The applicant should be permitted to demonstrate or explain how he or she would perform the essential functions of the job.
- Be accessible. Individuals with disabilities need access to the employment process. Use your TDD telephone number in classified ads. And make it possible for employees to work at your inn. You are required to make reasonable alterations to your work spaces when employees' disabilities demand it.
- Ask about cash incentives. A company that works with a local vocational-rehabilitation agency can receive partial reimbursement for the wages of disabled employees. For more information, contact your local agency. Under the

Job Training Partnership Act, an employer can set up on-the-job training and be reimbursed for half of the first six months' wages for an eligible disabled person. Contact your chamber of commerce.

The IRS and You

The U.S. Internal Revenue Service has taken a serious look at bed-and-breakfast operations, even creating a special publication for agents on how to examine them (*Industry Specialization and Market Segment Specialization Programs*). One thing is clear: the more you treat your inn like a business, the more the IRS will. If you run a ten- or twenty-room inn with completely self-contained owner's quarters, full-time staff, and year-round demand, the IRS is less likely to question your business status. If, however, you prepare your own dinner in the same kitchen where guests' breakfasts are cooked, do all the work yourself, and store Aunt Agatha's furs in the back closet of the Rose Room, you're in the gray area of the home-based business.

In 1988, the IRS tightened home-based-business rules. The chief intent was to prevent for example, attorneys who prepare briefs at home a couple of nights a week from writing off their home office—guest bedroom. According to IRS Publication 587, *Business Use of Your Home,* you must meet specific conditions in order to take a deduction for the business use of your home. The IRS rule says, "To deduct expenses related to the business use of part of your home, you must meet specific requirements. Even then, your deduction may be limited." The agency lists these requirements; the relevant factors for an inn are: exclusive use, regular use, principal place of business, and place to meet customers. How will these criteria apply to your property?

"Exclusive use" means use only for business. If a particular part of your home is used for personal purposes, it does not meet the exclusive-use test. So even though you had to completely renovate your kitchen to meet health department requirements, you cannot deduct or depreciate that expense unless you can show that the kitchen is for guests' meal preparation only.

Solution: Use a separate kitchen and dining area for yourself or develop a kitchen area in your quarters. You can get an apartment-type sink-stove-refrigerator combination unit that will fit in a small space. Exclusive use also means that friends and family cannot sleep in guest rooms for free, or the deduction is lost. (Those of you who plan to move from vacant guest room to vacant guest room, take note!) So create a place where family and friends can stay—a futon on the floor perhaps. Or establish a payment policy for these visitors.

"Regular use" means just that. Welcoming only occasional paying guests or guests only for seasonal or weekend business will not qualify, even if that part of your home is used for no other purpose. It is not deductible.

Solution: Keep good occupancy records to show you are doing regular business. If, in fact, you do not regularly receive guests because your business is still new, show your intentions by saving promotional and advertising materials. In your start-up years, you might keep track of tours given prospective guests by saving names, addresses, and dates in the guest book. If your occupancy is low, you may need to prove that your inn is a business and not a hobby.

"Principal place of business" is easy to justify for most inns, because you do business nowhere else. Factors to consider are the total time you regularly spend doing work there, facilities you need to complete the work, and relative amount of income you get from doing business at home.

"Place to meet customers" deals primarily with doctors who have offices elsewhere. If you have customers on a regular basis in your home, you can deduct expenses for that area used exclusively for such use.

LOOKING LIKE A BUSINESS TO THE IRS

In case you're focused more on the pancakes than on the profit and loss statements, here are some reminders about businesslike operations:

- Keep your personal checkbook separate from your inn checkbook. This seems logical to some folks, but sounds like extra work to others. Just do it.
- Keep separate records and receipts of all expenditures for the inn and for your personal life. For items such as food and utilities, this is crucial.
- Keep clean income records. Faithfully record receipts and deposits of cash, checks, and credit cards. The IRS has several key ratios they use to flag the possibility that cash is being skimmed. If the IRS doesn't catch it, your staff will, and might first help themselves to the cash and then, if disgruntled, report you to the IRS.
- Allocate appropriately in your tax records the fringe benefits like food, health insurance, and living quarters that you receive as an innkeeper.
- Keep tidy petty-cash accounts. Establish a standard balance, $50 or $100, diligently filing receipts as money is spent. When it's almost gone, write a check in the exact amount of the receipts, allocating those figures directly to the proper accounts, such as food and postage. When the check is cashed, the petty cash account returns to the initial balance. This system also keeps you in control of cash handling by the staff: no receipts, no reimbursement.

Hobby or Business? How the IRS Decides

IRS regulations list nine factors relevant to innkeepers among those considered in determining whether a taxpayer entered into or continued an activity with the objective of making a profit.

- *The manner in which the taxpayer carries on the activity. The fact that the taxpayer operates in a businesslike manner and maintains complete and accurate records may indicate that the activity is engaged in for profit.*
- *The expertise of the taxpayer or his advisers.*
- *The time and effort expended by the taxpayer in carrying on the activity.*
- *Whether there is expectation that the assets used in the activity may appreciate in value.*
- *The success of the taxpayer in carrying on similar or dissimilar activities.*
- *The taxpayer's history of income or losses with respect to the activity.*
- *The amount of occasional profits, if any, that are earned from the activity.*
- *The financial status of the taxpayer. The fact that the taxpayer does not have substantial income or capital from sources other than the activity may indicate that an activity is engaged in for profit.*
- *Elements of personal pleasure or recreation. The presence of personal motives in the carrying on of an activity may indicate that the activity is not engaged in for profit, especially where there are recreational or personal elements involved. However, the fact that the taxpayer derives personal pleasure from engaging in the activity is not sufficient to cause the activity to be classified as not engaged in for profit, if the activity is engaged in for profit as evidenced by other factors.*

- Use professional business materials. Letterhead stationery, brochures, business cards, registration cards, and guest registries all indicate that you are doing innkeeping for real.
- Pay local, state, and payroll taxes. Susan Hill, CPA, says state and federal agencies work together. If a state examiner picks up discrepancies during a review, the information will likely be sent to other governmental bodies. Also, if a state employment office review results in a reclassification of contract labor to employee status, it's an automatic ticket for IRS attention.
- Have at least two telephone numbers. One is automatically considered your personal phone: no deduction. List the inn phone in the phone book. Tax preparer Jim Carney observes that if you receive business only through a reservation

service and do not advertise publicly through the phone book, you are likely to lose any claim that you are running a business.

- Show your professional status by joining associations and attending seminars, thus demonstrating that you are developing skills and knowledge in your field. Add "conferences and seminars" to your chart of accounts.
- Keep an automobile log. Innkeepers typically use their cars for more than business. You can keep a record of business trips on your calendar and use it as the formal tally, or keep track of mileage in a log kept in the car. The exact format of this log is open, but how much you use the vehicle must be very clear.

MINIMIZE YOUR CHANCES OF BEING AUDITED

The IRS has developed mathematical formulas that prompt their computers to spew out returns for possible audits. For example:
- Huge losses "walk and talk" like tax shelters and are often flagged. These may be unusually high losses from a natural disaster or from extensive renovation. The IRS closely watches those B&B owners who renovate in a nice retirement area, deduct their expenses for a couple of years, and then retire—from the B&B business.
- High repair and maintenance costs, says CPA Susan Hill, are often shown on a tax return when actually the taxpayer should have capitalized them over a number of years.
- Skimming cash is detectable. According to Hill, if credit card charges in proportion to income and linen expenses in proportion to number of rooms sold are above a certain percentage, the IRS will look for unaccounted-for cash.
- Sole proprietorships making over $100,000 are much more likely to be audited than corporations earning the same amount, says Hill. If this is your situation, consider incorporating.
- Another red flag: basis too low for declared expenses. You must have invested more money in the corporation ("basis") than you claim as losses. Hills recommends handling this by taking out a personal loan and investing it in, or lending it to, the corporation rather than having the corporation borrow the money from the bank.
- The longer you record losses, the greater the risk of audit. If you lose money more than three out of five years, you can deduct the loss only to the level of your gross income.

So what if the worst happens and you're audited? Get Frederick W. Daily's books on dealing with the IRS (Nolo Press). And relax: you've done everything right.

Experience with the IRS

The days of the IRS trying to figure out whether B&Bs are real businesses are pretty much gone. Now inn owners are subject to the same random audits as other businesses and individuals.

In Susan Hill's experience with her subchapter S corporation inn clients' audits a couple of discoveries she made are helpful.

Mileage was examined very closely when the owner had purchased a car or claimed mileage. A clean log with the consistent recording of each trip's mileage and purpose was the saving item for this particular expense being honored.

But after the whole audit was completed, with all t's crossed and i's dotted, the auditor asked, "How do they live if they make so little money?" The owners had paid themselves a regular salary, though not a large one, and had been taking out employee benefits. They had been certain to pay rent to shareholders themselves and could show they were receiving interest on a shareholders loan.

Case Study: Rosewood Inn

Winnie and Dick Peer of the six-room Rosewood Inn in Corning, New York, had, since opening in 1980, taken lodging as serious business. Dick speaks with awe of Winnie's bookkeeping prowess. In 1989, the Rosewood, among numerous other inns in the Finger Lakes area, became a target for an IRS focus on the "business use of the home."

Tax adviser and former innkeeper Jim Carney, who represented not only the Rosewood but also several other Finger Lakes inns, is convinced that Winnie's organization and consistently businesslike practices won their appeal. (Carney stepped in when the Peers' original tax preparer panicked at the thought of an audit.)

When the IRS questioned the exclusive business use of the dining room and parlor, Carney showed that 80 percent of the days of the year a paying guest was staying in the house, thus making this area not available for personal use. He won this point.

When the IRS questioned their business-to-personal utility ratio, Carney used Winnie's guest records showing not only rooms rented but also number of people using each room to justify an 88 percent deduction of utilities.

Although the IRS did not allow the kitchen to be deducted, the Peers' 80 percent deduction claimed for expenses and depreciation of the building held on appeal—even though the auditor had originally disallowed it.

Insurance

An elderly guest has a heart attack and tumbles down three flights of polished stairs in your vintage Victorian. Are you liable?

It's an hour past checkout time, and your cleaning staff gets no response from repeated knocks at the door of a guest room. They open it and find the bed occupied. Is this an invasion of privacy?

A staffer, straightening the kitchen, slashes his hand on your bread knife. Can he apply for workers' compensation?

Mrs. Arnold in the Camellia Room chokes on your magnificent eggs Benedict, permanently injuring her voice. Was this a case of products hazard?

A guest leaves your dining room and on the way down the front steps slips and falls on an ice patch. Are you liable?

According to an attorney who works with innkeepers, "The question isn't *whether* you'll be sued, it's *when*." People with small businesses are among the most vulnerable. No longer a Jane or John Q. Citizen, innkeepers are viewed by juries as business owners with marketable assets. On the other hand, inns aren't big enough to have the protection of a corporate legal department or rich enough to keep an outside attorney on retainer. If you need to hire an attorney to defend you in a lawsuit—even just to have a "nuisance" lawsuit dismissed—you can plan on spending at least $10,000.

Dreary, isn't it? Fortunately, hospitality insurance has been designed to package appropriate protection for the contingencies faced by inns and innkeepers. Shop carefully. The inn packages are likely to get you the right coverage at a lower price than you could buy it in pieces. Whether packaged or not, policy prices vary widely. Ask for detailed comparisons of proposals and look into special payment plans.

Whoever insures you, you will need to prepare a complete inventory of your possessions, not only to determine how much insurance you need, but also to substantiate subsequent claims. It's wise to supplement a written inventory with color photographs or videotape records, separately held in a safe-deposit box.

If you lease your inn property, the building should be insured by its owner. Be sure it is. And whether the building belongs to you or to someone else, be sure your insurance protection begins right away. You'll need to be covered during remodeling, but you probably won't need all the coverages of an operating inn.

"I know what it says, but what does it mean?"

Let's start with a few terms and definitions, which may clarify the insurance language used in policies.

Property and Casualty. The standard insurance policy is divided into two sections: property and casualty (also called liability). When a policy is divided into two or more sections, it is referred to as a package. Property refers to the building(s), the equipment used to maintain them, and all the items contained within. Casualty refers to liability—any accidental injury or damage to someone other than an employee or relative who lives with you.

There are various property coverage types. *Special causes of loss* is the most comprehensive coverage form available, protecting your property against every peril unless the peril is specifically excluded. *Broad form* covers about eighteen perils, and *named peril*, the most limited, covers approximately six perils. In the last two coverage types, perils covered must be specifically named in the policy.

The casualty (liability) coverage you will need is commercial general liability. It is comprehensive, including overall limits and per-occurrence limits for products and completed operations, personal and advertising injury, and medical payments. See PAII's special report *Insurance, That Nine-Letter Word* for the most up-to-date discussion.

Actual Cash Value or Replacement-Cost Value. Property value is determined on the basis of one of these two concepts. Actual cash value takes depreciation into consideration; replacement-cost coverage replaces something without depreciating its value. Take a roof, for example. Let's say it cost you $8,000 to have it installed nine years ago, but it would cost $14,000 today. Supposing it were smashed by a tree. With replacement cost coverage, you would be paid $14,000. With actual cash value coverage, however, you would receive $14,000 less the cost of nine years of depreciation. Replacement-cost coverage is not more expensive than actual cash value, but you insure for a higher limit, which increases the premium. Under most circumstances, you will want to repair damages or replace objects, so replacement cost is the way to go. If you are not interested in rebuilding your inn on its present site in case of a loss, actual cash value may be more cost-effective.

Coinsurance Clause or Agreed Amount/Stipulated Amount. An insurance policy is a legal contract between two parties. Each has a role, and, legally, they are considered coinsurers. The insurance company agrees to pay for covered losses, less a deductible. The insured agrees in turn to pay the premiums, disclose necessary information to the insurance company, and insure to the full value of the property.

The coinsurance clause requires you to carry a specified amount of insurance based on the cost to rebuild the insured property; if you fail to comply with the clause, you will suffer a penalty in the event of a partial loss. Let's say your building has a value of $100,000 and an 80 percent coinsurance clause (80 percent being the most common). If you insure the building for less than $80,000, the amount you will receive in case of a loss will be the ratio of the amount of insurance carried to the amount required. For example:

$$\frac{\text{amount carried (\$50,000)}}{\text{amount required (\$80,000)}}$$

So if the insurance company finds that the building is insured for $50,000, they will only pay you five-eighths of the value of the claim, regardless of its total size. In no case will you receive more than the value of the insurance you bought, in this case $50,000.

Ordinance Replacement Coverage. This is insurance for what it would cost to reconstruct your building according to current ordinances. Inn-business insurance experts say it's one of the most important and most overlooked coverages. If you have to rebuild after a loss, code changes may require you to install sprinklers, firewalls, upgraded electrical service, and so on. Ask your contractor to give you a figure on what it would cost to replace your structure today; that is the amount of insurance you need to buy. For example, let's say that 60 percent of your building is damaged in a fire. Your town or county may require demolition of the undamaged part of your building and replacement with fire-resistant construction, sprinklers, firewalls, and Americans with Disabilities Act compliance—all of which would substantially increase the cost of preparing your building for reuse.

The extra cost to you is not covered by your policy unless specifically added by an endorsement. If you have a *replacement-cost* endorsement, the company will pay you for replacing with like kind and quality, but not for the legally required improvements.

Products Coverage. Products liability is designed to protect you from claims occurring as a result of injuries to your guests other than those caused by property. For example, products coverage would protect you from a suit by a guest who became ill upon finding half a worm in your baked apple.

Guest Coverage. *Guest injury* (liability) coverage is for medical payments. Most general liability policies have $5,000 medical payments coverage automatically built in to pay for doctor and hospital fees, regardless of your negligence. This is "goodwill" coverage, designed to relieve your guests of immediate payment responsibility for minor accidents on your property. *Guest property* coverage may need to be added by specific endorsement; check with your insurer.

Personal Liability. This term is a perfect example of the insurance industry's unique interpretation of the language. Personal liability does not cover injuries like broken arms, but does cover hurt feelings. The perils covered include libel, slander, invasion of privacy, unlawful entry, and so on. This is extremely important coverage for anyone dealing with the general public, especially in a business where it's possible to walk in accidentally on someone taking a bath.

Spoilage Coverage. Restaurateurs, take note.

Umbrella/Excess Coverage. This type of policy increases your total liability coverage. It is written as a separate policy that comes into force when your liability policy has been exhausted.

"How much liability coverage do I need?"

Whatever allows you to sleep well at night. Even small properties worth less than a million dollars can be sued for tens of millions. If you are held liable in such a suit, underinsurance could result in the loss of your business and even your personal assets. Worse still, most banks won't lend you the money you may need for legal costs if you're being sued for more than the amount of your insurance coverage.

Your liability limit should equal at least the value of your property. As a general rule, a liability policy should never be written for anything less than $1 million, and it is frequently recommended that an additional $5 million umbrella policy accompany it. Higher limits protect you in court. As long as the award sought in the suit is within your liability limit, the insurance company will have to pay all attorney and court costs even if, in total, the award and costs exceed your limits.

Talk with your agent or broker about your possible risks and the cost of liability insurance to protect against them. You need to reach a compromise between affordability and peace of mind.

Also, because you can be held liable for the acts of outside contractors who perform work on your property, be sure your policy covers you for this, and that the contractors you hire have adequate coverage themselves.

"As an innkeeper, should I have commercial coverage or homeowner's?"

If you have a standard homeowner's policy, which does not have a specific bed-and-breakfast inn or country inn endorsement, you could have serious problems in the event of a loss. A homeowner's policy will not cover bodily injury or property damage to guests or to their property. This means you are responsible for any medical bills, physical therapy, disability, and the like incurred by a guest because of an injury sustained on your property. In addition, you cannot insure for loss of income. You will not have any guest liability coverage and, in the event of a lawsuit, will be personally responsible for providing your own lawyer and paying for your own defense costs. Be aware that when selling rooms and food, your home becomes commercial property. If an insurance person promises that your homeowner's policy will suffice, request that assurance in writing from the carrier, not the insurance agent.

"What about punitive damages? Am I covered?"

Many states do not permit insurers to cover the costs of punitive damages, the award given the plaintiff to punish the defendant for gross negligence. Punitive damages can be awarded if the court decides there has been gross negligence in something like knowing your wiring is substandard or defective and nevertheless inviting the public onto your premises. You may not be able to insure for this peril, but you need to be aware of it.

"Is my garage covered?"

Under most business policies, appurtenant structures—garages and such—are covered. However, fences, signs, windows, and so on are usually not covered unless they are specifically listed. Ask your agent to do so.

"How do I figure out how much contents coverage I need?"

Most people underestimate the value of their furniture and other household contents. The best way to determine the value is to list your property room by room.

Here's an experiment that may help you judge whether your contents coverage is adequate. Sit at the kitchen table and make a list of the contents in some other room of the inn. Then put a value on each item; replacement value is best for this. Now go into the room you inventoried mentally and check your list. Most people find their original estimate low—as low as 50 percent.

If the contents of your inn are insured for only half their value, you've got a major problem on your hands in case of a loss. Have you priced sheets, mattresses, dishes, glasses, and so on lately?

An itemized list of all your contents will not only establish the proper level of coverage, it will also make the claim process a lot easier for you and your insurer. Trying to remember everything in a room and establish values for it is difficult enough on a tranquil afternoon. Imagine what it's like after a major fire.

"So if my contents limit matches my inventory, I'm okay, right?"

Wrong. Furs, jewelry, coin collections, silver, china, crystal, paintings, and things like camera equipment, musical instruments, and other tools that you use professionally are subject to specified limits in normal policies. Ask your agent to schedule such items if you wish to cover them.

"Am I financially responsible for guests' jewelry?"
Individual states have passed laws limiting your liability to a set dollar amount for property left in a guest room. These laws are for your protection. If guests give you property for safekeeping, and you accept it for safekeeping, inventory it and take special care of it until they want it back. *Innkeeper's legal liability* insurance covers this exposure only while the property is in your care, custody, and control.

"Is there insurance that would protect our guests from neighborhood crime and catastrophe?"
No. Even if you have innkeeper's legal liability coverage, damage or loss to your guests' property will be covered only when you are legally responsible for the damage or loss. The key phrase here is "legally responsible," which means that the law would find you responsible. Where neighborhood kids do damage, where contents are stolen from a guest car parked in your lot or in front of the inn, or where a guest is mugged two doors down the street, the law would most likely not hold you responsible, and therefore the insurance company won't pay for such losses.

There are nevertheless plenty of situations where innkeeper's legal liability coverage is very beneficial. If, for example, your child broke a car antenna, the damage would be covered. If faulty wiring caused a fire in one of your rooms, any loss of guest property would be covered.

The bright side of this question, from the guests' perspective, is that most guests would find that such situations are covered under their own homeowner or automobile policies.

"If we serve wine at our inn, do we need special liability coverage?"
If your guest consumes alcoholic beverages at your inn, leaves, and is involved in an auto accident causing serious injury to a third party, can the injured party sue you? Of course. Will your insurance provide your defense and pay a judgment? Not likely, unless you have purchased liquor legal liability coverage. "Liquor legal" provides liability coverage to you for the negligent acts of others arising from their consumption of alcohol provided by you.

If you charge a fee for alcohol, you must have a separate liquor liability policy. However, the issue is clouded when you provide complimentary alcoholic beverages. Are you in the business of "serving or furnishing"? Some insurance companies say yes, some say no. Find out the position your company takes and get it in writing from the underwriter (not the agent). All innkeepers need to be completely sure there is no gap or question in coverage. The innkeeper who has wine or other beverages available for guests—at a charge or not, with a license or not—is likely to be considered "furnishing and serving" alcoholic beverages to guests.

"Do I really need to have workers' compensation insurance?"

Better to be safe than sorry. Even in those states where workers' compensation insurance is not required, it is not worth the potential financial risk of exposure.

Workers' compensation provides coverage for an employee if injured on the job. The policy provides medical expense coverage, disability payments, life insurance, and unlimited rehabilitation. It entitles individuals to receive benefits for all job-related injuries, regardless of who is at fault (the employee or the employer). In many states you have to reach a certain threshold number of employees before the law applies to you; regardless of state requirements for insurance, if an employee is injured, you are responsible. You, as the owner, have the option of excluding yourself from coverage.

Workers' compensation protects the employer as well as the employee. It is an "exclusive remedy," which means that if employees are injured on the job, their only means of compensation is the workers' compensation policy. In other words, employees cannot sue you for further damages. (In rare cases where there is extreme negligence on the part of the employer, the "exclusive remedy" clause is waived and the employer can be sued.) Without workers' compensation insurance, employees are entitled to three times the amount they would have been awarded under a workers' compensation policy, and they may sue the employer for damages.

Benefits are calculated on preinjury, preillness, or predeath wages. The amount of benefits or the fixed weekly dollar amount that an individual might receive from a claim also varies according to a number of factors including the degree of impairment resulting from the injury.

Premium rates vary from state to state. Some states allow insurance companies to establish their own rates; in these states the rates are usually lower because of competition. Other states require insurance companies to use an established rate set by a ratings bureau that fixes rates at a cost per hundred dollars of gross payroll. In most of these states, many insurance companies will not offer workers' compensation insurance, and the employer must purchase a policy from a state agency or an assigned risk pool. Among these insurance companies in these states that do offer workers' compensation policies, the only competition among insurance companies is in the area of service. A rating bureau will also assign a percentage figure to your total premium based on your history of injuries and losses. This *experience-modification* rating, determined by a complicated mathematical formula, is intended to penalize businesses with high loss records and to reward employers with good safety records.

The *correct classification* for innkeepers is a complicated issue. Many states lump bed-and-breakfasts and country inns into a "hotel" category that covers a variety of tasks. However, if you have employees who do nothing except clerical work, they can be classified as "clerical." This may substantially reduce your premium. Do not cheat; your clerical person may not carry bags or help with breakfast, even occasionally. The state does audit workers' compensation.

"What about 'loss of income' and 'extra expense' insurance?"

As a business owner, you need it. If you experience a loss that is covered by your insurance policy, loss of income insurance will reimburse you during repair or rebuilding. For example, if an oak tree falls through the roof of the inn, you'll need to close for repairs. Loss of income insurance is designed to provide a reimbursement to you for continuing fixed expenses as well as the loss of income you suffer if no guests are able to come to the inn.

Be careful with this coverage, as it is written in various ways. The best form is *unlimited loss sustained.* "Extra expense" is an additional coverage.

"How high a deductible should I take?"

Insurance should be considered protection against a catastrophe, not just an everyday problem. Use deductibles wisely to lower or raise the cost of your insurance. For a commercial policy in most states, a $1,000-per-loss deductible on a commercial policy could result in an 18 percent lower premium in property rates as compared to the standard $250 deductible. A larger deductible is more attractive to your insurance company, assuring them that they will not be paying maintenance claims; they're willing to give a substantial credit for that.

GENERAL INSURANCE TIPS

- Ask questions. If you feel uncertain about any of the issues raised here, make an appointment with your agent. Insurance is supposed to give you security; think how secure you'll feel when you're sure you're covered.
- Report all losses. Insurance is confusing, and there are unquestionably occasions when what is covered and what isn't is unclear. Wind-driven rain damage, for example, is not normally covered. Rain damage because shingles blew off a roof

during a storm and then the rain caused further damage is probably covered.

Since these issues aren't clear-cut, it's a good idea to call your agent and report any loss. Any question you ask will help you make better decisions about limits, perils, and coverages.

- Keep records. Pieces of paper with numbers on them are very impressive to insurance claims people. Remember that they run into a lot of crooks, so they're probably as suspicious of you as you are of them. Keeping good records of contents, appraisals, and receipts makes things easier for everyone concerned.

- Risk management. Insurance is just one aspect of a complete program to protect you, your guests, and your inn property. Another element is risk management. Many insurance companies provide risk management information and consulting, even for small businesses. Something as simple as putting nonslip pads under the Oriental runners can avoid a multimillion-dollar lawsuit, and providing staff with instructions on the proper way to lift can avoid workers' compensation claims. Ask your insurance agent about information and assistance in this area.

Note: This short introduction to insurance issues does not provide all the answers. Many variations exist, and you need to be aware of the options to make an informed purchase decision. Your insurance agent or broker is your best source of information. Ask questions and fully disclose your activities and operations. The Professional Association of Innkeepers International's special report *Insurance: That Nine-Letter Word* is a great reference tool. Get it; use the insurance checklist, and then approach your insurance person to purchase the most cost-effective coverage for your bed-and-breakfast or country inn.

Special thanks to Christy Wolf, formerly of James Wolf (see Resources), for her invaluable assistance on this section.

Setting Rates

Setting your rates is anything but an absolute science. How do you decide how much to charge your guests or when to make a change in fees? For most innkeepers, rates are determined through trial and error at best. Now you can profit from their experience. Read on!

If the consumer price index is any indication, other businesses raise rates regularly, generally from 2 to 10 percent annually. So you might simply keep up with your area's CPI.

However, innkeepers tend to complicate things. As Hugh Daniels of the Old Miners Lodge in Park City, Utah, wrote shortly after his inn opened, "We went from comfortable upper middle class to abject poverty just by opening our inn." A personal economic plunge prevents innkeepers from really believing that anyone would pay $150 or more for a room. But just because you, the innkeeper, cannot afford such a price does not mean an average two-income couple cannot. Hey, these folks are desperate to drive their Porsche to a romantic weekend hideaway with a fireplace and whirlpool!

Even if you believe there are clients that can afford these rates, chances are your innkeeping partner won't. Often, one partner begins to lobby for an increase long before the other is ready to countenance it. "We just raised prices when Junior left for college," they'll say. Your reply may be, "But he graduates in June!"

These difficulties shouldn't surprise you. Simply acknowledging that you are in business to make money (among many other more altruistic reasons) is a big step for many innkeepers. Does it seem morally wrong to charge people you feel you would invite into your home? But wait! Guests are used to paying for good value. The experience in your inn is no doubt the best around, right? Why sell it short by undercharging? Usually, inns compare favorably with the finest lodging in town, offering at no charge services and amenities that others charge for, like all-day coffee and tea, homemade cookies, and complimentary sherry and hors d'oeuvres.

Innkeepers also tend to put off raising rates in anticipation of the terror they'll feel when quoting the new prices on the phone. You are convinced that the caller will screech obscenities and hang up as soon as you mumble the new rates. That just doesn't happen. (But if it does, the caller was looking for the YMCA and misdialed or has a six-year-old guidebook—relax!) Remember, rarely will you speak to someone who makes less money today than he or she did two or three years ago—unless it is an innkeeper who hasn't raised room rates in years!

So, you're still not psychologically prepared? You're ready for . . .

Ask yourself these questions, using your occupancy records, other relevant materials, and a pad and pencil. Use your calculator.

- How do your rates compare with those of other inns you have visited? Are the room features similar?
- When do you turn guests away? If you have a regular season when you could fill twice as many rooms, you have twice the chance of finding people who will pay a higher price. Does it really make a difference if you fill up eight weeks in advance, or two weeks, or even two days? As long you are full anyway, why not make a little more money when your rooms are at a premium? The old law of supply and demand keeps small entrepreneurs alive, just as it does corporations. Bill Oates, a New England inn business consultant, believes that if you're selling your rooms to the first person who calls, you can raise rates.
- What is your most popular, first-booked room? Raising rates does not need to be across the board. Your price range can be fairly wide. To assuage your guilt, have low to high prices, so both the economy- and luxury-minded will be pleased.
- Does a room's popularity vary with the season? In summer, a fireplace suite may not have the same appeal as it does in the dead of winter. Reducing the rate may be necessary. On the other hand, by adding a daybed or a futon during the summer months, you might increase a room's value by opening it up to families.
- Do you have one room that is the least popular? Probably you apologize for it and keep the rate low. But what is the problem? Perhaps adding a whirlpool, fireplace, queen bed, or canopy would solve it. Sometimes just paint and a quilt can spruce up a room. Don't keep prices low because of a problem you can fix.
- Are your prices so low that commissioning travel agents is painful and you resent discounting a room? Offering reductions to former guests during slow times or participating in a well-publicized discount program are good for business. However, if you feel that your already slim profit margin has been annihilated every time someone takes advantage of one of these deals, you will not be a gracious innkeeper.
- Do you like working harder for less money? Innkeepers often say, "But if my prices are higher, my occupancy will go down." Maybe. But even if it does, you will make—worst case—the same amount of money while working less.

Rates are a marketing tool, a reflection of your quality. If they are too low, potential guests may wonder what's wrong with the inn. If you frequently advertise $39 specials, for example, it will cheapen the inn's image. But if your room prices are high, guests will have high expectations, possibly higher than you're prepared to meet. Fortunately, once you've mastered the psychological hurdles, there's a sort of science to the setting of the rates.

STEP THREE: RESEARCH

The Professional Association of Innkeepers International's biennial *Bed-and-Breakfast/Country Inns Industry Survey* tracks inn prices and price increases. It has found, unsurprisingly, that guests expect to pay more for a room with a view, a fireplace, a whirlpool, or even extra space or privacy. As you evaluate the changes you want to make to your new or existing inn, look at what will bring you more income. A private bath can increase the room's value by $22 to $28, according to the study. A whirlpool tub in a room with its own bath will probably be worth an extra $41 to $100, and a fireplace, $11 to $50, depending on the season, the area, and the extravagance of the room.

Average Published Rate by Room Feature Based on Average Rates of the Inn

Room Feature	Under $80	Over $125	Overall
Whirlpool, Spa	$121	$188	$179
Cottages, Separate Building	$86	$189	$150
Balcony, Patio, Garden	$70	$178	$141
Suite	$86	$189	$160
Fireplace, Stove	$91	$166	$153
Audio/Video Equipment	$62	$140	$100
Kitchen, Wet Bar	$73	$154	$129
View/Window Seat	$81	$159	$138
Basic Room, Private Bath	$80	$135	$117
Basic Room, Shared Bath	$58	$112	$ 89

Room rates at inns ranged from $15 to $501 in the 2002 *Industry Survey*. Adding special features to a room not only increases the income per night, but also increases its rentability, further increasing income.

If your most popular room has a fireplace, can you add more fireplaces to the inn, perhaps even simple, freestanding, zero-clearance woodstoves or direct-vented gas fireplaces? If you invest $3,000 in a fireplace in a room with 50 percent occupancy, raising the room price a conservative $30 realizes a first-year increase of $5,475—enough to pay off your investment and go on vacation! And that's not counting the likely increased occupancy!

Why are some of the least responsible innkeepers the most enthusiastic about raising rates? Before you raise yours, take a close look at your property and services. If your rooms need paint and share baths, if your breakfast is no more than breads and fruit, if you offer no other special amenities like bikes or cookies, think twice before you hike the rates. Guests buy value for their dollar. Long-term success requires that you provide it.

Where Has All the Money Gone?
Cash Flow Management

Almost every inn has high seasons, months when income is high, and slower periods when income is low. Many expenses, however, remain more or less constant. Cash flow management is the art of staying solvent year-round. Planning is key. Here are some solvency strategies that work for existing inns.

- Establish a reserve account for large annual payments, such as property tax and liability insurance.
- Establish a credit line with your bank.
- Take out credit cards and use as necessary.
- Prioritize the order of bill paying. Take into consideration the cost of interest charged for late payments versus the cost of borrowing to pay now. Communicate with those whom you must pay later to maintain your good name.
- Take advantage of cash discounts for immediate payment in fat times to establish credibility for negotiating late or partial payment in lean times.
- Plan major purchases for the high season.
- Put money away regularly for such big-ticket items as washing machines that will eventually have to be replaced.
- Plan special events or a gift certificate push to bring money in for slow periods.
- Plan staffing with seasonal variations in mind; be realistic in the expectations you give your staff about hours.
- Consider taking a part-time job.
- Sell products at the inn—your homemade jam, note cards, or potpourri—or have a holiday bazaar.
- Barter for services such as printing, carpet cleaning, or legal advice.
- Collect deposits early for the fall-foliage season or for summer at the shore.
- Close off-season or midweek to cut expenses.
- Market harder.

The Inn Group: Innkeepers Associations

The existing inns in your area, your state, and your region can be a great resource. In many places, innkeepers have banded together on a variety of fronts for their mutual benefit.

- Group marketing, including advertising, brochures, media campaigns, and special events.
- A single referral or reservation number for area inns.
- Setting standards and administering inspection programs.
- Political clout.
- Group membership in high-cost visitors bureaus or chambers of commerce.
- Sounding board, professional support system, communications network.
- Establishing an image.
- Fun.

If you join an association that is already doing many of these things, expect to pay yearly dues. In addition, depending upon the association, you may pay extra fees for brochure printing and distribution, site inspections, special-event marketing, public relations campaigns, and so on.

There is a lot of strength in innkeepers associations, and this is evident, for example, in states where positive legislative changes for the industry were influenced by innkeepers. Problems do occur occasionally; like marriage, associations are no cinch. On the other hand, also like marriage, they have benefits you can't easily get elsewhere: common concerns, someone to share expenses with, and complementary interests and talents.

When problems surface, apply some marital strategies. Consider these:

- One of the biggest hurdles in marriage is making peace with the realization that, despite your expectations, your partner isn't responsible for your happiness or success. By the same token, no association can "fix" your occupancy rate or cash flow problems. But this doesn't mean that either the marriage or the association is a worthless relationship.
- When people in your group seem unreasonable, try really seeing them as the whole individuals they are, and not just as sources of support or frustration for your purposes. They too have goals and disappointments and babies that keep them up all night.
- If you feel you're doing more than your share in terms of time or money, either accept it or change it, but don't be a martyr. Being unhappy is dull, and it will cause you to create sideshow problems that will hamper the effectiveness of the group.

- Make it a policy never to talk about anyone. If people are behaving in ways you don't like, handle it with *them*. What's more destructive than the unbridled tongue?
- As to who's getting the glory, it's a waste of time to be jealous of anyone else's success. You do the best you can.
- Spend fun time together. Smiles do good things for the face. And as the saying goes, "By the time you're forty, you'll have the face you deserve."

Taking Care of Yourself

Burnout in the early years is one of the primary reasons innkeepers quit. Although every innkeeper experiences burnout sooner or later, and to a greater or lesser degree, there are several ways to recognize the danger signals and minimize the burnout.

The first step is believing that it can happen to you. Discuss with your partner the way you react to fatigue, and talk about how you would like to be treated in those situations. Maybe you want permission and encouragement to take time off. Maybe you prefer a nudge out the door. Make specific plans about how you can care for each other.

Unfortunately, instead of helping detect and defuse each other's burnout, partners often feed it. One demands an impossible performance of the other, or feels guilty when a partner outperforms him or her. Couples frequently run into problems when one partner works outside the inn. The innkeeping partner often wants more help in the inn while the outside partner feels that he or she is doing plenty by working to cover the income deficit. Or the outside partner won't know the inn procedures well enough to help out very satisfactorily, but may feel guilty about relaxing when the innkeeping partner is still folding laundry at 9:00 P.M.

Don't buy into these guilt trips. It's important for each partner to encourage and celebrate the care and concern from the other partner.

Burnout is cumulative and progressive. It is a depletion of personal energy that affects jobs and relationships. You cannot think it away, but you can take steps to avoid or reduce it.

SPACE

No matter how well you plan your living quarters, space may still be a factor in burnout, so hold out for the best living situation you can manage. Remember that if you share space with guests, you can't consider it inn footage for IRS purposes. Consider the matters below in your plans.

- Can you live with just a bedroom or will you need larger private quarters at the inn? Innkeepers who do not have their own space soon become impatient with the guests. When you are making a decision about living space, err on the side of generosity to yourself.
- Do you want a separate sitting area or living room or don't you mind being asked what's for breakfast when you're nine pages from the end of a Robert Ludlum novel?
- If you have an open kitchen where guests can freely come and go, be aware that you may be sharing your peanut-butter-and-onion sandwiches at midnight with some well-meaning guest who just meandered in looking for a doggie bag.
- Discuss how you will accommodate other family members who live at the inn or come home for vacations. Also take a look at where friends will stay. Will they always need to rent a room?
- Do you prefer to do paperwork uninterrupted, or will you be comfortable having your office or desk in the kitchen, available to staff? Keep your inn records out of guests' hands, not only because it takes away from their fantasy but because you don't want your blank checks or guests' credit card information available to just anyone who walks in. Be careful, too, about having your desk in your private space; it is too easy to bring your work into the bedroom.

Discuss these issues together before making space decisions. Respect both partners' needs for space; frequently one will need more distance or privacy, or need it in a different way. Acknowledge and appreciate these differences.

The less you accommodate your space needs initially, the bigger issue space will become. Even if you can't provide yourselves with the quarters you want and need at the outset, at least develop a plan for them and a timetable, so you will see a light at the end of the tunnel.

WORK SCHEDULES

Work patterns and responsibilities should be divided so partners can truly spell each other. If one partner prepares breakfast and rooms, greets guests, and supervises staff, he or she will get little time off, unless partners alternate being fully in charge from day to day. Another approach is to share the tasks, so that one person handles breakfast, then breaks for the afternoon while the other person supervises staff or cleans rooms; then the first person comes back on duty at three to greet guests.

No matter how you divide up the jobs, there is always more to do, so get a work schedule down on paper, *including breaks.* The work will get done; the breaks are what tend to be forgotten.

INN STYLE AND BURNOUT

Burnout-prevention strategies are often reflected in inn policies and procedures. Many innkeepers plan check-in and checkout times to meet their needs to take a breather, to leave the afternoon free for a concert or the evening for a dinner date instead of waiting around for a single late arrival.

Be cautious here. Although it is true that integrating innkeeping and your personal life is crucial for success, remember that your guests' needs are paramount. You cannot manage your inn just to meet your needs. Sound contradictory? In fact, it's not, but it may require hiring help with flexible hours to welcome guests while you take a break.

Extra services, such as afternoon refreshments and making dinner reservations, take extra time. But they are wonderful touches, and guests appreciate them. Try to evaluate whether the lack of any particular service will be a disappointment to guests, or whether providing it will really help bring them back again.

Some of the services you provide do not have to affect your personal time during the day. Be creative about the way you provide services. For example, self-serve beverages can be available all the time if you provide an instant hot-water faucet or insulated hotpots. You might develop materials for guests that will augment your presence. Instead of describing to every individual guest the process of renovating the inn, provide a scrapbook of before and after photographs. Make a folder of information about what there is to do in your area. Fill a basket with collected restaurant menus, and let guests fill a blank book with their own "reviews." Maintain a scrapbook of articles about the inn and the innkeepers. All these are ways to meet guests' needs for information without the every-moment personal involvement of the innkeeper.

Listen to what your guests tell you and respond accordingly. That's the key to success. When do your guests most need you? Planning their activities for the day? Selecting an evening activity or restaurant? Perhaps they want an afternoon debriefing after their hike? Set your personal time priorities accordingly.

Plan a reasonable way for guests to reach you or the innkeeper on duty. You shouldn't have to leap up every time someone appears in the parlor, and guests shouldn't have to wander around calling your name. A bell on the door to your quarters or a phone extension that reaches you will communicate to guests that you are available while preserving your privacy and theirs.

Marriage and Innkeeping

John and Maureen Magee, former owners of the Rabbit Hill Inn in Lower Waterford, Vermont, say, "Every day we experienced the challenge of balancing a business partnership in our inn/home with our love relationship. We had wanted the inn so much, and yet we watched it begin to take priority over our marriage; we wouldn't accept this. We made a plan to restore the balance.

"Together we identified the recurring pitfalls that heightened stress. We now plan ahead for these situations as much as possible. We took back control by creating and maintaining systems to handle them.

"We discovered that as long as we don't hear the ring of our business phone when someone else is scheduled to answer, we can separate emotionally from the job. We acknowledged our need for more staff, taking a financial risk to hire the right people. But it has paid benefits to our business and our love relationship many times over.

"Our next step required the most discipline. We recommitted ourselves to emotional intimacy. We discovered simple techniques for initiating personal conversations and closeness that preclude innkeeping talk. We went back to doing simple things for each other. Now we prayerfully begin each day with a commitment to each other."

PLAN FOR PRODUCTIVITY

Since burnout occurs when you're busy but don't feel productive, make long- and short-range plans that will help you minimize worry and see results. For example, if you want to increase occupancy this year by 5 percent overall, figure out what that means in terms of a daily or weekly increase in business. How many more rooms must you rent this week to accomplish your goal? Or say you want to replace all the drapes in the guest rooms this year. Plan a monthly schedule for doing it room by room, or for ordering fabric one month, purchasing hardware the next, and so on. Seeing the day's work in relation to a grander scheme makes the little jobs seem more meaningful and less routine.

Plan ahead to design your innkeeping lifestyle for stress prevention. Consider these questions:

- When will you get regular exercise? At least three days a week of thirty minutes of heart-pumping, heavy-breathing exercise will give you stamina, and you'll need it.
- How will you arrange time off for each working partner? Begin that pattern early, so it will feel like a right—which it is!
- How can you arrange unhurried, balanced meals? Plan for good nutrition and meals that are an event: a late breakfast in the kitchen, a sandwich in the park, a family supper around the fire when the inn is empty. This sounds easy now, but just wait!
- Don't finish off the breakfast coffee, the cocktail sherry, and the cheese and crackers without thinking. Moderation is healthy.
- Find an escape location outside the inn, perhaps a membership club, a gym, the woods, or the beach. You need a place where you can rejuvenate.
- Stimulate your brain as well as your body. Take a class or volunteer at your church, the local library, or the child abuse center. You need to feel good about yourself apart from the inn.
- Analyze your ways of becoming focused and centered; develop and make room for them. If attending church, writing, or getting a massage are important for you, don't let innkeeping push them out of your life. Because it will—if you let it!
- Know your limitations and honor them. If you don't want to host weddings and meetings or accommodate groups at your inn, don't.
- If you're an innkeeping couple, you will need to work at maintaining and enjoying closeness. Plan ways to nurture your relationship. Some innkeepers kidnap one another for a special day or night every month. Others play guest in various rooms of the inn on low-occupancy nights.

Sure, burnout is a problem. But you have solutions.

Confessions of a Former Innkeeper

I know that taking care of myself is my weakest skill, so every summer I would sit down and plan two days off every week so I would not end up relieved that high season was over and hoping never to see another guest.

The first week, I would get away, but I'd do inn errands for a day and a half—stopping in the big-city yardage store for curtain material and delivering brochures to the visitors center. Since these weren't my usual errands (I usually got the grocery store, the bank, and maybe—if I was lucky—the dog groomer), I told myself I did have a break from my routine.

Week Two: I decide to take my time off at the inn. Sure. Every time the phone rings, I jump. I go outside to read in the garden, and guests come and ask questions. Since I'm on my day off, I'm all theirs.

Back inside (it's just too difficult sitting outside with a box over my head, trying to look like I'm not there), I go through the kitchen and automatically start folding towels. I don't mind folding towels, except that now the staff wants to ask me questions.

So the third week I leave the inn and wander around town. I feel homeless and incapable of deciding what to do with this free time. I end up falling asleep in my car in the parking lot of the botanical garden. Then I go to the library and fall asleep in their chairs. Then I go to the movies and eat out alone because I don't even have enough energy to see friends. What fun!

The next morning I'm relaxed enough to stay in bed and read. Then I start writing a news release for the upcoming town gala—there it is again: work!

Week Four: I resolve to leave town for two days. Trying desperately to be spontaneous, I drive off in search of adventure. I decide to go bodysurfing and discover I've forgotten my bathing suit. I drive to Los Angeles to surprise my mom, but spend an hour on the phone solving inn problems. The next morning I vow to find an adventure, and I do stop for a short hike on my drive back.

Week Five: By the time my days off come, I'm just getting to full steam. Somehow, if I'm not desperate to leave, I don't think I need to do so.

And so it went. Unless I had an activity actually scheduled with someone or an appointment, I could not count on my actually taking time off. I sabotaged my own best intentions. I don't get a lot of satisfaction from physical activity. I just get tired and sore; but still I feel unproductive or unhealthy when I just read. That's my idea of a day off, but how do you make an appointment to read? I've been known to spend the night at friends' homes when they are away or at a local inn or camping just so I can read without interruption.

Probably the greatest truth I've learned about taking time off is that you have to schedule it so it will happen. If you don't, it won't.

If I Had Known Then …

If I had known then what I know now, I would:

Pat and Jo Ann's list:
- Replace every window that was even a little bit difficult to open or close.
- Use only one brand of one color of white paint and enamel paint on the doors.
- Have more money and brutally realistic financial projections.
- Plan 150 percent for renovation projections.
- Install all private baths from the beginning.
- Apprentice at an inn.
- Put in twice the number of electric outlets and be sure there's one on each wall. The plugs were never in the right place for clocks, lights, hair dryers, shavers, curling irons, heaters, and so on. And add another electrical panel to accommodate the outlets.
- Install three times the outlets I thought possible to use in the kitchen.
- Hire staff sooner.
- Cooperate with others sooner.
- Ask for more help from those who had already done it.
- Ensure that my private quarters were soundproof from inn activity.
- Heavily soundproof all guest rooms.
- Plan for and take vacations with my children, and even in the middle of our busy season.
- Put a refrigerator with an ice maker in an area where guests can help themselves.
- Buy a commercial dishwasher and save myself time.
- Install an instant-hot-water spigot in my kitchen and in a marble-topped buffet in the dining room for guests to make instant beverages or soups.

Susan's list
- Hire an architect and work out an overall plan of what my property could look like ten years from now, with maximum expansion.
- Prepare in advance a complete media package, so I wouldn't be running around getting pictures printed the night before a media representative is due.
- Be careful with initial room pricing. It's better to start high and discount than to try to inch your prices up from $50 to $120 a night.
- Develop a theme or gimmick early in the game so my inn would stand out more from the competition.

Mary's list:

- Furnish guest rooms with dressers with pull-out writing surfaces, to double as desks.
- Ask my assistant innkeepers to bring me breakfast in bed on my days off, and do it for them on their days off (for live-in staff, of course).
- Buy a larger property where I could build a separate cottage for myself and my family.
- Hire only staff members I really like, even if the ones I like less look better on paper.
- Even if I did nothing else different, my innkeeping life would be changed because my sister Marty finally said to me, "Righty tighty, lefty loosey." Invaluable advice for innkeeper handyperson jobs.

appendices

Property

Address_____

A. General Area

___ Proximity to large metropolitan area (within three hours)

___ Convenient public transportation to area, airport, train, bus

___ Close to major highways or interstates

___ Tourist attraction, good restaurants, entertainment, shopping

___ Good climate and environment

___ Businesses, manufacturers, government offices, retailers (commercial businesses)

___ Meets your family's environmental needs (weather, ocean, desert, mountains)

___ Meets your family's educational and employment needs

___ Cost of utilities, possibility for solar

B. Neighborhood

___ Close to, but not too close to, restaurants, retailers, tourist attractions

___ Low crime rate and safe environment

___ Convenient to freeways

___ Within service area for fire, police, medical utilities

___ Resale value

___ Zoned for B&B, dinner service, alcoholic beverage sale

C. Specific Structure: House, Barn, Inn-to-Be

___ Zoning, master plan_____

___ Structurally sound foundation_____

___ Curb appeal, charm, character, historical significance_____

___ Room for expansion_____

___ Adjoining property, dogs barking, type of neighbors_____

___ Outdoor area, patio, garden, spa, croquet, barbecue_____

___ Innkeeper's quarters, privacy, storage_____

___ Garage, parking for guests' and innkeepers' cars_____

___ Adequate heating, air-conditioning (if needed)_____

___ Plumbing, septic tank or sewer, water heater, potable water_____

___ Electricity, age, type, 220 available_____

___ Landscaping, big trees, sound insulation for traffic_____

___ Laundry facilities or in area_____

___ Storage facilities for linens, roll-away beds, cleaning equipment_____

D. Rooms: Size, Ventilation, Sun and Wind Exposure, Traffic and Neighbor-hood Noise, Entry and Exit

___ Living room or parlor_____

___ Space for dinner service if you need it_____

___ Kitchen, including equipment_____

___ Other common areas_____

___ Guest rooms and bathrooms (or spaces or closets to create bathrooms_____)

___ Room 1_____	Room 5_____
___ Room 2_____	Room 6_____
___ Room 3_____	Room 7_____
___ Room 4_____	Room 8_____

Sketch the basic floor plan while it's fresh in your memory.

Appendix 2
Personal Financial Statement: An Inventory

Assets

Liquid Assets (Cash is readily obtainable from these.)

Cash on hand	$_____
Checking account(s) (list banks and amounts)	$_____
Savings account(s)	
(passbook, money market, etc., list banks and amounts)	$_____
Stocks (list companies and cash values)	$_____
Bonds (list companies and cash values	$_____
Insurance (whole life; list companies and cash values)	$_____
Others (autos, jewelry, silver, gold, coins)	$_____
Total Liquid Assets	$_____

Nonliquid Assets (These take time to tap, due to rollover dates, the need to sell, etc. Can be used as collateral.)

Property/real estate (market value)	$_____
Location _____	$_____
Location _____	$_____
Time certificates of deposit	$_____
Pension fund	$_____
Name _____	
Other	$_____
Total Nonliquid Assets	$_____

Other Assets (Assets that are not necessarily liquid or useful as collateral, but show wealth.)

Personal property (china, silver, furs, art, clothing)	$_____
Furnishings	$_____
Livestock, pedigreed animals	$_____
Subchapter S or privately held stock	$_____
Total Other Assets	$_____
Total Assets	$_____

Liabilities

Property mortgages
(list current balances, banks and expiration dates) $_____
Loans $_____
Auto $_____
Other $_____
Credit accounts
(banks and department stores; list names
and current balances) $_____
Other $_____

Total Liabilities $_____

Net Worth

Total assets less total liabilities $_____

Annual Income

Employment (salary) $_____
Business operations
   (your own business) $_____
Spousal/child support $_____
Interest $_____
Rentals $_____
Dividends $_____
Other $_____

Total Annual Income $_____

Annual Expenses

Property taxes/assessments $_____
Income and other taxes $_____
Mortgage payments and interest $_____
Other contract payments $_____
Insurance $_____
Living expense $_____
Spousal/child support $_____
Auto payments $_____
Children's education $_____
Rent $_____

Other $_____

Total Annual Expenses $_____
(If income less expenses is a negative figure, credit cards and credit lines will be
high. If it's positive, back accounts will be high).

Credit Availability
(Itemize and state limits for each.)
Bank credit line $_____
Bank credit cards $_____
Department store credit cards $_____

Appendix 3
Property Evaluation Worksheet: Buying, Renovating, or Building

Property Type: _____

Address _____Owners_____

Research   Area occupancy rates and average daily room rates:

        Tourism bureau, visitors bureau, chamber of commerce_____

        Area bed-and-breakfast inns_____

        Area hotels and motels_____

        Derived area occupancy_____ Average daily room rate_____

        _____

        Comparable inn sales_____

A. Financial Needs Summary

    Original Building: no. of rooms _____ no. of baths _____

    Additional no. of rooms _____traditional/luxury   no. of baths _____

    Final: no. of guest rooms with baths _____traditional/luxury

    Owner/innkeeper rooms with bath_____

Cash Needed

Purchase price: land, building $_____

Mortgage _____%/years_____ ARM/Fixed Res/Comm.

        Monthly payment $_____

Down Payment $_____ (usually 20%–30% of price)

Closing costs, loan fees $_____ (get realtor's estimate)

Moving costs $_____

Working capital $_____ Exp. during const, marketing

Other costs, organizational, etc. $_____

Losses/gains first 3 years $_____

Select buying, renovating or building:

Buying an existing inn: Renovation, furnishings $_____

Other $_____

Buying Subtotal $_____

Renovating: Repairs and upgrade, incl. com. areas $_____ $15,000–$30,000 per room

Additional bathrooms (in existing space) $_____ $8,000–$20,000 each

Additional construction $_____ $100–$220 per square foot

Furnishings: total no. of rooms incl. common areas $_____ $7,000–$20,000 per room

Other_____ $_____

Renovation Subtotal $_____

Building: Construction Costs $_____ $100–$220 per square foot

Add for each bathroom beyond 2 $_____ $8,000–$20,000 each

Landscaping; outside patios, etc. $_____

Furnishings: Total no. of rooms incl. common areas $_____ $7,000–$20,000 per room

Other_____ $_____

Building Subtotal $_____

Total Cash Needed $ _____

B. Projected Income

_____ rooms x 365 days x average daily room rate $_____ = Income at 100% occupancy

Year 1 projection: 50% of area rate of _____% = _____% x Income at 100% occupancy *

Year 2 projection: 1st year_____% + 10% = _____% x Income at 100% occupancy

Year 3 projection: 2nd year_____% + 10% = _____% x Income at 100% occupancy

* Buying: use Seller's occupancy rate

C. Expenses

Traditional room $10,500 per room; luxury room $15,000 per room. (Does not include mortgage, depreciation, owner's salary or draw, income taxes.)

Year 1 projection: no. of rooms_____ x $ _____ ($10,500 or $15,000) = $_____

Year 2 projection: Year 1 projection $ _____ + 11% = $ _____

Year 3 projection: Year 2 projection $ _____ + 11% = $_____

D. Detailed Expenses

Standard Percentages of Total Revenue at 50% Occupancy	Expense Category	Column 1 Expense using Standard % at 50% Occupancy	Column 2 Seller's Actual Expenses or Adjustment For Reality (New Inn)	Column 3 Comments & $ Change in Expenses
16	Salaries/wages, incl. payroll taxes	_____	_____	_____
1	Auto expense	_____	_____	_____
2.5	Bank fees	_____	_____	_____
4	Taxes, fees (no bed tax)	_____	_____	_____
2	Interest: nonmortgage	_____	_____	_____
1	Dues, subscriptions	_____	_____	_____
7	Food, beverages	_____	_____	_____
2.5	Insurance	_____	_____	_____
1	Legal, accounting fees	_____	_____	_____
4	Maint., repairs, fixtures	_____	_____	_____
5	Marketing, advertising	_____	_____	_____
1	Office supplies, postage	_____	_____	_____
2	Outside services	_____	_____	_____
2	Housekeeping supplies	_____	_____	_____
1	Towels, linens	_____	_____	_____
2	Telephone	_____	_____	_____
2	Misc. expense	_____	_____	_____
1	Travel, entertainment	_____	_____	_____
5	Utilities	_____	_____	_____
62%	Total operating expense	_____ T	_____ T	_____
38%	Mortgage, Owner's salary	_____	_____	_____
100%	Grand total	_____ GT	_____ GT	_____

1. Multiply the number of rooms x $10,500 for a traditional inn and $15,000 for a luxury inn. Put this number in Column 1 T.

2. Divide this figure by .62 to calculate grand total expense GT for Column 1. The difference between the T and GT is the amount available for mortgage and owner's salary, expenses that are not included in operating expenses.

3. Take each individual percentage shown under standard percentage and multiply by the grand total GT to get the individual figures for Column 1.

4. Buying an existing inn: If you have been given itemized expenses, insert them in Column 2 for comparison.

5. If building or renovating a start-up, apply the reality test. Look at each item in Column 1 and see if it is logical and accurate for your personal circumstances and area. Put the changes in Column 2.

6. Use Column 3 for comments about changes and corrections.

E. Expenses Summary

	Year 1	Year 2	Year 3
Total operating expenses, T, from Column 2	_____	_____	_____
Plus mortgage expense	_____	_____	_____
Plus owner's salary	_____	_____	_____
Total Expenses	_____	_____	_____

F. Cash Flow and Breakeven

	Year 1	Year 2	Year 3
Gross income	_____	_____	_____
Less: operating expenses	_____	_____	_____
Net operating income	_____	_____	_____
Less: mortgage, owner's salary	_____	_____	_____
Income or loss (cash flow)	_____	_____	_____

Breakeven: $\dfrac{\text{(Total Expenses)}}{\text{(Income at 100\% occupancy)}}$ = _____ = Occupancy needed to break even

Your first year =

Comments:

_____
_____
_____
_____
_____

Appendix 4
Cash Flow Projection—Month by Month

	Jan.	Feb.	Mar.	Apr.	May	June	July	Aug.	Sept.	Oct.	Nov.	Dec.
Projected Occupancy %												
Income												
Room rental revenues												
Product sales												
Total Income												
Expenses												
Food												
Room and housekeeping supplies												
Hourly/part-time employees & payroll taxes												
Utilities												
Towels and linens												
Marketing, advertising, promotion												
Travel commissions & bank charges												
Office supplies and postage												
Telephone												
Travel and entertainment												
Dues and subscriptions												
Auto expenses												
Maintenance, repairs, and fixtures												
Outside services												
Insurance												
Legal and accounting fees												
Interest and/or lease expenses												
Salaried or permanent employees												
Total expenses												
Cash flow												

Appendix 5
State of California Form 55-037

Proposal and Contract

Date:_____, 20____

To: _____

_____

Dear Client:

_____propose to furnish all materials and perform all labor necessary to complete the following:

_____

_____

_____

All of the above work to be completed in a substantial and workmanlike manner according to standard practices for the sum of_____Dollars ($_____).

Progress payments to be made _____as the work progresses to the value of _____percent (_____%) of all work completed. The entire amount of contract to be paid within _____ days after completion.

Any alteration or deviation from the above specifications involving extra cost of material or labor will only be executed upon written orders for same, and will become an extra charge over the sum mentioned in this contract. All agreements must be made in writing.

Name and Registration Number of any salesperson who solicited or negotiated this contract:

Respectfully submitted,

By_____

_____

Name

_____

Address

_____

No.

Contractors are required by law to be licensed and regulated by the Contractor's State License Board. Any questions concerning a contractor may be referred to the registrar of the board, whose address is:

_____

Telephone

Contractor's State License No._____

You, the buyer, may cancel this transaction at any time prior to midnight of the third business day after the date of this transaction.

Contractor's State License Board
1020 N Street
Sacramento, California 95814

ACCEPTANCE

You are hereby authorized to furnish all materials and labor required to complete the work mentioned in the above proposal, for which _____agree to pay the amount mentioned in said proposal, and according to the terms thereof.

Accepted_____Date: _____, 20_____

Appendix 6
Room Planning Worksheet

Room name (or location): _____

Type of room: _____

Atmosphere desired :_____

Natural light:_____

Colors:_____

Items to Be Purchased or Installed

	Budgeted	Spent	Ordered	Installed
Bed				
Headboard				
Mattress/springs				
Dining table				
Light				
Chairs				
1				
2				
3				
Nightstands				
Table for lamps				
Bed lights				
Dresser				
Firewood container				
Armoire				
Desk or dressing table				
Mirrors				
Makeup				
Dressing				
Heating/air conditioning				
Wall treatment				
Window treatment				
Floor treatment				
Bed covering				
Fireplace tools				
Linens				
Accessories				

In the format above, make a master list of items needed in more than one room, such as beds, linens, carpeting, draperies, and accessories, which you may be able to purchase in quantity.

Appendix 7
Basic Information for Interim Innkeepers

Here's a beginning list of what should be discussed with the inn owners:

B&B layout and tour of the whole facility and grounds

Policy and procedure manual

Front office: Messages, answering machine, general operation of system

Computer
1. E-mail knowledge and experience
2. Reservation software knowledge and experience

Reservations
1. Both hard-copy and computer systems
   Confirmations
   Cancellations
   Gift certificates
   Check-in and checkout procedures
2. Accounting log

Guest hospitality

Food service
1. Breakfast, teatime, wine and cheese, snacks and beverages (including fees for extras)
2. Menus
3. Recipes
4. Kitchen and equipment
5. Staples
6. Food safety and sanitation
7. Nightly turndown with treat

Housekeeping
1. Guest rooms
2. Common areas
      a. Living room
      b. Dining room
      c. Halls
3. Laundry room
4. Kitchen
5. Office
6. Innsitter quarters

Laundry

1. Washer and dryer instructions
2. Spot removal chart
3. Laundry products
4. How to fold laundry
5. Laundry storage

Maintenance

1. Lights: day and night
2. Smoke detectors
3. Alarm system
4. Porches
5. Sidewalks and grounds
6. Parking area

Miscellaneous

1. Trash day
2. Background music
3. Security lighting: day and night
4. Gardening
5. Electrical panels
6. Main and secondary gas and water turnoffs

Emergencies

1. Fire extinguishers
2. Flashlights
3. First-aid kit
4. Sewing kit
5. Phone numbers for: police, fire, ambulance, hospital/quick care facility, electric, gas and water companies, plumber, heating/AC technician, electrician, appliances, well and septic system, insurance agent and incident procedure report, local neighbor or innkeeper

Special events

1. Details for meetings, conferences, receptions, parties, weddings, etc.

Information for Appendix 7 provided by the Bed & Breakfast Innstitute of Learning (www.bbinnstitute.com; info@bbinnstitute.com; 800-631-9080). *The Innkeeper's Notebook,* by Pam O'Connor (available from the Professional Association of Innkeepers International) provides additional helpful questions.

Resources

We wish to thank the consultants who contributed to this book. They are listed here with an asterisk (*). Also listed are other helpful services and products to get you started on the right track.

For additional resources of all kinds, go to the Professional Association of Innkeepers International's Web site (www.paii.org), where you'll find everything you need to know about running an inn or opening your own inn.

Accounting
* Theresa August–Selover, August Selover Accounting, LLC, 800-829-7703, theresas@augustseloveraccounting.com.
* Susan Hill, Hill and Thompson, PC (CPAs), 802-362-1880 April15 @together.net.

Business
* James W. Wolf Insurance, P.O. Box 510, Ellicott City, Maryland 21041; 800-488-1135; www.jameswolf.com; inns@jameswolf.com.
* Oates & Bredfeldt Inn Business Consultants, P.O. Box 1162, Brattleboro, Vermont 05301; 802-254-5931.
Phillips, Michael, and Salli Rasberry. *Honest Business.* New York: Random House, 1981. A good general introduction to doing any kind of business of your own.
Small Business Administration of the U.S. Department of Commerce, www.sba.gov. A good starting place for anyone thinking of opening a small business.
* Michael Yovino-Young, MAI, and Alison Teeman, LLV, Yovino-Young Inc., 2716 Telegraph Avenue, Berkeley, California 94705; 510-548-1210. Inn valuation and appraisal.
* Susan Brown and Nancy Donaldson, So You Think You Want to Be an Innkeeper? workshops and consulting, susanpbrown@aol.com, imawestylover@aol.com.
* Hugh Daniels, Ask Hugh Small Business Consulting, 435-645-3931, mail@askhugh.com, www.askhugh.com.
* John Sheiry, CEO, Distinguished Inns Alliance, and owner, Waverly Inn, Hendersonville, North Carolina; www.waverlyinn.com; info@waverlyinn.com.

Renovation and Decoration
National Trust for Historic Preservation, www.nationaltrust.org, 1785 Massachusetts Avenue NW, Washington, D.C. 20036; 202-588-6000. For your preservation questions.
The Old House Journal, www.oldhousejournal.com. Magazine, catalog, and on-line information on renovating and caring for an aging house.

Technology
Check out PAII's Suppliers Marketplace for the latest software companies as well as Internet support and marketing companies, www.paii.org.
Guest Management Software special report. Developers of inn-specific reservations software packages present their products. Also includes an overview of on-line availability and real-time booking options. Available through www.paii.org.
* www.easyinnkeeping.com.
* www.rezovation.com.

On-line Availability and Real-Time Bookings
- www.BedandBreakfast.com.
- www.availabilityonline.com.
- www.easywebrez.com.

Web Marketing
- www.netconcepts.com.
- www.blizzardinternet.com.
- www.inns.net.

Marketing and Promotion
Guide to the Inn Guidebooks. An annotated bibliography of the printed books and on-line directories published as guides for inn travelers; tells you where you'd like your inn listed. Available through www.paii.org.

Marketing Handbook. From the basics of writing a news release to writing brochure copy, this compilation of 140 pages of promotional ideas keeps your inn in the media's eye. Compiled from back issues of *innkeeping* newsletter. Available through www.paii.org.

* Marti Mayne, Maynely Marketing, www.maynelymarketing.com, 207-846-6331.
  Phillips, Michael, and Salli Rasberry. *Marketing Without Advertising.* Good practical ideas. Available through www.paii.org.
* Rusty Pile, TTA Advertising, www.TTAAdvertising.com; 888-699-1233.
* Sandra Soule, Editor, sandy@BedandBreakfast.com.

Food and Recipes
Greco, Gail. *Secrets of Entertaining from America's Best Innkeepers.* Hints collected from innkeepers. Available through www.paii.org.

* Wendy Denn, Trinity Inn and Conference Center, West Cornwall, Connecticut; triconfcen@aol.com.
* Debbie Mosimann, Swiss Woods B&B, Lititz, Pennsylvania; www.swisswoods.com, Innkeeper@swisswoods.com.
* Liza Simpson, Old Miners Lodge, Park City, Utah; www.oldminerslodge.com, stay@oldminers lodge.com.

Operations
Bed-and-Breakfast/Country Inns Industry Survey. PAII's in-depth biennial study of occupancy, amenities, marketing sources, prices, employees, revenues and expenses, rate of return on investment and break-even points. Broken out by geography, size, location (urban, rural, and village destination), and age of the inn. Available through www.paii.org.

Insurance: That Nine-Letter Word. This twenty-five-page report demystifies insurance while providing concrete information on why you need it, how much you need, the latest insurance trends, choosing an agent, and shopping for price. Available through www.paii.org.

George Washington Slept Here and Boy, Was He Messy! A twenty-eight-minute training video along with a training guide and employee checklists, done by American Hotel & Motel Association's Educational Institute with modifications by PAII. Revised and updated for inns, this is a training tool for new staff and a retraining tool for experienced staff. Available in both English and Spanish. Available through www.paii.org.

Staff Manual. Specifically written for bed-and-breakfast inns and country inns. Federal labor regulations, job descriptions, great ads for finding and selecting great staff, how to keep good staff, rightful termination, and more. Available through www.paii.org.

Nitty Gritty Innkeeping Book. Good stuff for operating your inn. Available through www.paii.org.

Politics

Anderson, Kare. *Cutting Deals with Unlikely Allies: An Unorthodox Approach to Playing the Political Game.* If you get into political trouble, this is the practical guide to getting out. A step-by-step approach to influencing decision makers. Available through www.paii.org.

Service

Barlow, Janelle, and Claus Møller. *A Complaint Is a Gift.* Barrett-Koehler Publishers, 1996.

Homestay How-Tos

Notarius, Barbara. *Open Your Own Bed & Breakfast.* New York: John Wiley & Sons.

Stankus, Jan. *How to Open and Operate a Bed & Breakfast Home.* Old Saybrook, Connecticut: Globe Pequot Press.

Newsletters

Yellow Brick Road. Insight for aspiring innkeepers.
P.O. Box 1600, Julian, California, 92036; www.yellowbrickroadnl.com; 760-765-1224

innkeeping. The national monthly newsletter for people who own and run bed-and-breakfast inns and country inns. With real-world information that you can put right to work in your own inn. Published monthly since 1982; included in PAII membership. Contact PAII, P.O. Box 90710, Santa Barbara, California 93190; www.paii.org; 805-569-1853. Ask for the index to back issues. This is your next step after reading this book.

"Of the fifty or so business and trade magazines we receive each month, *innkeeping* is one of the few publications read (and enjoyed!) by everyone in our office. The best ideas come from operators themselves rather than from those in ivory towers."
—William J. Hoffman, president, Trigild Corporation, California.

"Articles are germane and to the point, tips are useful. Yours is one of the best trade newsletters I've seen."
—Joan and Dane Wells, Queen Victoria Bed and Breakfast Inn, New Jersey

So You Think You Want to Be an Innkeeper? Workshops

The pioneer workshop (since 1981) for aspiring innkeepers, this semiannual workshop is held in Santa Barbara, California. Students are guided through three in-depth days of the delights and headaches of opening an inn. Conducted by Susan Brown and Nancy Donaldson, retired owner-innkeepers with over forty years in the business. Much of the content of this book grew out of the original framework of these workshops, although more detailed examples, personal attention to individual questions during nonclass time, and more depth in numerous areas typify this on-site workshop situation. Contact imawestylover@aol.com or susanpbrown@aol.com.

Professional Association of Innkeepers International

The trade association of the country inn and bed-and-breakfast industry, providing services and information to innkeepers, aspiring innkeepers, and innkeepers organizations. For information, contact PAII, P.O. Box 90710, Santa Barbara, California 93190. Call 805-569-1853, fax 805-682-1016, or visit www.paii.org.

Index

Food service. *See* Breakfasts; Dinners;
    Kitchens
Furnishings, 345
    estimating cost for, 72–75
    list of, 162–67

G
Gift certificates, 266
Giveaways, 266
Government officials, dealing with,
    60–62
Grandfathered conditions, 42, 111
"Green" rooms, 146–48
GRM (gross annual rent multiplier), 115
Guest management software (GMS),
    302–3
Guests
    business travelers as, 9, 35, 160, 178
    competition for, 10–11
    complaints by, 288
    with disabilities, 168–72, 267–69
    diversity of, 22
    expectations of, 10–11
    insurance and, 329
    international, 283
    organizing for arrival of, 301
    pretending to be, 229
    repeat, 111, 112
    researching potential, 34–35
    senior citizens as, 171
    sources of, 111–12
    speaking with prospective, 279–82
    tourists as, 34
Guidebooks, 7, 13, 256–58

H
Health, board of, 41–42, 57–58
Homestays, 3–4
Host homes, 3–4
Hotels
    bed-and-breakfast, 6
    boutique, 6
    inns vs., 7

Hot tubs, 12, 198
Humor, sense of, 23

I
Image, establishing, 232–33
Impressions, first, 199–200
Income
    and expense statement, 102–3
    gross, 116–17
    increasing, 117–18
    net operating, 85
    projecting, 76
Independent contractors, 155, 156,
    316
Innkeepers
    advice for, 344–45
    assistant, 128
    associations for, 13, 337–38
    burnout of, 338–43
    as chefs, 229
    interim, 125–35
    married, 341
    professionalism of, 286–88
    single, 15
    successful, 10, 19
    talking to, 38
    traits of good, 14–23, 19–23
    turnover of, 110
    work schedules of, 339–40
Innkeeping
    apprenticeship or internship, 30–31
    future of, 8
    support services for, 13
    trends in, 6, 40
    innkeeping newsletter, x, 363
Inns
    age of, 114
    buying existing, 38–39, 91, 110–22
    evaluating, 37, 69–95, 116–17,
        353–55
    as good neighbors, 42–44
    guidebooks for, 7, 13, 256–58
    hotels vs., 7